ML

REA

ALLEN COUNTY PUBLIC LIBRARY

3 1833 00276 2000

FRIENDS
OF ACPL

D0990297

12712

JUL 17 '80

VILFREDO PARETO

SOCIOLOGICAL WRITINGS

VILFREDO PARETO

SOCIOLOGICAL WRITINGS

Selected and introduced by
S. E. Finer
Translated by Derick Mirfin

ROWMAN AND LITTLEFIELD
TOTOWA, NEW JERSEY

© Introduction and editorial matter, S. E. Finer 1966
© Translation, Basil Blackwell, 1966

First published by Pall Mall Press Ltd., 1966
This reprint edition published in the United States 1976
by Rowman and Littlefield, Totowa, New Jersey

All Rights Reserved. No part of this publication
may be reproduced, stored in a retrieval system,
or transmitted, in any form or by any means,
electronic, mechanical, photocopying, recording
or otherwise, without the prior permission of
Basil Blackwell & Mott Limited.

ISBN 0-87471-855-4

Printed in Great Britain

Contents

2097415

Contents

Preface

It would be generally agreed, I think, that the length, prolixity, and arrangement of Pareto's Treatise on General Sociology make it unsatisfactory for readers coming fresh to his thought. This book is not meant as a substitute for the Treatise but as an introduction to it. Its object is to provide, by extracts from Pareto's own writings, a compendium of his theories, both in their development and their mature form.

But may I *beg* the reader not to plunge immediately into the thicket of Selections, but first to read the Introduction which expounds and makes cross-reference to key passages in the Selections and has been devised to interlock with them. For instance, the choice of extracts in Part One of the Selections ('The Preparation'), not readily intelligible at first glance, will, I trust, appear both coherent and apt in the light of that section (Section III) of the Introduction which discusses the *development* of Pareto's theory. Or again: without the Introduction a reader might well wonder why some particular concept—e.g. Elites—appears, not once, but at a number of places. This is not mere tedious repetition; each individual statement will be found to represent a stage in the development of the concept; and the relevance of each is expounded in the Introduction.

Amongst many colleagues at Keele, I am indebted to Professor Flew, to Professor Halmos, to Mr A. Iliffe and Mr R. Atkinson for helpful comment. Mr Stewart, the Librarian, and his staff gave me invaluable help in tracing and photocopying rare texts. I would additionally like to acknowledge three particular debts of gratitude: to Dr L. Ceriani and the Banca Nazionale di Lavoro of Rome for presenting me, when I was desperate, with the monumental de Rosa edition of Pareto's *Lettere a Maffeo Pantaleoni*—an indispensable work; to Mr Derick Mirfin, as much collaborator as translator; and to Mr Harold Lever, MP, whose affectionate generosity has made the production of this book possible.

S.E.F.

Introduction

BY

S. E. FINER M.A. F.R.HIST.S.
Professor of Political Institutions at
the University of Keele

1

The Climate of Opinion

I

The Climate of Opinion

Pareto was born in 1848, the *annus mirabilis* of liberalism. He died in 1923, ten months after the fascist March on Rome.

The age in which he grew up was dominated by belief in social and material progress, in human perfectibility, and in scientific positivism. The paths by which thinkers and believers reached these common conclusions were various, but the outcome was much the same. In their various ways the fashionable arguments reached a consensus for democracy and rationality, for free trade and the market economy, for pacifism and humanitarianism; and the very fact that these arguments were different seemed to make the final consensus all the more convincing. Counter-arguments existed, but ineffectually. Catholicism, at least as expressed in the Syllabus of Errors of 1864, might yet prevail; but its ultramontane wing had suffered a check with the downfall of the Second Empire in France and the Italian seizure of the Papal States. Social darwinism, for its part, could be interpreted in ways that ran counter to the prevailing meliorist philosophies. Lapouge and Ammon were demonstrating that ability and talent were unequally distributed in societies, and from this it was only a short step to argue that these aristocracies·of talent *ought* to rule the rest of society, or that the eugenically superior races *ought* to rule those less well endowed. In either case, the darwinian struggle for existence could be made to justify the rule of the strong over the weak, at home or overseas. But the full deployment of such arguments was yet to come. Hegelianism and marxism also stood outside the mainstream of meliorist positivistic theory. Both of these philosophies—the first in alliance with nationalism and the second in alliance with social war—were to help dig the grave of the liberal

3

democratic state. Yet for the moment even these served, in two major respects, to buttress the prevailing trust in reason and faith in human progress. For Hegel, humanity had spiralled upwards through the ages, becoming ever more rational and hence more free, driven unawares to its magnificent destiny by the immanent 'cunning of Reason'. For Marx also, humanity had spiralled upwards through the ages, but driven by the dialectical clash of class against class until this very moment when, the iron laws of human society having at least been revealed, the stage was set for the final class struggle from which must ineluctably emerge the era of material abundance in communities whence police and prisons and armies and all the agents of human coercion would have been banished for ever.

But by the end of the century, theories of progress, perfectibility and positivism were all under open attack. The liberal-democratic compromise was disintegrating into its two components which were now increasingly regarded as incompatible. That the many would not despoil the few (as liberals like Mill or Bagehot had feared) had been demonstrated, to tell the truth, only by miracles of philosophical ingenuity. By 1900 the argument had been diverted from a demonstration of why the 'masses' would not despoil the 'classes' to a demonstration by the conservatives as to why they should not, and by the socialists as to why they should. In the name of liberalism, the wealthy and the cultivated had denounced state intervention, whether this manifested itself in progressive income tax, in protective tariffs, or in welfare legislation; but the socialists, in the name of democracy, demanded precisely these measures. The vector of the two contending forces, the path actually followed by the professedly liberal-democratic states, was collectivism. On the one hand, the employer received tariff protection and subsidies; on the other, the worker received social welfare benefits. The free-trading, free-enterprising economy was on its way out, and its defenders, the mid-century liberals, increasingly became anachronistic survivals.

The political institutions of the liberal-democratic state were also disintegrating. Parliaments had seemed the ultimate in political invention and they were still so regarded in eastern countries anxious to emulate the materially successful western societies: in Persia, Turkey, Russia and even China. But in those European states which were popularly identified with the triumph of liberalism—namely republican France and monarchical Italy (for parliament was indigenous and traditional in Britain)—there was a growing disenchantment with parliamentarism. The French regime was insecure. It was alternately rocked by waves of clerical and conservative opposition from the Right, and by the direct action of militant socialists or syndicalists from the Left. It was tainted by a trail of financial scandals. And, after what appeared to its adherents to be its greatest hour—the Dreyfus years when defence of the regime seemed identical with the defence of justice and truth—many generous-minded persons, like Georges Sorel, were alienated for ever by the exploitation of the dreyfusard victory for political and sectarian ends.

As for the Italian regime, it was a sordid caricature of all the worst vices of the French. Utilising every device of pressure, coercion and corruption which a narrow electorate, abysmal poverty and widespread illiteracy made so easy, a selfish and short sighted clique of small-time politicians manipulated the whole commercial and industrial, as well as the political, life of the country. In pursuit of a mirage of national aggrandisement, they protected agriculture and so raised the cost of living, increased excises and so raised it still more, embarked on a heavy program of armaments and engaged in colonial wars. A succession of financial scandals in which leading politicians such as Crispi were involved completed the alienation of the intellectuals, while the insurrections of 1894, of 1898, of 1904 and 1914 amply attested popular desperation with the regime.

Still, these liberal-democratic regimes were only a manifestation, a practical application, of the underlying theories of evolution and progress. One might be disillusioned with these applications and yet subscribe to the tenets that underpinned them, much as the fact that a child falling from a bicycle does not invalidate the principles of mechanics. But by 1900 the very assumptions on which the philosophies of reason and progress had been erected were under attack. The house of Progress had many mansions—in the natural sciences no less than in philosophy. From the 1890s onward, voices began to grate out certain things which, if true, demonstrated that the seemingly solid and unshakeable foundations of the mid-century world outlook were so many deceptive quicksands, and the whole gigantic fabric a vast and ponderous mistake.

The new-found scepticism appeared simultaneously in every one of the fields in which the former views had held sway, even in the natural sciences themselves which one might have supposed to be the impregnable fortress of positivism. Each of the many new interpretations brought forward differed signally from the others, starting from different points, utilising differing concepts and ending with different solutions. Furthermore, with few exceptions, each of the major critics worked independently. Yet for all this, these diverse viewpoints all share one fundamental feature in common.

To this feature many names have been given. It has been called 'irrationalism' or 'anti-rationalism' or 'the revolt against reason' or 'anti-positivism'. All these terms are in some sense or another misleading and perhaps the best way to identify the common feature is to call it *subjectivism*. The reason is this: all these thinkers were in one way or another puzzled by the nature of what had hitherto been described as the *laws* which were said to operate in their respective fields of study—scientific laws, historical laws, economic or sociological laws. On the analogy of mid-nineteenth-century physics, these laws were believed to exist outside and independently of the observer. The laws of euclidean geometry, Newton's laws of thermodynamics, Comte's law of the 'three stages', Marx's dialectical law of social evolution—all claimed this objective and impersonal quality. The thinkers of the new generation were afflicted with a dreadful doubt: 'How,' they asked themselves, 'do we *know* that these are laws? By precisely what intellectual process do we ascertain them?' And all, in diverse ways, came up with a similar sort of notion. Laws are statements about the external world; but these statements are necessarily influenced—some said to a greater, others to a lesser extent—by our own psychic make-up. Into all these statements the personal had intruded. And hence in some degree or other these laws were not objective measures (*regulae*) of reality to which man like other beings and things conformed, but were subjective measures which man himself had moulded.

For instance: scientists had hitherto been wont to believe that all natural phenomena could be reduced to the laws of mechanics and that science would therefore—or could at any rate in principle—predict the future course of the universe. But Poincaré was to affirm that these famed general laws of science were neither statements of fact which could be checked by experiment nor *a priori* statements emanating, Kant-wise, from the categories of the human mind; that they were, instead, conventions which recommended themselves by their convenience or fruitfulness. Non-euclidean systems of geometry, the discovery of radio activity (the individual particles of which followed no predictable paths), the implications of the electro-magnetic theory of matter; all suddenly reopened the question of the logical status of the laws of nature.

Similar was the reaction taking place in the social and historical sciences. Of this Freud is so obvious and conspicuous an example that there is no need to elaborate; on his view most of human behaviour is the rationalisation or projection of drives and complexes stored deep in our unconscious. Bergson apprised the intrusive role of the subjective quite differently; but nevertheless he did apprise it. For him intelligence alone could not explain the whole of physical nature; it could not explain the nature of life and the process by which it had evolved and was continuing to evolve. Only the 'sympathetic communication ... between us and the rest of the living' could unveil that knowledge, and the sole path towards it lay not through the naked intellect but through intuition, akin to the aesthetic intuition of the creative artist regarding his subject.

At first sight, nothing could be more remote from this view than that of Durkheim. His works are empirical inquiries into limited topics like suicide or the social division of labour. In the course of them he elaborated his concept of 'collective representations': that is to say, society and its culture as externalised around us; and it was this, he argued, that shaped and gave content to our individual values through which in turn we apprehended society. The eyes through which we perceived our society were those with which it had itself endowed us. Once again, the personality had intruded between subject and object, between the observer and the phenomena he was trying to classify and reduce to laws. Likewise Weber: he reached the conclusion that the human sciences demanded special methods for their comprehension in addition to those appropriate for the natural sciences, and that they consisted in *Verstehen*, i.e. the cultivation of an empathy between the observer and his object of study. From across the Atlantic, William James affirmed that truth was not a final and fixed measure but shifted and changed, and that propositions became more or less true as they proved more or less useful to the individual making them. And it was James again who observed, in the first of his public lectures on pragmatism, that the temperament of the philosopher, however much he tries to sink it, 'really gives him a stronger bias than any of his more strictly objective premises', and that, trusting in his temperament, 'he believes in any representation of the universe that suits it'. Another example—eccentric though it be— is that of Georges Sorel. He distinguished, for instance, between marxism as a science and marxism as 'social poetry'; and it was in this second capacity that he found it formidable since it provided the proletariat with one of those great social myths which, irrefutable in proportion as they are non-rational, have, according to Sorel, incited men to action through the ages and provided the force which moves societies along.

Pareto was from ten to fifteen years older than either Freud or Durkheim or Bergson or Weber, but as his interest in social science awoke so late in life, he came to it at roughly the same time as they did—in the 1890s. At the outset he was a devout, albeit critical, believer in the dominant philosophies of reason, democracy and progress. Within ten years, however, in complete independence of these contemporaries, he had run up against their common problem and came up with a similar answer. Like them he sensed the intrusion of the human personality into the framing of what had hitherto been regarded as objective laws established by naked intellect.

Read in isolation from the intellectual movements of his day, his sociological works, and notably the million-word *General Treatise on Sociology*, sometimes seem idiosyncratic to the point of the bizarre. In the context of his time, however, Pareto must be regarded as not the least powerful of those who have been so well described as proposing 'views on human conduct so different from those commonly accepted at the time—and yet so manifestly inter-related—that together they seem to constitute an intellectual revolution': a revolution moreover 'from which there emerged the new assumptions characteristic of our own time'.[1]

II

Biographical Summary

Vilfredo Federico Damaso Pareto, born in Paris in 1848, came of a Ligurian family, ennobled in 1729. In 1835 (or 1836),[2] his father, the Marchese Rafaelle Pareto, while still a young man, fled Italy on account (so it is said) of his republican opinions and adherence to Mazzini and sought exile in France. There he took up the profession of civil engineer. He married a Frenchwoman, Marie Métenier, and it was in France that his three children—two daughters and the boy Vilfredo—were born.

He returned to Italy in 1855, to judge by a certificate attesting an award for his services in Genoa during the cholera epidemic of that year.[3] Shortly afterwards he entered the Piedmontese civil service in which he rose to high rank and honour. Meanwhile Vilfredo proceeded from school to the Turin Polytechnic to qualify in the same profession as his father. The five-year course in civil engineering which he followed there was of seminal importance to his later career as economist and sociologist. The first two years were devoted to mathematics in which Pareto was outstanding, and this proficiency was to lay the foundations for his success as a mathematical economist. His graduation thesis, *The fundamental principles of equilibrium in solid bodies*—an essay in mechanical equilibrium—was to become the paradigm for his conception of economics and, after economics, of sociology.

He graduated in 1870[4] and became a businessman. His first post was that of a director of the Rome Railway Company. He held this from 1870 to 1874 after which he became the managing director of the Società Ferriere d'Italia, a firm which extracted and processed iron and allied products, and which had its headquarters in Florence.

There Pareto moved in aristocratic salons—but professed extremist views in support of democracy, republicanism, free trade and disarmament. He despised the Italian aristocracy and regarded it as 'sucking the blood' of the Italian poor.[5] In 1876 the free-trading 'Right' fell from power; there followed the period of so called 'transformism' among the leftwing parties which led Italy towards protectionism and state intervention at home and military adventures abroad. Pareto now became an outspoken critic of the governing *consorteria*. In 1882 he stood as an opposition candidate for a constituency in Florence, but without success. He found his work as managing director increasingly handicapped by the necessity to negotiate 'deals' with influential deputies and government departments, and began to long to retire.[6] It was about this time that he started to conceive his notion of the Italian governing class as a great nexus of influence and pressure, using political power to win economic favours and economic favours to win political success, but concealing itself behind a façade of rigged elections and pliant legislatures.[7]

His father died in 1882; and after the death of his mother in 1889, the family household in Florence broke up and Pareto changed his entire way of living. He threw up the managing directorship of the firm and, instead, accepted a consultancy. Marrying a penniless Russian girl from Venice, Alessandrina ('Dina') Bakunin, he moved from Florence to a villa in Fiesole. He made use of his new leisure to launch a personal crusade against the government's foreign and domestic policies. Between 1889 and 1893 he wrote 167 articles, many of them scholarly, but the vast majority anti-government polemics. His public lectures in a working men's institute were closed by the police, and he became a marked man in government circles.

In the course of these activities, he became closely acquainted with other free-trading publicists and economists of the day and with one of these, Maffeo Pantaleoni, the economist, he formed a warm friendship which was to endure for the rest of his life. Through Pantaleoni, Pareto developed an interest in pure economics and became acquainted with the new, mathematically expressed equilibrium system developed by Walras, the professor of political economy at Lausanne. He soon began to contribute acute and learned articles expounding Walras's doctrine in the *Giornale degli Economisti*. For these his early mathematical training had equipped him superbly and they gained him international recognition. In 1893, with some intermediation from Pantaleoni, Pareto succeeded Walras in the chair of political economy at Lausanne; in 1894 this appointment was made permanent.

Pareto's first important publication was the two-volume *Cours d'Economie Politique* (1896), based on his university lectures. But during this period and until 1898, he continued to write his critical monthly 'Chronache' for the *Giornale degli Economisti* in which he maintained his passionately radical democratic and anti-interventionist critique of the Italian government. In his eyes the regime was going from bad to worse, and when the May Riots broke out in Milan in 1898 he ascribed the responsibility to the government's protectionism. He vindicated the forecasts which he and his free-trading colleagues had made by republishing a collection of their articles, with some of his own, in a book: *La Liberté économique et les événements d'Italie*. At the same time he sheltered and provided for the refugees, many of them socialists, who fled from Italy at that time. And when the Dreyfus affair exploded in that same year, Pareto became a dreyfusard and a passionate anti-anti-semite.[8]

Yet by 1900 his views had undergone a total revolution. He became an *anti*-democrat; and this new attitude intensified with every passing year. One cause was temperamental. Pareto's liberalism reflects a profound egotism. He was not gregarious; he was a cat who walked by himself. Furthermore, he loathed bullying and interference no matter for what purpose or from what quarter. The program of his liberalism was to strip the state of as many of its powers to intervene in social life as possible; in his own words, 'to end all privileges whatsoever'.[9] After 1898, partly owing to his disillusion with the sordid way in which the French dreyfusards had abused their victory and partly due to the way in which—in his eyes—the Italian and French trade unions were abusing their new-won right to unionise, he came to the conclusion that the extension of the suffrage and the rise of trade unions had merely replaced bourgeois privileges by working-class privileges, bourgeois oppression by working-class oppression. In the normal way, men have to choose the lesser of two evils. The only alternative is to turn one's back on the world and denounce it. This is precisely what Pareto was now in a position to do since, in 1898, his uncle had died leaving him a legacy the value of which at today's prices I estimate at about £200,000.

The other reason which contributed to the revolution in his thinking—and which incidentally also drove him to seek retirement from his teaching career for the sake of pursuing academic research—was an idea that had come to him in his reflections on the astonishing popularity of marxism in Italy. How was it that propositions which, in his view, were demonstrably false had come to be regarded by the best youth in Italy as—to use his own words—a 'new gospel'?[10] In 1897 the idea suddenly came to him that the bulk of human activitity is not due to rational processes at all but to sentiments. Men feel an urge and act; they invent justifications afterwards. He now burned to devote himself to writing a sociology based on this new principle.[11]

His new views were first expressed in 1900 in a long article for the *Rivista Italiana di Sociologia* and then in his book, *Les Systèmes Socialistes* (1901–2). They were further developed in his *Manuale di economia politica* (1906), published in French translation (*Manuel d'Economie politique*) in 1909.

By this date, his health had deteriorated. He had developed heart disease which caused him to confine himself more and more to his Villa Angora at Céligny whither he had moved from Lausanne, and in 1907 he retired from his chair at Lausanne (though he continued to deliver lectures on sociology until 1916). He had decided to write the long-meditated work on sociology. He began it in 1907 and, despite frequent bouts of illness, completed it in 1912. This is the *Trattato di Sociologia generale*, commonly known among English-speaking scholars as the *Treatise*. Publishing delays and the outbreak of war postponed its appearance until 1916. In the following year, the university signified its appreciation of his work by holding an international celebration in his honour.

The war had much impoverished Pareto and his health was now extremely precarious. Furthermore, his last years were preoccupied with personal difficulties. These sprang from the fact that in 1901 his wife Dina had betrayed him and absconded, and although Pareto was able to secure a legal separation, Italian law did not permit of divorce. Since that time a new woman, Jane Régis, had come into his life. It was to her 'affectionate care' that he dedicated the *Treatise*. He wanted to legitimise this relationship. In the end he succeeded, by taking Pantaleoni's advice and becoming a citizen of the city-state of Fiume, where the law permitted divorce. In 1923 he made Jane Régis his wife.

He continued to write until the last moment. Some of his articles were collected together and published in book form: the *Fatti e Teorie* (1920) and the *Trasformazione della Democrazia* (1921). They are, in most part, illustrations and adaptations of the themes advanced in the *Treatise*. He died in 1923, at the age of seventy-five, and lies buried in Céligny churchyard.

III

The Development of
Pareto's System

1. THE SYSTEM IN OUTLINE

Some of the matters discussed in the *Treatise* are better expressed in Pareto's previous works, while certain matters dealt with in these works are hardly discussed at all in the *Treatise*, because Pareto was by then taking them for granted. This is one reason for publishing passages from these works in Part One of these Selections. The second reason is that they illustrate the development of his doctrine. It is not easy to follow this, however, unless we already know the main outlines of his completed system. This is described in detail later on (see below page 31 *et seq*.), but it is necessary to give at this point a summary, albeit crude, and in this each main point is headed by a key word or phrase. This is to assist identification throughout the discussion.

1 EQUILIBRIUM. Society is to be regarded as a number of interdependent forces together constituting a system in moving equilibrium.

2 EXTERNAL FORCES. Some of these forces are external to the individual, e.g., soil, climate, race and external pressures both in space and time. Since all affect and enter into the next set of factors, they may be temporarily disregarded.

3 INTERNAL FORCES. These other forces are the internal drives of human beings, notably their inclinations, aptitudes and interests as manifested in their beliefs and theories.

4 SOCIAL HETEROGENEITY. By virtue of their psychic make-up, human beings are heterogeneous and unequal, and fall into different social strata and elites.

5 ELITE RULE. The most important societal distinction is between the governing elite (a minority) and the governed (the majority). Irrespective of the 'form' of the regime, all societies are governed by minority elites.

6 CIRCULATION OF ELITES. Individuals move in and out of these categories. In certain cases, one elite displaces another *en bloc*. Such movements constitute the 'circulation of elites'.

7 LOGICAL AND NON-LOGICAL BEHAVIOUR. Some human actions are logical (rational); other actions are non-logical (non-rational). This fact is concealed by the human tendency to 'logicalise' non-logical activity and make it seem logical.

8 SOCIAL UTILITY. A belief or theory may be useful to society however non-logical it may be, and vice versa. Its utility is not correlated with its scientific truth or falsity.

9 RESIDUE AND DERIVATION. Non-logical theories contain a constant element and a variable element. The constant element is called a *residue*, which (it is assumed) manifests human sentiments or states of mind. It lies at the root of otherwise very dissimilar theories, being tricked out and masked by a logical or pseudo-logical element called a *derivation*. The residue is non-logical and manifests some basic human impulse or attitude; as the unvarying element in multitudinous theories or activities, it is the true object of sociological enquiry, the derivations being mere masks or veils. There are six main classes of residues. The most important, socially, are the first two: Class I, which is the 'instinct for combining'; and Class II, which represents the propensity to conserve elements already combined and is styled 'the persistence of aggregates'. The first class is essentially innovatory, the second conservative.

10 RESIDUE DISTRIBUTION. Though the residues of one society usually differ from those of another, in any given society they change little for society as a whole; but their distribution between the social strata of that society changes markedly.

11 ALTERNATION OF ELITES. The relationship between the governing elite and the governed is determined by the way in which Class I and Class II residues are distributed between them. Governing groups with a preponderance of Class I residues tend to be mercantile, materialistic, innovatory; and they rule by guile. Governing groups in which Class II residues preponderate tend to be bureaucratic, idealistic, conservative; they rule by force. The proportion of Class I to Class II residues in the governing elite alternates through time. As the Class I residues preponderate in the rulers, so the Class II

residues build up among the ruled; the governing elite in this way comes to lose the propensity to use force, while the tendency to employ it builds up among the governed. So, ultimately, either by infiltration or revolution from below, the governing elite is displaced by a new elite drawn from the ranks of the former governed section of society. This process continues, the new governing elite in time being overthrown, for the same reason.

12 ECONOMIC-CULTURAL CYCLE. Other social phenomena—economic, intellectual and cultural—also alternate, their alternations being interdependent with the political cycle, as above.

13 INTERDEPENDENT FACTORS. As a first approximation to the form taken by the social equilibrium, the following factors should be isolated, and it is their interdependence which must be traced: (a) Interests; (b) Residues; (c) Derivations; (d) Social Heterogeneity and Circulation.

2. COURS D'ECONOMIE POLITIQUE (1896)*

Pareto was correcting proofs of this in June 1895. [12] It is his first major work. Although it is a treatise on pure and applied economics, it contains two chapters on sociology; both appear in the second volume. 'The General Principles of Social Evolution' forms chapter 1 of Book Two; 'Social Physiology' forms chapter 2 of Book Three. Pareto was already fully aware of the inadequacy of economic theory to describe and predict concrete social situations. He makes this perfectly explicit in the elaborate comparison between mechanical and social phenomena (Selections, p. 106).† To complete the picture drawn by economics, the other social factors had to be ascertained. Together, these factors constituted the *science sociale*—as he then called it. Indeed, Pareto goes further because at §629 he wrote that 'the science of utility is still very backward. We have indeed certain concepts of the utility of the individual, but our understanding of the utility of the species is most imperfect. Perhaps one day more progress will be made in this matter and maybe the time is not far

---

* Extracts from the *Cours* are given in the Selections, Part One, I, (pages 97–122).

† Hereafter the abbreviation *Sel.* is used for references to the translated extracts in Parts One, Two and Three. Where the square brackets contain only a reference to page or section numbers of a work of Pareto's, the matter cited is not included in the Selections. The following abbreviations are used in references to Pareto's works: *C.* (*Cours d'Economie politique*); *S.* (*Systèmes Socialistes*); *M.* (*Manuel d'Economie politique*); *T.* (*Treatise*); *FT.* (*Fatti e Teorie*); *Trasf.* (*Trasformazione della Democrazia*).

distant when the science of utility will, like the science of ophelimity, have a sure basis and scientifically rigorous method.' [*Sel.*, p. 103.] The suggestion that the conditions best conducive to the well-being of human societies could, in principle, be ascertained scientifically is a staggering one. It belonged to the early and sanguine 'do-gooder', not to the cynic of the *Treatise*.

For the *Cours* was written in the full flood of Pareto's liberalism. Individual liberty, free trade, private wealth are held to be goods. State interference is decisively repudiated. Pareto was still the preacher who believed that rational argument could affect social decision making. 'It is clear,' he wrote, 'that if a certain science can prove that protection will result in a destruction of wealth, the result thus obtained forms part of the very numerous conditions which determine social phenomena.' [*C.*, §607.]

The sociological chapters betray a powerful influence of the social darwinists and of Herbert Spencer. Although Pareto was critical of the former, he could find no better explanation for the shape of the distribution curve of incomes and aptitudes than zoological selection. [*Sel.*, pp. 112 *et seq.*] Spencer's thought is more pervasive. Throughout his entire discussion of social evolution Pareto utilises Spencer's concept of social differentiation. His notion of a cumulative increase in the degree of social differentiation from Roman times to the present also derives from Spencer; and, so we may surmise, does his basic concept of the mutual interdependence of all social phenomena.

One other general point is worthy of attention. In the chapter on 'Social Physiology', Pareto puts forward a theory which we may call his *theory of spoliation*. [*Sel.*, pp. 114 *et seq.*] This is the idea that in all societies at all times there exists a class of persons who seize on the goods of others, sometimes by legal and sometimes by illegal means. The 'governing class' which imposes protective tariffs is, in fact, indulging in legal spoliation. Pareto believed Marx's class struggle theory to be important and valid precisely because it brought the process of spoliation into the open. In the *Cours* Pareto puts his view forcibly; in the *Treatise* it becomes a subsidiary theory, to be found *inter alia* at §§2267, 2312–3. [*Sel.*, pp. 270, 277.] In the post-*Treatise* writings it appears again as an important part of his critique of 'pluto-democracy'. [*Transf. Sel.* 314–18, 320–2.]

What elements then of his mature system are already to be found in the *Cours* of 1896?

1 EQUILIBRIUM is fully developed as can be seen from chapter 1 of the second volume. [*Sel.*, pp. 103 *et seq.*] 2 EXTERNAL FORCES, *viz.*, soil, climate and race are all discussed more fully indeed than in any later

work. But Pareto rates them low. Obviously, since climate and soil are constant factors while social phenomena change, it is pointless to ascribe these changes to the constant phenomena—such is Pareto's view. As for race: he considered it of little or no sociological importance and to the end of his days remained an anti-racist. Among 3 INTERNAL FORCES, he devotes a great deal of time to the 'interests'—as befits a work on economics. For the rest, his recognition that men have different interests and aptitudes is used to establish his position on 4 SOCIAL HETEROGENEITY. This notion is fully developed here. [*Sel.*, pp. 110, 113–14.] He first considers the alleged differences between races only to reject them, as noticed. He then passes to social classes, which he accepts in something akin to a marxist sense. [*Sel.*, p. 117.] Here appears for the first time his famous curve of the distribution of incomes; and from this curve he goes on to consider a similar distribution for aptitudes in other fields. The income-distribution curve is taken as the paradigm. But Pareto has not yet taken to styling the top-bracket in each of these distribution-ranges the 'elite' of that particular range. His treatment of 5 ELITE RULE is still embryonic. He does not use the term 'elite' at all; instead, the chapter on 'Social Evolution' talks of 'aristocracy' (in its etymological sense of the 'rule of the best'), while the chapter on 'Social Physiology' uses the expression 'dominant class'.

The argument of the 'Social Evolution' chapter is spencerian: societies have moved from a homogeneous undifferentiated state to a state of heterogeneity and differentiation. Pareto asserts that despotisms (whether 'royal or jacobin') are not highly differentiated. The power of a despot is unlimited and extends over all branches of human activity. The subjects form an incoherent mass, and—politically at least—a homogeneous one. He concludes that 'liberty and heterogeneity are almost synonymous'. [*C.*, §658.] Historically, this differentiation usually begins with the emergence of an aristocracy. This differentiates the simple structure of the despotic regime. Differentiation proceeds further by the formation of more 'intermediary bodies between the individual and the state'. (This part of the argument derives directly from Montesquieu's *Esprit des Lois*.) 'These intermediary associations between the individual and the state are in fact one of the most powerful agents of social differentiation. . . . The instinct of despotic governments does not mislead them when it induces them rigorously to proscribe their subjects from forming associations.' [*C.*, §§659–60.]

Thus, so far the argument is a familiar pluralist argument, albeit tricked out in spenceresque terms. At this point it takes a sharp turn for Pareto goes on to discuss 'tutelage'. (We may note in passing that he seems to have introduced this under the influence of the *Précis d'Economie politique et de Morale* (1893) by Molinari, a man whom he admired till his dying day.) And here the 'aristocracy' is defined etymologically as a narrow group who are the best in physical and intellectual respects. [*Sel.*, pp. 109–11.] Such groups claim the *right* to rule the rest of society. Consistently with Pareto's anti-aristocratic and democratic sentiments of this period, he rejects this claim. He does so by arguing that the method by which the 'aristocratic' rulers are selected—whether by election or by heredity or co-option—is irrelevant to the problem of how to check their abuse of power. For, he says, 'The sole appreciable result of most revolutions has been the replacement of one set of politicians by another set.' [*Sel.*, p. 110.] Pareto is *assuming* that, by and large, 'aristocracies' are the essence of all forms of government, and that little social advance is to be expected from altering the methods by which they are selected. The true method lies in still further differentiation. It is social differentiation, up to the present time, which has hitherto been responsible for stripping the state of its former authority in matters intellectual, moral and religious, for substituting a spirit of innovation for the former neophobia, and for permitting the automatic play of the market to take the place of external compulsion by the government. In short, having asserted that societies are always or nearly always ruled by minorities, he argues that the only way to safeguard the public from them is to strip them of their powers, and to seek, in pluralism, the checks or balance of numerous social associations. [*C.*, §§686–9.] This conclusion is the one he was advancing at this time against protection, socialism, and state intervention.

Now, in the other chapter, 'Social Physiology', Pareto uses the expression 'dominant classes'. He conceives these as bodies with similar economic 'interests'. [*Sel.*, pp. 117 *et seq.*]; and thenceforward Pareto describes political struggle as, in practice, the struggle of the various economic classes to despoil one another. In doing so he specifically acknowledges his debt to Marx and Loria. But he once again makes the point raised in the earlier chapter, that this spoliation is not prevented by selecting the dominant class by one method rather than another. The important thing is to prevent all spoliation whatsoever [*Sel.*, p. 118], for the general tenor of his conclusion is, once again, that societies are always governed by a 'dominant class'.

Is the 'aristocracy' of the earlier chapter identical with the 'dominant class' of the later one? Pareto's private correspondence provides evidence that he was using them in an almost interchangeable sense. The term *classe dominante* (sometimes *classe dirigeante*) is a commonplace in his correspondence both before the publication of the *Cours* as well as afterwards; and in a letter of 1891 we find Pareto first contrasting 'dominant class' with 'the many' (from which we must infer that it itself is 'the few'); and then, a few lines later identifying 'the aristocrats of all ages' with 'the few'.[13] The conclusion must be that Pareto is taking it for granted that societies are, at least in general, ruled by minority groups irrespective of the purported *form* of their constitution, and that such groups have a natural tendency to exploit the remainder. The reason for his loose terminology and general lack of precision in defining these minorities is that, in this phase, his prime interest was to strip all governments, whatever their complexions, of as many powers as possible. And it is this which accounts for his switching interest to these 'aristocracies' in his next work, *Les Systèmes Socialistes*. For by that time he had become convinced that the battle against state intervention was lost.[14] There was no longer any point in campaigning against it. All that remained was merely to state and to analyse the process of exploitation. Furthermore, this conclusion gains further support from the fact that, in the *Systèmes*, Pareto uses the terms 'aristocracy' and 'elite' interchangeably. (See below page 22.)

The first indications of 6 CIRCULATION OF ELITES are also to be found in the *Cours*. [*Sel.*, pp. 111 *et seq.*] They occur where Pareto discusses the distribution of incomes in society and the corresponding distribution of abilities. Pareto asks himself why his curve takes the shape it does. He talks therefore of 'exchange' between its various levels; and he conceives this as a rise and fall of elements: a veritable circulation of them, similar (he says) to the circulation of the blood. But the explanation he gives is the process of zoological selection: a form of social darwinism. [*Sel.*, p. 112.]

Now follows an enormous gap as compared with the *Treatise*. There is a bare hint of 7 LOGICAL AND NON-LOGICAL BEHAVIOUR, but the notion of residues and derivations and their connections with the circulation of elites is totally absent. Again, in regard to 8 SOCIAL UTILITY, while the distinction between subjective desirability and objective utility is fully worked out [*Sel.*, p. 99], there is no suggestion that a belief may be socially useful though scientifically unsound, and *vice versa*. On 11 ALTERNATION OF ELITES we have nothing but the hints already mentioned, that one aristocracy or dominant class is simply succeeded by another. Finally, we are given a hint that the form of social phenomena is cyclical rather than linear [*Sel.*, p. 108] but Pareto does not elaborate this; nor does he maintain the proposition of 12 ECONOMIC-CULTURAL CYCLE, i.e., that all social phenomena occur in an undulatory form and that their undulations are all interconnected.

3. LES SYSTEMES SOCIALISTES (1902)*

A dramatic change occurred in Pareto's political outlook between the
completion of the *Cours* in 1896 and the appearance of the *Systèmes*
in 1902. He now despaired of halting the course of 'socialism',
whether of the bourgeois kind (protectionism and state intervention-
ism) or of the 'popular' variety, and henceforward he decided to
analyse and comment, but to participate no more.[15] Moreover, he
had developed his central concept: the paramountcy of the non-
rational in human affairs. From 1897, he began delivering a course on
sociology at Lausanne. 'The principle of my sociology,' he told
Pantaleoni in that year, 'rests precisely upon separating logical from
non-logical actions and in showing that in most men the second
category is far larger than the former.'[16] 'Reason is of little or no
importance in shaping social phenomena. The operative forces are
different ones; this is what I want to prove in my sociology.'[17] 'Men
think they are choosing their opinions, but instead these are imposed
on them by their mode of life just as it is imposed on fish that they
must breathe through gills and on mammals that they must breathe
through lungs.'[18]

The *Systèmes* owes its origin to a conversation with Pantaleoni
just as the second volume of the *Cours* was appearing. 'After our
discussion,' Pareto wrote, 'I saw the usefulness of giving a general
theory of these systems.'[19] He does not appear to have begun it,
however, until the spring of 1899 when he mentions it as 'the compendium of my *Cours* on social and socialist systems'.[20] He finished
it in September 1901.[21] Thus it overlaps with two other works he was
writing at that time: the second chapter of his *Manuale di Economia
politica* ('Introduction to Social Science') which he sent to Pantaleoni
in January 1900;[22] and an article for the *Rivista Italiana di Sociologia*, published in July 1900, entitled 'Some applications of sociological theory'.[23] The chapter from the *Manuale* was undoubtedly
reworked before its completion in 1904, and will be dealt with in the
next section. It makes some very considerable advances on the
Systèmes. But the first chapter of the *Systèmes* was probably completed in early 1900 *after* which Pareto would have drawn on it to
write his article in the *Rivista Italiana*; this, a long essay, is a notable
work: it foreshadows all the positions Pareto was to take up later.†
Long before he wrote the *Cours* Pareto had recognised marxism

---

* Extracts from the *Systèmes* are given in the Selection, Part One, II,
(pages 123–42).

† Internal evidence shows that this was retouched as late as 22 June
1900. It was probably written in April–May of that year.

and popular socialism as a kind of lay religion. 'This book,' he wrote, referring to *Capital*, 'is the gospel of an ever increasing number of men.'[24] Elsewhere he writes of 'these other believers who call themselves socialists. Have I never mentioned this to you? At Milan I saw youths like Rondani sacrificing their whole lives to become apostles of the new religion and who have a faith in the principles of Marx equal to that of the early christians in the gospel.'[25] The *Systèmes Socialistes* is an exercise on this theme. It examines various types of socialism both as practice and as sets of theoretical principles; it fully reflects Pareto's new-found belief that non-rationality is the principal spring of human activity. Non-rational beliefs are more important in spurring men to action than logical demonstration. Socialist theories are, precisely, such non-rational beliefs; they are a new form of faith, the faith of the lower class, representing its assault on the governing class. It is assisted in this assault by the defection of foolish or traitorous or time-serving elements of the governing class, and by this class's sentimental pandering to humanitarianism. In so far as this weakens the resistance of the governing class to the socialist assault, it represents decadence.

Pareto had always considered socialism and protectionism as two aspects of an identical movement, and he despised both equally. So, whereas the *Cours* is chiefly concerned to attack bourgeois state intervention, the *Systèmes* is concerned with the 'popular' socialist attempts to intervene in economic affairs. When he wrote it he was still a free trader and anti-interventionist, but he had lost the desire to persuade and advocate; his sole business now was to analyse. Despite this he could not suppress his private feelings and the book is shot through with shafts of irony and seethes with boiling gusts of invective at humanitarianism and the class treachery of sentimental or time-serving members of the bourgeoisie. Hitherto his sympathy had gone generously to the weak. In the *Systèmes* it is not extended to the strong, but, rather, to those who are willing to use what strength they have to stand their ground. Pareto by no means blames the proletariat for trying to get the better of the bourgeoisie; but he blames the bourgeoisie for playing the sheep. (One of the Genoese sayings with which he sprinkles his letters and his published work is: 'Play the sheep and you will meet the butcher.') His belief that rational argument can resolve the conflict has now disappeared; instead he now maintains that only self-interest and sentiments are efficacious. The veiled optimism of the *Cours* has totally disappeared.

The influence of Herbert Spencer has gone too, but social darwinism still leaves its powerful trace in explaining (as in the *Cours*) the circulation of individuals between the upper and lower levels of income and of ability. Pareto still quotes Marx approvingly as well as a new luminary, Sorel, with whom he had established the most friendly relations, which were to endure for the rest of his life. And the theory of spoliation, so important in the *Cours*, retains all its importance in the *Systèmes*. [*Sel.*, pp. 137–8, pp. 139 *et seq.*]

What advances towards the completed system does the *Systèmes* make, compared with those in the *Cours*?

Already fully treated in the *Cours*, 1 EQUILIBRIUM is not further developed, but is simply presupposed. Nor are 2 EXTERNAL FORCES developed further, except that the racist notions of Lapouge and Ammon are contemptuously rejected. Instead, the whole focus of the book is upon 3 INTERNAL FORCES—upon the human temperament. 'Interests' [*Sel.*, pp. 137 *et seq.*, and pp. 140 *et seq.*] are once again mentioned, and so are 'aptitudes' [*Sel.*, p. 131] as in the *Cours*, but for the first time great stress is laid on what Pareto calls 'sentiments', [*Sel.*, pp. 124, 128–9] and, finally, upon the vital importance to human motivation of *theories or beliefs*. [*Sel.*, Part One, II *passim*, esp. 1.] These theories and beliefs, linked as they are to 'sentiments', now move to the centre of the stage among the internal, psychic phenomena; and by the same token, reason is moved out.

The discussion of 4 SOCIAL HETEROGENEITY follows much the same lines as in the *Cours*. Racial groupings, economic classes, occupational groupings, as well as the groupings based on aptitudes and on wealth [*Sel.*, pp. 130 *et seq.*], are again recognised here. The treatment of the curves of ability and of wealth is lifted, as Pareto admits, from the *Cours* often in the self-same words; but with one important addition, that of a new nomenclature. For he has now reached a sharper definition of 5 ELITE RULE. In the *Systèmes* he first of all postulates that social and economic power is directly correlated with the possession of wealth: 'the classes called "superior" are generally also the richest'. He then says that 'these classes represent an elite, an aristocracy, in the etymological sense of ἄριστος, *the best*'. [*Sel.*, p. 131.] Thus the 'aristocracy' of the *Cours* is formally identified with the 'elite' of the *Systèmes* and the later works. Furthermore, the entire work proceeds on the assumption that all societies, irrespective of their form of government, are ruled by elites. A revolution, even in the name of socialism and the masses, is really only a battle between two rival elites and ends by the displacement of one in favour of the other. [*Sel.*, Part One, II, sections 4 and 5, especially the latter.]

Clearly, the laws governing the rise and fall of elites are of immense importance; and so postulate 6 CIRCULATION OF ELITES is more extended than in the *Cours*. Pareto distinguishes between hereditary and co-optative elites. He continues to ascribe the rise and fall of aristocracies of birth to zoological selection [*Sel.*, pp. 132–3]; but he finds the reason for the degeneracy of co-optative elites 'obscure', and attributes it to a waning of their idealism. [*Sel.*, p. 133.] This is a mere shot in the dark in the *Systèmes*; but the notion is to persist and find its way into the *Treatise*.

Pareto had grasped the distinction between 7 LOGICAL AND NON-LOGICAL BEHAVIOUR in 1897; but oddly enough, though he uses the terms 'logical actions' and 'non-logical actions' in letters to Pantaleoni,[26] he does not do so in the *Systèmes*. Even so, the early pages of the *Systèmes* are devoted precisely to drawing a distinction between subjective belief and objective occurrences, and to the rationalisations of the latter which produce the former. [*Sel.*, Part One, II, 1 *passim*.] This marks a completely new departure from the *Cours*, but is a mere sketch as compared with the *Manuale*, and bears no comparison at all with the massive elaboration of the notion in the *Treatise*. But he had grasped the point quite clearly enough to develop the postulate 8 SOCIAL UTILITY to its full extent. 'The diffusion of a doctrine depends hardly at all on its logical value. Quite the contrary ...' [*Sel.*, pp. 126, 127–8.]

He had still not arrived, however, at the analysis of non-logical behaviour into 9 RESIDUE AND DERIVATION. Yet there is here a hint of what was to come. He draws attention to certain persisting sentiments. Their 'hard core persists; the form in which they are expressed may be extremely variable'; and he goes on to state the problem of how to discover the common hard core under differing manifestations. [*Sel.*, p. 128.] This is the program of the *Treatise*! As to the differential 10 RESIDUE DISTRIBUTION between classes, this is quite absent, as one would expect; and hence 11 ALTERNATION OF ELITES is not yet explained in terms of sentiments. All the same, the analysis of the struggle between elites and of their replacement is much more complete and sophisticated than in the *Cours*. We find here certain propositions later fully developed in the *Treatise*. For instance, the *Systèmes* establishes the relationship between the circulation of the elites and their rise and fall: the open elite fends away revolution by creaming off the potential leaders of the counter-elite into its own ranks. Another point to be much developed later is the relationship of 'force' to the rise and fall of elites. If they are not prepared to use force they will be pushed aside by their opponents. This is why humanitarianism is a sign of decadence in an elite. [*Sel.*, p. 135.] And particularly to be noted is the statement that 'the lower classes are themselves incapable of ruling'. What they do, instead, is simply to produce a new elite. [*Sel.*, p. 135.] The way is cleared, in the preceding propositions, for a theory which will be able, in some way or another, to assert that elites are safest when they are 'open' to the subject classes, and at the same time virile enough to use force to preserve their position; and that in proportion as their conviction and willingness to use force weakens, so they will be pushed aside by a new elite drawn from the subject class.

In discussing the rise of one elite and the fall of another, Pareto introduces for the first time the notion of 12 ECONOMIC-CULTURAL CYCLE. The arrival of a new elite, he remarks, is accompanied by a burst of unusual prosperity and intellectual vigour. Elsewhere he talks of a rhythm of economic, moral and religious movements, especially the alternation between 'reason' and 'faith'. [*Sel.*, pp. 129 *et seq.*] But why such movements occur, and how all are linked together and with the political cycle, is not further explored.

4. MANUEL D'ECONOMIE POLITIQUE (1909)*

According to date of publication, a four-year period elapsed between the *Systèmes* and the *Manuale*, with its important sociological chapter, the 'Introduction to Social Science'. But the *Manuale* was in fact completed in 1904,[27] and we know that the sociology chapter was in draft in 1900. We also know that between the completion of the *Systèmes* in mid-1902 and the completion of the *Manuale* two years later, Pareto concentrated on the economic chapters, especially the mathematical appendix. Hence, although it would almost certainly be correct to surmise that the 'Introduction to Social Science' was reworked between 1900 and 1904, we ought not to expect any considerable advance in Pareto's sociology between these dates.

In 1906–7 the French translation was undertaken (published in 1909), and Pareto seized the opportunity to make a thorough revision of the mathematical appendix together with certain stylistic corrections to the text. But the main substance of the text is left intact; and it is this French text which has been used in this work, and is referred to throughout as the *Manuel* to distinguish it from the earlier Italian edition.

The first two chapters of the *Manuel* deal respectively with the nature of experimental science and of scientific 'laws', and with general sociology. By this time Pareto had totally abjured his free-trading zeal, and was now professing an entirely neutral attitude on this as well as on all other social questions. Yet his repugnance to socialism and every other form of state interference is most marked,

* Pareto's *Manuale di Economia politica* was published in 1906. Extracts from the French translation of 1909 (*Manuel d'Economie politique*), revised by the author, are given in the Selections, Part One, III (pages 143–64).

especially where he develops his thesis that the balance, formerly favouring the bourgeoisie, has now swung heavily in favour of the workers, and that these are assisted and abetted by the humanitarianism of one part of the bourgeoisie and the cowardice or cupidity of other parts. Whenever Pareto touches on this matter his supposed detachment entirely disappears and he spills over with fury and contempt.

Already firmly established in his previous writings, 1 EQUILIBRIUM is the guiding concept of the entire work, both in its sociological and its strictly economic sections. But 2 EXTERNAL FORCES are now totally ignored. All is reduced to 3 INTERNAL FORCES. The very first paragraph of chapter 2 'Introduction to Social Science' begins: 'Clearly psychology is the basis of political economy, and, in general, of all the social sciences'; and as before attention is concentrated on individual aptitudes, interests, beliefs and theories. It is worth noticing that in the *Manuel* the 'interests' receive a relatively large share of attention, whereas in the *Treatise* they drop to an altogether subsidiary place. This is because Pareto regarded political economy as the branch of social science directly concerned with interests; so that, having dealt with these in his economic writings, he chose to concentrate his strictly sociological research in the *Treatise* on non-rational beliefs and theories. Much of the 'Introduction of Social Science' is concerned with these, being a development of the earlier work, notably the *Systèmes*.

4 SOCIAL HETEROGENEITY follows the same pattern as before, but there are two advances towards the positions later taken up in the *Treatise*. First, the concept of elite is elaborated. For the first time Pareto defines the elite as simply *the best in any one particular field*—it can be 'an aristocracy of saints or an aristocracy of brigands', etc. [*Sel.*, p. 155.] In so far as a group of people possess qualities which promote their own welfare and domination in society, these are called the elite (without further qualification). [*Ibid.*] This conception opens the way to the distinction in the *Treatise* between the 'governing elite' and the 'non-governing elite'—a distinction foreshadowed at another point in the *Manuel* where Pareto observes that individuals at the top of the intellectual pyramid will not necessarily be at the top of the economic pyramid and so forth. [*Sel.*, p. 153.]

Secondly, the concept of 'class' in its marxist sense—a concept clearly used both in the *Cours* and in the *Systèmes*—is no longer sharply distinguished from the concept of the 'dominant' or 'governing' class, i.e., the *elite*. On the contrary, in the index to the book, 'Class struggle' refers, in all cases, to the ruler-ruled relationship. This elision of 'economic' class is the counterpart of the elision of 'interest' as a human motivation which is beginning to occur in the *Manuel*; and this is carried forward in the *Treatise* to the almost total exclusion of the concept of economic class and class struggle. (See below, pages 48–51.) The notion of 5 ELITE RULE is now complete in all essentials. All societies are ruled by elites, even democracies. [*Sel.*, pp. 155, 159.] On 6 CIRCULATION OF ELITES, Pareto still sets much store on zoological selection. [*Sel.*, pp. 158 *et seq.*] The interesting point about the treatment, however [cf. *Sel.*, Part One, III, section 4 *passim*] is that Pareto now pays far greater attention to the problem of the circulation of the elites. Obviously, if societies are always governed by an elite, the law regulating their rise and decline is the master-key to explaining social change. Hence Pareto's extended effort to suggest such laws, and the glimmerings of the notion of alternation. (See opposite page on 11 ALTERNATION OF ELITES.)

The *Manuel* further systematises the concept of 7 LOGICAL AND NON-LOGICAL BEHAVIOUR. These terms are here used for the first time. [*Sel.*, pp. 143 *et seq.*] Of considerable importance is the long passage of arms with ethical theories. In the 'Introduction' Pareto subjects these to a long damaging examination designed to show that from the 'logico-experimental' standpoint all of them merely reflect the personal sentiments of their propounder. This elaborate passage is not reproduced in our text, but its general purport is given in another passage. [*Sel.*, pp. 148–9.] So, whereas the *Cours* hopefully hailed the day when the objective utility of societies would be ascertained scientifically (see above page 16), the *Manuel* reaches the pessimistic conclusion: 'These problems (i.e., of social utility) have as yet no solutions, not even roughly approximate ones, when they concern actions depending on sentiments and on politics.' [*M.*, ch. 2, §97.]

By the same token, the proposition about 8 SOCIAL UTILITY, *viz.* that the truth and the social efficacy of a belief are not the same, is restated categorically. 'Faith alone strongly moves men to action. Nor is it desirable for the good of society that the mass of men, or even only many of them, should consider social matters scientifically.' [*Sel.*, pp. 150 *et seq.*]

Now follows a gap. The *Manuel* goes no further towards the concept of 9 RESIDUE AND DERIVATION than did the *Systèmes*. The term most frequently used is 'sentiment', and this is not differentiated. On 10 RESIDUE DISTRIBUTION or, in this context, the differential distribution of 'sentiments' between rulers and ruled, Pareto does make some significant advance. As can be seen from the Selections [Part One, III, section 3], he was now beginning to grope towards a key idea of the *Treatise*; i.e., that the motivations of the elite are different from those of the governed, and that this accounts for the rise and fall of governing elites. However, the view here put forward differs

from that in the *Treatise*. There the masses are said to be character-
ised by faith and idealism, to be emotional, and not to have a clear
view of their own interests. The *Manuel* ascribes to the masses not
simply neophobia but also materialism. [*Sel.*, pp. 153 *et seq.*] On the
other hand, Pareto was confronted by the brute fact that among the
working classes there had arisen, on his own showing, a 'new faith'—
socialism. Likewise he had continually quoted de Tocqueville as
evidence that the French Revolution was really religious in character,
an upsurgence of the religion of the masses against their sceptical
rulers. He therefore tried to reconcile this view with the materialistic
character of the masses, but the result [*M.*, ch. 2, §§55–73] is confused
and unconvincing. Its importance here does not lie in the solution
propounded—which is changed in the *Treatise*—but simply in that
Pareto propounds the problem for the first time.

Similarly with 11 ALTERNATION OF ELITES. In the *Manuel*, this
concept acquires definition for the first time. Pareto formulates it
many times in much the same way. 'When active, energetic and intelligent elements accumulate in the lower strata of society, while in
contrast the upper strata contain too high a proportion of degenerate
elements, a revolution breaks out which replaces one aristocracy by
another.' [*Sel.*, p. 162; cf. also p. 159.] He had hitherto argued that the
process was governed by zoological selection. Now, though still regarding this as a main factor, he adds that it is not the only one. The
'mutability' of a social system is also associated with social factors like
the laws of inheritance and private property, and the political power
of those already in positions of authority. These factors work against
the change in elites, and make for stability in social structure. [*Sel.*,
pp. 161 *et seq.*]

On 12 ECONOMIC-CULTURAL CYCLE, the *Manuel* makes little
advance. Perhaps the most striking evidence of how far the *Manuel*
falls short of the theory of the *Treatise* lies in its list of the chief
causally significant factors in social change. In the *Treatise*, as we have
noticed, they are: interests, residues, derivations, and social heterogeneity of society and its circulation. In the *Manuel* on the other
hand they are: natural selection, the average wealth per capita,
social hierarchy, and the succession of elites. [*Sel.*, p. 160.]

5. THE TREATISE ON GENERAL SOCIOLOGY (1916)*

Certain critics of the *Treatise* have written about it as though it were
a product of the post-1918 period, when the importance of the

---

* Extracts from the *Treatise* are given in the Selections, Part Two
(pp. 167–283).

irrational factors in human motivation had become understood, when the 'rationalisation' of such impulses was likewise widely accepted, when the role of force in government had become too apparent to need proving, when democracy was no longer regarded as the inevitable stage towards which all human societies must move —in short, when pessimism and doubts about 'progress' had become widespread. In fact, the *Treatise* was begun in 1907 and completed in 1912.[28] Seen in this light, its views on such matters were strikingly original.

The *Treatise* has had an unhappy reception. This is in a large measure due to its form and character, but in six respects it was unlucky. First: though completed in 1912, it did not appear until 1916,[29] in the midst of the world conflagration. Secondly: it was unfortunate that it appeared in Italian and French rather than in English. French texts do not circulate to the extent they should in areas where the great advances in sociology have been—and still are being—made. These two factors help to explain why the Anglo-American world paid little immediate attention to the *Treatise*. Moreover, the French for their part had their own Durkheim school of sociology, one alien to Pareto's approach, and to that school they were then, as to some extent they still are, parochially attached. In Italy, overwhelmed as it was by fascism in 1922, free thought in the social sciences suffered an eclipse.

This brings us to the third misfortune of the *Treatise*. Mussolini boasted that he had been one of Pareto's pupils at Lausanne in 1904. (This probably means no more than that he attended Pareto's lectures.) The fascist leader hailed Pareto as his inspirer and teacher; indeed, he insisted on making him (against his wishes) a senator of Italy.[30] The fascist party and its intellectuals followed the Duce's lead and canonised Pareto as a protofascist. Since no Italian scholar was permitted, let alone encouraged, to interpret Pareto in any other way than as pro-fascist, and since the Italian scholars in exile regarded him in that very light because of his contempt for humanitarianism and parliamentarianism, Anglo-American scholars tended to take the fascists' words at their face value. If they considered Pareto at all, it was as an enemy of their democratic convictions.

Fourthly: it was precisely when the anti-fascism and anti-nazism of such scholars was at its peak that Arthur Livingston's English translation (*The Mind and Society*, 1935) made the work widely accessible. The cynicism of the *Treatise* and its contempt for humanitarians accorded ill with what was known of concentration camps. Of the scholars reviewing the English translation at that time, the only ones approaching the book without an overt or unconscious 'anti-fascist' bias belonged to a small group of Americans who had founded a seminar at Harvard to study Pareto: Homans, Curtis, Henderson, Schumpeter and Talcott Parsons. Elsewhere, as in the work of Melvin Rader or Borkenau, the political bias engendered hostile criticism.[31]

Fifthly: the ideologies and political practices of the post-1930 period were just the reverse of those current at the time when the book was written. Then the prevalent ideas were of progress, of solidarity, of peaceful change by rational argument. But in the period of the 1930s and after, the current ideologies were, to use Pareto's terms, overtly '*anti*-intellectual' instead of '*pseudo*-intellectual'. They were the ideologies of nationalism, imperialism, racism, anti-semitism, and the like. In the *Treatise* Pareto condemns every one of these by name; but he pays by far the greatest amount of attention to the 'liberal' ideologies because these were predominant when he wrote the *Treatise*. In fact, he was the foe of all ideologies: in his own words 'an atheist of all religions'. But to progressive intellectuals living in the grim world of the 'entre deux guerres' he had attacked the *wrong* ideologies. Worse still, he had demonstrated that they *were* ideologies!

Sixthly: not only was the main point of the *Treatise*, the importance of the irrational, widely understood by the 1930s; it had also been given a—seemingly—far more convincing explanation by Freud. Consequently, the critics tended to argue that in the *Treatise* what was new was not true, and what was true was not new.

All the same, and making allowance for these unfavourable factors which prejudiced the work's reception, it has to be said that the *Treatise* is not a very satisfactory book. It is vast, lopsided and ill-conceived. The structure is none too clear. Its arguments are often fallacious. And, for all its vast length, it is a mere fragment. The argument of the book will be considered in detail later; here four points need to be noticed.

(i) Defects of form: these are threefold. In the first place, for all his vaunted impartiality, Pareto rarely passed over an opportunity for deriding democratic or humanitarian sentiments. Such interjections, it should be noticed, are not in the least necessary to support his argument. Indeed, they have the effect of hindering it for they irritate readers who do not share his views yet who would, otherwise, at least given them serious consideration. These interjections appear simply because Pareto enjoyed baiting his opponents.[32] In the second place, the arrangement is distracting. Arguments peter out, to be renewed at another place. Minor points receive vast and meticulous attention, whereas major points are often dismissed with short shrift. Footnotes of vast length—minor essays of great literary and argumentory artistry—are thrust into the text at unexpected places. 'The construction, fairly simple, disappears under a kind of vegetation which, beautiful as it may be, is as exuberant as that which envelopes a Maya ruin in the virgin jungle.'[33] Finally, for all its million words, the *Treatise* is not a treatise at all: it is a great, sprawling, untidy torso. The role of interests and economic classes is almost entirely excluded—not, as we know, because Pareto undervalued them but because he was assuming them as dealt with in his economic works. Yet for his system of sociology to be complete, these factors need to have a stress equal to that given to the non-rational impulses.

(ii) The external factors (climate, race, history and the like) are entirely excluded from consideration—again, not because he thought them unimportant, but because he was working, as he put it, on a 'first approximation'. (iii) Social conditioning is ignored. The notion that one's interests and theories, and one's non-rational attitudes (the residues) might be affected by the social environment as a whole was not alien to Pareto; but he did not make the slightest attempt to explain this relationship. (iv) He was so anxious to trace uniformities that he failed adequately to account for *changes*.

These grave omissions are partly explained by the antecedents of the *Treatise* in the previous works, and by Pareto's assumption that certain matters had been explained already. It will be recalled that by 1904, he had established in basic principle (of course, the matters are greatly elaborated in the *Treatise*) the following elements of his system: 1 EQUILIBRIUM AND INTERDEPENDENCE; 2 EXTERNAL FORCES; 3 INTERNAL FORCES; 4 SOCIAL HETEROGENEITY; 5 ELITE RULE; 7 the distinction between LOGICAL AND NON-LOGICAL BEHAVIOUR, and its corollary, 8 SOCIAL UTILITY (i.e., that it is faith, not scientific truth, which makes theories socially efficacious).

What Pareto sought when he started on the *Treatise* was the theory to link together the two already established parts of the system, *viz.*, the part relating to the importance of interests and beliefs on the one hand, and the part relating to social structure and rule by elites on the other. It is because of its strategic importance that Pareto dwelt on this and truncated all other discussions. And the master-solution lay in 9 RESIDUE AND DERIVATION, with its corollary, 10 DIFFERENTIAL DISTRIBUTION OF RESIDUES. These two elements explain alike the circulation of the elites, their alternation, and the way in which the political, economic and cultural cycles are interlinked. With them the other parts of his theory become coherent. Only the quest of this missing factor interested Pareto, and this is why three-quarters of the *Treatise* is concerned with the residues and their derivations and only the last two chapters deal with what would be generally held as the concern of a treatise on sociology, viz. 'The General Form of Society'.

IV

The System

1. EQUILIBRIUM

Pareto considered that he had the choice of two models for his enquiry: the model of society as an organism; and the alternative model of society as a system of mutually interacting particles which move from one state of equilibrium to another (i.e., the mechanical analogy). He chose the latter deliberately because, as he says in the *Cours*, 'the way in which living organisms are arranged is much more rigid and defined than is a system of material points. Now in political economy and social science our task is, precisely, to effect considerable variations in a continuous fashion in the motion of certain parts. . . .' The mechanical model 'alone permits an understanding of the very complicated actions and reactions of social phenomena . . . and in this way affords us a precise conception of social and economic equilibrium.' It also enables one to consider 'virtual' movements—that is to say, movements which arise in the system if we assume that one of its points has been artificially moved in a certain direction. The organic model does not permit this operation. On the other hand, it is the better of the two 'when the problem is one of forming an idea of the evolution of societies'. [*C.*, §619.]

'The form of society is determined by all the elements acting upon it,' he wrote at §2060 of the *Treatise*, 'and in turn it reacts upon them.' [*Sel.*, p. 251.] Further on he wrote: 'Action and reaction follow one another indefinitely as in a circle.' [I, §2207, *Sel.*, p. 261.] 'Think,' he said in one of his letters, 'of so many little bits of lead attached together by elastic threads which interlace in a thousand ways. You cannot move one of these pieces of lead without altering the form of the whole system.'[34]

31

These movements and countermovements adjust themselves to one another to produce a state of equilibrium. 'Accidental movements arising in a society are neutralised by the counteracting movements they provoke; and ultimately, as a rule, they die away and society reverts to its previous state. A society where this occurs can therefore be considered as being in a state of equilibrium, and of *stable* equilibrium.' Real societies, however, are in continual motion: their condition is one of *dynamic* equilibrium—'society in its entirety being borne along by a general movement which slowly modifies it'. [*C.*, §§585–6; *Sel.*, p. 104.]

In the science of mechanics, the observer can apply the concept of dynamic equilibrium. The social scientist cannot; instead, he has to consider society as moving from one static equilibrium to another static equilibrium, in a continual series. Imagine, says Pareto, two men descending a mountain side. One slides down, the other picks his way down from rock to rock. The first illustrates dynamic equilibrium, the second the series of static equilibria which is appropriate to social enquiries. [*C.*, §587; *Sel.*, p. 104.] In selecting this mechanical analogy, with its central concept of equilibrium, Pareto was applying to sociology—as he had already to economics—the method and concepts of mechanics. How selfconsciously he did this can be seen from the lengthy parallels he draws between mechanical and social phenomena at §592 of the *Cours*. [*Sel.*, pp. 106–7.]

2. ELEMENTS OF THE SOCIAL SYSTEM

So numerous are the elements which together determine the form of society that only the most important can be considered in the first instance. Those which Pareto elects to consider are, on the one side, the psychological characteristics and motivations of men, and on the other, the reflections of these in the stratification of society. All others are put aside. Although, as we have noted above, he affirmed that the form of society reacts upon all the elements acting on it, he never considered the way in which this reaction occurs, nor did he consider the way in which a given society is conditioned by its past history; although he recognised that both of these affected the form of society. Likewise he put aside the considerations of race, natural selection, geography and climate, although well aware of their relevance, for they formed three fifths of the course in sociology he was delivering at Lausanne.[35] Instead, in the *Treatise* he subsumes all these elements under those he selects for consideration. For instance, he reduces the significance of race by deliberately confining himself to

Europe and the Mediterranean littoral. Again, he sets aside the question of geographical environment by assuming that its effects will already have manifested themselves in the psychological traits of the societies under review. [*T.*, §§2064–5.]

Which elements, then, are deemed worthy of investigation? At first sight, they appear to vary from one part of the text of the *Treatise* to another. [*Cf.*, 'Index Summary of Theorems': 1b.] The definitive list at §2205, however, comprises only four: residues, interests, derivations, and social heterogeneity and circulation. [*Sel.*, p. 260.] This list of four operative elements breaks into two. On the one side stand the psychological states or motivations: i.e., residues, derivations and interests. On the other stand the results of other states, conditions and motivations—*viz.*, the stratification. These are variously listed elsewhere as interests, inclinations, capacities for reasoning and observation, appetites [*cf. T.*, §2060, *Sel.*, p. 251, and 'Index of Theorems': 1b]. These two parts are locked together by Pareto's concept of vertical social mobility, i.e., 'the circulation of elites'. This *relates* to structures, but is *explained* in terms of the residues, the derivations and the interests.

3. RESIDUES, DERIVATIONS, INTERESTS

Human activities are of three types. First, men perform certain purely instinctive actions, without the intermediation of any process of reasoning. Secondly, there are purely rational actions (though Pareto always uses the term 'logical' instead of 'rational'). Such actions involve a relationship of means to end which appears identical both to the performer and to any experienced, disinterested observer of the act. The natural sciences, strategy, technology and economics comprise many such actions of logical behaviour. Thirdly—and most numerous—comes the class of non-logical actions. This is a residual class. Such actions often *seem* to be logical, and men go to great pains to convince themselves and others that they are logical; but in fact they are not.

'Human beings,' writes Pareto, 'often fail to recognise—they do not know, they disregard—the fact that many of the verbal manifestations which go to make up (this class of action) are mere manifestations of instincts, inclinations and so forth. One of the purposes of this work (the *Treatise*) is to strip realities of these emotional veils.' ['Index Summary of Theorems': 1b.] Ignored, under-rated or misunderstood in the past, the class of non-logical actions is of major, perhaps of maximum, importance among the various elements determining the social system.

(i) *Logical and non-logical actions*

Logical actions are those which are 'logically linked to an end, not only in respect to the person performing them, but also to those other people who have more extensive knowledge: that is to say . . . behaviour which is subjectively and objectively logical in the sense here indicated. Other actions we shall call non-logical.' [*T.*, §150; *Sel.*, p. 184.] Thus:

> 1. The relationship of the action to the desired end must be established in the actor's mind by a scientifically verifiable theory; or, supposing he does not know this theory, his behaviour's efficaciousness must be verifiable in terms of such a theory.
> 2. The 'subjective end', i.e., the state of affairs the actor wishes to bring about must coincide with the end actually brought about as seen by the detached scientific observer.

Pareto illustrates this concept and the residual category of non-logical actions by the synoptic table at §151. [*Sel.*, p. 184.]

Of these, Class II-2 has occasioned much controversy. In this the actor has an aim but as far as the observer is concerned achieves no result. Borkenau, for instance, comments that in this class come the actions in 'which the performer's aim and the actual result obtained differ' and continues: 'Science and economics are (according to Pareto) specifically logical. Religion and metaphysics (are) specifically non-logical. Is it really the case that science and economic behaviour always achieve their aim, and religion, etc., do not? Such a statement is more than doubtful.'[36] The criticism is misplaced because there are two ways in which the actor may act purposefully and yet, as far as the observer can see, achieve no result. It may be that he is working on an erroneous hypothesis. If that were the only possibility, Borkenau would be perfectly right. But there is a second way in which the condition can be met, namely where the performer's aim, as Pareto says, is 'an imaginary end' outside the field of observation and experience. [*T.*, §151; *Sel.*, p. 184.] In that case no outsider could possibly say whether that end has or has not been reached. It is precisely for this reason that Pareto treats metaphysics and religion as non-logical. It is not that religious and metaphysical systems are erroneous; it is simply that the aims they are out to achieve are non-verifiable. The theories are not unscientific; they are non-scientific.*

---

* *Cf.* M. Ginsberg, *Reason and Unreason in Society*, London, 1947, Vol. II, p. 86 for what may be a similar misunderstanding. 'Why . . . is it more logical to pursue honour and consideration than to satisfy other social impulses, or let us say, the desire for knowledge?' The answer is, surely, that

(ii) *The analysis of non-logical actions*

Thus the criterion as to what is logical and what is non-logical is a comparison: a comparison between the ends-means relationship as seen by the performer and as seen by the observer. Where the two correspond, the action is logical. Where they fail to correspond the action is non-logical. What accounts for a failure to correspond? It may be that the deductive chain of reasoning is at fault. It may also be that the basis from which the deductive reasoning starts is not clear, precise and testable. A large part of non-logical activity is of this second kind. It starts from a private state of mind, some ultimate and non-rational attitude or impulse. To the performer it seems as though he is first cogitating and then acting. In fact, says Pareto, the reverse is true; he acts first, from his attitude or impulse, and cogitates afterwards. The theory he elaborates as to why he is performing the action is *ex post facto*, a 'logical veneer' or justification of the urge to act. It is what today is widely called a 'rationalisation' of the prior impulse or attitude.

Human beings, Pareto observes, have a marked tendency to make their behaviour logical, to 'logicalise' it. So, given the relationship represented by the diagram, this tendency makes them believe that action B is the result of theory C. In fact, the relationship between B and C is indirect in that each of them is a manifestation of the state of mind A. Suppose, for instance that a man has a horror of murder (A). Therefore he will not commit murder (B). He tells himself, however, that 'the gods punish murderers' (C). And he imagines that this is *why* he refrains from murder.

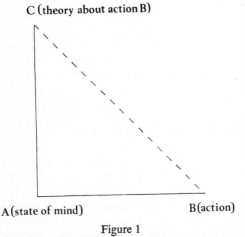

C (theory about action B)

A (state of mind)   B (action)

Figure 1

the pursuit of honour and consideration is logical to the extent that the attainment of these states is verifiable by the observer. In certain circumstances the pursuit of knowledge would also be verifiable and hence logical activity: e.g., satisfaction of the desire to speak French. But attainment of a moral or religious satisfaction would be inaccessible to outside verification, and hence this activity ranks as non-logical.

(a) *Theories as mere masks.* Clearly, if these theories are merely manifestations of states of mind, it is the latter not the former which constitute the true social force, the true 'element of the social equilibrium'. 'We have to see how far reality is distorted in the theories and descriptions of it that are to be found in the literature of thought. We are shown a curved mirror; our problem is to discover the form of the object so distorted.' [*T.*, §253; *cf.* also §249, *Sel.*, p. 194.]

(b) *Method.* Beyond recognising that these theories manifest psychic states, however, Pareto refused to go. 'It is for psychology,' he writes, 'to study this psychic state; in this inquiry we accept it as a fact without seeking to go any further than that.' [*T.*, §161, *Sel.*, p. 185.] Instead he chooses to study the overt conduct which reflects the existence of these psychic states, and he narrows down this conduct to the verbal theories about it. The inductive part of the *Treatise*, therefore, consists of its chapters 2, 3 and 4, in which he analyses a great number of theories, so as to find out more about the states of mind which they manifest. This part of Pareto's system is therefore, 'psychologism',[37] but a paradoxical psychologism without the psychology. For this he has been much reproached, but the reason is obvious enough: states of mind as such were the province of the psychologist, while he himself was concerned only with their outward and directly observable manifestations. He made this clear in chapter 2 of the *Manuale* (written by 1904 and drafted in 1899). In its very first paragraph he states that his kind of sociology, working backwards from overt behaviour to the threshold of the psyche, would meet the work of the psychologist, pressing forwards and outwards from the inner workings of the psyche to the realm of social behaviour. When this meeting occurred, the science of society would begin to form a united corpus of principles; but that time was not yet and for the moment he was resolved to limit himself only to the external acts. [*M.*, ch. 2, §1.]

This resolve is all of a piece with the way Pareto had developed value theory in economics. Edgworth's indifference curves assumed the existence of measurable human satisfactions. Pareto turned the idea back to front. Observing—or affecting to observe—the choices made by an individual, he plotted these on a graph and obtained indifference curves from these observations, thus dispensing with any prior assumptions about what went on in the subject's mind. 'The new idea,' as Schumpeter puts it, 'was to replace "utility" postulates by postulates about observable behaviour,'[38] and this is precisely Pareto's intention when dealing with the elements of the social equilibrium in the *Treatise*. (*Cf. T.*, §§2078, n1, 2408, 2409, n 2.]

(c) *The quest for uniformities.* The conclusion so far, then, is that theories are so many social facts, and as such are manifestations of underlying psychic states and attitudes. These are the true operative forces in society. But there are hundreds of such theories, and if there were as many as there are states of mind, nothing would have been gained. Hence the inductive inquiry in chapters 3, 4 and 5 which is primarily a quest for uniformities among such theories.

This inquiry achieved—to Pareto's satisfaction at least—one negative and four positive results. The negative result is incidental to Pareto's main purpose but must have afforded him a mischievous satisfaction: it is the altogether destructive analysis of the great metaphysical, moral and religious systems, both of the past and of his own time. To all of them he applies the rigorous test of verifiability; and, not unnaturally, nothing at all survives of their claim to scientific status. The entities with which they work, such as 'liberty' or 'equality' or 'progress', are fictitious and imaginary, and the reasonings with which the theories are elaborated are often shown to violate the rules of logic. Pareto's sympathisers have thoroughly welcomed this exercise and cheered on what has seemed to them a welcome step towards intellectual hygiene.[39] The hostile critics have had to admit its ruthless efficacy, and confine their criticism to complaining that it is irrelevant to sociology.* The vast majority, however, have simply continued to debate the old theories like that of the General Will and erect new ones as though the demonstration had never taken place. This is, ironically, just what Pareto's theory would lead one to expect. If theories are indeed mere manifestations of psychic states, and if the latter tend to endure, then the theories will continue to be held and new ones spun, irrespective of any logical refutation.†

The first result of the inquiry is, in Pareto's eyes, to verify his view that theories are manifestations of psychic states. The second is to satisfy him that these theories have failed to stand up to his logico-experimental criterion and therefore that in human affairs the

---

* E.g., F. Borkenau, *Pareto*, London and New York, 1936, chap. IV *passim*, and: 'The bulk of his considerations in this case are not sociological nor purely psychological but mostly logical with a certain amount of the psychology of paralogisms' (p. 86).

† P. Winch (*The Idea of a Social Science*, London, 1958) has tried to prove that Pareto's demonstration is unacceptable *in limine*, since each branch of thought—theological, moral, political, scientific and the like—has its own internal 'rules' and is only intelligible by these canons. Hence it is improper to apply the canons of one to the other, hence improper to apply the canons of scientific intelligibility to say, theology. For a specific, and in our view convincing, refutation see E. J. Baker, 'The philosophical "refutation" of Pareto', *Mind*, Vol. LXIX, 1960; and for a general rejection of Winch's view see M. C. Bradley, review article, *ibid*.

non-logical vastly preponderates over the logical. The third is to cause him to observe why this vast preponderance has not hitherto been perceived. [*T.*, §261, *Sel.*, pp. 195 *et seq.*] The fourth result is the vital one. It marks a quite new stage in the development of his doctrine, absent from all his previous writings up to and including the *Manuel*: the view that these theories contain certain *constant* elements. This step enables him to take his argument to its next stage, because it provides the uniformities with which a scientific theory can proceed. He now writes that there is in the theories 'a constant, instinctive and non-logical element', and also 'a deductive element the purpose of which is to explain, justify and demonstrate the constant first element'. [*T.*, §845, *Sel.*, p. 216.] The deductive element, which is highly variable, serves only to mask the constant elements, which are to be taken as indices of highly permanent psychic states.

Thus, if you strip from the theory its variable part you are left with a residuum. This is the constant element and Pareto therefore calls it a *residue*. From this constant element, much as from some root in philology, there 'derive' certain variable arguments, explanations and justifications. Pareto calls these—the variable deductive elements of theories—the *derivations*. The total theory is a *derivate* or *derivative* (Italian: *derivata*) but he hardly ever has recourse to this term [*cf. T.*, §868, *Sel.*, p. 216], and it can be ignored and the discussion carried forward in terms only of *residues* and *derivations*.

(iii) *Residues and derivations*

Of these residual elements Pareto at first found no less than fifty-two varieties: an unmanageable number. Some, however, are cognate with others. In the end Pareto reduces them to six classes or groups. Even he admitted that his classification was provisional[40] and it has found no defenders even among his champions.

Two of these classes seem comparatively unimportant in determining the social equilibrium. Class III consists of the residues impelling men 'to express their emotions by means of outward acts'. The often functionless and purposeless marching and countermarching of the nazi Brownshirts or the fascist militia might well fall into this class of residues.[41] Class VI is the residue of sex. Like Freud (of whose work Pareto was entirely ignorant), Pareto attaches great importance to the fact that many theories and ideals flow from the instinct of sex; but although he collects some fascinating and curious details of such matters as phallic worship, flagellation and so forth, he is concerned simply to illustrate the connection between the sex instinct and certain literary and religious ideologies instead of claiming for it a transcending and indeed unique social import-ance.*

The two most important classes of residues are Class I and Class II. When Pareto came to apply his theory to European history he did so almost exclusively in terms of these two classes.

Class I is translated by Livingston[42] as 'the instinct of combina-tions' and this has now achieved such wide currency that we have followed it; but a better term would have been 'the instinct for combining' or perhaps some such coinage as 'the Ulysses complex'. By the 'instinct of combinations', Pareto means the propensity to take disparate elements out of their familiar contexts and unite them together in new combinations. It takes the most diverse forms. Guided by certain hypotheses, scientists indulge this propensity; but since their means and end are both verifiable this leads them into logical activities. Other people express this same basic propensity quite differently—by associating together the most diverse elements under the prompting of fantastic analogies: as, for instance, in the 'doctrine of signatures' and sympathetic magic. But the effect of the propensity in all cases is to create a new entity or association out of disparate elements. [See table of residue-classifications, *Sel.*, pp. 222 *et seq.*] Thus Class I residues lead to *innovations*.

Class II, on the other hand, leads to conservatism; it is the *obverse* of Class I as Pareto makes quite clear. It is called 'the per-sistence of aggregates' (translated by some writers as 'aggregate-persistence'). Once combinations have been set up, an 'instinct' often operates to prevent the breaking up of the things thus joined to-gether; and if, nevertheless, they do break apart, the instinct tries to disguise this fact by preserving the image of the aggregate. [*T.*, §§991–2, *Sel.*, p. 228.] As an example of the relationship between Class I and Class II, one might perhaps cite the course of events in Russia from 1917. At the beginning all is made anew. Later, the rulers cease striving for new combinations, arguing that the revolu-tion has been made and they bend their energies to conserving it. From innovators and iconoclasts they become conformists and arch-conservatives of the new pattern they have established. As an example of the secondary manifestation of the instinct which dis-guises the break-up of aggregates by preserving their image, the Holy Roman Empire springs to mind; Rome has collapsed, its figment is preserved. The various classes and subclasses of these two main Classes are defined in Pareto's tables. [*Sel.*, pp. 222–3.]

We are left with Classes IV and V, styled, respectively 'the

---

* Hence Pareto's attack on the efforts to prohibit 'immoral' literature in his *Mythe Vertuiste*, 1911.

residues of sociality' and 'residues connected with the integrity of the individual'. There is an implied contrast between the two. Class IV comprises the propensities which relate to men's self-subjection to the requirements of society, and without which no society could exist. Among them are the willingness to conform and by the same token to enforce conformity on others; the willingness to sacrifice oneself for the whole; sympathy and pity for one's fellows; the willingness to defer and the expectation of being deferred to. Class V, on the other hand, comprises the propensities relating to the individual's determination to preserve his position and his interests against the rest of society—which is very often the same as preserving the existing form of society and resisting changes in it. To the extent which these two classes of residues tend to keep society together and resist changes in it, their role is similar to Class II residues, those of the 'persistence of aggregates'. Indeed, some of their subclasses could equally well have appeared as subclasses of Class II. For instance Class V-a—'sentiments opposing alterations in the social equilibrium'—or Class IV-b—'the need for uniformity'—could easily pass as subclasses of Class II. This is one of the reasons why Pareto, in the last resort, conducted his analysis of society in terms of Class I and Class II, and played down the role of the other classes of residues. 'Not a few of the residues of sociability, of personal integrity and so forth have their counterparts among the class of persistence of aggregates, so that they are taken account of indirectly in discussion of Class I and Class II residues.' [*T.*, §2415.]

Despite their rare appearance in Pareto's social analysis, Classes IV and V of the residues are essential to his theory. They serve as a kind of flywheel or makeweight in the social equilibrium. This is obviously true of the Class IV residues, for these—the residues of sociality—are what prevents society from breaking up, either under the stress of innovation or, equally, of violent reaction to such innovation. And as for the Class V residues, they are central to his notion of equilibrium. This he specifically recognises. 'If an existing state of social equilibrium is altered, forces come into operation which tend to re-establish it; this is precisely what "equilibrium" means. These forces, in the main, are sentiments which manifest themselves as residues of the V-a type . . . They prompt us to repel, remove and counteract the causes of the alteration.' [*T.*, §1210, *Sel.*, p. 234.] 'If (such sentiments) did not exist, then every slight nascent alteration in the social equilibrium would meet little or no resistance and could therefore with impunity go on developing to the point where it came to affect a large enough number of individuals to arouse resistance on the part of those directly concerned to avoid the evil.' [*T.*, §1214, *Sel.*, p. 235.]

One of the Class I residues (the instinct of combinations), Subclass I-e, has a special importance. It is the urge to appear to be acting rationally, or as Pareto puts it, 'logically'. It is due to this residue that the residues in general are tricked out with 'derivations', by 'logical arguments, unsound arguments and manifestations of sentiments used for purposes of derivation'. All these are 'manifestations of the human being's hunger for thinking . . . This is satisfied in any number of ways: by pseudo-logical arguments, by words which stir the emotions, by fatuous and inconclusive chatter.' (*T.*, §1401.]

(iv) *The nature of residues and derivations*

The residues are inarticulate imperatives of an extremely vague kind which lie at the root of whole families of apparently diverse kinds of activity to which they stand in the same relationship as does a root to the family of words derived from it. For Pareto these are the ultimate inspectable data.

He is indeed prepared to assume [*T.*, §1690; *Sel.*, p. 219] that there *is* some mental or physical state to which these imperatives correspond, but he will not be drawn into any hypothesis concerning what kind of condition or state this may be. The residues 'correspond to' these mental phenomena, or 'manifest them' in the sense of making their presence known, just as mercury in the thermometer manifests the presence of heat without necessitating a physical theory as to the nature of heat. [*T.*, §875; *Sel.*, p. 217.] Later, however, Pareto states that he is henceforth going to use the term residue, not only to mean the observed root of a family of modes of overt behaviour, but *also* the sentiments or psychic states which (by inference) they manifest. (This new usage, however, does not require him to affirm that for each separate residue there exists a separate and corresponding mental or physical condition or process.) In this sense the residues are discovered by inspecting their outward manifestation in human theorising. It is in this latter sense that they are, to Pareto, overt and inspectable phenomena. (This assertion is, really, equivocal; see below, pp. 72 *et seq.*)

Professor McDougall, in an egregious article, asked: 'Are all manifestations of sentiments residues?'[43] Obviously, no. Residues are the constant element in *theories* (the variable element being the derivation). Where there is no derivation, there is no residue at the root of it; and where there is no reasoning, argument, justification, there is no derivation. So sex, *qua* simple appetite, is not comprised in a residue; but sex, in so far as it gives rise to human theorising, to asceticism and the like, *is* a residue (Class VI). 'If the (residue) corresponds to certain instincts, it is very far from reflecting them all. This is obvious from the very way whereby we discovered it. We analysed specimens of thinking, on the look-out for a constant element. We may therefore have discovered only the instincts which underlay such thinking. Following this path there was no opportunity to meet instincts which were not so rationalised. Still unaccounted for would be the simple appetites, tastes, inclinations and—in social relationships—that very important class called "interests".' [*T.*, §851, *Sel.*, p. 217 n.]*

Why, then, are *interests* not included in the residues? Broadly speaking, by interests Pareto means material wants. These may indeed give rise to reasoning, but often this is of a *logical* nature. The satisfaction of a material want is a specific imperative, and its attainment is verifiable. Hence, the interests tend to give rise to logical conduct. On the other hand, it is observable that men often invent theories about equality, justice and other 'metaphysical entities'—as Pareto calls them—and which are not verifiable by an external observer when, objectively, these same men are impelled by a desire to satisfy a material want. In the *Manuel* Pareto cites the propaganda of the English protectionists as an example. [*M.*, ch. 9, §§62–5.] When this happens, the interest is surely giving rise to a derivation; is not the interest playing the same role as the residue is said to play? In such a case, ought not the interest to be considered as a residue? And to this Pareto specifically agrees. Dealing with Class V residues—those pertaining to the 'integrity of the individual and his appurtenances'— he writes: 'That sum of the sentiments called "interests" is of the same nature as the sentiments to which the residues of this present class correspond. Sentiments of "interests", therefore, ought strictly to be included in this classification, but they are of such great intrinsic importance for the social equilibrium that it is better to consider them separately from residues.' [*T.*, §1207, *Sel.*, p. 234.]

A final point of clarification is raised by Pareto's terminology, which has led some commentators to suppose that the residues are innate, invariate and biologically determined. For instance, Class I residues are styled 'the *instinct* of combinations', and he writes also that a residue 'corresponds to certain *instincts* . . . of men'. [*T.*, §850.] 'Instinct' is nowadays defined very precisely as a biologically determined characteristic or drive; but in 1912, the date of the completion of the *Treatise*, it was used very elastically and was held to comprise matters which we are told today are not inherited but are acquired and socially conditioned.[44] Furthermore, there is no evidence that

---

* It will be noted that this passage provides the answer to McDougall's question in perfectly clear and unambiguous terms. The reader may wish to ask himself why McDougall did nevertheless ask his question.

Pareto used the term *instinct* as meaning an unalterable biologically determined characteristic or drive such as Borkenau, for instance, attributes to him, and there is very powerful evidence to the contrary. Talcott Parsons' masterly and minute exegesis makes this quite clear.* But in addition to exegesis we have certain statements by Pareto himself. In the *Manuel*, he roundly declares that it is pointless to inquire whether the sentiments are innate or socially acquired; they are both. And he added that 'the standard morality is only the product of the sentiments of those who frame it, sentiments which, for the most part, are taken over from the society in which they live, and *belong properly to its authors only to a small degree*'. [*M.*, ch. 2, §18, *Sel.*, pp. 148–9.] Again: 'These sentiments originate in man's nature *combined with his life-circumstances* and it is not open to us to assert *a priori* that the two are logically connected'. [*M.*, ch. 2, §22.]

The fact is that some of the tastes, sentiments, instincts, appetites, etc., which Pareto indifferently cites as corresponding to certain residues are today held to be 'true' instincts, notably the residue of Sex. Others are not. For this reason Parsons suggests that Pareto's residues fall into two distinct classes: those prompted by instincts and the others—best described as 'normative' residues—which are, more simply, value-attitudes. When Pareto says that the residue manifests the former of the two, the word 'manifests' is to be taken as 'indicating the presence of'. When it 'manifests' the latter however, it means 'expresses it in verbal or ritual behaviour'. This distinction, a useful one, is consistent with Pareto's system as a whole.

On inspection, Pareto claims that the six classes of residues have remained very constant throughout the two-thousand year span of western history (with which alone he is concerned). It is for this reason that he surmises—but certainly does no more—that they correspond to certain 'instincts'. [*T.*, §850.] On the other hand, he claims, the subclasses of each main class are much less constant, and indeed a sort of compensation seems to have occurred in them by which the rise of one subclass is offset by the decline of another. Thus some of the Class I residues making for magic and ritual combinations have declined, but others, making for scientific experiment and inquiry, have offset them. Among the Class II residues those relating to religion have declined but their place has been occupied by those

---

* *The Structure of Social Action*, New York, 1937, chs. V, VI. This analysis makes entire chapters of Borkenau completely irrelevant, notably ch. III (Residues) and ch. VI (Derivations), both of which are spirited reaffirmations of the anti-instinct critiques of Boas, Benedict and Mead, but have no bearing on Pareto whom Borkenau quite mistakenly helds to be an 'instinctivist'.

making for the secular faiths of nationalism, socialism, and the like.
[*T.*, §§1699–1717.] The main classes are more constant than their
individual subclasses, and these are in turn more constant than the
derivations. [*T.*, §1718, *Sel.*, pp. 243–4.]

Derivations are not, however, unimportant. On the contrary:
they have the power to make the residues more or less *intense*. They
satisfy the craving to appear logical but also may, and often do, make
people more conscious of the residue that is in play and give it
emotional overtones. In this way they can greatly increase its social
effectiveness. Pareto calls the process 'the intensification of the
residues'. [*T.*, §1747.] It 'lends them strength and aggressiveness'. For
instance, nationalist propaganda makes people more self-conscious
of their Class II residues of group-solidarity and the like, and thereby
makes them more effective. His theory of propaganda stems from
this thought. Newspapers, he says, are important, not because of
their logico-experimental reasonings, 'which are mostly childish', or
because they can force their views on the public; their influence is
'due to (their) art . . . for working on the residues *via* the derivations.
Strictly speaking the residues have to be there in the first place. That
determines the limit of the influence of the newspapers; it cannot run
counter to sentiments; it can only utilise them for some purpose or
another.' [*T.*, §1755.]

(v) *The social role of the residues*

The social importance of the residues is, consequently, enormous.
Outside natural science and technology, strategy and the field of
economics, almost all social conduct is dictated by the residues, not
by reason. Rational argument is in most cases an appearance which
serves only to justify action or heighten the basic residues from which
this action springs. Nowhere is this more apparent than in the ruler-
ruled relationship, as we shall see in further detail below. All governments rule by a mixture of force and persuasion, and this persuasion
consists of so many derivations. 'It is always an oligarchy which
rules and finds ways of expressing such "will of the people" as the
(ruling) few wish to see expressed.' [*T.*, §2183.] ' "Divine right", be it
of prince, aristocracy, people, proletariat, majority, or any other
imaginable divine right, has not the least experimental validity. We
must accordingly consider (it) only extrinsically, as facts, as manifestations of sentiments . . .' [*T.*, §2239, *Sel.*, p. 266.] Hence Pareto's neo-
machiavellianism. 'The art of government lies in finding ways to take
advantage of . . . sentiments, not in wasting one's energies in futile
efforts to destroy them, the sole effect of which, frequently, is to
strengthen them.' [*T.*, §1843, *Sel.*, p. 244.] When sections of the

population contend for the right to rule, the conflict lies between their sentiments, not between the arguments they use. This truth is not obvious 'for the conflict becomes a conflict between derivations'. [*T*., §2248.] The most absurd of mistakes is to suppose that it is possible to alter an opposing point of view by refuting its arguments. If one derivation is knocked out, the effect will simply be to encourage a different one to take its place.

Pareto's views have met with much criticism. 1. To begin with, criticism has been levelled at his proposition that the scientific truth of a theory bears no relation to its social efficacy. It is not true, he states, that 'whatever is not rational is harmful'. [*T*., §2239, *Sel*., p. 266.] The derivations of government, such as divine right, majority rule, 'the new god called universal suffrage' and the like, though they are mere derivations are yet of priceless social utility in so far as they reinforce the residue that 'social stability is a good thing. . . . Indeed', comments Pareto, 'it is *so* good a thing that, to maintain it, it is well worth while enlisting the aid of fantastic ideals and this or the other ideology (including among others the theology of universal suffrage) and resign oneself to certain actual disadvantages.' [*T*., §2184.]

This, of course, assumes that we know what is good or useful for our society, and in these passages Pareto is writing as though certain that stability is a good thing. It is however a cardinal feature of his system that we cannot know this, only assign certain values arbitrarily. He distinguishes between the maximum utility *of* and the maximum utility *for* a community. The former is the point where each and every individual has attained his maximum private satisfaction, and governments can make crude approximations to this condition by assuming that certain desirable things like food, shelter and clothing are 'goods'. The latter, however, is the maximum utility not of the individuals but of the entity as a whole. Now, for the pure economist, society is *not* an entity. It is an aggregate of dissimilar individuals whose individual satisfactions cannot be added together. It does not exist. But in *sociology*, Pareto says, 'society can be considered, if not as a person, at least as a unit'. [*T*., §2133, *Sel*., p. 254.] This is a subjective estimate. [*T*., §2131, n. 1.] It is *assumed*; and this assumed maximum utility for the society as a whole need by no means coincide with the maximum private satisfaction of any or of each of its constituent members. Thus it may be assumed that wealth is of the maximum utility for the society; but this may involve great individual inequality, and even poverty in certain strata. [*T*., §§2131–7, *Sel*., pp. 253–5.] Thus, in assigning a maximum utility for the community as such, one is always making a private judgement. If *Herrenvolk* were in power, they might assign a huge utility coefficient for the rich or the blond or the white, and a zero coefficient for the poor or the dark or the coloured races. And here, says Pareto, 'there is no criterion save sentiment for choosing one or the other'. [*T.*, §2135; *cf.* also *T.*, §2136, *Sel.*, p. 255.]

2. It has also been said that Pareto's system devalues the social importance of 'ideas'. For instance, Borkenau writes: 'He completely lacks the feeling that ideas are powerful driving forces of the historical process. For him ideas are either logical . . . or they are empty talk without any real importance. . . . His views can be summed up in one sentence: Ideas except scientific discoveries are of very little importance in social life.'[45] Pareto argued precisely the reverse. As he puts it, 'selling' a social policy is not the same as selling a machine. Given a good machine, the engineer-salesman can use logico-experimental arguments. The statesman however must resort to derivations, for in social matters sentiment is the most powerful factor by far, especially if the sentiments be 'aroused' to the point where they become a religion. Where this occurs, the case for the policy is best expressed in enthusiastic derivations which 'transcend cold realities'. This is (as Pareto acknowledges) similar to Sorel's views 'that a social doctrine . . . if it is to have any influence, has to take the form of a "myth" '. [*T.*, §§1866, 1868, *Sel.*, pp. 245, 246.] Nor is this all. Pareto devotes many pages to demonstrate that societies are able to innovate only, or largely, because men are moved by ideals. [*T.*, §1869 *et seq.*, *Sel.*, pp. 246–7.] Pareto certainly deflates the scientific status of ideas and ideals in society; but he accords them an altogether major role in spurring men to action.*

3. Nor is it altogether true that he considered reason powerless. As we have seen, in an illustration about the imputing of utility *for* society (I., §2135 above), Pareto argues that it is a matter of sentiment as to whether we should or should not assign a 'zero coefficient' to the lower orders and a maximum coefficient to the master-rulers. To this a critic has rejoined: 'Is reason really helpless in the face of such a problem?', and goes on to suggest that reason could assist in such an issue by clearing up certain questions of fact which greatly limit the scope of the non-rational. It could, for instance, ascertain just what is the extent of the differences between the rulers and the lower orders. 'Ultimately,' admits this critic, 'value judgements *will* have to be discussed but it may be doubted whether they would loom so large in the minds of the disputants.'[46]

---

* *Cf.* also his remark in *Le Mythe Vertuiste*: 'There has never been in history any great, strong and flourishing society which has not exhibited deep and active sentiments expressed in an ideal, a religion, a myth, a faith. . . . One might in a sense advance this paradox: nothing is so real and practical as the ideal (p. 183).

This passage has to be compared with those in which Pareto considers the proper way of approaching social problems. For instance, suppose the question is the use of force in society. It is improper, says Pareto, to answer in such terms as that the use of force is justified because it preserves existing uniformities in society, or alternately that it is justified precisely because it will overturn such uniformities. This way of answering is far too general. First, these various uniformities have to be appraised to see whether they are beneficial or harmful to society. Then the utility of preserving a harmful uniformity peacefully must be put against the utility of introducing a beneficial uniformity in a violent fashion. 'All the advantages and all the drawbacks, direct or indirect, have to be computed.' [*T.*, §2174.] He underlines this point when he remarks that solutions are more frequently found to specific problems than to grand general ones, precisely because the more specific the problem, the less the part that general theory has to play in its solution. [*T.*, §§2175–6.] It is not reason which Pareto is condemning but doctrinairism.

This is why he preferred the practical wisdom of the man of affairs to the predictions of the social scientists. For he had little faith in the predictive value of any sociology, including his own. To make a successful kill on the Stock Exchange, it was better to trust the hunch of the successful stockbroker than the skills of the academic economist, for the same reason that the experienced traveller with no map is more likely to be able to traverse the Peloponnese than a clever fellow with a poor topographical map. [*T.*, §§2411, n 1. Pareto emerges, not as the opponent of the use of reason in society, and still less as the fatalistic exponent of a biological determinism, but as the opponent of ideology and all its claims to be scientifically true, by virtue of which it takes on its cloak of authority.

4. Again, it seems an exaggeration to claim that he supposes human nature and human society to be constant and changeless. He holds, rather, that it is far less changeable than is usually supposed, that the form changes more markedly than the substance, and that the march of humanity is not, as was currently supposed at the time he wrote, inevitably onwards and upwards. For the classes of residues, though slow to change, do change nevertheless. Surveying the last two thousand years of western history, Pareto claimed to discern a constant general decline in Class II residues (the persistence of aggregates) and a corresponding general increase in Class I residues (the instinct of combinations). This was chiefly evidenced by the enormous expansion in the natural sciences. 'If we consider modern life as a whole,' he writes, 'we may safely conclude that Class I residues and the conclusions of logico-experimental science have enlarged the field

of their sway. To that fact, indeed, is largely due the great variety of traits in our modern society as compared with the societies of ancient Greece and Rome.' 'It is no great mistake, therefore, to conclude that "reason" is coming to play a more and more important part in human activity.' [*T.*, §§2392, 2393; *Sel.*, p. 283.] He does, however, qualify this view. The average trend, he affirms, conceals considerable variations over time; and in any case the advance of the Class I residues is distributed very unevenly over the different branches of social activity. Whereas the advance in science and technology and economics has been marked, it has hardly appeared at all in social and political conduct.

5. Criticism is also voiced over the role of the interests in Pareto's system. To judge solely by the *Treatise* itself, interests seem unimportant compared with the residues. But this view cannot be sustained in the light of Pareto's previous writings. It is to be understood by the breakdown of his original scheme for the *Treatise*.

For his original plan for the 'sociology' was a five-volume work embracing economics as well as sociology. To assist him in this ambitious enterprise, Pareto relied on a young disciple, Guido Sensini, who had begun to correspond with him in 1904. The basis of the work was to have been the *Cours d'Economie politique*, which was then out of print, and would have comprised: 1 Sociology; 2 Pure economics (without mathematical formulae); 3 Mathematical economics; 4 and 5 Applied economics.[47] Such a work would have put the logical actions, i.e., the interests, on an equal footing with the non-logical ones. But at this time Barbéra the publisher was asking Pareto to write him a Manual of Sociology. After some reflection Pareto decided that the five-volume plan was too ambitious, given his precarious health. He dropped it, abandoned all intention of revising the *Cours*, and began the work that was to grow into the *Treatise*.[48]

The importance he attached to the interests is clear from his parallel statements that, while the influence of the residues on the circulation of the elites, the interests, and the derivations 'provides a very substantial part of the social phenomena', the influence of the interests on these other factors '*also* provides a considerable portion of the social phenomenon', and it too is also similar to the influence of residues in that it 'fosters social continuity, varying but little and slowly in time'. [*T.*, §2206, *Sel.*, p. 260.] Interests rank *pari passu* with the residues. The marxists' error is not that they lay stress on the importance of interests but that they suppose them to be the sole important factor. To form a just estimate of Pareto's system therefore it would be necessary to try to build back into it what he left out: namely the importance of interests, of the economic factor.

(vi) Interests

That the interests are only lightly touched on in the *Treatise* is one of the most misleading features of its gigantic malproportion, for their presence is everywhere assumed; and when Pareto comes to illustrate social analysis according to his conceptual scheme [*T.*, §2203 *et seq.*, *Sel.*, pp. 260–1], they are brought in fully and explicitly for the first time—but also, for the last.

Interests are 'self-interests' or 'individual interests', prompted by tastes and appetites. Pareto does not define them closely and gives two kinds of definition. The first, ostensive, definition is that they are desires 'to acquire possession of material goods which are of useful or just pleasurable importance for purposes of living; and also to seek consideration and honours'. [*T.*, §2009.] The functional definition is that interests are 'a means to some personal end'. [*T.*, §1138.] These two definitions are quite compatible. If we follow Parsons and distinguish residues into those arising from instincts and those describable as 'value attitudes'—i.e., propensities towards certain ultimate ends—then the interests can be defined as means to achieve any of these ultimate ends; and wealth and power and consideration are the most important of such means.[49]

Such tastes or appetites for power and wealth, etc., work themselves out in three ways. 1. They may do so by simple and direct satisfaction, as we pointed out in connection with sex, and so, in the same way, for food and drink. (See pages 41–2 above.) 2. They may give rise to logical conduct. By and large this is what usually occurs. (*Cf.* page 42 above.) 3. From this arises the implication that the activity arising from individual interest will tend to be logical in proportion as the interest is apprehended by the performer. The hazier his notion of where his interest lies, the greater the scope for non-logical action on his part. Only in so far as these tastes and appetites give rise to logical behaviour are they to be called *interests*. Where tastes and appetites give rise to non-logical actions they are so many residues. (See page 42 above.) This is why Pareto wrote that they ought properly be regarded as a subclass of the residues of 'individual integrity'. (See same page above.) Now tastes and interests sometimes do give rise to just such non-logical activity. Thus, the cry for *equality*, and the derivations (Class V-b) to which it gives rise, are 'related to the direct interest of persons who seek to free themselves from certain inequalities which operate against them and to set up new inequalities in their favour. This last is their principal concern.' [*T.*, §1227, *Sel.*, p. 236.]

This analysis prompts the question as to what makes a given taste or appetite an interest for one man, but a residue for another.

Pareto never raised this question. However, materials for an answer lie in the *Treatise*, and it is possible to provide one that is quite consistent with the rest of his system.

The answers turn on whether an individual is *aware* that his motive is the satisfaction of his material or honorific desires. 1. He may be unaware of this. In such a case he acts, as in the examples of 'justice' or 'equality' already cited, from a *residue* and constructs or adopts derivations. 2. He may have only a foggy notion that his self-interest is involved and may play down or even reject the belief that his self-interest is involved, acting therefore from a *residue* and invoking derivations. Pareto holds that individuals in whom Class I residues preponderate tend to be more self-aware of their interests and more ready to make public acknowledgement of 'naked' self-interest than those people in whom the Class II residues are preponderant. The latter, more concerned with ideals, are less clear as to where their interest lies. They therefore seek to persuade themselves that their self-interest is not involved, and therefore they tend to act through residues rather than interests. For instance: Pareto alleges that the Italians declared war on Turkey in 1911 as a matter of self-interest. But the Italians themselves suppressed this, acting instead from Class II residues, and invoking the sentiments of justice by harping on alleged atrocities, on christianity, on the liberation of the Arabs from the Turkish yoke, and so forth. [*T.*, §§1707–8.] 3. Finally, an individual may be perfectly aware that his motive is self-interest and yet deliberately conceal this and expound his claims by means of derivations. In such a case, the use of the derivation is a deliberate strategy to achieve his own interest, and his action is perfectly logical. According to Pareto, this is precisely how the governing class have to act in order to get their own way, for he avers that the multitude are richly endowed with Class II residues and so unresponsive to appeals to their own self-interest, let alone that of their rulers. They can best be persuaded by an appeal to their 'sentiments'—i.e., the residues—in the name of some lofty ideal. [*T.*, §§1864–5, *Sel.*, pp. 244–5; *cf.* also I., §§1867, 1869, *Sel.*, p. 246.]

Thus there can certainly be, as Marx argued, 'ideologies' of self-interest and even of class interest. Indeed, in the *Manuel* [ch. 9, §§62–5] Pareto analyses the campaign of the British protectionists in precisely these terms. His major difference from Marx is that he rejects interest as the unique basis of ideology, and insists that interest is in its turn modified by other autonomous social factors, such as the residues. But of the importance he attached to economic motivation there can be no doubt as his analysis of the 'protectionist cycle' [*T.*, §§2208–18] very well illustrates. It is a great pity that Pareto dwells so exclusively on the residues and fails to expand on the role of the interests in the *Treatise*, for his conceptual scheme both requires such an amplification and was designed to take it, and its absence greatly weakens the second part of his system, the concept of the elites and their circulation.

4. THE THEORY OF THE ELITES

(i) *Social heterogeneity*

Individuals are not intellectually, morally or physically equal, and society is not homogeneous. On the contrary, it is composed of vastly numerous social groups, mixing in innumerable ways. In any particular grouping, some people are more capable than the others. Those who are most capable in their peculiar branch of activity, whether this be playing chess or playing the prostitute, thieving or defending thieves in the lawcourts, writing poetry or governing the country, are *le classi elette*, the 'select' persons of their particular grouping: in the French tongue, *l'élite*. And this word 'elite' has been taken over into the English language. [*T.*, §§2025, 2027, 2031, *Sel.*, pp. 247–8.]

The elite and the non-elite shade into one another by imperceptible degrees; but that is no reason why, as a first approximation, one cannot recognise—albeit by some arbitrary line—that some of the population are elite in their various branches of activity and others are non-elite. So we can, crudely, divide society into (*a*) the lower stratum and (*b*) the superior stratum. This latter in turn can be divided into two groups: those who 'directly or indirectly' play some considerable part in governing (and who are referred to as the governing elite and later—and more frequently—as the *governing class* or the *governing classes*), and the rest of the elite, not in government: the 'non-governing elite'. [*T.*, §§2032–4. *Sel.*, pp. 248–9.]

The governing elite (or governing class) may be closed, or open to a greater or less degree, to accessions from the non-elite section of the population. The Spartiates, or the Venetian oligarchy, are cited as examples of closed governing classes; the governing classes of contemporary democracies as examples of open ones. [*T.*, §§2494–50.] In so far as members of the non-elite part of the population accede to the governing elite, and members of the governing elite sink into the mass of the non-elite, we have a so-called 'circulation of the elites'—a term and a process which must be further explored below.

It is bootless to object that modern parliamentary democracies have no 'governing class' and that personal autocracies, by definition, represent rule by one single person and not by a 'governing class'. For Pareto 'everywhere there exists a governing class, even in a despotism'; it is the forms under which it appears that differ. 'In absolute governments, there is only one figure on the stage—the sovereign; in so-called democratic governments, it is the parliament.' But behind the scenes all the time are people who have very important functions in the actual work of government. [*T.*, §2253, *Sel.*, p. 268.] 'Whether universal suffrage prevails or not, always it is an oligarchy that governs.' [*T.*, §2183.]

(ii) *How is rule maintained?*

The *Treatise* says two contradictory things about the governing elite. In one place this is *defined* as those most qualified to govern, and the statement that the elite governs is an analytic one and value-free. Elsewhere, however, we are told that those who wear the 'label' of ruler do not always possess the capacity to govern; while others who do possess this capacity do not always wear the label. [*T.*, §2051.] However, if these passages are compared with certain in the *Manuel* [*M.*, §§106, 111, *Sel.*, pp. 161, 162], it becomes clear that for Pareto the proposition that 'the governing elite = those best capable of governing' is true only in a condition of perfect social mobility. In such conditions the label of ruler and the capacity to rule would coincide. In fact obstacles like inherited wealth, family connections, social rank impede the free circulation of talent. In so far as this happens those wearing the label and those possessing the capacity diverge.

What then is this capacity? It consists in the will and ability to blend the two means by which rule is maintained—force and consent. And the capacities to use one or other of these two methods are on the whole mutually exclusive; a governing class tends to use one or the other method but not both; and a governing class is ejected from office because it lacks the ability and will to use one or other of these methods in sufficient degree.

Forms of government are not to be compared by reference to constitutions but to their operative practice. All are oligarchies. All govern by force and/or consent. But they differ from one another first, by the relative proportions in which force and consent are utilised to maintain rule, and secondly, by the ways in which the force is exercised and the consent obtained.

(a) *The use of persuasion.* As we have seen, Pareto affirms that the two great sources of human activity are sentiments (residues) and interests. Both rank equally in his scheme. The two chief methods, then, of persuading the masses by non-violent means are by appealing to their interests and/or their sentiments—and in the latter case this will have to be achieved by means of some 'derivation' which is attuned to the particular residue or residues that have to be harnessed. We have already seen the importance Pareto attached to the derivations as a mode of 'intensifying' the activity of the residues, and his theory of propaganda. (See page 44 above.) 'The policies of government are the more effective the more adept they are at utilising residues.' [*T.*, §2247.] And along with these residues 'come interests and sometimes these are the only available agents for modifying residues'. [*T.*, §2250, *Sel.*, p. 267.] In his own terminology, the masses are always rich in the Class II residues (persistence of aggregates). Hence naked interests may well make an appeal to the ruling classes and modify its residues, but not to the idealistic masses. To gain their approval, the interests will have to be dressed up in fictitious derivations which will appeal to their sentiments; and—since the government's policy may well be in their interests after all—'this deception may well prove beneficial to the subordinate class'. [*Ibid.*]

The 'derivations' of Pareto are much the same as the 'political formulae' of Mosca, and a wider genus of which Sorel's 'myths' are but a species. 'Human beings are effectively guided,' affirmed Pareto, 'not by sceptical reasonings of a scientific nature, but by "living faiths" expressed in ideals—theories such as the divine right of kings, the legitimacy of oligarchies, of "the people", of "majorities" of legislative assemblies. . . .' [*T.*, §2182.]

(b) *The application of violence.* Thus the statesman must judiciously mix appeals to self-interest and to popular residues by the use of the appropriate derivations. What is *not* possible is to try to suppress the residues by force, short of one limiting case—where all those who possess such residues can be physically exterminated. In some cases this might be possible. In most cases the residues would be too widespread to make it practicable. In some intermediate cases, such physical extermination might be possible but would have such weakening effects on the social fabric that even the ruling class would perceive that it was too unwise to risk. Instead of the application of force to suppress the residues—indeed, 'instead of fighting or trying to modify them'—the task of the statesman is to 'utilise them as tools of policy'. Folk must be governed, in fact, by their own prejudices. Pareto draws special attention to the folly of trying to combat nationalism by force of arms. He compares the Russian and German efforts to suppress Polish nationalism (which he maintained to be unsuccessful) with the Austrian policy (claimed to be successful). Similarly, according to him, with British rule in India and French in Tunisia: 'there,' he comments, 'the sentiments, usages and customs of the natives have been respected. . . . The art of government lies in finding ways to take advantage of such sentiments, not in wasting one's energies in futile efforts to destroy them—the sole effect of which, frequently, is only to make them stronger.' [*T.*, §1843, *Sel.*, p. 244.]

But this is by no means to aver that force is unnecessary in ruling. Far from it. The vehemence with which Pareto expresses this view partly derives from his own personal predilections; but it also springs from his recoil from the sentimental ideologies of his day which, in one shape or another, appeared to affirm that violence was never necessary, that persuasion, sweet reasonableness, enlightened self-interest, the habit of compromise and the like were all that were necessary to bring about a form of rule from which the sanction of violence was forever banished.

The need for governments to apply force arises from the fact that 'a small group of citizens, if prepared to use violence, can impose its will upon ruling circles which are not willing to meet violence by equal violence'. [*T.*, §2178, *Sel.*, p. 257.] To argue that it is always disadvantageous, even in exceptional cases, to meet stratagems with violence could only be proved by demonstrating that the use of such stratagems has always been, even in the exceptional cases, more advantageous than the use of violence. [*T.*, §2190.] As far as Pareto is concerned, history has confirmed the opposite. In that case, the use of force is shown to be necessary, at least on some occasions. Of course, he says, the issue has been tricked out with all manner of ethical derivations; but the use of force against the government or by it is not in itself an ethical question. Those who want to preserve existing uniformities will use force to do so; so therefore must those against whom the force is directed. The situation is dressed up in derivations —'on the one hand theories which condemn the use of violence by the subordinate classes in all cases whatsoever, and on the other, theories which censure its exercise by the public authority [I., §2181, *Sel.*, p. 260]; but these do not alter the essence of the situation, the struggle between the Outs and the Ins.

(c) *Force, persuasion and durability of the governing class.* Thus, a governing class can only maintain itself in power and exercise its authority effectively if it is prepared to use both force and persuasion. If a governing class could apply both of these in the appropriate proportions it could, in principle, maintain itself for ever. No governing class has ever succeeded in doing so. 'History is a graveyard of aristocracies.' [*T.*, §2053, *Sel.*, p. 249.] This is because the type of person who favours recourse to violence is usually unwilling or unable to have recourse to persuasion and *vice versa*. The two styles of governing are, on the whole, mutually exclusive. In this lies the key to the rise and fall of governing classes. Broadly speaking the explanation is this: the self-confidence and willingness to use force, which has been shown to be essential to the maintenance of power, gradually diminishes in the governing class 'until now and again they are reinforced by tides welling up from the inferior stratum of society'. [*T.*,

§2048.] 'The governing class is renovated, not only in numbers but also—and this is more important—in quality, by recruiting to it families rising from the lower classes, bringing with them the energy and proportions of the residues necessary for maintaining them in power. It is renovated also by the loss of its more degenerate elements.' [*T.*, §2054, *Sel.*, p. 249.] In other words, it is kept going by the 'circulation of the elites', i.e., by social mobility. The greater this mobility, the better the 'health' of the governing class, from which it also follows that the more open the governing class the more likely it is to maintain itself, and the more caste-like it is the greater its tendency to decay. So, except for the limiting case of totally closed aristocracies or governing castes, 'the governing elite is in a state of continuous and slow transformation'. Revolutions, however, do from time to time occur. Why? They occur 'because—either through a slowing down in the circulation of elites or from other causes—the upper strata accumulate decadent elements which no longer retain the residues appropriate to the maintenance of power and which shrink from the use of violence; while, among the lower strata, elements of superior quality are increasing which do possess the residues suitable for governing and are prepared to use force.' The revolution merely supplants the old governing class by a new one. Thereafter this new class in its turn is slowly transformed. 'The governing elite . . . flows like a river. Every so often . . . the river floods and breaks its banks. Then, afterwards, the new governing elite resumes again the slow process of self-transformation. The river returns to its bed and once more flows evenly on.' [*T.*, §§2056–7, *Sel.*, p. 250.]

In Pareto's view, this cycle of rise and decay is ineluctable and necessary. It is one of the laws ('the uniformities') of human society. What is the reason for it? We have already noted that from the *Cours* of 1896 down to the start of the *Treatise* in 1907, Pareto had been searching for the answer to this question, without making much advance. (See pages 26–7, 30 above.) The *Treatise* supplies the answer.

(iii) *The rise and fall of governing classes*

In its completed form, that of the *Treatise*, Pareto's theory asserts that: 1. The rise and decay of governing classes is due to the alteration in them of the proportions of Class I residues (combinations) to those of Class II (the persistence of aggregates). 2. This rise and decay reflects a rhythmic and necessary alternation, now of a preponderance of the Class I, now of the Class II residues. 3. To each of these two classes of residues there corresponds a definite style of government, *viz.* to Class I residues a relative preponderance of persuasion and guile, to Class II residues a relative preponderance of coercion.

(a) *Residues and governmental style.* The residues of combination—the Class I residues—supply, according to Pareto, 'precisely the skills and flair for expedients which are necessary for devising ingenious ploys as substitutes for open resistance ... The policies of the governing class are not planned very far forward in time. The predominant influence of the instincts of combination and the weakening of the sentiments of persistence of aggregates have the effect of making the governing class more satisfied with the present and less inclined to take thought for the future. The individual comes markedly to prevail over the family, the community, the nation. Material interests and the interests of the present or of the very near future come to prevail over the ideal interests of the community and nation and over the interests of the distant future.' [*T.*, §2178, *Sel.*, pp. 257–8.]

The Class II residues—those of the persistence of aggregates—supply qualities just the opposite of these. They resist innovation, and seek to preserve old forms and traditions. They are aggressive, authoritarian, reliant on force and threats of force, and contemptuous of manoeuvre, persuasion and compromise. They give rise to ideals, and are embodied in religions whether supernatural or secular, among the last being such religions as nationalism, socialism, imperialism. The goals are set for a distant future. Self-sacrifice for the community and the future, the subordination of the individual's interest to both of these, courage and persistence in striving for them—these also are the characteristics of the Class II residues.

(b) *Varying proportions of Class I and Class II residues.* Just as intelligence and aptitudes are not evenly distributed throughout society, neither are the residues. Furthermore, not only are they unevenly distributed in the various strata of society, but their *intensity* varies in different strata. The masses as a whole are rich in both Class II residues and Class III residues (manifestation of sentiments by activity). They are deficient in other kinds—notably, says Pareto, in Class V residues, those of the integrity of the individual. 'The neophobia and supersitition of the masses have often been noticed,' he says, and 'it is a well-attested historical fact that they were the last to abandon faith in the religion which derives its very name, paganism (from *paganus*, country dweller) from them. [*T.*, §1723.]

The governing class is, however, much smaller than the masses. A small *absolute* number of withdrawals from the masses will cause little or no change in the balance of its residues; on the other hand the accession of this small number of individuals to the relatively tiny governing class is sufficient to upset the relative balance of its residues very considerably indeed. The circulation of the elites, by accession or by violent overthrow, thus unbalances in a shorter or longer interval, the characteristics of the governing class. [*T.*, §2179,

Sel., p. 258.] So, if A is the index of the force in society of the Class I residues, B the index for the Class II residues and q the phenomenon under consideration, what has to be considered is the relation between them, as in the equation

$$q = \frac{B}{A}$$

It is not enough to know that B has increased to conclude that q has increased because A may have also increased so as to offset the increase in B. [*T.*, §2466, n 1.]

(c) *Alternation of governing classes: 'lions' and 'foxes'*. The outline of the theory of alternation is stated in its most basic form at §2227. With appropriate deletions it runs as follows: 'A predominance of interests which are mainly industrial and commercial makes the governing class richer in individuals who are cunning, shrewd and well-endowed with instincts of combination, and poorer in individuals of bold, resolute character and well-endowed with instincts of aggregate-persistence. This may also come about for other reasons; taking them into general consideration . . . we might well opine that, if the exercise of government consisted solely of astuteness, cunning and artful devices, then the power of the social group in which Class I residues greatly predominated would be very long enduring and would come to an end only if that group destroyed itself through senile degeneration of the breed. But force also is essential to the exercise of government. As within the governing group there develops a gradual intensification of Class I residues and a corresponding weakening of Class II residues, so those who govern become less and less adept in the use of force. This produces an unstable equilibrium and revolutions ensue, like that of protestantism against the governing class of the Renascence and of the French people against its rulers in 1789. Such revolutions succeed for reasons somewhat similar to those through which a rude and uncultivated Rome was able to conquer a civilised and cultivated Greece. . . . The populace, in whom the Class II residues predominate, carry them upwards into the governing class either by infiltration (circulation of the elite) or in sudden bursts through revolutions.' [*Sel.*, p. 263.]

But once the new governing class which is so rich in the Class II residues has acceded, why does it, in its turn, ultimately lose its power? There seem to be two reasons. The first is external pressure. States which are governed by the Class II residue type of governing class, after a brief burst of energy and prosperity due to the replacement of an effete elite by a new upthrusting and bustling one, become petrified ('*irrigidite nelle sue istituzioni*'). That is to say they become hidebound, bureaucratic, and unadaptable [*T.*, §2274, *Sel.*, p. 274]— like Sparta or Byzantium. Other things being equal, a state of this kind is no match for a state in which the masses, rich in their

Class II residues, are yet led by the imaginative, unscrupulous and highly adaptable Class I residue type of governing class. This, to Pareto's mind was why the Thebans were able to beat the Spartans, and it is the reason he gives in *Fatti e Teorie** (1920) for the Entente powers' beating the hidebound and overweening Germans and Austrians in the 1914–18 war. [*Sel.*, pp. 287 *et seq.*] The other reason is internal. Class II type governing classes do not possess the technical and money-making skills which societies require. Hence, very often, they 'readily accept individuals who are well-endowed with Class I residues and devote themselves to economic and financial pursuits because usually these persons are great producers of wealth and so increase the wealth of the governing class. . . . The immediate effect of their accession to power is therefore useful to many people, and they strengthen the governing class. Then, little by little, they act like the woodworm, impoverishing the governing class of the elements in it who are well-endowed with Class II residues and are capable of using force. So the "speculators" in France first brought about the triumph of the absolute monarchy and then its ruin. Nowadays in certain countries they have helped on the victory of the so called democratic (better described as demagogic plutocratic) regime and are now preparing its ruin.' [*T.*, §2227, n. 1.]

Such is the theory in outline. It is set out in brief in §§2178–9 of the *Treatise*. [*Sel.*, pp. 257–9.]

(d) *Typology of political regimes*. So, finally, Pareto comes to recognise two basic types of regimes, with intermediate cases partaking of the characteristics of both.

Type I. Governments relying chiefly on physical force, and on religious and similar sentiments.

The examples given are Greek tyrannies; Sparta; Rome under Augustus and Tiberius; Venice in its last centuries; and the absolute monarchies of Europe in the eighteenth century. In all of them the governing class contained a predominance of Class II over Class I residues. The circulation of the elites is usually slow, the governments are inexpensive but on the whole fail to stimulate economic pursuits. Where the instincts of combinations still survive among the population, there would be moderate prosperity if the governments did not harm their enterprise; but in the long run this is just what they tend to do, because they 'petrify', i.e., become of a bureaucratic and regulatory type. They can grow precariously wealthy by exploiting conquests abroad, but this is shortlived. Such governments in the past

---

* Extracts from *Fatti e Teorie* will be found in Part Three of the Selections, pp. 287–98.

have shown a tendency to degenerate into praetorianism; military rule of this kind is parasitic and wastes such wealth as is produced. [*T.*, §2274, *Sel.*, pp. 273–4.]

Type II. Governments relying chiefly on intelligence and cunning.

These are of two subtypes. 1. *Theocratic governments*. Here intelligence and cunning are chiefly used to influence the sentiments of the subordinate class. In modern Europe this type has disappeared. 2. *Demagogies*. Here intelligence and cunning are used to play on interests, as well as sentiments. Examples are the Athenian democracy, some epochs in the Roman Republic, the regimes of many medieval republics, and finally, modern mass democracies. All such governments have governing classes in which the Class I residues predominate over those of Class II. Confining ourselves only to the 'demagogic' subtype, the circulation of the elites is high, and in modern democracies very high indeed. They are expensive governments—but they are also economically very productive so that there may well be an excess of production over costs, and hence great prosperity. The difficulty is to guarantee that the ever increasing cost of such governments will be matched by corresponding increases in production. Another difficulty is that such governments, divested of the Class II residues, may degenerate into cowardice and easily be overthrown from outside or from within. [*T.*, §§2275–6, *Sel.*, p. 274.]

Type III. Mixed types.

These also are of two subtypes: 1. *Subtype II-2 + strong dosage of Type I*. Example: the earlier Roman Empire. The chief hazard here is that the II-2 elements will dwindle and the regime resemble the Class I type and become bureaucratic and 'petrified'—as happened in the later Roman Empire. 2. *Type I + strong dosage of subtype II-2*. Carthage is an example. These regimes can last a long time because they have a capacity for self-defence against their internal and external foes. Their hazard is lest they should tip over more and more into a type in which only the Class I residues predominate, i.e., become a pure subtype II-2. This exposes them to foreign conquest. Carthage seems to have suffered this kind of development. [*T.*, §2277, *Sel.*, p. 275.]

(iv) The relationship of the political and the economic forces: Speculators and Rentiers

Just as there is a political cycle—the flux and reflux of Class II residues into and out of the governing class, resulting in the cycle of 'lions' and 'foxes', so there is an economic cycle; and the two cycles are interconnected. The discovery of their inter-relationship marks one of the advances of the *Treatise* over the earlier works. Between trade cycle and political cycle the linkage is accomplished through Pareto's concept of the 'rentiers' and the 'speculators'.

The distinction between these two categories turns on that of the conflict of outlook and of self-interest between those who live on fixed incomes and those who have the opportunity to increase their incomes. The 'capitalist' class of Marx contains both of these groups, and is by no means a homogeneous body. Furthermore this division of interests extends beyond the possessing classes to the employees dependent on either of the two subgroups. There is a clear clash of interest, for instance, between workers in industries which are exposed to external competition or which are in a declining state on the home market, and workers in industries which are in a protected condition or which enjoy a monopoly or near-monopoly at home. The latter category of workers can secure higher wages from their employers because these are in a position to pass on such wage-increases to the consumer in the form of higher prices, whereas the former, working for employers who cannot do this, must bear like other consumers the brunt of rising living costs. Likewise there are savers among the masses, and persons living on pensions and other fixed or fairly fixed benefits. All these have, paradoxically, an economic interest similar to that of members of the 'capitalist' class who live on fixed incomes in the shape of returns on debentures, rents and other fixed-interest property.

Opposed to these are the 'business men'—the entrepreneurs in the full sense of the word. They may include small shopkeepers or the workers who can enforce their wage demands on their employers, but above all they are those employers, industrialists, financiers or merchants who can see and manipulate business opportunities so as to increase their incomes and their capital. To do this they have to rely, largely, on the savings effected by the first type, i.e., the fixed-income group. Pareto never ceased to affirm that saving was a non-rational activity; that persons who save do so because this reflects a value-attitude, a character-trait. (It is not a far cry from this to Keynes' 'propensity to save' which is independent of the rate of interest.)

Those who can and do increase their incomes Pareto calls, 'speculators'—a most ill chosen word. 'Enterprisers' would be a much better choice. Those who save and live on fixed incomes he calls the 'rentiers'—another ill-chosen word, suggesting obese cigar-puffing millionaires collecting their dividend slips.* Now the speculators and

---

* A study of British management (*Thrusters and Sleepers*, PEP, London, 1965) divides managers into two classes: 'thrusters' and 'sleepers'. These terms express Pareto's meaning far better than his own chosen terms.

the rentiers not only have conflicting interests: they represent different and incongruous temperaments; and these temperaments reflect the distribution of residues in their psychic make-up. These types are economic rather than political men; there is no *identity* between the lions and the rentiers and between the foxes and the speculators but there is an important *overlap* in that those people in society who have a preponderance of Class II residues in their make-up include (but are not congruent with) the rentiers, while those with a preponderance of Class I residues include (but are not congruent with) the speculators. 'The speculator category is primarily responsible for changes and progress in social and economic affairs. The rentiers on the other hand are a powerful element making for stability. . . . A society in which the rentiers almost exclusively predominate remains immobile and so to speak petrified. A society in which the speculators predominate lacks stability and is in a state of uneasy equilibrium which can be destroyed by a trifling accident from outside or from within.' [*T.*, §2235, *Sel.*, p. 265.]

Neither speculators or rentiers are, we must repeat, part of the political elite. In so far as they have a political interest it is derivative from their economic pursuits. Neither 'are very good at using force, and both categories are fearful of it. Those who wield force make up a third category (which finds) it easy to despoil the rentiers but somewhat more difficult to despoil the speculators since (these), defeated today, return to power the day after. . . .' [*T.*, §2313, *Sel.*, p. 278.] But, though they do not themselves use force, and fear it, both categories may on occasion lend support to those who are prepared to use it, and this is particularly true of the rentiers. It is not a question of political affinities but of temperaments with which we are concerned.

The rentiers, who as we have seen tend to be the dogsbodies of the community, despoiled by the speculators in the economic field and by any group or government which uses force against them, may indeed become revolutionaries. There are 'evolutions, innovations and revolutions which the rentier will support, particularly movements tending to restore to the governing class certain residues of aggregate-persistence which had been eliminated by the speculators. A revolution may be made against the speculators—for instance, of the kind which founded the Roman Empire.' One is instantly reminded of the fascist revolutions in Italy and Germany, supported to such a large extent by a middle class that had been ruined by the inflation—in Pareto's words, 'despoiled' of their savings. And indeed, the fact that this passage [*T.*, §2235] was added in the 1923 edition, suggests that Pareto may have had Italian fascism in mind.

Thus, in Pareto's words, 'the different proportions in which speculators and rentiers are combined amidst the governing class correspond to different types of civilisation'. [*T.*, §2236, *Sel.*, p. 265.] For this proportion is linked with the predominantly Class I residue or Class II residue characteristic of the politicians, and each type of person—the 'political' men and the 'economic' men—interacts upon the other in real life.

In the last chapter of his *Treatise*, Pareto interprets western history in terms of this linked economic-political cycle. His illustrations are too lengthy to be abridged in the extracts. But two major instances of his interpretation may be noted, examples of which are given in the *Treatise* and elsewhere. One is the interconnection of economics and politics in the 'military cycle'. [*T.*, §§2223–6, *Sel.*, pp. 261–3; *FT.*, xxix, *Sel.*, p. 292; *Trasf.*, p. 76, *Sel.*, p. 315.] Another is his analysis of the protectionist cycle. Pareto first makes the usual classical economic analysis showing that this will tend to reduce the total national product. It will also have indirect effects, *viz.*, the transfer or redistribution of wealth. Wealth is lost in this process also; but since some wealth may be transferred into the hands of more adventurous and risk-taking economic types (i.e., 'speculators'), there may be a subsequent increase of wealth which is greater than the loss. Nor is this all. In so far as it enriches these speculator-types, it brings men of Class I residues to reinforce the governing elite. Furthermore, the transference of wealth and the new opportunities created for getting rich quickly stimulate the circulation of the elite—i.e., protection creates avenues and opportunities for speculator types which simply do not exist in a static agricultural economy. For all these reasons, the governing class becomes richer in Class I residues; and this gives it an interest in economic activity and industrialisation which the former Class II-ridden governing class, with its horizons limited to a static agricultural economy, never previously possessed. The resulting increase in the national product may more than offset the destruction of wealth which the protection causes. [*T.*, §§2208–22.]

(v) The relationship of political and economic cycles to intellectual and artistic cycles

There remains to link up the socio-politico-economic cycles with those of intellect, belief and artistic creativity. All of these spheres are concerned with 'derivations', and as such are far more dependent on interests and residues than the other way about. These derivations alternate also, in what can be crudely expressed as periods of 'faith' alternating with periods of 'scepticism'. This is correlated, chiefly, with the fluctuation of Class I and Class II residues in society.

Individuals can and do experience alternations in their psychic make-up. So, 'at times there will be persons in whom the Class II residues have declined in strength while the combination-instincts (Class I) have waxed'. [*T.*, §2340.] Such individuals will increasingly view the conclusions drawn from the residues of persistence of aggregates (i.e., the Class II residues) as at odds with realities. They will regard them as outworn prejudices, and will strive to destroy and then supplant them by what they think are scientifically grounded and logical theories and programs. They will see this as making 'faith and prejudice' give way to 'reason'.

In a society dominated by these now triumphant *pseudo*-intellectual theories a countertrend will arise. To the individual whose combination instincts have weakened and whose sentiments of the persistence of aggregates have grown stronger, these pseudo-intellectual theories will begin to seem as at odds with realities. Their conclusions will be held to be false; but as they are, ostensibly, derived from logic and reason, the only way they can be *shown* to be false is to launch an attack on the use of logic and reason. Thus *anti*-intellectualist or mystical theories or species of intuitionism arise, to displace the old positivistic and rational theories.

However, continues Pareto, this argument is incomplete, in so far as it implies that individuals make a considered appreciation of their beliefs. This is true only for a few refined intellects. Furthermore once these rare individuals have stated their position, it remains for this to gain wide popular acceptance. [*T.*, §§2343-4.] But popular acceptance takes us back to the residues and the relative proportions of Class I and Class II residues in society as a whole. It is with this proportion that the general adoption of faith or of scepticism is correlated.

But with what is this proportion itself correlated? At first sight it might seem as though the relative wealth or poverty of a society provided a good correlation with the state of its residues; but not so. On the other hand, the rise of rationalism and scepticism does seem, Pareto asserts, to be correlated with a *quickening* in the increase of wealth; and this in turn with the quickening of the circulation of the elites. The two latter factors, we have already seen, are interdependent. Pareto now shows that the rise of scepticism is dependent on them in its turn. To take one of his illustrations: as wealth began to increase in the later Middle Ages, so the catholic governing classes became more sceptical, more inclined to temper their religion with the findings of science and rational philosophy. 'Then,' says Pareto, 'a religious reaction sets in and as usual it comes from the masses.' This is one 'of the usual reactions by which Class II residues force a retreat upon Class I residues'. [*T.*, §2367.] However, in this case, the economic conditions continued to stimulate the circulation of the elites and bear individuals with Class I residues upwards into the governing class. And so, in the eighteenth century—especially in England in the latter eighteenth century as it underwent the beginnings of the industrial revolution—a reaction against 'superstition' and in favour of reason took place. Then a counter-reaction developed, signalised in England by the rise of evangelicalism, and in France by the lay-religions of the great Revolution which, Pareto never ceased to insist, was essentially a religious revival. The tendency reached its high point after 1815 with the florescence of christian moral and political philosophy. Then, with the rapid growth of economic prosperity as large scale production became widespread through Europe, there was a stimulus to class circulation and a rise in the proportion of Class I residues in the elites. And so came in the era of positivism, scientism and free thought. [*T.*, §§2386–7, *Sel.*, pp. 281–2.] And at the time of writing, Pareto, observing the state of Europe in 1912, discerned another temporary cycle supervening, as such cycles tend to do, on the wide cycle which he has been describing: a temporary cycle of reaction against the positivistic and rationalistic theories that had so far dominated the scene, and which was embodied in the return to catholicism on the one hand, and the adoption of rival lay-religions—nationalism, imperialism and socialism—on the other. [*T.*, §§2390, *Sel.*, p. 282.]

And so we come to the close of the system. It began by postulating the interdependence of phenomena. In this theory of the way in which political, economic and intellectual and cultural changes are interconnected in a characteristic wave form, from the Graeco-Roman origins of western civilisation to his own day, Pareto had, for better or for worse, demonstrated the how and the why of his opening proposition. The serpent's tail had come to rest in the serpent's mouth.

(vi) Pareto's system and pluto-democracy

The theory that society is governed by more or less well-defined groups—governing class, political class, ruling elite—has obvious applicability to autocracies, aristocracies and such regimes as one-party systems wherein ruling authority is vested in the upper echelons of a party hierarchy. What has always been at issue is whether, as Pareto and others claimed, modern mass democracies also are ruled, in effect, by such narrow groups. In Pareto's case the issue has been blurred in two ways. To begin with Pareto had nothing but scorn and contempt for the parliamentary regimes of his own day, and permitted his feelings to spill over into his scientific analysis. To do justice to that analysis one ought to separate the two. This course has not always been the one followed. Secondly, in many quarters Pareto seems to be regarded as expressing similar views to those of Mosca. This is not correct. His definition of the 'governing class' is by no means the same. It is necessary therefore to devote a special section to Pareto's notion of the governing class and the role he held it to play in a modern mass democracy. This should be regarded as a specific application of the system that has been expounded in the previous pages.

The first matter to be dealt with is Pareto's private prejudice against parliamentary democracy. He was always reiterating that he held no such prejudice, that his work was scientific, not subjective. This is absurdly false. In some cases he lets his prejudices obtrude by slipping in implicit value-judgements, in others by using loaded terms, by sarcasms, abuse and imputations of baseness. The explanation lies in his own private concepts of the criteria for social utility and his own personal preferences in the matter of means. As to the second we know what these were. He was a man of noble traits, but soured by his experiences, and he applied them out of context to the political manners of his time. As a pugnacious man he could not stand the continual retreat of governments in the face of threats and their timid gestures of conciliation and compromise. To him these governments lacked guts. They were under attack. Why did they not hit back? Again, he was a man of austere habits, who cared little for material pleasures. He preferred those with the faith of their own convictions to those who were motivated by their own material interests. And he was an honest man. Thus, these two sentiments made him detest the materialism and the corruption of the governments of his own day. There is much truth in Giacalone-Monaco's contention that Pareto was a puritan who wanted to 'moralise' government.[50] It is borne out by Pareto's admiration for Swiss democracy: 'the best government now in existence and better than countless others that have so far been observable in history'; a country whose regime, democratic, 'has nothing in common with the governments also called democratic of such countries as France and the United States'. [*T.*, §2240, n 1.]

In regard to the first factor—his private criteria for social utility—Pareto nowhere makes these explicit, but it is not difficult to collect them from references and inferences in the *Treatise*. It is clear that he privately believed the necessary conditions of social utility to be (a) the maintenance of public order, (b) national independence, and (c) an increase in national wealth. In so far as a governing class becomes 'humane' (i.e., determined never to use force until the very last moment and then in insufficient degree), Pareto has no difficulty in showing that such a governing class fails to secure public order, and likewise fails to meet aggression. In more than one footnote he repeats with relish the Italian saying that 'he who plays the sheep will meet the butcher'. Furthermore, from this standpoint, the governing class is bringing peril upon itself, for almost by definition it is inviting overthrow from the outside or from its insurgent masses, rich in the aggressive Class II residues.

But these personal prejudices of Pareto must not be taken as his scientific theory of parliamentary democracy, or as he called it, 'plutodemocracy'.

Pareto's views are nowhere collected into one comprehensive statement. They have to be collected from the sprawling corpus of the *Treatise* and from the post-*Treatise* writings. It will help to clarify his views if, paradoxically, we start off with six main objections which American scholars have brought against the view that there exists in the highly pluralistic democracy of the United States a 'ruling class' in any precise sense. These objections have been summarised by Harold D. Lasswell as follows:

> 1. Important decisions are not in fact made or executed by a *sufficiently restricted* body of decision makers to justify the use of the term 'elite'.
> 2. Top decision makers *do not stay* in control positions *long enough* to justify the use of the term elite.
> 3. They do not act together with *sufficient cohesion* to protect their current position or to control the selection of successors.
> 4. They do *not act covertly* (or conspiratorially) to maintain or extend their control.
> 5. They compete with one another for the popular support which they are not able to obtain by traditional obedience or the use of coercion.
> 6. The members of the body politic ... expect to be able to make themselves effective in the decision making process whenever they become genuinely involved ...[51]

First: it must be underlined that Pareto is painting with a very broad brush indeed. His 'governing classes' each cover whole historical epochs. They cover the period of the rise and collapse of the Roman Republic; the rise and collapse of the Roman Empire; the period of the Reformation and Counter-Reformation; the period between the latter and the French Revolution; and the whole post-Revolutionary era. His governing classes, therefore, are by no means to be equated with the ins and outs of the Labour and Conservative parties or the Republican and Democratic parties and the general rise and fall of ministries in constitutional forms of government. Hence objections 2 and 5—particularly the latter—are wide of the mark.

Secondly: the concept of the governing elites, of the governing classes, is not exhausted by the concept of rival political parties. Pareto draws a distinction between two types of political parties. 1. Parties which alternate with one another in government; when one is in power the others are in opposition. 2. Intransigent, uncompromising parties which never participate in government. [*T.*, §2268, *Sel.*, p. 271.] The latter are made up of sincere fanatics—men of great faith and idealism, who will not compromise. [*Ibid.*] In paretian terms, they are replete with the Class II residues. The compromising parties are rich in Class I residues, those of combinations. It is absolutely clear from Pareto's examples that 'compromising' parties are synonymous with 'transformist' parties—i.e., those which are themselves part of a governing class, rich in the residues of combinations, supplying merely a variant leadership. In so far as one group of the Italian socialists was prepared to work with the system, Pareto regards this group simply as part of the governing elite—albeit not necessarily its 'inner government'. Only the other activist faction 'which wished to wreck and overturn the system' did he regard as a genuine counterelite. [*T.*, §2256.] In our day we have seen the triumph of precisely these 'intransigent' parties which Pareto regarded as incapable of obtaining power: the Russian communists, the Italian fascists and the German nazis. These would, in his mind, constitute the triumph of a new elite; the alternation of the British Labour and Conservative parties or of the American Democratic and Republican parties are, in the paretian analysis, merely alternating faces of a single governing class.

Thirdly: the governing class is not a tight well-knit and clearly circumscribed organisation. It is a very unsystematic system—much like the concept of the feudal *system*. Its essence (in democracies, it must be clearly understood) is the patron-client relationship, a relationship based for the most part (and increasingly) upon economic interests. It is an order or system of a vast number of mutually dependent hubs of influence and patronage, which keeps together by the fact that each such hub is dependent to some extent on the good graces of another such hub. It can fairly be described a *class*, because it has a certain amount of cohesion which comes about in three main ways. The first, as already stated, is that all its principal members— i.e., the patrons in the patron-client relationships—live by taking in one another's washing. We can see what Pareto is driving at when he launches a bitter attack on the Italian bourgeoisie (his own words) in a letter to Pantaleoni in 1896. 'Whom do I call the *bourgeois*? I call *bourgeois* all those who live comfortably and enjoy protective tariffs, get government jobs for their children and make gains through the contractors and, when the occasion arises, despoil the banks; and besides these, many wealthy or well-to-do persons, honest in their private lives but who think it necessary 'in order to support their class and so as not to dry up the well-springs of money for their friends' to support any knavery on the part of the government.'[52] The second is that its members, in so far as they are actuated by economic interests, naturally tend to see what is their economic advantage and hence to act in a certain common sense or common direction, without any preconcerted design to do so. The third is that this governing elite, this quite widespread network of affiliations, has its own 'government'. This Pareto describes either as a visible (hence formal) body or an invisible, informal one. This governing body is 'a more exclusive, class, or a leader or a committee, which exercises control in effect and in practice'. It may be the Spartan Ephors or the Venetian Council of Ten, or the parliamentary leadership of a modern democracy (here the 'inner government' is overt and formal); or it may be covert as was, at the time when Pareto was writing, the Liberal Caucus in Britain or the party Conventions in the United States. [*T.*, §2254, *Sel.*, pp. 268–9.]

The task of such a body—let us suppose it be the parliamentary leadership—is to aggregate the various centres of patronage—let us call them the various clienteles—in such a way as, by broadly satisfying all these, to maintain itself in power. But the governing class is not, quite emphatically not, conceived as a 'concrete unity', as a 'person'. The governing class does not have a 'single will', does not implement 'pre-conceived plans by logical procedures'. 'The main factor in the matter is really the system . . . not the conscious will of individuals, who may indeed in many cases be carried along by the system to positions they would never have arrived at by deliberate choice.' [*Ibid.*] So much for objections 3 and 4.

Fourthly: the governing class of Pareto is not congruent with a particular socio-economic class, taken in the marxist sense of the word. There is no doubt that as originally conceived by Pareto, who was taking Italy as his paradigm case, the governing class was more or less identical with the marxist 'bourgeoisie'—as the letters of 1891 and 1896 to Pantaleoni make clear.[53]

But in the *Manuale* (1906) [*Manuel* (1909)], the *Treatise* and the *Trasformazione* (1921)* Pareto argues that in the mass democratic state, the governing class is a tacit alliance of the entrepreneurs and their workmen against the fixed-income groups in the community— from property owners to those living on savings, pensions, public

---

* Extracts from *La Trasformazione della Democrazia* are given in the Selections, Part Three, pp. 299 *et seq.* For Pareto's argument on this point see: page 60 above; *M.*, ch. 9, esp. §§34–5; *I.*, §§2231–2, *Sel.*, pp. 263–4; *Trasf.*, pp. 73–4, *Sel.*, pp. 314–15.

assistance, and those working in depressed or highly competitive industries where increased wage costs cannot readily be passed on to the consumer and where accordingly the wages tend to remain low. However much the workers and the employers may struggle over other matters, in this fundamental issue there is a tacit bond. This alliance forms the basis of the governing class of the modern mass democracy.

Fifthly: the role of the 'inner government' of this alliance or governing elite is to keep all the clienteles reasonably satisfied and the statesman who can do so successfully is the one who will remain in power. What are the means at his disposal? The least important are those which are most censured ethically: bribery of voters, deputies, officials or newspaper proprietors either by money or by honours and awards. The most important of the means is 'looking after' the various clienteles. There need be no explicit understanding with them at all. 'A protectionist government, for example, wins the confidence and the support of the manufacturers (whose products) it protects without necessarily making an explicit agreement with all of them, although it may come to a direct understanding with leading individual manufacturers.' [*T.*, §2257, *Sel.*, p. 269.] And 'even if economic protection were abandoned, there would still be other fields for corruption such as military supplies and munitions, fortress construction, shipbuilding, public works, state concessions, the administration of justice . . . the distribution of honours and awards within the gift of the state, the apportionment of taxation, "social" legislation and so forth'. [*T.*, §2265.]

In the course of this vast redistribution of wealth great opportunities are created for the entrepreneur. [*Trasf.*, p. 85, *Sel.*, p. 318.] One effect of this system is to increase the circulation of the elites prodigiously, so that although this vast shuffling and reshuffling of incomes destroys a great deal of wealth, it produces a situation where there rise to the governing elite even larger numbers of people who produce wealth; and to this Pareto ascribes the mounting economic prosperity of Europe in the second half of the nineteenth century. [*T.*, §2301.] But this very fact is what makes the pluto-democratic regime so vulnerable. 'Modern governments are kept in power less and less by resort to force and more and more by a very expensive art of government (and so) they have a very urgent need of economic prosperity in order to carry on their activities and . . . are also much more sensitive to variations in prosperity.' [*T.*, §2305, *Sel.*, p. 276.] Older types of government, reliant on force, also tottered when scarcities occurred; but that was because their force was met by a counterforce born of despair. In the pluto-democracies, the worsening of economic conditions can have effects long before it reaches such desperate limits. The difficulties which the pluto-democracy faces come in periods of economic depression 'and they would be far worse if such a depression were to prove protracted. The social order at the present time is such that probably no government could remain unaffected during such a period; and tremendous catastrophes could well occur more intense and extensive than any yet known to history.' [*T.*, §2307, *Sel.*, p. 276.] On the other hand, Pareto could write after the first world war that 'as long as the increment from savings is not too severely curtailed, the price of food and rent kept low and all the other benefits are on tap which the plutocracy can make available to its supporters and dependants, there is nothing in all this to prevent the plutocrats from continuing to make fat profits.' [*Trasf.*, p. 85, *Sel.*, pp. 317–18.]

But all this requires political skills of a high order. The ingenuous think that pure knavery will suffice. They are quite wrong. 'In fact, exceptional talents are required: shrewd intelligence and a marked aptitude for combinations of all kinds. Ministers do not have at their disposal great treasure chests which they can dip into at any time to scatter largesse among their adherents. They have to survey the world of business and industry with a shrewd eye to devise subtle combinations of economic favouritism, adroit ways of being agreeable to banks and business corporations, of promoting monopolies, of manipulating the incidence of taxation and so forth.' [*T.*, §2268, *Sel.*, p. 272.]

It would seem that objections 5 and 6 (at page 60 above) are to a large extent discounted by this confession that the system, to endure, has to procure what are or appear to be extensive economic benefits to its supporters, and by the tacit admission that the particular group which will form the 'inner government' of the governing elite will be the one best able to conciliate the clienteles competing for its favours.

Pareto's final view of modern parliamentary democracy is expounded in the *Trasformazione*. If the emotive language is disregarded, it amounts to this: over the last century in the industrialised countries of the West there have occurred (a) a vast increase of wealth, (b) the continued unequal distribution of that wealth, and (c) the predominance of the two classes of 'speculators' and workers over the fixed-income groups and the military classes of the community. The importance of the 'speculator' elements in society warrants the term 'plutocracy', that of the workers the term 'democracy': hence Pareto's composite term, 'pluto-democracy'. Both economically and politically there has occurred a tacit alliance between these two predominant classes (see page 68 above), partly 'to get the upper hand over the state' (Pareto's notion of the 'new feudalism' of trade unions and employers' associations), and partly to exploit the fixed-income groups in the community. In the latter the 'persistence of aggregates' is strong; the former—whether workers or capitalists—are rich in the 'instinct of combinations'. Thus the community is led by a governing class of 'combiners', and for their type of rule parliament is so fitting an instrument that Pareto argues that the fate of the one is linked with that of the other. For an elected parliament acts as the forum or market place for cementing alliances and concluding transactions between the various components of this ruling class, and at the same time as the platform from which the masses are persuaded to consent to these. [*Trasf.*, pp. 44–57, 73–6, *Sel.*, pp. 307–11, 314–15.] Thus the governing class in a modern democracy is very widespread indeed, comprising the trade union bosses as well as employers, the captains of pressure groups as well as the party leaders, social democrats as well as conservatives.

The result is a vast and largely impersonal system. Personalities enter into it only in so far as one political caucus or another is better able to conciliate the various clienteles that clamour for satisfaction. The governing class does not despoil others of their property solely to enrich itself: it does so to share the spoils with those in the governed masses who defend and sustain it, standing towards it in the relationship of clients to patron. Furthermore although in an objective sense this governing elite 'defrauds' or 'gulls' the governed, this is not necessarily how it appears to them—or to the governed either. In most cases, states Pareto, neither is entirely aware of violating social morality and in some cases the governing elite earnestly believes that its rule is in the best interests of the country. [*T.*, §2267, *Sel.*, p. 270.] The system, in full working order, brings about so open a governing class and so rapid a circulation of the elite, that the talent for 'combining' has ready access to the key posts in government and the economy; and the result is to generate more wealth than is lost in the clumsy process of income redistribution which the 'democratic' nature of the system demands. As long as these conditions obtain, so long the pluto-democratic regime can endure. [*Trasf.*, pp. 73–7, *Sel.*, pp. 317–18.]

V

Critique and Assessment

In what follows we propose, first to criticise Pareto's system *qua* system, and then to indicate some of the areas where he made original or significant advances.

1. A CRITIQUE OF PARETO'S SYSTEM

Pareto's completed system is attackable at many points: its mechanistic and atomistic nature, its definition of what is 'non-logical', its over-sharp dichotomy between ends and means, its assumption that ends are random and unsusceptible to any 'logic of ends', and so forth.[54] Here we propose to concentrate on two matters only: the residue theory and the elite theory, since these are the system's two main pillars.

(i) Residue theory

The central problem here is to decide whether the residue is a psychic cause of overt actions or merely a description of these. Pareto himself recognises both senses of the word, and warns that he will use it to mean both the cause of actions and the description of them. (See page 41 above.)

   If we are to assume that the residues are psychic states and hence causes, two difficulties arise. In the first place, Pareto himself admits that the only way he can establish the existence of the 'residue-cause' is through examination and classification of overt actions, not from any other and independent source. He also admits that he infers their existence from these overt acts: he does not *know* it (cf. page 41 above). Thus the only evidence for the existence of this 'cause' is the overt action which is alleged to be its effect. The argument runs like this. Emperor William II of Germany is observed to be choleric; this sort of temperament is classified as part of the Class II of residues (the persistence of aggregates); hence it is caused by a psychic state to which we impute (with no independent evidence) the property of giving rise to choleric actions; hence we assert that the cause of the German Emperor's choler is that he possesses Class II residues. But this is the argument of animism. The native asserts that the movements of a tree are the movements of the god that possesses it. He then proves the existence of the god by pointing to the movement of the branches. Or, if one likes, it is the argument of the *médecin malgré lui*. Opium makes one sleepy; the doctor is asked the reason; the answer he gives is: 'opium possesses a sleep-inducing quality'. The only reason Pareto gives for asserting that residues are causes is the assertion that actions are their effects! He 'puts these residues into a man and later on deduces from them whatever he likes'.[55] Causal explanations such as Pareto gives [*FT.*, xii, *Sel.*, p. 292; *Trasf.*, p. 31, *Sel.*, p. 304] may be correct. But he provides no proof. In the absence of such proof, they are simply labels.

This does not mean that they are useless to sociology. To establish that some actions form syndromes in the sense that a man who performs one is usually observed to perform the others is not a senseless exercise. At the worst it has some predictive value; at the best, it permits 'typing' men according to the peculiar syndrome of actions they perform. This is precisely what underlies such conceptions as 'introvert-extrovert', or Znaniecki's 'Bohemian', 'Philistine' and 'Creative' types of character, or Reisman's 'tradition-directed', 'inner-directed' and 'other-directed' types.

Let us assume, then, that the residues are labels. Still the difficulties do not entirely disappear. When Pareto asserts that a given man possesses a predominance of Class I residues, he does not mean that such a man may be expected to perform actions falling in subclasses I-a, I-b, I-c, etc.; he is saying more often than not that such a man may perform actions of subclasses I-a and I-d though not I-b and I-c; or of subclasses I-b and I-d and not I-a and I-c. By saying that the man possesses a predominance of Class I residues, he is saying that he may perform actions belonging to all or *some* of the subclasses of that class. So the syndromes of behaviour are somewhat fluid and indefinite and so, therefore, are the 'types' of social character based upon them. Is Pareto perhaps saying, however, that a man who performs an act belonging to one of the subclass I-a activities may or may not go on to perform activities falling within the other

subclasses of Class I residues, but will *not* go on to perform *any* of
the activities falling within the Class II or any other class of residues?
To some extent, yes. His difficulty here is that, by his own admission,
some of the activities classed as those of the Class IV and Class V
residues are identical with those falling inside Class I or Class II
residues. Significantly, however, there is no overlap between activities grouped under Class I and those under Class II.

The most satisfactory inference we can draw from these considerations, then, is that the Class I and Class II residues are shorthand expressions, labels, for two mutually exclusive syndromes of
behaviour, and by extension of two mutually exclusive character
types. This conclusion is compatible with the main argument of
Pareto's thesis which indeed, as we have seen, works very largely in
terms of only these two classes of residues. This is a position not so
far removed, in principle, from the three character-types of Znaniecki
or of Reisman which we have already mentioned. The problem now
becomes: what is Pareto's evidence for asserting the existence of
these two character-types, the distribution of which in society
accounts for social change?

In principle, the correct way to establish their existence would be
to enumerate and define their respective traits very carefully, and then
devise some psychological of psycho-analytical test which could be
administered to statistically valid samples of the population. Today
such methods are not only conceivable but have become regular
practice, as the work of Adorno, Sheldon, Eysenck, Rokeach and
others bears witness. This method was not open to Pareto. The
method he did employ is unacceptable: it is the appeal to the so-
called facts of history. This is subject to a criticism similar to that
which we have directed against his proof of the existence of residues
as causes of human behaviour. Pareto puts these two character-types
into history and then explains history by them. Were the British
cabinets of the nineteenth century 'lions' or 'foxes'? As far as Ireland
was concerned, they alternated between violence and blandishment.
If they were a 'judicious mixture' of both types, then Pareto's assertions are never falsifiable!

This criticism of Pareto's appeal to the 'facts of history' is borne
out by an examination of his associated thesis: that the course of
history is dictated by the relative changes of Class I and Class II
residues in the governing elite. At §2466 of the *Treatise*, he sums this
proposition up by an equation:

$$q = \frac{A}{B}$$

where *q* represents the pheno-
menon we are examining (let us say, Germany's breach in 1914 of

Belgian neutrality). A represents the force of the Class I residues, and B the force of the Class II residues. To find the absolute values of A and B—which alone will give us their relative proportion—we do not, according to Pareto, inspect for A and B empirically. No; he says (*Ibid.*) we are best placed to judge of the relative variations in A and B when 'we can find phenomena directly dependent upon q, and therefore give some notion of the manner of *its* (our italics) variations'. We set out to explain q in terms of $\frac{A}{B}$. Instead we are told we infer $\frac{A}{B}$ from changes in q!

The circularity of the reasoning is most convincingly brought out, however, by a passage in the correspondence. On March 15, 1918, Pareto wrote to Pansini: 'Thus, even if Germany *is* defeated, the fact that she has for so long resisted the forces of the entire world proves once again the efficacy of a governing class rich in residues of Class I (combinations) and of a governed class rich in Class II of residues.'[56] But when the war was over, Pareto wrote in *Fatti e Teorie* [*Sel.*, p. 292]: 'In Germany's rulers Class II residues (persistence of aggregates) were potent, while among the rulers of the Entente nations, with the exception of Russia, Class I residues (instinct of combination) predominated'—the diametrically opposite conclusion!

The conclusions so far must be: 1. there may indeed be six basic psychic impulses which, in combination, account for our activities, but Pareto does not prove this; 2. there may also be two mutually exclusive character types whose social distribution explains the course of history—but, again, Pareto does not prove this. Supposing, however, that we give him the benefit of the doubt and assume these two propositions are established, we are still not out of the wood.

Pareto asserts that, by and large, the six main classes of residues have remained constant over the last two thousand years of western history. Such social changes as have taken place have occurred through the preponderance of Class I over Class II residues in the governing class, or of Class II over Class I. The form of society has merely *alternated*. 'Is this all that has happened?', we may well ask. Is our present condition just a latterday version of the later Roman Republic? No, Pareto answers. Perhaps the greatest difference between our day and the Graeco-Roman period is the increase in natural science and its extrusion of superstition and magic [*T.*, §2392, *Sel.*, p. 283.] Now, both of these are subvariations of Class I residues, (the instinct of combinations); and it is a cardinal point of Pareto that as one subclass of residues increases, others decline so that the force of the total class of that kind of residue in society remains the same as before. [*T.*, §1718, *Sel.*, p. 243.] Thus, a basic and admitted difference between ancient times and our own is ascribed not so much to a relative change in the force of Class I and Class II residues* as to a relative 'intensification' of one subclass of Class I residues and the corresponding diminution of another.

In that case, the course of social change is not exhausted by the relative proportions of the classes of residues; some parts of it, at least, are only explicable in terms of the relative intensification of one *sub*class at the expense of others. Pareto does indeed discuss 'intensification' of subclasses, but he never gives us a pattern for it. As far as the *Treatise* is concerned, the intensification or diminution of subclasses of the residues is unexplained and arbitrary. So, if his system explains anything, all it explains is why western society has alternated between two forms. No explanation is afforded for any changes occurring *within* either of these two forms. The dilemma this creates can be expressed thus. If the form of society is to be explained in terms of six classes of residues and their relative proportions, then these classes operate only as *limits*, within which such dramatic contrasts as superstition or natural science can equally prevail. If, on the other hand, it is to be explained in terms of the relative variations of the fifty-two subclasses of residues, then we must be told what determines these variations—and we are not.

This dilemma reasserts itself when another, and for our purposes, a last objection is put. It concerns the allegedly constant, or fairly constant force, of each class of residue over the last two thousand years. This implies that in western societies, over this time span, 'human nature' has remained constant. In the 'twenties and 'thirties the cultural anthropologists demonstrated how plastic human nature is under the influence of the culture surrounding it. For this reason they disputed Freud's theory of personality. Later, when the *Treatise* was translated into English (1935), similar criticism was levelled against Pareto's theory of personality.

As we know, Pareto's residues are not instincts. (See page 43 above.) On the other hand they are as constant as instincts might be supposed to be. For Pareto the residues were 'both innate *and* socially acquired'. But in so far as they are socially acquired, and are also constant through time, only one conclusion is possible: that society has not changed through time. And except in one respect this

---

* It may be argued that Pareto has covered himself on this particular point by asserting that Class I residues had expanded over the last two thousand years, and were now greater than in Graeco–Roman times. This does not affect the point of the argument but, if another example is felt to be preferable, *cf.* the alleged changes in subclasses of Class IV residues. [*Trasf.*, p. 31, *Sel.*, p. 304.]

is indeed Pareto's position. The exception is, of course, that the relative proportions of persons of Class I or Class II residues in the governing elite *alternate* over time, so that society *alternates* also. But this is the extent of its change: from one polar type to the other and back again.

In details, Pareto tells us, 'history never repeats itself'. [*T.*, §2410.] Equally, 'in certain respects that *we may call the main ones* [our italics] history does repeat itself'. [*Ibid.*] What are 'the main' respects? They are simply those which reflect Pareto's personal judgement. So we learn that all wars are 'numberless copies' of the Peloponnesian war; that western Europe is the same as republican Rome. The fallacy here is the same as in marxism. 'All history is the history of class struggles' turns out, under inspection, to mean that 'all history that is worth calling history [*scilicet*, the causes, course and results of class struggle] is the history of class struggles'. Similarly with Pareto: 'The sentiments (residues) which have varied but slightly between Aristotle's day and our own' are the 'main element' in historical events [*T.*, §2194]; but the only events Pareto is prepared to consider as 'the main' ones are those related to and explicable by the residues.

(ii) *Elite theory*

Unlike the residue theory, Pareto's theory of the elites has exercised a massive influence, and has proved altogether more acceptable. But as he states it, his theory is but the beginning of wisdom. To begin with, Pareto concentrates solely on the qualities of inferiority-superiority and of psychological type; he makes no effort to relate his elites to social groupings and classes. His concept will apply to a tribal gerontocracy as well as to the presidium of the Communist Party of the Soviet Union. In particular, Pareto declines to relate his notion of governing elite to the concept of socio-economic class. This was not his original attitude. In the *Cours* he accepted Marx's socio-economic classes and his notion of class struggle; but the *Treatise* extrudes the marxist notions and replaces theory by a distinction between 'rentiers' and 'speculators'. (See pages 59–62 above.)

This intellectual evolution reflects Pareto's preoccupation with the ideas of Karl Marx. The *Treatise* is a gargantuan retort to Marx. However, Pareto's strategy is not confrontation but envelopment. He constructs social concepts and categories so broad as to reduce marxist propositions to the status of mere special cases of a much more general theory. He does not contradict marxism but denatures it. The trick is worked by transcending the marxist categories. For instance: the concept of ideology is so expanded that marxism itself rates as an ideology; the concept of class rule is transcended by that of elite rule; the concept of class exploitation is transcended by the more generalised concept of 'spoliation' of 'rentiers' by 'speculators'.

The result, however, is to denature Pareto's own sociology. It could have developed into a valuable supplementation and extension of marxist analysis, but it purports to be a substitute. Its simple message is that the many are always governed by the few, the less able by the more able. Only the psychological differences between strata are admitted: socio-economic classes and all other groupings of the population are excluded. But Pareto's 'governing elite' is no substitute for these; it is in fact composed of the governing elites of all or some of these. Moreover the 'style' and consequences of a governing elite drawn from the aristocracy are likely to differ greatly from those of one drawn from the managerial class or the bureaucracy; an elite drawn from the church is likely to govern differently from one drawn from the military. Furthermore the success of any of these groupings in pre-empting political power depends on such factors as their corporate self-consciousness, their material interests, their indispensability to society, and these factors will help determine the style of the political struggle between them, as it will also determine the 'derivations' to which they are susceptible. The interplay of such factors as these creates differences between regimes which are as real as any similarities discovered by Pareto—and, some sociologists would say, equally important. To assert that all societies are governed by minorities, and that these minorities are either 'lions' or 'foxes' is, at best, only a first step on a long, long journey.

But in any case, the doctrine that 'lions' alternate with 'foxes' is open to serious objection. We have already seen that it is very difficult to establish the existence of two such mutually exclusive psychological types (pages 74–5 above). Suppose, however, that it be granted that the will to use violence does arise from a specific type of human character; even so, the *need* to apply it surely arises from characteristics of society? For instance, it varies with the amount of disagreement provoked. A government that tries to regulate everything will, *caeteris paribus*, provoke more disagreement than one which limits its functions. Likewise a society in which dissensus prevails is likely to require more governmental coercion than one in which there is consensus. But this in its turn is related to the social structure, to the existence and corporate consciousness of classes and organised groups of all kinds; in short, to precisely those factors which Pareto chooses to exclude.[57]

A further criticism of Pareto's concept of a governing class is that it is too inclusive. Paradoxically, this is also its virtue. Most current criticism of what is called the 'ruling elite model' fastens on the term *class* in such expressions as Mosca's 'political class' or Pareto's 'governing class'. It is admitted that there are rulers, but denied that in western democracies these rulers behave consciously, coherently and conspiratorially enough to warrant their being styled a 'class'.[58] This criticism is unquestionably valid for Mosca's 'political class'. Pareto's concept escapes this particular criticism—but only to run into another.

On examination, Pareto's concept discloses a typology of regimes —and the key to this is Pareto's appreciation of the fact that, to govern, folk must somehow or other be mobilised. Accordingly he sees regimes as lying on a continuum between two polar types of mobilisation. At one extreme is what—for want of a better term—we may call the bureaucratic autocracy. In this the governing elite is a tightly organised and identifiable minority, of which the territorial or sectional subleadership is either the nominee or functionary; institutions and status are rigidly defined and conserved; and all authority to act emanates from the power and authority of the governing group (see Pareto's examples at pages 57–8 above). The limiting case of this type of regime would be the oriental despotism as conceived by Wittvogel.[59] A modern totalitarian state approaches it.

Significantly, Pareto spent little time in describing such regimes. His efforts are chiefly directed to the other polar type, and especially its modern form, the 'pluto-democracy'. Mosca derived his concept of the 'political class' from the lessons of history and from extra-European examples, and then applied it to contemporary democracies; he then spent the rest of his life trying to adjust the over-narrow concept to fit the characteristics of democracy.[60] But Pareto, as the correspondence makes clear, evolved his own concept from democracy itself: from the *consorteria* which emerged after the fall of the Italian Right in 1876. This model of a *consorteria* is the basis of the other polar type of regime which we may call the patron-client state. Pareto's contention is that the feudal state, the late Roman Republic, the modern pluto-democracy all share in common the characteristic of being organised as a loose consortium of patrons each with their own clienteles to satisfy. Two illustrations from very diverse works will make this notion more concrete. Skinner, examining the Chinese community in Thailand, speaks of the leaders 'who by virtue of their interrelations in commercial enterprises and non-profit community organisations constitute important loci or clusters of influence. On the basis of common memberships, these clusters of leaders are shown to be related more or less closely to one another and are grouped in blocks each held together by a "key leader". The blocks in turn . . . are shown to be either isolated or united with one another to form one or more structures . . .'[61] Hunter, examining the

United States, observed: 'In the nation as in the community there is a power structure inside and outside of government—not synonymous with government or any other formal organisation—influencing policy development. The national power structure is not a single pyramid of influence and authority but rather a kind of informal executive committee of the many major influence groups. It represents different geographic sections, different segments of the economy, and different organised groups. While disagreements may arise on specific issues the common aspirations of the larger corporate interests bring about a working unity . . .'[62]

Pareto saw parliamentary democracies precisely in this way; and his notion of 'the governing class' is correspondingly broad. This loose conception permitted him to handle the phenomenon of its fragmentation into 'the new feudalism' [*Trasf.*, pp. 41–57, *Sel.*, pp. 305–11] without self-contradiction. The various pressure groups, the regional and sectional groupings, the opposing political parties (providing they are of the 'transigent' type) are viewed as so many different clienteles whose leaders collectively form the governing class. The public authorities and politicians (part of this class) have the task of trying to accommodate as many of these sections of the ruling class as possible at the same time. The successful politicians, the Giolittis, achieve this; the Crispis, who fail, are ejected from office. (See page 69 above.) The strength of this concept of a 'patron-client' regime is that it points to somewhat unsuspected affinities between apparently diverse regimes. We all recognise that Britain, the United States, France, Italy belong to the same family of regimes; but we do not usually ask ourselves how the role of the American boss is related to the role of the *coronel* in Brazil, the *cacique* in nineteenth-century Spain, the tribal sheikh in pre-1958 Iraq, the tribal chief in contemporary Nigeria.[63] It is not always grotesque to compare very different objects in respect to one particular parameter; on the contrary this procedure can often cast new light on the respects in which the objects differ, and the reasons for this. In this regard, Pareto's typology deserves to be explored further: it contains interesting implications for research.

But this very flexibility of Pareto's concept of the 'governing class' is also its fatal weakness. It tells us in what respects regimes as dissimilar as, say, the Brazilian oligarchy and modern Britain, are similar: it fails to provide any differentiating criteria except, possibly, the degree of elite circulation. It distinguishes Britain, France, the United States from, say, the Soviet Union; so far so good; but it provides no criteria to explain the differences between these western regimes. For Pareto they are all simply pluto-democracies. The crucial difficulty in all elite theory is that the governing elite, as defined, is either too narrow or too broad. Mosca's conception of a closely knit and self-conscious organised minority is demonstrably too narrow to fit modern democracies; but Pareto's network of 'leading minorities'[64] is too broad to distinguish between them.

2. PARETO'S CONTRIBUTION TO SOCIOLOGY

Pareto was a concept-maker. This is by no means every sociologist's idea of what a sociologist should be. Sociology falls into two main and opposed types. One great tradition, which may be called the *empiricist*, disregards all generalisation which is not firmly tied to data secured by controlled observation; the other, the *interpretive*, concerned with what it regards as the essentials of the social process, is interested only in data on which to ground a general theory. The first accepts data because they exhibit statistical significance, the second because they permit the construction of types and of models. The empiricist tends to concern himself with microsociology, i.e., the study of the contemporary, the localised, and the specific area of culture; the interpreter with cross-cultural and historical comparison. The former is concerned with any typical or deviant patterns of behaviour that offer themselves, without reference to any prior interest in the pattern of society as a whole; the latter, however, is primarily concerned with political control, with decision making, the stability of the social system, which it sees as central to the social processes. It is evident that Pareto belongs to the latter tradition.[65]

It must be obvious from what has gone before that the system he erected will not do. But although it will not stand up, *qua* system, some of his perceptions have great value.

Notable among these is Pareto's explicit vision of society as a system of mutually interacting factors, with all that this implies. In the first place, it implies equilibrium, in the sense that interacting forces always tend towards balance, even if they never reach it owing to changes in some of the basic conditions, e.g., population, technology and the like. Secondly, it implies that policies arise from the interaction of the different forces and are not final products but incidents in a continuing process. A third implication is the abandonment of the notion of simple cause-effect in favour of variables standing towards one another in varying states of mutual dependence. Fourthly, it also obviously implies that the forces in society are many. Fifthly, and equally obviously, it implies that each element is to be understood only after examining the part it plays relative to the others.

The first concept—equilibrium—is by no means unanimously

accepted by sociologists (though it is fair to ask, 'what concept is?').
It is undeniable, however, that it is a widely influential concept and
that certain important works which apply it have done so under the
direct influence of Pareto.[66] The second implication—of process—is
now universally held and has had the most far reaching effects on
what Pareto called 'special sociology', i.e., political science. Herein
modern analysis starts with a model of classes, groupings, sections
and strata interacting upon one another, with policies as the result.
In this respect, however, Bentley* is likely to have had a far more
direct influence than Pareto. The third and fourth implications have
had a massive effect. They have killed the quest for, and vogue of,
monist, unicausal theories of social change such as those of Spencer or
Tarde or Marx. In this respect it is best to regard Pareto's *Treatise*,
not as the last of the 'great systems', but as an anti-system: a system
to kill all systems. The fifth implication, that of the role which each
part of the system plays, makes Pareto one of the fathers of function-
alism. Because, then, of the importance of each of the several
implications of viewing society as a system, it is easy to understand
why Parsons has said that 'the attempt to delineate the social system as
system was the most important contribution of Pareto's great work'.[67]

It may seem strange to single out Pareto's views on human
personality as a great contribution since we have already rejected
them—the more so since the important current developments in
characterology owe nothing to him but have developed autochthon-
ously from psychology, psycho-analysis and cultural anthropology.
But the most important point about Pareto's theory of personality is
surely that he had one at all. He is the first *sociologist* to recognise
that a complete science of social relations must include the personal-
ity-system as well as the multiplex factors of the social system, and
correspondingly to make his theory of personality an overt and
integral part of his system. We showed, indeed, that one principal
reason for the inadequacy of his whole system was precisely the
inadequacy of his theory of personality; but this emphasises how
central a part it plays.

Furthermore, though the detail of his personality-theory is imprecise and inadequate, its general upshot is certainly not. Contrary
to, say, Marx—for whom the well-springs of motivation are in the
last resort the 'interests'—Pareto drew attention to other, autonomous and equally important sources of motivation, to what we might

---

* A. F. Bentley: *The Process of Government*, Bloomington, Ind., 1949.
(First edn. 1908.) Yet Bentley's work only became influential in the 1940s
because American political science had by then reached the point from
which he had started forty years back.

today call human predispositions and attitudes. And, in directing attention to these, Pareto brought home to social theorists a fact that they had hitherto been singularly reluctant to acknowledge: that vast tracts of human activity are non-rational. It is fair to say that from that point onward sociological theory has never been the same. Here again, the concept of the *Treatise* as an 'anti-system' is most appropriate. Whatever else it did, it killed stone-dead the positivistic-rationalistic types of theories which preceded it and foreclosed all further attempts on those lines. One of the greatest tributes to the fundamental correctness of Pareto's emphasis on human irrationality is the faint praise of the critic who remarked in 1935 that it was 'hardly revolutionary'.[68] Nor indeed was it—by 1935. The point is that Pareto developed his notion of residues, and the consequent irrationality of much human action, between 1897 and 1912—at the same time as, but in complete independence of, Freud. When sociologists discuss the importance of irrationality,[69] they nowadays increasingly couple the two; and thirty years after writing the criticism quoted above, its author felt compelled 'in reflecting on his arguments' to couple Pareto with Freud (and also with Marx) 'as contributors to the growing distrust of the part of reason in human affairs'.[70]

The principal difficulties in Pareto's own theory of the personality lie, as we have shown, partly in their detail—which as such is not precise—and partly in his failure to provide proofs. But something, at least, ought to be said on the other side. Consider, first, Pareto's residues in the sense of 'psychic states'. We reject this because, as we have seen, Pareto's method of proof is circular. Nevertheless this does not prove that something like these psychic states do not exist. As a *general* contention Pareto's view has, if anything, been reinforced by current developments in psychology. It is now widely accepted that we possess 'predispositions', a generic term for 'habits, dispositions, sentiments and dispositions of other orders'[71] by which we act or through which we interpret our experiences. By the time the 'nuclear personality' comes to grips with its surrounding culture, so we are told, it acts out its internal conflicts and interprets outside experience in its own terms. It is this mediation of experience by the mind that accounts, so we are told, for the now recognised phenomena of warped thinking, for what is called 'rationalisation',[72] for 'prejudice',[73] for 'the authoritarian personality',[74] for the 'open and closed mind',[75] and so forth.

Consider next Pareto's residues simply as generic *descriptions* of classes of overt actions. Ought they to be dismissed out of hand? The classification is confused and the whole appearance bizarre. Yet as one familiarises oneself with them, they 'lose a good deal of their incongruity', as Sorokin pointed out long ago:[76] examples from everyday experience come crowding in. For instance, a teenager is asked why his generation indulge in gang fights, and replies: 'It is not a question of intelligence. So often violence or a similar sort of behaviour is the only way you can express yourself, the only way you can feel you have an identity.'[77] This is a Class III residue: the 'need to manifest sentiments in external acts'; and examples can be multiplied. How applicable Pareto's categories are as shorthand descriptions of repetitive types of activity is well attested by one of the earliest works on Pareto to appear in English: *Pareto's General Sociology* by Homans and Curtiss. This book is, for the most part, a set of everyday illustrations and examples of the subclasses of the residues.[78] Of course, merely to hang labels on repetitive types of activity does not explain their genesis; but it does focus attention on them *as* repetitive. In this respect, as Madge remarks, the classification 'was . . . and remains, an aid to clarity'.[79]

Something can even be retrieved from Pareto's antithetical character-syndromes, the 'lions' and the 'foxes'. We have shown that whether this antithesis really exists is never established by Pareto, because his method of proof is, once again, circular. But today, when statistical techniques and the use of psychological scaling have at last made the validation of statements about character-type possible, lines of research give some justification to Pareto's inspired guess. For the antithetical types, Lions and Foxes, are not altogether dissimilar from Eysenck's tough-minded and tender-minded, just as the Lions resemble the 'authoritarian personality' of Adorno.[80] Likewise his contention that the masses tend to be authoritarian, neophobic and intolerant finds depressing confirmation in Lipset's *Political Man* and the literature there cited.[81]

Involved in the concept of the residues is the concept of the derivation: and this corresponds, closely enough, with what we now conceive of as 'ideologies'. This aspect of Pareto's residue theory is a major contribution which has exercised on contemporary political science an influence which is direct as well as profound. Indeed, in so far as the founding fathers of Italian fascism looked to Pareto as one of their antecedents, it can be claimed that it exercised a direct influence upon contemporary political practice. The expression 'ideology', first used during the napoleonic period, owes most of its contemporary meaning to Marx. For him ideology was the 'false consciousness' which sees the world upside down, unlike 'science' (including marxism itself) which sees it truly. Pareto widened the meaning into roughly what we mean today: a system of thought which masks and rationalises human predispositions and urges—and not simply the ones that are due to their economic interest or class position. Five sixths of the *Treatise* are, after all, concerned with the origins, nature, critique and social role of the ideologies. The purely negative aspect of this exercise, that is to say the chapters in which Pareto subjected existing social philosophies to critical examination and demonstrated their non-scientific status is itself a great contribution to the understanding of ideology. Even more important, however, has been the associated distinction between the inherent truth or falsity of a belief and its social utility, for this is the key to understanding the social role of beliefs. Pareto's position resembles Plato's doctrine of the 'noble lie'; and, of course, his position was shared by Sorel and Mosca. But the general propositions that men are moved to act by emotively coloured beliefs rather than by logical demonstrations, and that the social effect of such beliefs has no necessary correlation with their intrinsic truth or falsity, would be regarded nowadays as central propositions in political science and the theory of propaganda. These disciplines have learned to regard beliefs as objective facts in a social situation; as far as social and political action is concerned, what matters is whether and how deeply the beliefs are held. The truth or falsity of the belief is certainly relevant to the wisdom or unwisdom of the action; it is clearly of importance in evaluating the action; but these are different questions.

We may note that Pareto makes a contribution to the last problem by his distinction between the utility *of* a community and the utility *for* a community (pages 45–7 above). This distinction has had a direct and important influence upon welfare economics[82] but seems to have been neglected in political theory. This seems a pity, for many such theories have tried to demonstrate that to will the common good is to will one's own good, or vice versa. Rousseau, for instance, put the former view, Bentham the latter. Neither distinguished, as Pareto did between these two meanings of 'good' (utility), which convincingly demonstrates that the two will not necessarily coincide. At its lowest, application of Pareto's distinction to these and similar theories effects a considerable clarification.

Finally, we come to the best known and most directly influential of Pareto's contributions: his concept of the elites and of their circulation. It is Pareto's term 'elites' and not Mosca's 'political class' which has passed into general circulation (though the two conceptions are by no means identical); and in relating the governing elite concept to psychological type, and even more importantly to vertical mobility (neither of which Mosca attempted), Pareto stood alone. Contemporary political science finds the elite concept indispensable if only as a hypothesis to be rejected. For the notion, common to Mosca and Pareto, that all societies have been and necessarily are governed by an oligarchy can neither be proved nor disproved without the preliminary question 'who runs this place?'. And then, if the interlocutor chooses to answer 'everybody' or 'nobody', he must qualify that answer by showing 'how' this takes place and what the words 'rule' or 'govern' mean in that particular context. This has led to entirely more realistic definitions of what we understand by democracy. The facile concept of some hypostatised 'People' which 'governs Itself' simply blanketed all such discussions. By analogy, it 'governed Itself' as a person 'governs himself', so that there were few questions left to answer. (Incidentally, it led to metaphysical discussion, derived from the same analogy, of the 'higher self' versus the 'lower self', the 'real will' versus the 'actual will'.[83]) From the paretian approach have sprung such radical reappraisals of democracy as that of Schumpeter for whom it is a system in which elites publicly compete for the authority to govern; the work of Aron, interrelating elites, government and social structure; the studies of community power structure of Hunter (arguing for the presence of an identifiable elite) and of Dahl (arguing the contrary); and the great program of comparative elite studies of Lasswell and his school.[84]

After all this, what place ought we assign Pareto in the development of social and political theory? The difficulty in answering such a question lies in deciding what criterion of worth to adopt. If we ask ourselves what direct influence Pareto has had upon his successors, we can certainly point to a batch of distinguished names; but it has to be admitted that by this criterion his place is relatively small. If, on the other hand, we ask ourselves what indirect influence he has had, no precise answer is possible because of the very way the question is posed. Perhaps the best criterion to adopt is the extent to which Pareto pioneered propositions which have since become commonly accepted or widely influential. By this standard his contribution is substantial in sociology and even more so in political science. In the former field, his three major contributions are the postulate of society as a system, together with the important associated concepts; the destructive critique of positivistic-rationalistic theories and corresponding stress on the role of the irrational in social behaviour; and the emphasis on the importance of social stratification and social mobility.

In political science, however, the positions he took up are today's governing hypotheses. In this field, moreover, his influence has been, to a large extent, direct. The interconnection of political and other forms of social behaviour; the interdependence of political institutions and associations with social institutions and associations; the pluralistic model—the hypothesis of a political 'process', consisting in the interaction of these political and social factors; the elite concept, and the significance of a vertical mobility; the importance attaching to the 'political formula', by which the elite derives its authority over the governed, and the corresponding role of ideology and propaganda—these are now the starting positions in the comparative analysis of government and politics. They have enormously reinvigorated the discipline and made it far more realistic. Many tributaries have fed into the general movement. The notion of pluralism derives more directly from Bentley than from Pareto, irrationalism owes more to Freud, the elite concept owes much to Mosca and Michels, the role of ideology derives from Sorel and Mosca and well as from Pareto. But Pareto's work is the only one that incorporates every one of these positions. By this criterion— admittedly not the only criterion, as we have shown—it claims to rank as the most pregnant work of political science in the last half century.

References for Introduction

ABBREVIATIONS

CP: *Carteggi Paretiani*, G. de Rosa (ed.), Rome, 1962.

MP: *Vilfredo Pareto—Lettere a Maffeo Pantaleoni*, G. de Rosa (ed.), 3 vols., Rome, 1960.

SP: *Corrispondenza di Vilfredo Pareto*, Guido Sensini (ed.), Padua, 1948.

PP: *Vilfredo Pareto dal Carteggio con Carlo Placci*, T. Giacalone-Monaco (ed.), Padua, 1957.

SECTION I

1. H. S. Hughes, *Consciousness and Society*, London, 1959, p. 33.

SECTION II

2. CP, p. 205.
3. *Ibid.*, p. 206.
4. *Ibid.*, p. 211.
5. PP, 28 May 1894.
6. MP, 28 October 1896.
7. *Cf.* Pareto's articles: 'L'Italie Economique', *Revue des Deux Mondes*, 15 October 1891, p. 904; and 'The Parliamentary Regime in Italy', *American Political Science Quarterly*, 1893, p. 677.
8. PP, 30 August 1898.
9. V. Pareto, 'Il Crepuscolo della Libertà', *Rivista d'Italia*, February 1905, pp. 193–205; quoted MP, Vol. II, p. 436.
10. MP, 18 April 1893.
11. MP, 17 May 1897; 11 November 1897.

SECTION III

12. MP, 17 June 1895.
13. MP, 6 December 1891.
14. MP, 22 February 1898.
15. MP, 16 May 1898; 20 July 1898.
16. MP, 17 May 1897.
17. MP, 11 November 1897.

18. MP, 10 April 1898.
19. MP, 25 September 1896.
20. MP, 29 April 1899.
21. MP, 18 September 1901.
22. MP, 3 January 1900.
23. V. Pareto, 'Un' Applicazione di Teorie Sociologiche', *Rivista Italiana di Sociologia*, July 1900, p. 401.
24. MP, 18 April 1893.
25. MP, 23 December 1896.
26. MP, 17 May 1897.
27. MP, 20 July 1904; 10 December 1904. The printer was extraordinarily slow.
28. MP, 20 December 1906; SP 6 November 1912.
29. SP, 18 August 1916.
30. MP, 17 August 1922; 23 December 1922; PP, 5 January 1923.
31. F. Borkenau, *Pareto*, New York and London, 1936; M. Rader, *No Compromise*, London, 1939; F. Alexander, *Our Age of Unreason*, London and New York, 1942.
32. *Cf.*, for example, MP, 8 March 1907.
33. G. H. Bousquet, *Pareto, Le Savant et l'Homme*, Lausanne, 1960, p. 147.

SECTION IV

34. MP, 17 June 1895.
35. SP, pp. 143–62.
36. Borkenau, *op. cit.*, pp. 30–2.
37. N. S. Timasheff, *Sociological Theory*, New York, 1957, pp. 131–84, where it is classified along with the vastly dissimilar theories of Cooley, Thomas and Max Weber.
38. J. A. Schumpeter, *Ten Great Economists*, London, 1952, pp. 128–9.
39. Schumpeter, *op. cit.*, pp. 138–9; T. Parsons, *The Structure of Social Action*, 2nd edn., New York and London, 1961, p. 269.
40. G. H. Bousquet, *Pareto, sa vie et son oeuvre*, Paris, 1928, p. 136.
41. *Cf.* H. Rauschning, *Germany's Revolution of Destruction*, London, 1939.
42. The Livingston-Bongiorno translation, published as *The Mind and Society*, New York and London, 1935.
43. W. McDougall, 'Pareto as a Psychologist', *Journal of Social Philosophy*, Vol. I, 1935, p. 42.
44. For an example, *cf.* William James's list of Instincts in his *Principles of Psychology*, 1891, ch. XXIV.
45. Borkenau, *op. cit.*, pp. 89, 90.
46. M. Ginsberg, *Reason and Unreason in Society*, London, 1947, Vol. II, pp. 88–9.
47. SP, 9 April 1905.
48. MP, 20 December 1906.
49. Parsons, *op. cit.*, p. 263.
50. T. Giacalone-Monaco, *Pareto e Sorel: Riflessioni*, Padua, 1961, II, pp. 169–70,

51. H. D. Lasswell, 'Agenda for the study of Political Elites', in D. Marvick (ed.), *Political Decision-Makers*, New York, 1961.
52. MP, Letter 246, 23 December 1896.
53. MP, 6 December 1891; 23 December 1896.

SECTION V

54. The best single source is M. Ginsberg, 'The Sociology of Pareto', in *Reason and Unreason in Society* (*op. cit.*).
55. P. Sorokin, *Contemporary Sociological Theories*, New York, 1928, p. 61.
56. CP, pp. 142–3.
57. For an exercise in such fields, *cf.* S. E. Finer, *The Man on Horseback: the Role of the Military in Politics*, London, 1962; New York, 1963.
58. *Cf.* for instance: C. J. Friedrich, *The New Image of the Common Man*, Boston, Mass., 1950; R. A. Dahl, 'A Critique of the Ruling Elite Model', *American Political Science Review*, Vol. 52, 1958, pp. 463–9; *Modern Political Analysis*, Englewood Cliffs, N.J., 1963, pp. 15–18, 32–5; *Who Governs?*, New Haven, Conn., 1961; and Renzo Sereno, *The Rulers*, New York, 1962.
59. K. A. Wittvogel, *Oriental Despotism*, New Haven, Conn., 1957, ch. IV, pp. 101–24.
60. *Cf.* J. H. Meisel, *The Myth of the Ruling Class*, Ann Arbor, 1962—a full account of the way in which the concept, first formulated in 1882, was successively adapted. The result was most unsatisfactory.
61. G. W. Skinner, *Leadership and Power in the Chinese Community in Thailand*, Ithaca, N.Y., 1958, pp. 208–9.
62. Floyd Hunter, 'Studying Associations and Organisation Structures', in R. Young (ed.), *Approaches to the Study of Politics*, London, 1958, pp. 250–1.
63. C. Moraze, *Les Trois Ages de Brésil*, Paris, 1954.
G. Brennan, *The Spanish Labyrinth*, Cambridge, 1960.
M. Khadduri, *Independent Iraq*, Oxford, 1960.
64. This phrase is taken from G. Sartori, *Democratic Theory*, Detroit, Mich., 1962, p. 131, note 28. The whole of ch. VI, 'Democracy, Leadership and Elites', is most valuable and contains an excellent discussion of Pareto's concepts.
65. This distinction is based on the essay, 'David Riesman and Interpretive Sociology', by P. Kecskemeti, in S. M. Lipset and L. Lowenthal (eds.), *Culture and Social Character*, New York, 1961, pp. 3–14.
66. E.g., E. Mayo, *Human Problems of Industrial Civilization*, New York, 1933; G. C. Homans, *The Human Group*, London, 1951; T. Parsons, *The Social System*, London, 1952.
67. Parsons, *op. cit.*, p. vii.
68. Ginsberg, *op. cit.*, p. 85.
69. E.g., C. Madge, *Society in the Mind*, London, 1964, pp. 72–93; *cf.* also T. Parsons, *The Structure of Social Action*, preface *passim* to 2nd edn., New York and London, 1961.
70. M. Ginsberg, *The Psychology of Society*, 9th edn., London, 1964, p. xxii *et seq.*

71. G. W. Allport, *Personality*, London, 1937, p. 48.
72. Coined by E. Jones in 1908.
73. *Cf.* G. W. Allport, *The Nature of Prejudice*, New York, 1954.
74. *Cf.* T. W. Adorno and associates, *The Authoritarian Personality*, New York, 1950.
75. *Cf.* M. Rokeach, *The Open and Closed Mind*, New York, 1960.
76. Sorokin, *op. cit.*, p. 49.
77. 'Confessions of a Teenage Delinquent', *The Listener*, London, 5 November 1964, p. 709.
78. G. C. Homans, and C. P. Curtis, *An Introduction to Pareto: His Sociology*, New York, 1934.
79. Madge, *op. cit.*
80. H. J. Eysenck, *The Psychology of Politics*, London, 1954.
81. S. M. Lipset, *Political Man*, New York, 1960—esp. ch. IV, 'Working Class Authoritarianism'.
82. I. M. D. Little, *A Critique of Welfare Economics*, 2nd edn., Oxford, 1957, ch. VI.
83. *Cf.* B. Bosanquet, *Philisophical Theory of the State*, London, 1899.
84. Floyd Hunter, *Community Power Structures*, Chapel Hill, N. Ca., 1953; H. D. Lasswell, *Politics: Who Gets What, When, How*, New York and London, 1936; 'Agenda for the study of Political Elites' in D. Marvick (ed.), *Political Decision-Makers*, New York, 1961; and the bibliography there cited, pp. 281–7; R. Aron, 'Elites and Social Structures', *British Journal of Sociology*, Vol. I, No. 1, 1950; and J. A. Schumpeter, *Capitalism, Socialism and Democracy*, 4th edn., London, 1952.

SELECTIONS

Part One
The Preparation

I

Cours d'Economie Politique
(1896)

1. SOCIAL SCIENCE PROCEEDS BY ABSTRACTIONS*

Human behaviour reveals *uniformities* which constitute *natural laws.* If these uniformities did not exist, then there would be neither social science nor political economy, and even the study of history would largely be useless. In effect, if the future actions of men have nothing in common with their past actions, our knowledge of them, although possibly satisfying our curiosity by way of an interesting story, would be entirely useless to us as a guide in life.

If we try to put some order into the extremely various and complex motives of human behaviour, we see that they are divisible into three categories. 1. Certain acts of behaviour simply have as their motive the procuring of an agreeable sensation. 2. With others, the motive is to procure for the individual performing them certain conditions of health and of bodily and mental development. 3. A further category consists of behaviour whose motive is to procure these conditions for a whole group of people and to ensure their perpetuation.

Distinct terms need to be given to the abstract qualities manifested by the things relevant to the attainment of the motives indicated above. The term *utility* may properly be used for the qualities relative to the second and third categories of motive. We will term 'individual utility' the abstract quality of the things which are appropriate to realising and perpetuating the physical, intellectual and moral development of the individual. We will apply the term 'utility of the species'—or, if we are considering only one section of the species, 'utility of the group'—to the abstract quality of the

---

things which serve to ensure the perpetuation of the species, or group, and of its physical, intellectual and moral well-being.

Having pre-empted the term 'utility' for the second and third categories, we must find another term for the first category. Since a suitable one cannot be found in everyday language,* it behoves us to follow the practice of the natural sciences and derive terms from the Greek. We have therefore chosen *ophelimity* to designate the abstract quality of the things which satisfy a desire or need, legitimate or not.† All that is necessary is to have fixed clearly in our minds what this quality is; the term designating it is of no importance. It is only 'literary economists' who quibble over such otiose questions; people dedicated to the study of the positive sciences are concerned with facts, not words.

Studies in ophelimity, individual utility and utility of the species or group, taken together, constitute social science. Political economy is but one branch of this science and is governed specifically by the study of ophelimity.

Sentiments of justice and morality have the effect of making us look for ophelimity in behaviour the real purpose of which is utility of the individual, the species or group.

In any study of concrete phenomena, man is obliged to proceed by analysis and by abstraction. He identifies certain properties and studies them separately. Thus, the chemical properties of substances and bodies are isolated from their physical properties. A further selection is made amongst the physical properties: heat, electricity and light are made the objects of separate studies; while a further abstraction leads to the study of forces and motion under the name of mechanics. Proceeding thus, from abstraction to abstraction, we arrive at the study of rational, 'pure' mechanics which is concerned solely with material points and inextensible connections.

We have thus worked downwards from concrete phenomena to certain highly simplified notional phenomena. We can now follow this process in reverse. Working upwards from simplified notional phenomena to complex concrete phenomena we are enabled to employ a system of successive approximations.

Such are the methods of enquiry used by all the positive sciences: methods whose employment is also indispensable for the social sciences. First we separate the study of *ophelimity* from that of the various forms of *utility*; then we direct our attention to man himself, stripping him of a large number of accretions, ignoring his passions, whether good or bad, and reducing him eventually to a sort of molecule which is susceptible solely to the influence of the forces of ophelimity. By following this procedure we shall achieve a science: pure economics, equivalent as a science to pure mechanics.

---

* In English, 'agreeability' could perhaps be devised to supply the term desired, but, as Pareto points out, such word-coining is not possible in French or Italian.

† See below, page 177, footnote on ophelimity and utility.

2. UTILITY, OPHELIMITY AND THE TASKS OF SOCIAL SCIENCE*

(4) Amongst the writers who have discussed new theories, *utility* generally has the sense of a relationship of convenience between a thing and a man. But because, in everyday language, 'useful' is the converse of 'disadvantageous', and since a good many ambiguities arise from the same term's having two different meanings, we are obliged to give a new term to the utility we wish specifically to study.

(i) Ophelimity

(5) We shall employ the term *ophelimity*, derived from the Greek ὠφέλιμος (useful or serviceable), to designate the relationship of convenience which makes a thing satisfy a need or a desire, whether legitimate or not. This new term is all the more necessary because *utility* will be required for use in its ordinary accepted sense as the property which makes a thing favourable to the development and well-being of an individual, a community or the whole human species.

(6) A few specific examples will make clearer the differences of meaning we want to emphasise.

Gold had a certain ophelimity for the Caribbean Indians. It is doubtful if it ever was *useful* to them, and certainly—in that it aroused the cupidity of the Spaniards—it became very harmful to them. Is the diamond *useful* to the human race? One can make out a case equally well for or against; but there is no question about its ophelimity for a great many people. Corn made into bread has an ophelimity for almost all men, and a great utility for the human race. Medicines have no ophelimity for a child, but they do have an ophelimity for an adult who knows, or believes, that they will cure the child given them. And if they really do have such curative power, then they are useful, have *utility*, to the child as well as to the adult. Learning to read is rarely ophelimous for any child; nevertheless it is extremely useful. The study of astronomy seems to have had no ophelimity for Socrates, according to Xenophon. If it had had an ophelimity for Nikias, it would have been outstandingly *useful* for Athens. The Athenian army would have been able to escape out of the harbour of Syracuse when the eclipse occurred (August 27, 413 BC) which was interpreted by the augurs and by Nikias as signifying the opposition of the gods to the army's withdrawal. In the event, missing the opportunity for safe escape, the Athenian army was encircled and utterly destroyed.

Fortunately for the human species, the study of science is ophelimous for a large number of people. Some, it is true, question its *utility*, but the mere fact that ignorant people have doubts about it is perhaps one of the best proofs of the utility of science.

(7) Ophelimity is a wholly subjective quality. For it to exist, there must at the least be a man and a thing. If the human race were to disappear from

---

* From Vol. I ('Principles of pure political economy'), §§4–17. The arabic numerals in curved brackets refer to the section numbers of the original.

off the face of the earth, gold would still be a rare metal, soft, and with a specific gravity of 19·26; but its ophelimity would exist not at all.

(8) There is nothing to prevent our envisaging a state of scientific knowledge so advanced as to enable us to deduce, from the chemical and physical properties of a substance and from the bodily and mental qualities of a man, the relationship of convenience (ophelimity) subsisting between that substance and that man. But, though such questions as these may be extremely interesting, they are of no concern to us in our present enquiry. They should properly be the concern of other sciences. The science of ophelimity has its starting point in the findings of these sciences and the facts requiring explanation which they produce.

(9) Why do people like fermented drinks? Why do many of them prefer the *grands crus de Bordeaux* to gut-rot concoctions? These are questions for the psychologist and the chemist or other experts to resolve. The science of ophelimity takes its point of departure from the facts themselves. There are things which are ophelimous for one man only; others which are so for many men; and yet others which are ophelimous for almost all men. In the last case, ophelimity comes very close to being an objective quality. This explains how it comes about that, in political economy, ophelimity (which has been called 'subjective utility') has almost always been confused with an objective quality.

Certain cherished objects have ophelimity for a very small number of people. Wine is ophelimous for the great majority of christians: it is not so for the great majority of moslems. Bread is ophelimous for almost all civilised men; but, generally speaking, it is more so for Frenchmen than for Englishmen. The art of divination was ophelimous to a high degree for the armies in ancient Greece; it was still ophelimous for Wallenstein; it is no longer so for the armies of today. This subjective characteristic of ophelimity is fundamental. It must be borne in mind throughout this enquiry.

(ii) Utility

(10) We accept ophelimity as a plain fact: it presents no difficulties. Such is not the case with utility. In this context problems arise which for the most part are not resolved; progress in the social sciences depends, probably, on their solution.

Air, water, sunlight and warmth are certainly useful to the human race. Corn also seems to be so. Is the potato? It is accused of being, to some extent, the cause of Ireland's woes. Is there a utility for human beings in the use—not the abuse—of fermented drinks? Many people will say, *No*. But it must be admitted that the proofs they offer have not the least scientific value. For example, even if they should succeed in demonstrating that the use of alcoholic beverages shortens life, this still would not prove that such drinks are harmful. The shortening of the lifespan might well be compensated for by its intensity.

(11) The difficulty in these problems of utility is further increased by the vagueness of definitions. What fundamentally is a 'prosperous nation'? Is it the nation in which the greatest number of citizens enjoys material and moral well-being? Or the nation which makes conquests and covers itself

with military glory? Should Athens be taken as a model, or the kingdom of Macedon? According to the answer made to these questions, certain things will lose or acquire the characteristic of utility. Leroy-Beaulieu, in his *Essai sur la répartition des richesses* says (p. 127) that 'the ideal of society is not a human antnest'. Such indeed is my impression also; but if someone takes the contrary view, I know of no criterion which I could apply to determine which of us is right and which wrong.

(12) Some people, who perhaps see things optimistically, regard ophelimity and utility as one and the selfsame thing; others, who perhaps take a gloomier view, think that the two things are and ever will remain entirely separate. The ascetics of the past certainly thought so, and we have no scientific proof that they were wrong. Buddhists seem to identify utility with the entire destruction of any sort of ophelimity in the individual.

(13) We intend to keep wholly aloof from questions of this kind. When we have occasion to speak of utility, we shall take as criterion material well-being and scientific and moral progress as generally understood by men in civilised nations. We accept received usage, leaving to others the labour of determining the question further.

(14) Different sorts of utility are distinguishable according as they ensure the development and progress of different aspects of human nature. *Economic utility* would be that utility which should ensure material well-being; *moral utility* that which should conduce to the most perfect moral development; and so on. Ophelimity lends itself to similar distinctions; in measure as it satisfies material, moral, religious and similar desires, we term it *material ophelimity, moral* or *religious ophelimity,* and so forth.

(15) Notwithstanding the difficulties inherent in them, the problems involved in the matter of utility have initiated highly important enquiries. Herbert Spencer's work on the social sciences contains, in addition to his studies on evolution, far-reaching investigations into the utility of certain things and certain institutions. The most thorough work so far done on utility, mainly on economic utility, is that of G. Molinari. What firm ground we have to stand on in this very difficult matter is made up of his findings.

(16) Among the social sciences, the science of ophelimity is the only one whose results attain a degree of precision and certainty comparable to that of the propositions of natural sciences like chemistry, physics and so forth. It is well, therefore, to make a special study of it, if only to avoid mixing propositions which are almost certain with those which are less certain. In this book, we shall make a special study of ophelimity and deal only secondarily with economic utility. This latter, strictly speaking, may be regarded as including the former, for fundamentally ophelimity is only a kind of subjective utility. Where there is no need to distinguish these utilities from each other, we shall deal with them under the general term of the 'science of utility'.

(17) For a people developing and prospering materially, economic ophelimity, generally speaking, must rarely deviate to any appreciable extent from economic utility, with which the other types of ophelimity— moral, religious, etc.—must be reconciled. But we must guard against thinking that this coincidence of ophelimity and utility can be complete.

For every being endowed with reason, ophelimity corresponds very closely to present well-being. Consideration of utility for the individual involves future well-being. This distinction corresponds to that which many writers have made between a maximum present felicity and a maximum future felicity.

(iii) *Adaptation to environment**

(628) Adaptation to environment assuredly occurs, but from the point of view of social science there is to be noted a radical difference between the two ways in which the adaptation can be conceived as operating. If the individual is altogether unmodifiable, and if the process of selection operates only by destroying those individuals who deviate too much—for the worse—from the average type of the race, then the sum of individual sufferings will always be very great, and it is hardly possible to conceive how this sum of suffering could be reduced without at the same time worsening the conditions of the race. In other words: there is in these circumstances an absolute opposition between the ophelimity of a great number of individuals and the utility of the race. On the other hand, if the individual is capable of slight modifications; if these modifications are transferable by heredity; and if the process of selection, albeit suppressing the weakest or most defective individuals, has at least the effect of preserving the best—then the sum of individual sufferings may be much less than in the first hypothesis. Ophelimity of the individual and utility of the race will conflict with one another only in regard to a fairly restricted number of individuals; for the great majority they will be in harmony.

Adaptation is never perfect. The divergence between the real phenomenon and the phenomenon corresponding to maximum utility may, in certain cases, be very considerable and entail the destruction of living organisms or societies.

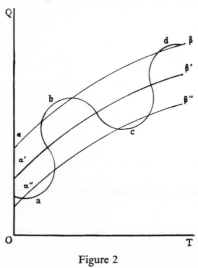

Figure 2

In dealing with this subject we must decisively separate ophelimity from utility. But more than this is necessary. We need also to distinguish utility for the individual from utility for the species. Let us take for an example an economic or social phenomenon capable of being measured. In the graph (figure 2) the axis O–T represents time, the axis O–Q the dimensions of the observed phenomena. We thereby obtain a line *a–b–c–d*, which

---

* Vol. II, chapter 1, §§628–9.

represents the concrete phenomenon. Now let us determine the ideal phenomena and trace the curves corresponding to them. The curve α–β represents the phenomenon which gives the maximum utility for the species. The curve α′–β′ represents the maximum utility for the individual. Finally, the curve α″–β″ represents the phenomenon which procures the maximum ophelimity.

There is a tendency for all these curves to approximate to one another. One can discuss whether or not this tendency varies in intensity, but it cannot be denied that the tendency exists or, alternatively, be asserted that the curves are absolutely identical. On the one hand, it is clear in effect that individuals and species which practice what is highly harmful to them must eventually perish. On the other hand, it cannot be concluded from the simple fact that an individual or a species exists that either of them desires and practices only what is useful to them. There are unuseful and even harmful instincts.

(629) . . . The science of utility is still very backward. We have indeed certain conceptions of the utility of the individual, but our understanding of the utility of the species is most imperfect. Perhaps one day progress will be made in this matter, and maybe the time is not far distant when the science of utility will, like the science of ophelimity, have a sure basis and a scientifically rigorous method.*

(iv) Comparison of utilities†

(655) Comparing utilities is much more easy than comparing ophelimities —at least, if there can be agreement on the meaning to be given to the term *utility*. If, as has generally been the case, it is held that, for a people, *utility* is co-terminous with its material prosperity and its moral and intellectual development, then we have a criterion for making comparisons between different peoples. But there still remains a difficulty, deriving from the fact that society has to be considered as a complex whole, as a system, as an organism. It may therefore happen that one of these organisms is in certain respects superior to others, in other respects inferior. But be that as it may: if the comparison does not hold good for the whole, it may at least be valid for details. For example, one can say that, as concerns military power, it has been of utility to the Japanese for them to adapt the organisation of European fleets and armies.

3. INTERDEPENDENCE AND MECHANICAL EQUILIBRIUM OF SOCIAL PHENOMENA‡

(580) It is easy enough for us to form a general idea of the mutual dependence of social phenomena: it is more difficult to gain a clear and precise conception of it.

---

* But see *Treatise* §2271 (footnote page 177 below) for Pareto's later view that the concept of 'needs' is experimentally undefinable.

† Vol. II, chapter 1, §655.

‡ Vol. II, chapter 1, §§580, 585–90, 593, 591–2.

Suppose we take for general consideration certain phenomena A, B, C, D. Our knowledge of their interdependence may pass through three successive stages. 1. We may know only that this interdependence exists: that the presence of A and variations in its extent and intensity influence B, C and D; that the presence of B influences A, C and D; and so on. 2. We may also have an idea of the connections subsisting between A, B, C and D: knowing, for example, that when A increases, B decreases, C increases and so on. In other words, we may know the direction of variations of B, C and D produced by a given variation of A. 3. Finally, we may be able, not only to know the direction of these variations, but even to calculate exactly their extent and intensity. If we reach this stage, our knowledge of the totality of the phenomena A, B, C and D is complete and perfect.

Economic and social equilibrium

(585) We observe that the state of society generally changes very slowly. Every society invariably offers considerable resistance to external or internal forces which tend towards its modification. Accidental movements arising in a society are neutralised by the counteracting movements they provoke; and ultimately, as a rule, they die away, and society reverts to its previous state. A society where this occurs can therefore be considered as being in a state of equilibrium, and of *stable* equilibrium.

(586) To be exact, what is involved here is not a static but a dynamic equilibrium—society in its entirety being borne along by a general movement which slowly modifies it. This is the movement which is usually called evolution.

In mechanics, D'Alembert's principle enables us to study fully the dynamic state of a system. In political economy, we can still only make shift to catch a glimpse of an analogous principle. In social science even this dim light is lacking. In the case of both these sciences, we are obliged to consider a series of static equilibria rather than the dynamic equilibrium.

(587) To give a rough but adequate idea of this, let us take the example of a man sliding down a slope on a sledge, while another man descends the same slope on foot, stopping at every step. The two men leave the top at the same time, travel down together and arrive at the bottom at the same time. In a general sense, their movements are pretty well much the same. But the movement of the man on the sledge is a continuous movement which, if we study it, involves us in a problem of dynamics. The movement of the man descending on foot represents a series of successive positions of equilibrium. He passes from one to the other in broken movement. It is precisely this—a series of positions of equilibrium—which we study in political economy.

(588) Knowledge of the conditions which are necessary and sufficient for equilibrium brings us to stage 2 referred to in §580. In effect these conditions establish relationships between the phenomena A, B, C, etc., and thereby apprise us how the variations of any one of these influence the others. But to be able to do this, we really need to have *all* the conditions of the equilibrium, and these must be neither too many nor too few. This is one of the reasons why it is necessary to employ mathematical analysis,

this alone being able—in the existing state of our knowledge—to tell us if this requirement is fulfilled.

(589) The human intellect proceeds from the known to the unknown. Thus, where we have extensive knowledge of the equilibrium of a material system, this equilibrium can serve as an example to help us gain a conception of economic equilibrium. This latter in its turn can help us to form an idea of social equilibrium.

(590) In such reasoning by analogy there is, however, a pitfall to be avoided. Its use is legitimate, and perhaps highly useful, as long as what is involved is only the elucidation of the sense of a given proposition. But this method of reasoning can lead us into grave errors if we presume to use it to demonstrate the proposition itself, or even simply to establish a presumption in its favour. Examples and analogies should serve only to make clearly understandable the statement of a proposition. Thereafter, when its meaning and bearing have been grasped, it is for facts—and facts alone—to determine if the proposition is true or false.

(593) Several kinds of errors are frequently committed in connection with the dependence of economic phenomena.

1. This dependence is entirely ignored. ... Reformers almost invariably neglect to take into consideration the effect of the reforms they envisage on the complex movement of society.

2. The attempt is often made to determine the factors constituting economic equilibrium by taking situations which are either too many or too few to provide the number necessary and sufficient for the task. This kind of error could, strictly speaking, be classed with the foregoing, for it is precisely the interdependence of economic phenomena which provides the number of necessary and sufficient situations and conditions.

3. The equation which economic equilibrium establishes between certain quantities is taken as if it were an identity, or rather it is taken for a relationship of cause and effect. Under a system of free competitition, and in a state of equilibrium, the cost of production is equated with the selling price. It is concluded from this that the cost of production is commensurate with the value, or rather that it is the *cause* of the value. In this situation, the net interest of capital becomes equal to the yield of savings. The one has been confused with the other.

(591) The interdependence of economic phenomena is rarely denied in abstract theory but many writers ignore it in practical application; and in all cases it is apparent from the way they express themselves that they have only very vague ideas about the relationships of dependence which establish the conditions of economic equilibrium.

(592) It would not be necessary to stress this point if political economy were studied only by those with a knowledge of pure mechanics. The equilibrium of an economic system offers striking similarities with that of a mechanical system. An understanding of the latter helps to give us a clear idea of the equilibrium of an economic system. But those who have not studied pure mechanics will want a little clarification of the point we are here making.

We shall find it useful, therefore, to tabulate the analogies existing between mechanical and social phenomena. It must be understood very clearly that such analogies do not *prove* anything: they simply serve to elucidate certain concepts which must then be submitted to the criterion of experience.

Mechanical Phenomena	Social Phenomena
Given a certain number of material bodies, the relationships of equilibrium and movement between them are studied, any other properties being excluded from consideration. This gives us a study termed *mechanics*.	Given a society, the relationships created amongst human beings by the production and exchange of wealth are studied, any other properties being excluded from consideration. This gives us a study termed *political economy*.
This science of mechanics is divisible into two others:	This science of political economy is divisible into two others:
1. The study of material points and inextensible connections leads to the formulation of a pure science—rational pure mechanics, which makes an abstract study of the equilibrium of forces and motion.	1. The study of *homo economicus*, of man considered solely in the context of economic forces, leads to the formulation of pure political economy, which makes an abstract study of the manifestations of ophelimity.
Its easiest part is the science of equilibrium. D'Alembert's principle enables dynamics to be reduced to a problem of statics.	The only part we are beginning to understand clearly is that dealing with equilibrium. A principle similar to D'Alembert's is applicable to economic systems; but the state of our knowledge on this subject is still very imperfect. Nevertheless, the theory of economic crises provides an example of the study of economic dynamics.
2. Pure mechanics is followed by applied mechanics which approaches a little more closely to reality in its consideration of elastic bodies, extensible connections, friction, etc.	2. Pure political economy is followed by applied political economy which is not concerned exclusively with *homo economicus*, but also considers other human states which approach closer to real man.
Real bodies have properties other than mechanical. Physics studies the properties of light, electricity and heat. Chemistry studies other properties. Thermodynamics, thermochemistry and the like sciences are concerned specifically with certain categories of properties. These sciences all constitute the physico-chemical sciences.	Men have further characteristics which are the object of study for special sciences, such as the sciences of law, religion, ethics, intellectual development, esthetics, social organisation, and so on. Some of these sciences are in an appreciably advanced state; others are extremely backward. Taken together they constitute the social sciences.

Mechanical Phenomena	Social Phenomena
Real bodies with only pure mechanical properties do not exist.	Real men governed only by motives of pure economics do not exist.
Exactly the same error is committed *either* by supposing that in concrete phenomena there exist solely mechanical forces (excluding, for example, chemical forces), *or* by imagining, on the other hand, that a concrete phenomenon can be immune from the laws of pure mechanics.	Exactly the same error is committed *either* by supposing that in concrete phenomena there exist solely economic motives (excluding, for example, moral forces), *or* by imagining, on the other hand, that a concrete phenomenon can be immune from the laws of pure political economy.

The difference between practice and theory arises precisely from the fact that practice has to take account of a mass of details which theory does not deal with. The relative importance of primary and secondary phenomena will differ according to whether the viewpoint is that of science or of a practical operation. From time to time, attempts are made to synthesise all the phenomena. For example, it is held that all phenomena can be ascribed to:

The attraction of atoms. The attempt has been made to reduce to unity all physical and chemical forces.	Utility, of which ophelimity is only a type. The attempt has been made to find the explanation of all phenomena in *evolution*.

These are fascinating studies. But we must school ourselves to resist the attractive lure of certain hypotheses, and depart from the solid ground of experience only with the very greatest circumspection.

4. FORM OF SOCIAL PHENOMENA*

(578) With the intention of dispensing with the deductive method, which is quite mistakenly associated with the metaphysical method, many writers have recourse to what they think is pure empiricism, but is in fact the old sophism: *post hoc, ergo propter hoc*. Let us take as example a measurable phenomenon. [Figure 3 overleaf.]

In the graph, the axis o–t represents time; o–q represents quantities. The line m–n represents present time; o–n is the past; the shaded section m–n–t is the future. We want to predict the form the phenomenon will take in this part of the graph. If its curve is similar to that of α–β, we should be able to predict with a great degree of probability that its future curve will resemble α–β–γ, since the fact that α–β is a regularly ascending curve makes it probable that β–γ will likewise continue to ascend. But if

---

* Vol. II, chapter 1, §578.

the curve of the phenomenon is similar to that of *a–b–c*, we can make no certain prediction of its future form because, although this curve describes an ascending form up to *c*, its overall configuration is such as to suggest the possibility of a decline after *c*.

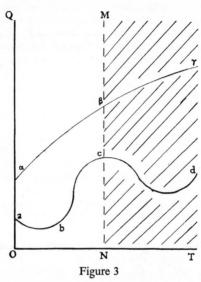

Figure 3

Now, social phenomena are generally of the form *a–b–c–d*. The empirical method, which judges *post hoc*, is therefore of no use.

5. ARISTOCRACIES; CIRCULATION OF ELITES; THEORY OF SPOLIATION

(i) Tutelage*

(661) When the use of coercive force is not limited exclusively to the advantage of the person or persons deploying it, their exercise in securing advantage is called *tutelage*. It may be to the direct advantage of the dependent person, or to his indirect advantage if the exercise of tutelage is of direct advantage to the social aggregate of which he is a part. The first type can be termed *private tutelage*, the second *public tutelage*. Private tutelage originates from the difference between ophelimity and direct utility for the dependant; public tutelage mainly originates from the difference between direct utility for the individual and his indirect utility consequent upon direct utility for the aggregate. In cases where tutelage brings no utility, direct or indirect, for the individual, it should not be confused with tutelage in its proper sense.

(662) Within certainly limits, tutelage appears indispensable. Where it is utterly absent, it clearly appears that the individual and aggregate perish.

---

* Vol. II, chapter 1, §§661–6.

Private tutelage is obviously necessary for the child and for the mentally deranged adult. As concerns the aggregate, we find from observation that there exists no people, civilised or barbarous, which lacks at least some element of government in its society. Anarchism, which wishes to destroy all forms of tutelage, no more merits serious discussion than a fairy-tale for the nursery. Of course, if we set the imagination free of all restraint, we can certainly envisage a time when men will desire only what is truly advantageous to themselves, their nation and their species. But it is clear that men of this kind will be wholly different from men as we know them; there is no point, therefore, in occupying ourselves with them.

(663) Three conditions are necessary if private tutelage is really to increase the sum of utility for the dependant:

1. The guardian must be superior, intellectually or morally, to the ward;

2. The guardian must employ his authority in the ward's interests and not to his detriment;

3. The tutelage must not, of itself, be an obstacle to the development in the ward of the faculties which would enable him to take charge of himself.

(664) These three conditions are realised more or less fully in the case of child-tutelage. Yet even here serious deficiencies are noticeable. A considerable number of fathers abuse their authority, and this has made it necessary to pass laws regulating the employment of minors. Unfortunately, such laws do not seem so far to have been very efficacious. It is strange that employers should be held exclusively responsible for abuses in the committing of which they must necessarily have the child's guardians as accomplices.

(665) The tutelage of persons who are retarded in intellect or mentally deranged gives rise to grave abuses. Often the only reason why people so afflicted are committed to asylums is the greed of relatives who see in this a way for acquiring the property of the helpless person.

(666) Evils such as these, which occur in the most necessary forms of tutelage and in circumstances where strong natural feelings can act as a corrective, make very evident how great are the defects in other forms of tutelage where the correctives against abuse are much less strong. It is questionable if the private tutelage of an adult possessed of intellectual and moral faculties not very much below the average has ever been advantageous to the dependant. Males have almost always exerted exclusively to their own profit the tutelage they arrogate to themselves over females; and the same is true for the tutelage of master over slave, of lord over serf.

(ii) Aristocracy*

(667) The theory of 'natural servitude', as conceived by Aristotle, deserves careful examination for, although slavery has happily disappeared from western societies, this theory has survived and it occurs in the most diverse forms. It could be termed the theory of *aristocracy*, understanding this

---

* Vol. II, chapter 1, §§667–72; chapter 2, §§1001.

word in its etymological sense of ἄριστος, the best. It rests on an indisputable fact: human beings are not equal physically, intellectually or morally. But its defect is that it embraces only the first condition mentioned above (§663) as justifying private tutelage in so far as it increases the sum of utility for the dependant. It wholly neglects the second and third conditions. Certainly, from the fact that men do exist who are intellectually and morally better than other men, it can legitimately be argued that these men of superior qualities *could* be capable of increasing the sum of utility in acting as guardians of their inferiors. But there is nothing to justify replacing a conditional by an affirmative proposition, claiming that this increase in the sum of utility does actually occur. This matter has to be resolved by observation.

(668) The reason for the general neglect of the second condition springs from two factors. On the one hand, the guardians feel the need for a certain prestige in order to exercise their functions, and therefore they try to exclude from the minds of their wards the mere thought that they are capable of abusing their authority. Herein is one of the originating reasons for restrictions on the freedom of the press. On the other hand, it is of prime importance to those hostile to the guardians to demonstrate the ignorance and immorality of these high and mighty people. This their opponents seek to do either because they think that by destroying the prestige of the guardians they will be able to seize power from them; or because, envisaging only a change of persons, not of systems, they are careful to avoid using fundamental arguments which could rebound against themselves.

(669) It is for reasons akin to these that we find much more discussion in social and political questions about the manner of selecting the guardians than about the second and third conditions of tutelage. It seems to be agreed on as an axiom that a formula must exist for selecting guardians in such a way that they will be unable to abuse their power; and that the evils seen occurring in practice derive simply from the fact that this wonderful formula has yet to be applied. This error occurs in those theories which ascribe an exclusive influence over social phenomena to the form of government or to the method for recruiting its personnel. These factors are indeed interdependent, but to a much smaller degree than is generally supposed. To appreciate this it is enough to make a comparative study of the facts observable in societies which have changed either the method of recruiting their governors or the form of government itself. Such a study makes it clear that, while the facts observed are variable in form, the fundamental substance remains pretty much the same. The sole appreciable result of most revolutions has been the replacement of one set of politicians by another set.

(670) Since human beings have a well-nigh absolute need to live in society, and since society cannot subsist without some form of public tutelage, it would seem then that this type of tutelage always brings with it utility for the individual, but that it may be of a greater or lesser degree. The worst government is a lesser evil for a people than the total absence of government. On every page of history we see men resigning themselves to enduring the heaviest sacrifices and tolerating the most heinous govern-

ments so long as some measure of order and security at least is assured them.

(671) Public tutelage seems indisputably to have brought more utility than private tutelage. It is not difficult to understand why this should be so. In private life, effect generally follows cause more swiftly than in public life. An average dose of foresight is therefore sufficient to guide one in private life. But a much greater dose is needed in public.

If a workman spends all of his wage on payday, then hunger and privation the day after will impress on his mind the utility of thrift. On the other hand, it will be extremely difficult for him to perceive that the evils afflicting him are the consequence, for example, of alterations in the value of money. In this matter, tradition often supplements the defective knowledge of the individual, substituting for the experience of a single individual the collective experience of a long series of generations. Herein indeed is the reason for the utility of religious precepts to the degree that they have strengthened the authority of government. Since the majority is incapable of associating particular effects with their real causes, it has been useful to invent fictive causes which are within the understanding of the masses. And let it be said here that the motives governing the political decisions of modern peoples are often no more rational than those derived from the auguries sent by Zeus or Athena.

(672) The existence of society being assumed essential, what governmental organisation will guarantee it the maximum utility? This is an unanswerable question in the present state of science. In most cases, the best we can do is to conserve those forms of government which have been tested by experience, at the same time endeavouring to improve them as much as possible. To seek to change everything in obedience to abstract considerations is as absurd as to seek to conserve everything in obedience to a sentiment of plain neophobia. Herein lies an argument of great weight in favour of economic liberty for, if we do not know what may be the best form or organisation for government, we do nevertheless know that existing systems of government are heavy and complicated machines. . . . It is advisable therefore to restrict to a minimum the work of the governmental machine.

(1001) It is not easy to understand in what sense many writers use the term *aristocracy*. Sometimes they seem to be giving it the usual meaning: that is, a group of men occupying the summit of the social hierarchy. But at other times, when it is made apparent that such groups may be, intellectually and morally, below the average obtaining in the given society, these writers protest and declare that the term 'aristocracy' simply means the *wellborn*. This rather mysterious term ends up by playing the same role in new doctrines as 'vital force' did in ancient medicine.

(iii) Circulation of elites *

(1002) Let us consider a community in which incomes are represented by the following graph. The community is represented by the surface *m–n–t–*

---

* Vol. II, chapter 2, §§1002, 1004–5, 1025–7, 1039–41.

b–b'–s–a'–a–m, individuals being the elements of this surface. We know that the form of the curve n–t–b–s varies only slowly. This form may be

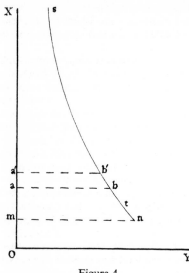

Figure 4

supposed almost constant on average and for a fairly short period. But the molecules composing the social aggregate are not at rest: some individuals are becoming rich, others poor. Appreciable movements therefore are occurring within the figure m–n–t–b–s–a–m. In this the social organism resembles a living organism. The external form of a living organism—a horse, for example—remains almost constant, but internally extensive and varied movements take place. The circulation of the blood is putting particular molecules in rapid motion; the processes of assimilation and secretion are perpetually changing the molecules composing the tissues. The analogy goes even further. It is only the *form* of the curve n–t–b–s which remains constant; the absolute dimensions of the figure may, and do in fact, change. Thus the foal becomes an adult horse. Similarity of form is maintained, but the size of the animal changes considerably.

(1004) Taking this graph to represent the distribution of wealth for every million inhabitants in the given society, there is indicated on the surface m–n–b–s–a–m the small section a–b–b'–a'. Changes of two kinds occur within this section:

1. An individual dies and is succeeded by his son. The income remains the same; only the ownership has changed. In general, birth introduces new individuals into this section and death removes individuals belonging to it.

2. An interchange, often very active, occurs between the section a–b–b'–a' and neighbouring sections, whereby it receives from lower sections individuals who are growing richer and from higher sections individuals who are growing poorer. It loses to the higher sections those individuals within itself who are growing richer, while those within it who are growing poorer pass down to the lower sections.

In short, changes of the first kind are attributable to changes in the 'personnel' of society, and those of the second kind to changes in wealth.

(1005) Let us consider these variations cumulatively. If their outcome is an increase in the number of individuals comprised in section a–b–b'–a', this increases in breadth and, since the total number of individuals represented in the graph is assumed to be constant, this increase must be accompanied by a reduction in the breadth of some other section, and this will change the form of the curve *n–t–b–s*. Now experience shows that the form of the curve only changes with great slowness; in fact, remaining well-nigh constant. We therefore conclude from this that each social stratum receives almost as many individuals as it loses. In other words: there are, for example, almost as many individuals every year entering the class of those who have an income of 4,000 to 5,000 francs as there are individuals leaving this class.

It must clearly be understood, as we have already strongly emphasised, that what is involved here is only an average phenomenon. It would be utterly absurd to claim that the number of persons in a month, or even in a year, who join the class of people with an income of 4,000 to 4,010 francs, or even of 4,000 to 5,000, is exactly equal to the number leaving these income groups. To recur to a previous comparison: when we say that the form of an adult animal remains almost constant, we are speaking of an average phenomenon. Not only age, but a host of secondary phenomena ensue to modify this form. Mammals moult hair and birds their feathers; snakes shed their skins, stags their horns, and new ones grow; and so on.

(1025) The causes, whatever they may be, which determine the distribution of the ownership of income may operate with variable intensity. An extreme case would be that in which each individual found himself infallibly placed in that income level which corresponded to his capacities. Another extreme case would be one in which each income level was a closed caste, no exchange taking place between one level and another. The cases occurring in reality are intermediary between these two extremes.

(1026) The capacities just mentioned are to be understood both in the good and the bad sense. If, for example, we were considering a community of thieves, we would perhaps find a distribution of income similar to that revealed to us by general experience of life. The distribution of the ownership of income would be determined by aptitude for theft. Conversely, it would be aptitude for work, the capacity for order and good management, which would determine the distribution of income in a community where the production of wealth was the sole means for procuring income. Some people will inherit or receive in gift a fortune which will assign them a place in a class other than that which would be assigned to them in virtue of their capacities, good or bad.

The main fundamental factor affecting the form of the income curve could well be the proportion in births of choice individuals.* This would explain how it comes about that the form of the curve varies little from one country to another. It would also explain why inequalities of income diminish and the minimum income increases only if wealth becomes more abundant. If the total quantity of wealth is very small, only the most gifted individuals will be able to acquire a notable amount of it. If the total quantity of wealth is very great, it is more easily acquired and individuals who are but moderately gifted will be able to acquire an appreciable amount. In short: if there is only one prize in the contest, obviously it will

---

* Earlier in the *Cours* Pareto says: 'By "choice individuals" we mean simply those individuals in whom the activity of life is most intense. But this activity can be exerted to bad as well as to good purposes.'

be the strongest contestant who gets it. If there are two prizes, then a contestant less strong than the first will get the second prize. Moreover, the first contestant being already satisfied with what he has won will be less inclined to run additional risks to despoil the second contestant.

(1027) The rejected elements of each level fall down to the lower level. But what becomes of the rejected elements of the bottom level—of that section whose lower limit is described by the line *m–n* in our graph? Evidently they are removed from society by death. If we consider society as a living organism, then the surface forming the base of the social pyramid figured in our graph represents the organ of excretion. If the production of rejected elements cannot be prevented in any way, then the very life of the whole system requires the elimination of these elements.

(1039) Differentiating individuals by occupation is not the most rational division, since the same person may, and very often does, belong to more than one class of occupation. In this respect certainly, human societies bear little resemblance to animal societies in which—as, for example, in the case of termites—functional differentiation corresponds to a material differentiation of individuals. In dealing with human societies, therefore, it is advisable to differentiate, not individuals by functions or occupations, but the functions or operations themselves. These are classifiable as follows:

1. Occupations directly producing economic goods and services;

2. Occupations indirectly contributing to the production of economic goods and services; or producing some utility for the aggregate;

3. No occupation; idleness;

4. Occupations aiming at the appropriation of the goods of others, by legal or illegal means.

(1040) The first class of occupations is studied specifically by economic science. It constitutes the services of personal capital. The second class includes tutelage; when adult wards demand tutelage, its services may belong to the category of those which, being ophelimous, are subject to the general laws of exchange. But when, as most frequently happens, the tutelage is imposed, or when it envisages a utility which the wards only vaguely perceive, its services are entirely unregulated by the laws governing the exchange of economic goods. . . .

(1041) The unoccupied or idle are far from being useless creatures. Children answer to this description: but they will be producers later on. And this class includes old people who, in their prime, were producers. The possessors of invested funds and landed capital, when they administer their own fortunes, fulfil a very important function. . . .

*(iv) Spoliation**

(1042) In considering the fourth class of occupations (§1039), we should note that the general condemnation of spoliation has meant that econo-

---

* Vol. II, chapter 2, §§1042, 1046–50.

mists on the whole have refrained from studying it. In this they act like those amateur entymologists who are interested only in the most beautiful butterflies. The serious naturalist, on the other hand, does not avert his gaze from any insect, however repulsive it may be. Science must study all the phenomena which are germane to it. Spoliation has always existed in human societies. One may hope for it to be considerably reduced, but it is by no means certain that it can ever be made entirely to disappear.

(1046) Illegal appropriation by violence is easily explained by the law of the strongest. Likewise it is understandable that the majority which makes the laws is in a position to exact for itself whatever tribute it pleases. What is less easily understood is how a small number of individuals is able, by underhand methods, to get the majority to pay tribute to a minority. Why does the majority allow itself to be despoiled of its possessions?

First and foremost, it is by ignorance. Very many economic matters are so complicated that few people have even a superficial understanding of them. Amongst the people who use sugar there is not one in a thousand who is aware of the appropriation of wealth that goes on under the system of production-subsidies. Similarly, only a handful of people in the United States were in a position to understand the benefits—at the expense of the community—which would accrue to certain individuals, and the crisis which would be provoked in the country, in consequence of the Bland Bill and the Sherman Act.

Further—and this is the main reason—the intensity of human activity is not proportional in the same degree to losses as to gains. A hundred men from each of whom is exacted one franc will not react to defend their own with as much energy as one man moved by the desire to get hold of those one hundred francs. There has, of course, to be some pretext for this appropriation, otherwise—even independently of the loss threatening them —a certain instinct of equity and justice, existing in all human beings, would spark off resistance to it. But if a more or less plausible pretext can be found—the degree of plausibility is not very important—it is pretty well certain that the operation will not miscarry through any resistance on the part of the despoiled.

(1047) Let us suppose that in a country of thirty million inhabitants it is proposed, under some pretext or other, to get each citizen to pay out one franc a year, and to distribute the total amount amongst thirty persons. Every one of the donors will give up one franc a year; every one of the beneficiaries will receive one million francs a year. The two groups will differ very greatly in their response to this situation. Those who hope to gain a million a year will know no rest by day or night. They will win newspapers over to their interest by financial inducements and drum up support from all quarters. A discreet hand will warm the palms of needy legislators, even of ministers. In the United States there is no necessity to resort to such underhand methods; there deals are made in the open: there is an open market in votes just as there are open markets in cotton and grain. On the other hand, the despoiled are much less active. A great deal of money is needed to launch an electoral campaign. Now there are insuperable material difficulties militating against asking each citizen to contribute a few centimes. One has to ask a few people to make substantial contributions. But then, for such people, there is the likelihood that their individual contribution to the campaign against the spoliation will exceed the total amount they stand to lose by the measure in question. Only pure philanthropy could induce an individual to subscribe ten francs in the hope of thereby helping to defeat a proposal which would cost him but one franc. Economically, it is a bad bargain. When election day comes, similar difficulties are encountered. Those who hope to gain a million apiece have agents everywhere, who descend in swarms on the electorate, urging the voters that sound and enlightened patriotism calls for the success of their modest proposal. They will go further if need be, and are quite prepared to lay out cash to get the necessary votes for returning candidates in their interest. In contrast, the individual who is threatened with losing one franc a year—even if he is fully aware of what is afoot—will not for so small a thing forego a picnic in the country, or fall out with useful or congenial friends, or get on the wrong side of the mayor or the *préfet*! In these circumstances the outcome is not in doubt: the spoliators will win hands down.

... Cobden's Anti-Corn Law League succeeded because manufacturers in Manchester and other places realised that free trade was to their advantage. It is probable that the consumers on their own would have been unable to get the Corn Laws repealed, or would only have achieved this much later.

(1048) There is a further reason to explain how cases of the transference of wealth from one pocket to another can grow apace. The loss of a small sum of money by several instalments is more easily accepted than the loss of the same amount in one disbursement. A man will object much more strongly to being made to pay five francs in one swoop than to paying out first one franc, then another, and yet another, and so on. It would be difficult to get a duty of seven francs on every hundred kilos of grain accepted all at one go. One has to start by, say, a duty of three francs, and after a time increase it to five francs, then eventually to seven. It is this factor in combination with ignorance which maintains the very high level of indirect taxation in the major European countries. If the attempt were made to raise the same amounts by direct taxation as are raised by indirect taxation, the taxpayers would become aware of the heavy sacrifices they were making and would in the end compel their governments to cut expenditure.

(1049) Limitations on spoliation seldom come from resistance by the despoiled; they come rather in consequence of the losses spoliation inflicts on the whole country, part of which falls also on the spoliators. These may, as a result, end up by losing more than they gained. If they are intelligent enough to appreciate the consequences, they call a halt. But if they lack the good sense to see what is happening, the country goes further and further down the road to ruin. This is exactly what has happened in certain South American republics, in Portugal, in Greece and in other countries.

(1050) It is clearly mistaken to hold certain individuals exclusively responsible for the ills afflicting a particular society; for, save where the people are under the yoke of brutal force, the spoliators are able to ply their trade only because of the ignorance, the apathy and the vices of the

despoiled. We must be quite clear in our minds about this: social phenomena are the product of all the forces operating in society, the result of the
virtues and defects of all the citizens in a given community. People everywhere love to find some scapegoat on which to unload all their faults. But
this is nothing more than pure illusion.

(v) *Economic interests and class struggle**

(1053) Different economic classes have different economic interests. This
arises from the nature of things. It is quite obvious that an ordinary workman does not have the same economic interests as a great landed proprietor
or the owner of a large personal fortune. When it comes to the question of
taxes and levies, each class endeavours to the best of its abilities to shift the
burden on to other classes. When it is a question of disbursements of
public money, each class seeks to corner the cash for itself. The socialists
are therefore entirely right in emphasising the great importance of
the 'class struggle', and in stating that it is the great dominant fact in
history. In this respect, the works of Marx and Loria deserve the greatest
attention.

(1054) The class struggle at all times takes two forms. One is plainly
and simply economic competition. When this competition is free, we
find that it produces the maximum ophelimity. Each class, like each
individual, although looking exclusively to its own advantage, indirectly
comes to be useful to the other classes. Nor is this all: since free competition, far from destroying, produces wealth, it indirectly contributes to
raising the minimum income level and to reducing inequalities of income.
The other form taken by the class struggle is that whereby each class
endeavours to get control of the government so as to make it an instrument
for spoliation. The struggle of some individuals to appropriate the wealth
produced by others is the great factor dominating all human history.

(1055) The dominant class not only directly harms the class it despoils:
it also harms the nation as a whole for, since spoliation is as a rule accompanied by a destruction of wealth, the minimum income level must fall and
inequality of incomes increase. From this point of view, it matters little
whether the dominant class is an oligarchy, a plutocracy or a democracy.
All one can say—though there are exceptions to this—is that the more
people there are in this governing class, the more severe the evils arising
from its domination, for a numerous class consumes a greater amount of
wealth than a class restricted in numbers. This is probably the reason why
demagogic regimes have always been of shorter duration than tyrannic or
oligarchic regimes. This factor will probably prove to be the great obstacle
to the establishment of popular socialism. Bourgeois socialism, which
operates by means of customs protection, export subsidies and devaluation
of the currency, has in its favour the circumstance that it has only a small
number of adherents to satisfy. Hence it can enrich them without entirely
destroying the wealth of the country.

(1056) Many writers confound two questions which are absolutely

---

* Vol. II, chapter 2, §§1053-62, 1064-5.

different: the existence of a dominant class; and the way by which it is recruited. It seems to such writers that when the subject class has the right to choose its masters in accordance with a certain method of selection, it has nothing more to desire and must be deemed to have attained perfect happiness in this world. It never occurs to them that it would perhaps be more useful to prevent spoliation altogether than to restrict themselves to determining who is to profit from the practice of spoliation. Certainly, when the dominant class is recruited by heredity or by co-option, its yoke is more odious than when it is recruited by election. But it does not follow from this that an hereditary or co-optative governing class is also more burdensome to the subject classes. In no way can it be presumed that an oligarchic administration would have been more corrupt than the municipality of New York, based on universal suffrage, has shown itself to be. The people of Tuscany were happier and less despoiled under the absolutist government of Peter Leopold than they are under the present constitutional government of Italy. In most countries nowadays election plays a more or less preponderant part in the selection of the governing class. But this is no new thing in history. In Rome towards the end of the Republic it was election which conferred power; but those chosen were so deplorable and oppression was so great that military despotism seemed to the vast majority of Romans a lesser evil. The situation had reached such a point that, in a sense, Caesar and Augustus were truly the benefactors of the subject class. In saying this I do not intend to make a judgement of what type of government is preferable; a particular type which, at a given time, is found inferior to another type, may contain within itself seeds of reform which will make it superior in the future. What I want to establish is that form must not take precedence over substance, and that altering the names which bedeck spoliation in no way changes the amount of wealth it destroys.

(1057) From time to time dissensions break out in the dominant class, or between that class and another which seeks to replace it. While these dissensions last, they tend to alleviate the yoke weighing down on the subject classes, the weaker of the contending parties trying to win their support in order to gain power. But when it has achieved its ends, it hastens to assert its domination and employs, albeit under new names, the same methods it had formerly condemned.

(1058) This situation occurs repeatedly in history and there are instances of it in our own day. Towards the end of the eighteenth century and at the beginning of the nineteenth, the bourgeoisie fought to gain power. At that time, the demand was for independence of the judiciary, guarantee of individual rights, freedom of the press, institution of the national guard and the jury system; and these were claims which then admitted of no compromise or abatement. But ever since it gained control of government, the bourgeoisie has forgotten them. Its ideas have been profoundly modified, and it is beginning to discover that the *ancien régime*'s methods and practices, hitherto held to be so reprehensible, were not so bad after all.

(1059) Crudely interpreted, this factor has given rise to the belief that the standstill or regression which has occurred in the movement of economic liberty was due to defects inherent in it. But in fact this impediment to the movement is only the outcome of a reflex action caused by something else quite different. The change of opinion which has taken place in regard to certain abuses is governed solely by changes in the persons profiting from them. The same privileges which were judged abominable when a sovereign bestowed them on his favourites are now considered perfectly right and proper when a parliament hands them out to politicians. The inhabitants of the United States rebelled against England over the imposition of a tax which is utterly insignificant in comparison with the tribute money paid by their descendants to the owners of silver mines and to manufacturers who have laid out hard cash to get the benefits of protective tariffs.

(1060) At all times, and even under democratic regimes, the rich classes have exerted a marked influence on the government of their country. The ways whereby these classes are recruited—that is to say, how the recipients of income are selected—is therefore a highly important factor in the determination of social phenomena. The qualities which make for man's success in the struggle against the forces of nature are not the same as those which ensure success in the wiles and stratagems resorted to in spoliation. A society in which (as in Switzerland and England) wealth is achieved only by work, industry and trade, will differ considerably from a society in which wealth is, to a considerable degree, the fruit of fraud and political intrigue.

(1061) Moreover—and this is not the least of its evils—spoliation deflects the productive work of a large number of a country's most intelligent citizens. Let us suppose there are, in France, two industrialists who are equally active, intelligent and hard working. One is constantly on the iob in his factory, wholly concerned with improving production and cutting costs. The other goes off to Paris to pay court to the politicians and their chosen ministers. The results are very different. The first industrialist, with great effort, will manage to save 2 or 3 per cent on his expenses; the second will be able to obtain a protective duty of 50 per cent and more. What improvements and careful management in the growing of wheat could reduce the cost of this cereal by 60 per cent? Yet a protective duty of exactly this amount has been obtained quite easily by Italian farm interests, thanks to political intrigue. . . .

(1062) The numbers of highly capable people engaged in the production of wealth is, in some countries, diminished further by recruitment into a large body of state employees. For such countries, it is literally a question of *lucrum cessans et damnum emergens*. One of the main reasons for the wealth of England and Switzerland lies in the fact that, for the present at least, the politician class and the state functionary class are limited in size and cannot, therefore, attract away from the production of wealth the greater part of the country's enterprising elements. The reverse is the case with Spain and Italy, which helps to account for their general poverty. In France, the destruction of wealth is not less, but is compensated for by the French people's truly marvellous capacity for work and saving and, above all, by the fall in the birth rate. The French are unable to raise as many children as the English because the economic resources and products necessary for rearing a larger number of children are consumed, squandered and destroyed by politicians and by protectionists of all shapes and sizes. For there to be a rise in incomes and a decrease in inequalities of income, wealth must grow in relation to population. In France this effect is achieved by acting on the second term of the equation: that is, by impeding the growth of population. In England the same effect is achieved by stimulating, through economic liberty, a substantial increase of wealth.

(1064) Because the rich classes so frequently despoil the poor classes, some conclude that it is the ownership of land and personal capital which is the 'cause' of spoliation, and that collectivism alone can remedy the evils of society. There is a radical error in such arguments ... which consists of ascribing to 'capital' or 'wealth' (savings) effects which are not germane to them. It is not the simple possession of private wealth which puts certain individuals in a position to despoil others: it is the use to which they put that wealth; for example, by employing it to win favours from public authorities instead of transforming it into 'capital' in the economic sense. ...

(1065) It is certainly the case that wealth is not only the end but also one of the means of spoliation, but this of itself does not suffice to condemn the possession of economic goods, for if it did one would have to conclude from the fact that iron is used by murderers and thieves that this metal is harmful to the human race, and that, because ships are used by pirates, navigation must be abandoned.

Wealth is not the only basis of the strength of the spoliators: they use many other means, and cunningly make recourse to the most worthy things and those intrinsically most useful to society. The maintenance of order and security being the most pressing need of society, they make use of it and glibly deploy it as a pretext in order to ensure the success of their operations. Spoliation has also been given the sanction of religion and morality. In the eyes of the dominant class, the things most abominable are those which may threaten its power, and often enough they manage to get those subject to them to accept this viewpoint. The thing most indispensable to men, after morality, is justice: hence at all times the dominant class has sought to make justice serve its ends. The mere idea of an absolutely independent judiciary is repugnant to it, and it senses instinctively that it must make the judiciary serve its behests in order that it may fix its power on a secure base. This is fundamentally the real motivation behind the contemporary movement against the jury system. Not that there are lacking sincere opponents of the institution who criticise it solely from an objective viewpoint; but they do not reflect on the fact that it is the sole institution which, for all its defects, gives to accused persons who are not on good terms with the dominant class some prospect of acquittal. It is precisely this which accounts for the aversion of politicians to the jury system: their motivation differs not at all from that which prompted the Roman *equites* to gain control of the judiciary. Highly honourable people let themselves be deluded by the ingenious pretexts which are never lacking in such cases. Misled by the false principle that the end justifies the means, they believe they are serving the cause of order and justice: in fact they are doing it the most brutal injury.

6. ECONOMICO-POLITICAL DOCTRINES AND SOCIAL SCIENCE*

(1066) The abuse made of things which in themselves are perfectly reputable and highly beneficial engenders dangerous doctrines which reject the use to avoid the abuse. Communism, collectivism, protectionism, state or 'pulpit' socialism, bourgeois socialism, anti-semitism, nihilism, anarchism—all such are offshoots of the same stem. They spring directly from an incomplete observation of the laws of social science—and very often from passion serving in the stead of reason. At all times men have given imaginary causes to evils that were only too real. Ancient Rome rang with the cry: 'To the lions with the Christians'; in medieval cities it was: 'Death to the Lombards'; today it is: 'Down with the Jews'. These are blind revulsions with no more reason in them than in the action of a child belabouring the inanimate object it has stumbled against. At a slightly higher intellectual level, these feelings of resentment and hatred against certain abuses find expression in systems and theories. The owners of landed property, gaining control of the state, have fastened a heavy yoke on their fellow citizens: landed property must therefore be abolished and common ownership of land be established. Certain possessors of private wealth, instead of transforming it into capital, have used it to oppress the community: private wealth and savings must therefore be abolished. Some businessmen, instead of attending to their function—the best means of production—have induced the public authorities to bestow privileges on them: private business therefore must be abolished and only the community be allowed to possess 'the means of production', i.e., capital in the form of land and property, investments and personal wealth. Socialists stop at this point but —as Prince Kropotkin has told them—they are not logical in so doing. It is the anarchists who, scorning half-measures, imperturbably go on to deduce the logical consequences of the premises laid down by the collectivists. 'From the day when private property is struck down in any one of its forms—land or industry,' they say, 'one will be forced to strike at it in all its other forms.' Since the organisation of justice has served to cover up misdeeds, we must entirely abolish it. Family, government, morality—all have to pass away for the same reasons. But the anarchists in their turn are also compelled to call a halt at some point, for if they really sought to push this extraordinary theory to its ultimate conclusion, they would have to let themselves die of hunger, since food itself, by its abuse, is capable of engendering all manner of evils.

(1067) It often happens that a theory exaggerated in one direction gives rise to another theory exaggerated in a contrary direction. Certain socialists, preaching the absolute physical and intellectual equality of men, thereby arrive at the point of seeking to waste in manual labour, of no importance or skill, the exceptionally rare and precious talents of learned and brilliant men. The neo-aristocrats, without much expenditure of imagination, have simply adopted the antithesis of this doctrine. According

---

* Vol. II, chapter 2, §§1066-8.

to them, the whole of mankind exists only to produce a few superior beings; it is merely a dungheap on which a handful of flowers blossom.

All such sects have, naturally, some economic system whose merits they laud to the heavens: a system which has no more relationship to reality than had the cosmologies of the ancients.

(1068) For such utterly defective analyses, science substitutes a large and comprehensive survey of the facts, not limiting itself to studying them qualitatively, but going further into studying them quantitatively. For baseless abstractions it substitutes realities, and replaces vague and inconsistent aspirations by the strict investigation of the necessary relations of things. Above, far above, the prejudices and passions of men soar the laws of nature. Eternal and immutable, they are the expression of the creative power; they represent what is, what must be, what otherwise could not be. Man can come to understand them: he is incapable of changing them. From the infinitely great down to the infinitely small, all things are subject to them. The sun and the planets follow the laws discovered by Newton and Laplace, just as the atoms in their combinations follows the laws of chemistry, as living creatures follow the laws of biology. It is only the imperfections of the human mind which multiplies the divisions of the sciences, separating astronomy from physics or chemistry, the natural sciences from the social sciences. In essence, science is one. It is none other than the truth.

II

Les Systèmes Socialistes

(1902)

1. DISTINCTION BETWEEN SUBJECTIVE BELIEFS AND OBJECTIVE OCCURRENCES*

It is, as a general rule, necessary always to distinguish between the concrete *objective* phenomenon and the form in which our mind perceives it: a form constituting another phenomenon which we may call *subjective*. To cite an everyday example: a straight stick immersed in water is the objective phenomenon. As we see it, this stick seems to be bent; and we would in fact say it was bent if we did not know it to be otherwise. This represents the subjective phenomenon.

Livy is taking for bent a stick which in reality is straight when he relates an anecdote to explain certain facts signalising the rise of plebeian families to power in Rome. A trifling event occurred, he says, which, as is often the case, had far-reaching consequences. One daughter of M. Fabius Ambustus married a patrician; his other daughter married a plebeian. The animosity between the two sisters was such that in the end it led to the plebeians' being granted privileges hitherto denied them. But modern historians have straightened this particular bent stick. Niebuhr was one of the first to understand clearly the upwards movement of the nobility, the new elite, in Rome. He was guided mainly by the analogy of the struggles in our own societies between the bourgeoisie and the mass of the people. This is a realistic analogy for it relates to particular cases of a single and consistent general phenomenon.

The notion that great historical occurrences are attributable to small personal causes is now almost wholly discarded, but it is frequently

---

* Vol. I, Introduction, pp. 15–18, 21–29; chapter 6, pp. 264, 304–5.

replaced by another error, that of denying the individual any influence at all on circumstances. Unquestionably, the battle of Austerlitz could have been won by some general other than Napoleon if this other had been a great battle commander. But if the French had been led by an incompetent general, they would have lost the battle well and truly. The way to avoid one error is not to embrace the opposite error. Because straight sticks on occasion appear bent, it must not be assumed that bent sticks do not in fact exist. The subjective phenomenon partly coincides with the objective phenomenon and partly differs from it. Our ignorance of the facts, our passions and prejudices, the ideas in vogue in the societies in which we live, the events which powerfully affect us—all these with a thousand other circumstances conceal the truth from us and prevent us from getting an exact impression of the objective phenomenon giving rise to them. We are like a man who sees objects in a curved mirror; their outlines and proportions are to some degree altered. We must realise that most often we are aware only of this subjective phenomenon—i.e., the objective phenomenon in distorted form—knowing it either directly through investigation or the state of mind of the men witnessing a given event, or indirectly through the testimony of a historian who has conducted such an investigation. The problem which historical criticism has to resolve is therefore quite other than that involved in textual criticism. It amounts first and foremost to reconstituting the object itself, the image of which has been distorted.

This is a difficult and delicate operation, and is made even more formidable by a particular circumstance: very frequently, individuals and groups are unaware of the forces prompting their behaviour. They ascribe to their actions imaginary causes which differ considerably from the real causes. It is mistaken to believe that those who thus deceive others are always acting in bad faith. Most often such people start off with self-deception, believing with all the sincerity in the world in the existence of these imaginary causes which they claim to be determining their actions. The testimony of men who have witnessed, and even of those who have taken part in, a particular social movement, is not to be accepted without reservation when considering this movement's real cause. Unwittingly they may be induced to disregard the real causes and to assign imaginary causes to it.

... Given the conditions in which an individual lives, certain opinions can be expected of him; nevertheless he may not be aware of this relationship between his opinions and his circumstances, and will seek to justify the former on quite different grounds. Many people who are socialists are not socialists because they have been persuaded by a particular line of reasoning; quite the reverse: they acquiesce in this line of reasoning because they are socialists.

The sources of men's illusions about the motives determining their behaviour are manifold. A main one lies in the fact that a very large number of human actions are not the outcome of reasoning. They are purely instinctive actions, although the man performing them experiences a feeling of pleasure in giving them, quite arbitrarily, logical causes. He is, generally speaking, not very exacting as to the soundness of this logic, and is very easily satisfied by a semblance of rationality. Nevertheless, he would feel very uncomfortable if there were lacking a smattering of logic.

This figure will perhaps make the matter clearer: A is a real cause and its resulting phenomenon, B, is equally real. People are, or wish to be, ignorant of the existence of the relationship of reality between A and B, but they do feel the need to connect B with some cause, and so they make B the consequence of C. There may be several variants of this relationship between B and C.

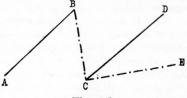

Figure 5

1. C *exists in reality, but B is not its consequence.* This is very often the case with hasty generalisations, with badly made observations, and with defective rationalisations. The C–B link exists only in the imagination of those describing it. In reality—but the people concerned are unaware of it—the consequence of C is D. In other cases this C–D relationship may be perfectly well known, but it is desired to avoid accepting D as the consequence of C, and so the C–B link is established. Herein is one of the origins of casuistry.

2. C *is imaginary, but the link connecting C with B is strictly logical*: that is to say, if C did exist its consequences would be B. Why does water rise up in a pump? Because Nature abhors a vacuum. The fact B, that water rises in a pump when the latter is worked, is real. The consequence—abhorrence of a vacuum—is logical. But Dame Nature and her feelings of abhorrence of a vacuum are imaginary entities. The facts which were explained by reference to *vital force* were often real, and the rationalisations of it could be tolerably sound; but *vital force* is a thing unknown. Sometimes it is with deliberate intent that recourse is made to an imaginary cause C: in legal fictions, for example.

3. *Not only is C imaginary, but also its link with B is not logical.* This error is common amongst metaphysicists. Thus in Hegel's *Philosophy of Nature* we see appear certain unknown entities from which, by incomprehensible rationalisations, is deduced the explanation of real phenomena. In their extreme form, disquisitions of this sort degenerate into pure reveries. One reason why Greek mythology proves attractive to intelligent minds repelled by oriental mythologies is perhaps due to the fact that Greek mythology comes close to the second variant, while oriental mythologies belong to the third. The gods of Homer and Aeschylus are imaginary, but —their existence once admitted—they are seen to behave not too illogically; whereas with the oriental gods, it is not only necessary to make a pronounced effort to accept their existence, but this effort has to be renewed continually, for their manner of behaviour is utterly incomprehensible.

4. It remains finally to consider cases in which the thing which it is desired to explain, B, *the event or situation itself, is imaginary.* Again, it may be linked to a real cause or to an imaginary cause by strictly rational arguments, or by arguments lacking strictness and precision of reasoning.

In studying the objective phenomena we seek to discover the relationship of interdependence between the real facts A and B. In studying the subjective phenomena, the aim is to discover the C–B connections which men substitute for the real relationships, and also such connections as C–E which writers establish between two facts, C and E: relationships which are equally imaginary.

In our enquiry, all these questions will, as far as possible, be considered successively from this double viewpoint, that is to say, from a viewpoint we will term objective and from one which we will term subjective. On one hand, we will seek to discover what are the real facts which have favoured the establishment of certain social systems, or gestation of projects of social systems; in other words, what are the facts and features revealed by them. On the other hand, we will examine the methods of reasoning employed in justification of these systems or projected systems, and we will consider to what extent the premises of such reasoning are drawn from experience and the degree to which the deductions are logical.

The respective scope of the different sections of this study cannot, unfortunately, relate to their practical importance. In this regard, we are pretty well limited to the objective study and, at the most, to that part of the subjective study which brings to light the arguments resorted to by adherents of different systems. It is absorbing and interesting *qua* philosophic speculation to study the logical value of such arguments—and a large part of this book will be concerned with studying them from this aspect—but it must be clearly understood that the practical importance of such a study is extremely limited. The diffusion of a doctrine depends hardly at all on its logical value. Quite the contrary; and any one trying to assess the social effects of a doctrine according to its logical value would expose himself to enormous errors.

It is not thus that the phenomenon is reflected in the awareness of men. When they feel drawn by certain religious, moral or humanitarian movements, human beings believe—and almost all of them entirely in good faith—that their convictions have been formed by a series of strict syllogisms deriving from real and incontestable facts. We shall guard against falling prey to this illusion, and shall make every effort to reveal its origins. This enquiry will frequently impress on us the fact that economic factors modify social institutions and doctrines, and as such are reflected in the awareness of men, as is claimed by the materialist theory of history. But frequently we shall also find that there are other factors which are not reducible, at least in the present state of our knowledge, to purely economic categories.

The materialist theory of history, indeed, has its point of departure in a principle which is true; but it errs in trying to claim too much: a claim taking it beyond the conclusions which are legitimately derivable from experience. This tendency to claim too much is, it seems, natural to the human mind, for a similar defect is to be found in the theory of Malthus, in Ricardo's theory of rent, and in many other theories. It is only by successive rectifications and by pruning away propositions which are found to be false that the truth is reached.

Human beings habitually make all their actions dependent on a small number of rules of conduct in which they have a religious faith. It is inevitable that this should be so, for the great mass of men possess neither the character nor the intelligence necessary for them to be capable of relating these actions to their real causes. Indeed, even the most intelligent men are obliged to condense their rules of conduct into a few axioms for, when one has to act, there really is not time for indulging in long and theoretical deliberations.

Yet the causes of social phenomena are enormously greater in number and variety than the small number of religious or other axioms which are posited. The desire—indeed it is an obligation—to relate all one's behaviour to these axioms necessarily leads to assigning fictive causes for one's conduct; hence, among other consequences, the need for a casuistry. Social life makes it impossible to accept all the logical consequences of the principles one seeks to respect. A way therefore must be found for interpreting these principles in such a way that their consequences do not conflict with the circumstances of real life. A certain principle x, in which individuals have a religious faith, has—let us say—as its logical consequences the actions M, N etc. which are useful to society; and also other actions, P, Q etc., which would clash too strongly with the conditions of social life. To deny x in order to avoid P, Q etc. is generally a bad way out, for x would inevitably be replaced by z, and this might have logical consequences worse than P, Q etc. The dilemma is usually resolved by giving a few gentle twists to logic in such a way as to exclude P, Q etc. from the consequences of x. This is the task of casuists and exegetists. If judged from the viewpoint of logic, it has no value at all; but judged from the viewpoint of practical life, it is indispensable, and in fact is seen to have been operative at all times. At a certain stage in the evolution of Graeco-Roman polytheism, the attempt was made, by elaborate feats of interpretation, to reconcile a purified morality with the legendary crimes of the gods. When christianity experienced an enormous increase of proselytes in the Roman world, it had to make considerable efforts to reconcile precepts, which were obviously relevant solely to people in very humble stations of life, with the conditions of life in a society embracing the rich and the powerful. Socialism in its turn is now beginning to enter this phase.

. . . As noted earlier, although we shall have occasion to examine at some length the logical value of certain concepts, we must guard against thinking that the logical value of a concept has much practical importance. In our enquiry, we are working rather like a grammarian studying the structure and form of Homer's verses. The morphology of Homer's poetry has fundamentally little or no connection with its beauty which has given delight to men generation after generation, for reasons quite unrelated to the poet's usage of this or that verbal form.

. . . One of the most widespread sophistries is that which seeks to prove the experimental and logical reality of certain beliefs, offering as proof that they are good and useful for men. This last proposition may be true, but it has logically nothing to do with the first. It was useful for the Greeks to consult the Delphic oracle when they wished to found a colony, but this neither proves the existence of Apollo nor that he gave oracles. In reality, there was collocated at Delphi a mass of information enabling Apollo's priestess to give well-founded advice in the matter of setting up a colony. The origin of the sophistry under discussion lies in a concept which, in another context, has led some people to imagine that science could replace religion, reckoning that what is scientifically true may be, of itself, useful to man. This identification of the 'true' with the 'useful' being established, two different kinds of conclusion are drawn from it.

1. Since what is useful is scientifically true, once we have proved the utility of a thing, we have also proved that it is verified by experience and logic. This is the sophistry we have just referred to.

2. Since only that which is true scientifically is useful, everything which cannot be proved by logic and experience is harmful to man. As it is of the very essence of religion that it is beyond experimental proof, then all religion therefore is harmful. Those who argue thus succumb to the rambling errors of the philosophers of the eighteenth century and of the 'materialists' of our own day.

This need for identifying the non-real and the real is strong in human beings; and as the non-real is sometimes useful, it follows that even those who are perfectly aware that this identity does not exist, are obliged to speak as if they believe it does exist so as not to run counter to and damage sentiments and attitudes which are useful to society. Other people in these circumstances end up by deceiving themselves, their notion being, more or less explicitly, that it would be useful if a certain thing were scientifically true: consequently it must be accepted as such. This is the state of mind in which certain educated and intelligent marxists find themselves at the present time in regard to the theory of value. From the logical viewpoint, they are certainly wrong; from the viewpoint of practical utility to their cause, they are probably right.* The main thing is not to misuse something which, within certain limits, may be beneficial to mankind. And it is above all necessary to understand that in this respect there are great differences between one man and another, that what moves some people in no way persuades other people, and that what—in certain circumstances—acts strongly on one type of person acts feebly or not at all on another type. Studies in mass-psychology offer examples of this last fact, the incidence of which is general.

2. PERSISTENCE OF BASIC SENTIMENTS†

The hard core of sentiments persists; the form in which they are expressed may be extremely variable. One of the difficulties facing social science is precisely that of recognising this common hard core, hidded under different forms. It is like having to deal with the same proposition written in different languages. In both cases a translation is necessary.

Institutions and doctrines which in appearance are strikingly different

---

* Cf. *Manuel*, p. 150 below; *Treatise*, §§401 and 843–4, pp. 207, 216 below; and *Trasformazione*, p. 300 below.

† Vol. I, Chapter 2, pp. 132–4.

and even antagonistic to one another may have at bottom the same origin. In former times, the same sentiment which, for some men, took the form of stoicism, with others took the form of christianity. Some modern writers, rectifying the errors of their late eighteenth-century predecessors, have made it appear that the Emperor Julian was far from being a free-thinker, and that fundamentally his revival of paganism was an attempt to create a rival sect to christianity. All unwitting, he was subject to the same mystical influences which found expression in the cult of Mithras, in christianity and in other doctrines. . . . In our own day, a similar mystical and ascetic sentiment is to be found in certain manifestations of socialism, in the propaganda of the total abstainers, of the vegetarians, and of those rigid censors who will not allow their fellow citizens to read erotic literature unless *librorum quaerendorum causa*. It is evident in the lucubrations of those people whose enormous capacity for pity is exercised exclusively on behalf of delinquents and systematically withheld from their victims.

3. UNDULATORY FORM OF SOCIAL PHENOMENA*

The great currents which carry men along, and which are revealed to us through the concepts and opinions dominant in a given period, and through the state of mind and the behaviour of individuals and groups, these currents are not uniform. They vary considerably in intensity and present great differences from one period to another. For reasons partly known and partly unknown, but some of which seem to be connected with the psychological nature of man, the moral and religious movement—like the economic movement—is rhythmical. The rhythm of this latter movement produces economic crises which, in our day, have been carefully studied and are now fairly well understood. The rhythm of the moral and religious movement, on the other hand, often passes unperceived. And yet one has only to traverse history to recognise it very distinctly. We see, for example, that in the self-same country many periods of faith and unbelief succeed one another repeatedly. The movement sometimes attains considerable dimensions; it is then noted by all historians. But more often than not they see in it only one particular fact, whereas in effect it is a manifestation of the general law of rhythm.

It is because social movement takes an undulatory form that it is difficult to predict, from the evidence of the past, the future direction of this movement. You find a certain characteristic which, in literature, in morality, in law, is more and more accentuated as time passes; you would be wrong to conclude therefrom that this movement will continue indefinitely and that the society concerned will keep moving towards a certain objective. A reaction against the prevailing trend may well be in the offing, and the emergence of a movement in a contrary direction may not be long delayed. Furthermore, when a movement is going to change direction, it does not usually start by diminishing in intensity, which would facilitate prediction;

* Vol. I, Introduction, pp. 30–2.

on the contrary, it often happens that the movement attains its maximum intensity on the very eve of a change of direction.

All the scholars who have studied Roman history have remarked on the great oscillation from unbelief under the Republic to credulity under the Late Empire. Friedländer has observed that unbelief scarcely affects any save in high society. This observation is of universal relevance and can be applied generally. Such movements are felt principally in the higher classes of society and affect much less the lower classes; even so these eventually experience the effects of them. . . .*

Renan saw the religious movement very clearly as including philosophical doctrines such as stoicism, and ending finally in the triumph of one of the competing religions. The writings of pagan philosophers often contain 'christian' thoughts, but no direct borrowing is involved here. It is simply a matter of similarity of form among the ideas common to men at that time. The religion which triumphed is thus revealed to us as a synthesis and culmination of the general movement in ideas and sentiments. Moreover, to succeed it had to modify itself profoundly and to take over many features of its rivals.

4. ARISTOCRACIES; CIRCULATION OF ELITES; SPOLIATION

(i) Aristocracy†

The curve of the distribution of wealth in western societies varies very little from one period to another. What has been called the 'social pyramid' is, in reality, a sort of upturned top. The figure here gives an idea of it. The rich occupy the summit, the poor the base. Only the section A–B–C–G–F is at all known to us, thanks to statistical data. The section A–D–E–F is purely conjectural. We have adopted the form of it given here from Otto Ammon whose suggestion seems probable enough.

The form of the curve is not due to chance, of that we may be certain. It probably relates to the distribution of the physiological and psychological characteristics of human beings. On the other hand, it can partly be associated with theories of pure economics; that is to say, with human choices (these choices being in strict relationship with physiological and psychological characteristics), and to the obstacles encountered by production.

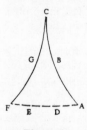

Figure 6

If we imagine men as disposed in strata according to their wealth, the whole figure represents the exterior form of the social organism. As we have just said, this form hardly changes; on average and over a short period it may in fact be supposed to be well-nigh constant. But the molecules composing the social aggregate are not

---

* Here Pareto cites Gibbon's description (in chapter 15 of *The Decline and Fall of the Roman Empire*) of the effects on the masses of the rejection of belief in the gods by the superior classes.

† Vol. I, Introduction, pp. 6–8.

stationary. Some individuals are growing rich, others are growing poor. Movements of an appreciable extent are therefore taking place within the social organism, which in this respect resembles a living organism. In a living organism the circulation of the blood carries along certain molecules in rapid motion; the processes of assimilation and secretion are incessantly changing the molecules composing the tissues, but the exterior form of the organism, of an adult animal for example, undergoes only insignificant changes.

Supposing men to be disposed by strata according to other characteristics, for example, by intelligence, by aptitude for mathematics, by musical, poetic and literary talents, by moral characteristics and so on, we shall probably get curves whose forms are more or less similar to that which we have just found by ordering men according to the distribution of wealth. This wealth-curve results from a large number of characteristics, good or bad as it may be, which taken together are favourable to the success of the individual who seeks wealth or, having acquired it, conserves it.

The same individuals do not occupy the same positions in the same figures which hypothetically we have just traced. In fact it would clearly be absurd to assert that the individuals occupying the upper strata in a figure representing the distribution of mathematical or poetic genius would be the same as those occupying the upper strata in the figure representing the distribution of wealth. This different distribution in relation to moral qualities (or those regarded as such), and in relation to wealth, has given rise to endless denunciations. Yet it is wholly understandable. The qualities, for example, of a St Francis of Assisi, are quite different from those of a Krupp. People who buy steel cannon need a Krupp, not a St Francis.

But if human beings are disposed according to the degree of their influence and political and social power, then it will be found that in most societies, to some extent at least, the same men will occupy the same position in a figure relating to influence and power as in our figure representing the distribution of wealth. The classes called 'superior' are also generally the richest.

These classes constitute an elite, an aristocracy (in the etymological sense of ἄριστος, *the best*). So long as the social equilibrium is stable, the majority of the individuals composing these classes appear highly endowed with certain qualities—good or bad as may be—which guarantee power.

A fact of extreme importance for social physiology is that aristocracies do not last. They are all subject to a more or less rapid decline. We do not have to go into the reasons for this here; it is enough to note the existence of this fact, not only in regard to elites perpetuated by heredity, but also—albeit to a lesser degree—in regard to elites which are recruited by co-option.

(ii) Circulation of elites*

War is a powerful cause of the extinction of military elites. This has always been realised, and some even have been inclined to see in war the only

---

* Vol. I, Introduction, pp. 9–15, 34–41.

cause of the disappearance of elites. But this is not the case. Even in the depths of the most profound peace, the movement of the circulation of elites continues; even the elites which suffer no loss through war disappear and often very quickly. It is not only a question of aristocracies' being extinguished through the excess of deaths over births, but also of degeneracy in the elements composing them. Hence aristocracies can subsist only by the elimination of these elements and the adhesion of new ones. Here is involved a process similar to that observed in the living animal, which survives only by eliminating certain elements and assimilating others to replace them. If this circulation is halted, the animal is destroyed: it dies. The same applies to the social elite. If its destruction may be slower, it is none the less sure.

Merely a slowing down of this circulation may have the effect of considerably increasing the number of degenerate elements within the classes still possessing power, and—by contrast—of increasing the number of elements of superior quality within the subject classes. In such case, the social equilibrium becomes unstable; the least shock to it from within or without destroys it. A revolution or a conquest leads to the overturning of everything, bringing to power a new elite and establishing a new equilibrium which will remain stable for a longer or shorter period.

Ammon and Lapouge in their writings go too far when they séek to give us the anthropological characteristics of these elites, dealing with them as eugenic groups and identifying them in particular with the dolichocephalous fair-haired races. At present, this point remains obscure and much more research will be necessary before it will be possible to decide whether the psychic qualities of elites are indicated by external, anthropometric characteristics, and what precisely these characteristics are.

For contemporary European societies, conquest by foreign eugenic groups has been of no significance since the last great barbarian invasions, and it no longer exists as a factor in the European social organism. But there is nothing to indicate that it cannot appear again in the future. If European societies were to model themselves on the ideal dear to the humanitarians, if they should go so far as to inhibit selection, to favour systematically the weak, the vicious, the idle, the ill adapted—the 'small and humble' as they are termed by our philanthropists—at the expense of the strong, the energetic who constitute the elite, then a new conquest by new 'barbarians' would by no means be impossible.

At the present time in our societies, the adhesion of the new elements indispensable to the subsistence of the elite comes from the lower classes and principally from the rural classes. These are the crucible in which are being formed, in the dark, the future elites. They are the roots of a plant the flower of which is the elite. The flower droops and withers, but it is soon replaced by another if the roots are healthy.

The fact is certain: the reasons for it are still not clearly understood. However, it seems highly probable that the rigorous selection occurring in the lower classes, especially in regard to children, has a significant effect. The rich classes have few children and almost all of them survive; the poorer classes have many children and lose a great number of those who are not particularly robust and well equipped for life. Similarly we find that highly bred plants and animals are very delicate in comparison with ordinary breeds. Why are Angora cats much more delicate animals than alley cats? Because they are surrounded by constant attention; care is taken to save all the kittens in an Angora mother's litter, whereas of the litter of a wretched starved alley cat only the kittens who are in very good health survive. The care taken with wheat over many centuries has made this plant unable to withstand the competitition of natural life; wild wheat does not exist.

The high-minded people who would persuade the rich classes in our societies to have many children, the humanitarians who—wishing (for good reasons) to avoid certain modes of selection—give no thought to replacing them by others, are working without realising it for the enfeeblement of the race, for its degeneracy. If the rich classes in our societies had many children, it is probable they would save almost all of them, even the sickliest and the least gifted. This would increase further the degenerate elements in the upper classes and delay the emergence of the elite coming from the lower classes. If selection no longer exerted its influence on the lower classes, these would cease to produce elites and the quality-level of society would fall considerably.

It is less easy to explain why, amongst the lower classes, it is especially the rural classes which seem to have the privilege of producing choice individuals. There are a good many analogous phenomena in regard to plants and animals which also, for all that they are well known, remain inexplicable. It is essential to use Riga flax seed to produce linen of a certain quality. The corn seed which, cultivated in Tuscany, produces the straw called Florence, comes from the Romagna and degenerates rapidly. The most beautiful hyacinth bulbs are grown in Holland and degenerate in other countries.

It may be that the simple fact that the rural classes develop their muscles and let their brains rest has the precise effect of producing among them individuals who can let their muscles rest and work excessively with their brains. At all events, rural life seems eminently suitable for producing the reserves for the devouring, excessively active life of the great centres of civilisation.

There are different and somewhat obscure reasons for the decadence of the elites which recruit by co-option or some other similar method. The example which most readily comes to mind in this connection is that of the catholic clergy. What a profound decadence this elite underwent between the ninth and eighteenth centuries! Heredity plays no part in this phenomenon. The decadence originates from the fact that the elite, in recruiting itself, chose subjects of increasingly mediocre calibre. This is partly due to this elite's gradually losing sight of its ideal, being less and less sustained by faith and the spirit of sacrifice; and partly also to external circumstances: the emergence of other elites and their attracting choice individuals away from the elite in decadence. The proportion of these choice subjects to the rest of the population varies very little, so that one social sector's gain is another's loss. If commerce, industry, administration and so forth offer them a large outlet, they will necessarily be rare in any other elite, for example in the clergy.

This phenomenon of new elites which, through an incessant movement of circulation, rise up from the lower strata of society, mount up to the higher strata, flourish there, and then fall into decadence, are annihilated and disappear—this is one of the motive forces of history, and it is essential to give it its due weight if we are to understand great social movements.

Very often the existence of this objective phenomenon is obscured by our passions and prejudices, and the awareness we have of it differs considerably from the reality.

. . . The circulatory movement which carries to the summit elites born in the lower strata, and leads to the decline and disappearance of the elites in power, is very often concealed by several factors. As it is in general a fairly slow movement, it is only by studying history over a long period of time— for several centuries, for example—that one can perceive the general direction and the main lines of this movement. The contemporary observer who brings his gaze to bear only on a short period of time perceives only the secondary circumstances. He sees the rivalry of castes, the oppression of tyrants, popular uprisings, liberal protests, aristocracies, theocracies and ochlocracies*; but the general phenomenon, of which these are but particular aspects, often wholly escapes him. Amongst the illusions thus produced are some which, because very common, deserve to be singled out for attention.

It is very difficult to avoid the influence of sentiment in dealing with a concrete example; to prevent our discussion from being clouded by this influence, let us deal with the matter in an abstract way. Let A be the elite in power, B the social element seeking to drive it from power and to replace it, and C the rest of the population, comprising the incompetent, those lacking energy, character and intelligence: in short, that section of society which remains when the elites are subtracted. A and B are the leaders, counting on C to provide them with partisans, with instruments. The C on their own would be impotent: an army without commanders. They become important only if guided by the A or B. Very often—in fact almost always—it is the B who put themselves at the head of the C, the A reposing in a false security or despising the C. Moreover, it is the B who are best able to lure the C for the simple reason that, not having power, their inducements are long-dated. It sometimes happens, however, that the A endeavour to get the better of the B, seeking to content the C with apparent concessions without going too far in the direction of real concessions. If the B gradually take the place of the A by slow infiltration, if the movement of social circulation is not interrupted, the C become deprived of the leaders capable of spurring them to revolt, and there ensues a period of prosperity. The A usually strive to resist this infiltration, but their resistance may be ineffective and amount in the end only to an inconsequent resentment. But if the resistance of the A is effective, the B can wrest the position from them only by open conflict, with the help of the C. If they succeed and get into power, a new challenging elite, D, will be formed and

* I.e., mob-rule.

will play the same role vis-à-vis the B as the B played vis-à-vis the A, and so on.

Most historians do not perceive this movement. They describe the phenomenon as if it were the struggle of an aristocracy or an oligarchy, always the same, against a people, likewise always the same. But in fact:

1. What is involved is the struggle between one aristocracy and another;
2. The aristocracy in power changes constantly, that of today being replaced, after a certain lapse of time, by its adversary.

When the B attain power, replacing the A elite in full decadence, it is generally observed that a period of great prosperity follows. Certain historians ascribe all the merit of this to the 'people', that is, to the C. Such truth as there is in this observation subsists only in the fact that the lower classes produce new elites. So far as these lower classes themselves are concerned, they are incapable of ruling; ochlocracy has never resulted in anything save disaster.

But more significant than the illusion of those who see things from afar is that of those who are involved in the movement and take an active part in it. Many of the B genuinely believe that they are pursuing, not a personal advantage for themselves and their class, but an advantage for the C, and that they are simply struggling for what they call justice, liberty, humanity. This illusion operates also on the A; many among them betray the interests of their class, believing they are fighting for the realisation of these fine principles all to help the unfortunate C, whereas in reality the sole effect of their action is to help the B to attain power only to fasten on the C a yoke which may often be more severe than that of the A. Those who finally understand that this is the outcome sometimes make accusations of hypocrisy against the B or the A—as the case may be—who claimed they were guided solely by the desire of helping the C. But on the whole, this accusation of hypocrisy is ill-founded, for many of the B as well as the A are irreproachable in point of sincerity.

A sign which almost invariably presages the decadence of an aristocracy is the intrusion of humanitarian feelings and of affected sentimentalising which render the aristocracy incapable of defending its position. Violence, we should note, is not to be confused with force. Often enough one observes cases in which individuals and classes which have lost the force to maintain themselves in power make themselves more and more hated because of their outbursts of random violence. The strong man strikes only when it is absolutely necessary, and then nothing stops him. Trajan was strong, not violent: Caligula was violent, not strong.

When a living creature loses the sentiments which, in given circumstances, are necessary to it in order to maintain the struggle for life, this is a sign certain of degeneration, for the absence of these sentiments will, sooner or later, entail the extinction of the species. The living creature which shrinks from giving blow for blow and from shedding its adversary's blood thereby puts itself at the mercy of this adversary. The sheep has always found a wolf to devour it; if it now escapes this peril, it is only because man reserves it for his own prey. Any people which has horror of blood to the point of not knowing how to defend itself will sooner or later become the prey of some bellicose people or other. There is not perhaps on this globe a single foot of ground which has not been conquered by the sword at some time or other, and where the people occupying it have not maintained themselves on it by force. If the Negroes were stronger than the Europeans, Europe would be partitioned by the Negroes and not Africa by the Europeans. The 'right', claimed by people who bestow on themselves the title of 'civilised' to conquer other peoples, whom it pleases them to call 'uncivilised', is altogether ridiculous, or rather, this right is nothing other than force. For as long as the Europeans are stronger than the Chinese, they will impose their will on them; but if the Chinese should become stronger than the Europeans, then the roles would be reversed, and it is highly probable that humanitarian sentiments could never be opposed with any effectiveness to an army.

In the same way, for right or law to have reality in a society, force is necessary. Whether developed spontaneously or whether the work of a minority, law and order cannot be imposed on dissidents save by force. The utility of certain institutions, the sentiments they inspire, prepare the ground for their establishment, but for them to become established fact it is quite obvious that those desiring these institutions must have the power to impose them on those who do not desire them. Anton Menger fancies he proves that our present law needs to be changed because it 'rests almost exclusively on traditional relationships based on force'; but such is the characteristic of all laws that have ever existed, and if the law desired by Menger ever becomes reality, this will only be because he, in his turn, will have at his disposal the force to make it so; if he hasn't, then it will always remain a dream. 'Right' and 'law' originated in the force of isolated individuals; they are now maintained by the force of the community; but it is still force.

In considering successful changes of institutions, persuasion should not, as is so often the case, be contrasted with force. Persuasion is but a means for procuring force. No one has ever persuaded all the members of a society without exception; to ensure success only a section of the individuals in a society need to be persuaded: the section which has the force, either because it is the most numerous or for some quite different reason. It is by force that social institutions are established, and it is by force that they are maintained.

Any elite which is not prepared to join in battle to defend its positions is in full decadence, and all that is left to it is to give way to another elite having the virile qualities it lacks. It is pure day-dreaming to imagine that the humanitarian principles it may have proclaimed will be applied to it: its vanquishers will stun it with the implacable cry, *Vae Victis*. The knife of the guillotine was being sharpened in the shadows when, at the end of the eighteenth century, the ruling classes in France were engrossed in developing their 'sensibility'. This idle and frivolous society, living like a parasite off the country, discoursed at its elegant supper parties of delivering the world from superstition and of crushing *l'Infâme*, all unsuspecting that it was itself going to be crushed.

Parallel with the phenomenon of the succession of elites, another of great importance is observable among civilised peoples. The production of economic goods goes on increasing, thanks mainly to the growth of personal capital, the average amount of which per head is one of the surest indices of civilisation and progress. Material well-being is thus expanding more and more. On the other hand, foreign and civil wars, becoming less and less lucrative as an industry, are diminishing in number and intensity. In consequence, habits are growing softer and morals becoming purer. Outside the vain agitations of politicians, there is being accomplished what G. de Molinari has called 'the silent revolution'—the slow transformation and improvement of social conditions. This movement is impeded, sometimes halted, by the squanderings of state socialism and by protectionist legislation of all kinds, but it is not the less real for that, and all the statistics of the most civilised peoples bear traces of it.

Having noted the importance in history of the succession of elites, we must not fall into the kind of error which is only too common, and claim that all is explained by this single cause. Social evolution is extremely complex; we can identify in it several main currents, but to seek to reduce them to one is a rash enterprise, at least for the present. For the time being, what is necessary is to study these great classes of phenomena and endeavour to discover their relationships.

(iii) Spoliation*

We must again stress the point . . . that historians often see these events only through the veil of their passions and prejudices, depicting to us as a battle for liberty what is a straightforward struggle between two competing elites. They believe—and wish us to share the belief—that the elite which in reality is seeking to get hold of power to use it and misuse it in just the same way as the elite it is opposing, is moved only by pure love of its fellow men; or, if we prefer the phraseology of our day, by desire for the well-being of the 'small and humble'. It is only when they seek to join issue with certain adversaries of theirs in historical and political debate that such historians alight on the truth, at least so far as these adversaries are concerned. Thus Taine produces the declamations of the Jacobins and shows us the greedy interests lurking beneath them. Likewise Jan Jensen shows us theological dissensions which are no more than very transparent veils cloaking exclusively worldly interests. His work is a remarkable description of how new elites, when they achieve power, deal with their allies of the day before, the 'small and humble', who discover that they have merely exchanged yokes. The socialists of our own day have clearly perceived that the revolution at the end of the eighteenth century led merely to the bourgeoisie's taking the place of the old elite. They exaggerate a good deal the burden of oppression imposed by the new masters, but they do sincerely believe that a new elite of politicians will stand by their promises better than those which have come and gone up to the present day. All revolutionaries proclaim, in turn, that previous revolutions have ultimately ended up by deceiving the people; it is their revolution alone which is the *true* revolution. 'All previous historical movements,' declared the *Communist*

---

* Vol. I, Introduction, pp. 58–62.

Manifesto of 1848, 'were movements of minorities or in the interest of minorities. The proletarian movement is the self-conscious, independent movement of the immense majority, in the interest of the immense majority.' Unfortunately this *true* revolution, which is to bring men an unmixed happiness, is only a deceptive mirage that never becomes a reality. It is akin to the golden age of the millenarians: for ever awaited, it is for ever lost in the mists of the future, for ever eluding its devotees just when they think they have it.

Socialism is motivated by certain factors, some of which are present in almost all classes of society, while others differ according to the classes.

Among the first we should reckon the sentiments which move men to sympathise with the troubles and misfortunes of others, and to seek a remedy for them. This sentiment is one of the worthiest and most useful to society; indeed, it is the very cement of society.

Today almost everyone pays court to the socialists because they have become powerful. But it is not very long ago that many people were reckoning them to be scarcely better than criminals. Such an attitude could not be more false. So far, the socialists have certainly not been morally inferior to the members of the 'bourgeois' parties, especially of those parties which have used legislation to exact tribute from other citizens and which constitute what one may term 'bourgeois socialism'. If the 'bourgeois' were being animated by the same spirit of abnegation and sacrifice for their class as the socialists are for theirs, socialism would be far from being as menacing as it actually is. The presence in its ranks of the new elite is attested precisely by the moral qualities displayed by its adepts and which have enabled them to emerge victorious from the bitter test of numerous persecutions.

The sentiment of benevolence men have for their fellows, and without which society probably could not exist, is in no way incompatible with the principle of the class struggle. Even the most energetic defence of one's own rights may perfectly well be allied to a respect for the rights of others. Each class, if it wishes to avoid being oppressed, must have the force to defend its interests, but this does not at all imply that it must aim at oppressing other classes. On the contrary, it should be able to learn from experience that one of the best ways of defending these interests is in fact to take account, with justice, equity and even benevolence, of the interests of others.

Unfortunately, this sentiment of benevolence is not always very enlightened. Those who have it at times resemble the good women who crowd round a sick friend, each recommending a remedy. Their desire to be useful to the unfortunate is beyond question; it is only the efficacy of the remedies which is doubtful. How ever great their devoted concern for him, this cannot supply them with the medical knowledge they lack. When they find themselves in like-minded company, all of them advocating their own special nostrums, they usually end up by choosing a remedy almost at random, because really 'one must do *something*', and the ailing victim is lucky if his malady does not grow worse.

5. SOCIALISM AS A PARTICULAR CASE OF SPOLIATION*

Societies which admit private property—which is to say almost all and every society known up to the present—offer men two essentially different ways of acquiring wealth. One is by producing it directly or indirectly through the work and services of the capital they possess. The other is by acquiring the wealth thus produced by others. These two methods have at all times been employed, and it would be rash to believe that they will cease to be employed in the foreseeable future. But because the second method is generally under moral reproof, people willingly close their eyes to its employment, holding it to be something sporadic and incidental. In fact it is a general and enduring phenomenon.

Social movements generally follow the line of least resistance. The direct production of economic goods is often a very laborious process, whereas appropriating these goods produced by others is sometimes a very easy matter. It has become considerably more easy ever since the idea took root of accomplishing the spoliation, not by transgressing the law, but by using the law. In order to save, to refrain from consuming all he earns, an individual has to have a certain degree of control over himself. Tilling a field to produce corn is an arduous labour; lurking at the corner for a passer-by to rob is a dangerous venture. On the other hand, going along to the polling station to vote is a very easy business, and if by so doing one can procure food and shelter, then everybody—especially the unfit, the incompetent and the idle—will rush to do it.

From another point of view, it may be said that of the two procedures by which the property of others can be appropriated, i.e., directly by violence or fraud or indirectly by the help of the public powers, the second is much less harmful to social well-being than the first. It is a refinement and improvement on fraud and violence, just as the rearing of domestic animals is a refinement and improvement on hunting wild animals. The socialists who are willing, when collectivising the means of production, to grant fair compensation for expropriation of property to the existing owners, cannot be accused of seeking to employ either of these two procedures. Other socialists, who would expropriate gradually or immediately without indemnifying the existing possessors, clearly intend to appeal to the second procedure, but they cannot truly be represented, as some legislators have done, as wishing to have recourse to the first. It is solely by means of the law that the socialists and communists seek to alter the distribution of wealth, to give to some what they take away from others. In this sense, their systems do not in any way differ from the various protectionist systems. These latter, properly speaking, represent the socialism of the entrepreneurs and the capitalists.

Classical political economy has only incidentally, and in order to condemn it, been concerned with appropriation occurring with the assistance of the law. Every science necessarily has to limit its field of enquiry. In this respect there is nothing to be said against the method used by

---

* Vol. I, Chapter 2, pp. 115–22, 128–9.

political economy. But after separating, by analysis, the various parts of a real phenomenon in order to study them in isolation, there must then be a synthesis, bringing them together again to obtain an idea of reality. Political economy may not study appropriation by aid of the law, but this study must be undertaken by some other science if we wish to understand the concrete phenomenon. So important a part of it cannot be neglected.

The class struggle, to which Marx has specially drawn attention, is a real factor, the tokens of which are to be found on every page of history. But the struggle is not confined only to two classes: the proletariat and the capitalist; it occurs between an infinite number of groups with different interests, and above all between the elites contending for power. The existence of these groups may vary in duration, they may be based on permanent or more or less temporary characteristics. In most savage peoples, and perhaps in all, sex determines two of these groups. The oppression of which the proletariat complains, or had cause to complain of, is as nothing in comparison with that which the women of the Australian aborigines suffer. Characteristics to a greater or lesser degree real— nationality, religion, race, language, etc.—may give rise to these groups. In our own day the struggle of the Czechs and the Germans in Bohemia is more intense than that of the proletariat and the capitalists in England. People who are engaged in the same occupation naturally tend to group together. In many countries, the makers of sugar have banded together to exact tribute from their fellow citizens. This phenomenon is similar to that occurring in former times when armed bands levied tribute from the peasants, and it is only a variant of the same thing. The shipowners combine to get shipping bounties; the retailers act in concert to crush the big shops by taxes; fixed stallholders cabal to prevent or hamper itinerant street-sellers; business men in one region unite to do down those of another region; 'organised' workers to deprive 'non-organised' workers of jobs; the workers of one country to exclude from the 'national market' the workers of another country; the workers of one town to keep out the workers of another. In Italy the shoemakers in certain towns have attempted, by imposing municipal import duties, to keep out the footware of shoe-makers living outside these towns.

Past history and contemporary observation show us men at all times and in all places divided into groups, each of which generally procures economic goods for itself partly by producing them directly and partly by despoiling other groups, who despoil it in their turn. These activities inter-act in a thousand ways and their direct and indirect effects are extremely varied. One could draw up a sort of balance sheet for each group. For example, some manufacturers produce merchandise of a certain type; through protective duties on the materials they use, they pay tribute which goes to other groups of manufacturers, to farmers, merchants, etc. Other tribute is exacted from them by the circulation of paper-money or by government measures of monetary policy; they pay tribute money to politicians, laying out cash to maintain certain prejudices which they judge favourable to their interests. In compensation they receive tribute from the consumers in the shape of protective duties on foreign products which might compete with theirs, and from the workers through the issuing of paper-money or through measures taken by the government to prevent the workers from freely negotiating the sale of their labour. They levy toll on the tax payer by getting favourable terms in supplying government departments, etc. With certain industrial groups, it is easy to see to which side the balance tips; with others it is difficult to know whether, on balance, they are gainers or losers by this system—one which, moreover, entails an enormous destruction of wealth for society in general. Cases are by no means rare in which those concerned are deceived into thinking that they end up on the right side in the balance of gains and losses produced by this system of mutual spoliation. For certain groups state socialism may well bring with it cruel disillusion.

There are groups for which the question is simpler, for example, those which produce nothing of importance, pay no tribute, or almost none, but which simply receive tribute. Other groups, the most numerous and important, directly produce goods and very often pay tribute without getting any in return or only to an insignificant degree. Such has often been the fate of the workers; such also is the fate which certain regimes would reserve in time to come for the entrepreneurs and the capitalists.

Generally, for individuals to be able to constitute a group and to win for themselves the possessions of others, certain conditions are necessary.

1. The members of the group must not be too widely dispersed; they must have an easily recognisable common characteristic, such as the same race, the same religion, the same occupation, and so forth. Herein lies one of the most effective reasons why the consumers can scarcely ever organise themselves successfully to resist the producer combines. For example, in our societies, we are all to a greater or lesser extent consumers of cloth and clothing, while there is only a very small number among us engaged in making cloth and clothing. The fact that we all wear clothes cannot serve to determine a group, whereas the fact of making cloth and clothes can perfectly well determine a group.

2. Centuries of civilisation have impressed on man's mind the sentiment that he should refrain from seizing the goods of others. This sentiment must not be directly impugned, so an indirect method has to be employed for appropriating these goods, and some reason must be found to justify it. But there is never any very great difficulty on this point, for the most paltry reasons find acceptance when they serve powerful interests or minister to fixed inclinations. Since most men make convictions of their interests, one is preaching to the converted. A hollow phraseology, empty, high-sounding, emotional formulas, abstract and repetitive phrases, vague and airy expressions with never a firm meaning—this is all that men ask for when they are looking, not for truth, which they wouldn't know what to do with, but only for a justification of actions which are advantageous or simply agreeable to them. There are periods, like the end of the eighteenth century in France and the present epoch, in which the despoiled themselves give reasons for justifying and increasing spoliation by their ethical declamations about 'sensibility', 'solidarity', etc., etc.

. . . It is a curious circumstance, and one meriting attention, that men are often observed to act with much more energy in appropriating the property of others than in defending their own. As we have noted elsewhere [*Cours*, §1047; p. 115 above] if, in a nation of thirty million, it is proposed to levy one franc per annum on each citizen and to distribute the total to thirty individuals, these latter will work night and day for the success of this proposal, while it will be difficult to get the others to bestir themselves sufficiently to oppose the proposal, because, after all, it is only one franc! Another example: it is proposed to establish a 'minimum salary' for the employees of a public administration. The people who in consequence of this measure will receive an increase of salary are perfectly well aware of the advantage this proposal has for them. They and their friends will exert themselves all they can for the success of the candidates who promise to provide them with this manna. As for the people who are going to have to pay for this salary increase, each of them has great difficulties in working out what this is going to cost him in tax, and if he manages to assess it, the amount seems of small significance. In most cases, he doesn't even think about it. He follows discussions about this measure with an inattentive ear, as if it were something which in no way affected him. One of the hardest things to get tax payers to understand is that ten times one franc makes ten francs. Provided the tax increases occur gradually, they can reach a total amount which would have provoked explosions of wrath had they been levied at one swoop.

Spoliation therefore seldom meets with a really effective resistance from the despoiled. What sometimes stops it is the destruction of wealth consequent upon it, which may entail the ruin of the country. History shows us that more than once spoliation has finished by killing the goose that lays the golden eggs.

The behaviour of these groups, each of which tries to get hold of the goods produced by others, would in all probability survive radical changes in the social organisation, like, for example, the abolition of private property. But experience suggests that private property inevitably emerges again after its destruction. However perfect the profoundly thought-out rules for the distribution of goods which have to be consumed, these rules will have to be applied by human beings, and their conduct will reflect their qualities and their defects. If today there are arbiters who always decide against persons belonging to a certain class and in favour of persons belonging to certain other classes, there will very likely be 'distributors' in this society of tomorrow who will share out the loaf in such a way as to give a very little piece to A and a very big piece to B.

III

Manuel d'Economie Politique (1909)

1. LOGICAL AND NON-LOGICAL ACTIONS DISTINGUISHED*

(2) To put some order in the infinite variety of human behaviour we have to study, it will be useful to classify the variations according to certain categories. Two come immediately to mind. A well-bred man enters a drawing-room; he removes his hat, utters certain words and makes certain gestures. If we ask him why he does this, his only reply will be: because it is customary. He observes a similar pattern of actions in certain matters of much greater importance. If he is a Roman Catholic and attends mass, he will perform certain actions 'because that is what one has to do'. He will justify very many other, different actions by saying that 'morality requires it'.

But let us suppose that this same individual is in his office, engaged in buying—let us say—a large quantity of grain. He will no longer say that he is doing such-and-such because that is the custom. His purchasing of grain will be the last stage in a process of logical reasoning based on certain data of experience. If these data were to change, the conclusions also would change, and it could happen that he would refrain from buying grain, or even sell it instead.

(3) By abstraction we can therefore distinguish: 1. non-logical behaviour; and 2. logical behaviour. We say 'by abstraction' because in actual behaviour the different categories are nearly always mixed, and a given action may to a large extent be non-logical while yet being to a smaller

---

* Chapter 2, §§2–4, 6, 9–19: The page references relate to the French edition of 1909, from which the translation has been made, not to the first, Italian, edition of 1906. The arabic numerals in curved brackets refer to the section numbers of the original.

extent logical; or vice-versa. For example, the behaviour of a speculator on the stock exchange is certainly logical. But it also depends, if only to a minor degree, on the character of the individual concerned; to this extent the behaviour has a non-logical element in it. It is a known fact that some speculators usually do business when the market is high, and others when it is low.

It must be clearly understood that 'non-logical' does not signify 'illogical'. A non-logical action may well be one which can be found, from the observation of facts and logic, highly suitable in adapting means to ends. But this adaptability has been obtained by a process other than that of logical reasoning. For example, it is known that the cells of bees have a pyramidal formation. With the minimum of surface—that is, with the smallest expense of wax—the cells have the maximum of volume—that is, they are able to contain the greatest possible amount of honey. Yet no one supposes that this is because the bees have solved a problem of maxima by syllogisms and mathematics. Their cell-construction is clearly a form of non-logical behaviour; yet, since the means employed are perfectly adapted to the end, their behaviour consequently is far from being illogical. The same observation holds good for a good deal of the behaviour of animals and human beings which is ordinarily called 'instinctive'.

(4) We must further note that human beings have a very marked tendency to regard as logical behaviour which is non-logical. A tendency of a similar kind induces them to animate and personify certain material objects and phenomena. These two tendencies are observable in ordinary speech which, preserving traces of the sentiments subsisting when the language was formed, personifies things and facts and represents them as the outcome of a logical will.

(6) ... Let A be a real fact and B another real fact; and let us assume that between the two of them there is a relationship of cause and effect or, to express it better, of interdependence. This we will call an *objective* relationship. In the human mind, there is a correspondence between this relationship and another, A'–B', which is properly a relationship between two mental concepts, whereas the A–B relationship is between two things. This A'–B' relationship we will term *subjective*.

If we find in the minds of men of a given society a certain A'–B' relationship, we can enquire: 1. What is the nature of this subjective relationship, whether the terms A' and B' have a precise meaning or not, and whether there is, or is not, a logical connection between them. 2. What is the objective relationship A–B which corresponds to this subjective relationship A'–B'. 3. How does this subjective relationship A'–B' originate and how is it determined. 4. What is the effect on society of such A'–B' relationships, whether they correspond to some objective thing A–B, or whether in fact they are entirely imaginary.

When A'–B' corresponds to A–B, the two phenomena develop in parallel. When this development becomes somewhat complex, it is termed a *theory*. This is true when in all its development A–B corresponds to A'–B' —that is to say, when theory and experience agree. There is not, nor can there be, any other criterion of scientific truth.

Moreover, identical facts may be explained by an infinite number of theories—all equally true, for all reproduce the facts in their explanation. It is in this sense that Poincaré is able to say that the moment a phenomenon is capable of a mechanical explanation, it is capable also of an infinity of explanations.

Almost invariably it is observable that establishing a theory amounts, so to speak, to passing a curve through a certain number of determined points. An infinity of curves can be projected to pass though these points in an infinite number of ways.

(9) . . . The objective phenomenon presents itself to our mind only in the form of a subjective phenomenon; hence it is the latter, not the former, which is the causation of human behaviour. For the objective phenomenon to be operative on human behaviour, it must first be transformed into a subjective phenomenon.* Hence the great importance to sociology of the study of subjective phenomena and their relationships with objective phenomena.

The relationships between subjective phenomena are seldom a faithful copy of the relationships subsisting between the corresponding objective phenomena. The following difference is very commonly to be found. Certain actions P . . . Q are performed under the influence of the circumstances of life; then, when thought is given to them, it is discovered—or believed to be discovered—that the actions P . . . Q share a common principle; and so it is imagined that these actions P . . . Q are the logical consequence of this principle. But in reality P . . . Q are not the consequence of the principle; rather it is the principle which is the consequence of P . . . Q. It is true that, when the principle is established, the actions R . . . s ensue as derivatives of it—so the disputed proposition is only partially false. The laws of language provide us with a good example. Grammar does not precede the formation of words: it follows after their formation. But, once established, the rules of grammar give rise to certain forms which then come to be attached to the existing forms.

To sum up: we distinguish two groups of actions. The first, P . . . Q, the most numerous and important, pre-exists the principle which seems to govern actions in this group. The second, R . . . s, which is subordinate and often of small importance, derives from the principle, or—in other words—it is an indirect consequence of the same causation which has directly produced P . . . Q.

(10) The phenomena A' and B' referred to in §6 [page opposite] do not always correspond to the real phenomena A and B. It very often happens that A' or B'—or even both of them—corresponds to nothing real and is an entirely imaginary entity. Moreover, the relationship between A' and B' may be logical only in appearance, not in reality. So there are varying cases which need to be differentiated.

(11) Let A be a real phenomenon, of which another phenomenon, B, also real, is the consequence. There is an objective relationship of cause and effect between A and B. If an individual has more or less roughly approximate notions of A and B, and supposing that he links these notions by a relationship of cause and effect, then he obtains a relationship A'–B'

---

* Cf. *Systèmes Socialistes*, above p. 124.

which is a more or less faithful image of the objective phenomenon. The relationships discovered by the scientist in the laboratory belong to this class.

(12) It may not be known that B is the consequence of A. It may on the contrary be thought of as the consequence of another real fact, C.

Figure 7

Alternatively, though B may be known to be the consequence of A, it may for some reason be desirable to think of B as the consequence of C. Scientific errors are of the first type, i.e., cases where it is not realised that B is the consequence of A. There will always be cases of this since man is subject to error. Examples of the second type—wherein B is deliberately made out to be the consequence of C, although its derivation from A is known—occur in *legal fictions*, in the arguments used by political parties in their efforts to get the better of one another, and in other similar circumstances. It is thus that the wolf in the fable reasons when he seeks to devour the lamb. Most of the arguments used to justify the imposition of taxes belong to this type. It is asserted that taxes B are motivated by certain principles of justice or by the general interest; but in fact B is connected—by a relationship of cause and effect—to A, which represents the interests of the dominant class. We can also at least partly associate the origin of casuistry with this type of rationalising.

(13) We have just now referred to three real factors: A, B and C. But in human speculation there very often intervene factors which are completely imaginary. One of these imaginary causative factors, M, may be put into a logical relationship with a real factor, B. This error—which is still common in the social sciences—was formerly prevalent in the physical sciences. Take, for instance, the question of the displacement of air contained in a tube connected with a vessel filled with water. The pressure of air on the surface of the water is fact A; the rise of the water up the tube is fact B. Now, at one time this fact was explained by another, and completely imaginary, fact, M—i.e., by 'nature's abhorrence of a vacuum', the logical consequence of which is B, the water's rising in the tube. At the beginning of the nineteenth century, an enormous number of biological facts was explained by 'vital force'. Similarly, contemporary sociologists explain and demonstrate an enormous number of things by the intermediation of the notion of 'progress'. 'Natural rights' have played, and continue to play, an important part in explaining social facts. For many people who have learned socialist theories parrot-fashion, 'capitalism' explains all and everything, and is the cause of each single evil in human society. Others speak of 'freeing the land'—although no one has ever seen this thing, 'free land'—and tell us that all the ills which afflict society were born on the day when 'man was separated from the means of production'. When was this day? Nobody knows the answer; perhaps it was when Pandora opened her box, or perchance in the time when animals talked and pigs had wings.

(14) When imaginary facts M are brought into play, then—since one's choice in the matter is free—it would seem that one should at least make the nexus between M and B logical. Yet this is not always the case, either because some people are resistant to logic, or because the intention is to

operate on sentiments. As a result the imaginary fact M is often made to relate to another imaginary fact, N, by means of a logical nexus or even by a non-logical nexus. We find numerous examples of this type of development in metaphysics and theology, and also in certain philosophical works, like Hegel's *Philosophy of Nature.* . . .

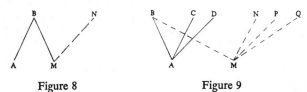

Figure 8   Figure 9

(15) If an objective relationship A–B coincides approximately with a subjective relationship A'–B' in someone's mind, this person will be able, by reasoning logically, to derive from A' other consequences, C', D' etc., which will be not too far removed from the real facts C, D, etc. But in the case where M is an imaginary fact or even a real fact different from A, if the objective relationship A–B corresponds to the subjective relationship M'–B' in someone's mind, then this person will, still reasoning logically, derive from it certain consequences N, P, Q, etc., which will be devoid of any reality. If he then compares his deductions with reality, assuming he is intent only on discovering the truth and is unmoved by any strong emotion, he will perceive that M is not the reason for B. So little by little, by experiment and by comparing his theoretical deductions with reality, he will modify the subjective relationship M–B' and replace it by another, A–B, which comes closer to reality.

(16) The experimental enquiries of the scientist belong to this type, together with many of the practical activities of men, including those studied by political economy. Actions of this kind are repeated a very great number of times in scientific enquiry, and conditions are made to vary so as to permit the examination of a large number of consequences of A or of M, attaining thereby an exact idea of objective relationships.

(17) On the other hand, people who rarely respond to the relationship A–B, or who consider it always in the same set of conditions, or let themselves be dominated by their sentiments, may have of the relationship A–B a partly imaginary notion, M–B', and sometimes a wholly imaginary notion, M–N.

(18) The theory of this first type of behaviour is essentially different from the theory of the second type. We will give only a few indications of the second type, since this Manual is primarily concerned with studying the first type.

We note that, in social life, this second type of behaviour is very widespread and of high importance. What are called morality and custom are entirely dependent on it. It is an indisputable fact that up to now no society has had a scientific or experimental morality. The efforts of modern thinkers to give morality a scientific or experimental basis have come to nothing. But even if their efforts had achieved their designed purpose, they would be of concern only to a very limited number of individuals, and would be ignored completely by the majority of men, indeed by almost all of them. From time to time, the anti-scientific, anti-experimental character of this or that custom is pointed out. While this may give rise to a good many books and articles on the subject, it cannot have the slightest influence on such customs; these can only be changed by quite different influences.

Certain phenomena exist termed *ethics* or *morals* which every one thinks he understands perfectly, and yet which no one has been able to define with any precision. They have hardly ever been studied from the purely objective viewpoint. All who have to do with them uphold some principle which they would like to impose on other people, esteeming it superior to any other principle. Hence they do not enquire about what the people of a given time and place have called 'moral'; their concern is limited. to what, in their view, must be understood by this term. Should they deign to consider some other morality, they conceive of it only in reference to their own preconceptions and confine themselves to comparing it with their own notion of morality, this being the model and measure for all others. There accordingly devolves from this comparison a certain number of implicit or explicit theories. The 'standard morality' has been considered as something absolute, revealed or imposed by God (according to most) or deriving from the nature of man (according to some). If there exist societies which do not observe this morality, it is because—so the argument runs—they do not know of it, and therefore missionaries have to teach it them and open the eyes of these unfortunates to the light of truth. Or philosophers must endeavour to remove the heavy veils which hang between weak mortals and knowledge of absolute *Truth*, absolute *Beauty*, absolute *Good*: words in common use though no one has ever understood what they signify or to what realities they correspond. Those who go into the subtleties of these matters perceive in the divers types of morality—some would add the divers types of religion—an effort by *Humanity* (another abstraction of the same sort as the foregoing, though a little less unintelligible) to attain to knowledge of the supreme *Good*, the supreme *Truth*.

Such ideas have been modified in our day, more perhaps in the form than in the substance, but at least to the extent that they approach a little nearer to reality. As a result, an evolutionist morality has developed. The idea of a 'standard' morality, however, has not been abandoned; it has simply been posited in terms of evolution, of which it is either the absolute or the provisional outcome. It is quite obvious to its advocates that this standard morality, as elaborated by them, is better than any which has preceded it. This superiority may be demonstrated, if desired, with the help of another very fine (and in our day very powerful) metaphysical entity: *Progress*, which ensures that each stage of evolution marks a better state than the preceding stage. Moreover, thanks to certain virtues it has, hidden but nonetheless efficacious, Progress is such that it prevents deterioration in the state achieved in a particular stage of evolution.

But in reality—and discarding all empty and baseless arguments of this kind—this standard morality is only the product of the sentiments of those who frame it: sentiments which, for the most part, are taken from the society in which they live and belong properly to its authors only to a small degree. Their standard morality has no other value than that of being the manifestation of these sentiments and of this method of reasoning. Such, however, is not the opinion of its authors. They accepted this morality under the influence of sentiment and then put to themselves the question: how to prove it by experience and logic? Hence they inevitably fall into pure logomachies because, by its very nature, this problem is insoluble.

(19) Human beings, and probably those animals which live in communities, have certain sentiments which, in particular given circumstances, serve as the norm for their behaviour. These sentiments affect various classes of human activity, amongst which are to be considered those called 'religion', 'morality', 'law' and 'custom'. We cannot, even today, mark with any precision the limits of these different classes; at one time all these classes were undifferentiated and constituted an almost homogeneous whole. They have no precise objective reality, being only the product of our mind. This is why it is vain to enquire, for example, what, objectively, are morality and justice. Even so, men have at all times reasoned as if morality and justice existed in their own right—in this acting under the influence of that very strong tendency which leads human beings to confer on subjective facts an objective character, and under the influence also of that imperious need which prompts them to give a logical varnish to relationships of sentiments. From this originate most theological controversies, likewise the truly monstrous notion of a scientific religion.

Morality and justice were at first made dependent on a divinity; later they acquired an independent existence, and it was even sought, by an inversion of terms, to submit the Omnipotent himself to their laws. This is a clear indication of the changeable character of faith in the human mind. When faith is all-powerful, the idea of a divinity predominates. When faith diminishes, the idea of a divinity gives place to metaphysical concepts and later to experimental notions. This movement is not always in one direction; it is subject to large oscillations. Plato drew up an indictment against the gods of Olympus in the name of metaphysical abstractions; later there followed a return to faith which eventually was subjected to further oscillations; and now, for certain theologians of our time, God is no more than a belief in 'solidarity' and religion is a nebulous humanitarianism. They imagine they are reasoning scientifically because they have erased all notions of positive religion from their outlook. They do not perceive that their conception of things, having no more of an experimental basis than has religion, consists merely of words void of all meaning and capable only, by the noise they make, of arousing in certain individuals vague and imprecise feelings—like those we have when we are drowsy. If we compare the *Vitae Sanctorum* of the Middle Ages with these empty discourses, we find that both rest on no experimental concept whatever; but the former are at least intelligible: the same cannot be said of the latter.

2. DIFFERENTIATION BETWEEN THE TRUTH AND THE EFFICACY OF BELIEF*

(101) . . . Faith alone strongly moves men to act. Nor is it desirable for the good of society that the mass of men, or even only many of them, should consider social matters scientifically. There is antagonism between the conditions of *action* and those of *knowledge*. This is a further argument serving to demonstrate how little wisdom there is in those people who want everyone, without distinction or discrimination, to participate in knowledge. It is true, of course, that the evils which would arise from this would be to some extent corrected by the fact that what they call *knowledge* is simply a particular form of sectarian faith; and we should perhaps be advised to worry less about the evils deriving from scepticism and more about those resulting from such faith.†

The contrast between the conditions of action and those of knowledge appears also in the fact that, in order to act, we conform to certain rules of conduct and morality. It would indeed be impossible to do otherwise, if only because we would have neither the time nor the means to trace back to its origins the principle governing our actions in each particular case and make a complete theory for it. Contrariwise, in order to understand the relationships of things, to *know*, it is necessary to do precisely that: to subject these very principles to deliberation.

For example, the habits and customs of bellicose peoples are such as to sustain warlike sentiments. If it is accepted that such people should remain bellicose, then it is useful to a society of this kind that, within certain limits at least, the behaviour and activities of individuals should be in accord with these warlike sentiments. It is therefore right—still within these limits—to judge a given activity or form of conduct as harmful to society by the mere fact of its being in opposition to such sentiments. But this conclusion would not be valid if the object of the enquiry were to find out if it were good for this people to be bellicose or pacific.

Similarly, where private property exists there exist also sentiments which are offended by any violation of the rights of property. As long as it is considered useful to maintain the right of private property, it is logical to condemn conduct which is in opposition to these sentiments. These thus become a proper criterion for determining what is good and what bad in a society which admits the right of private property. But they can no longer fulfil this role if it is a question of deciding whether private property should be maintained or abolished. Certain writers in the first half of the nineteenth century attacked socialists as criminals because socialism seeks to destroy private property; but this is really to argue in a circle and make oneself judge in one's own case. The same error would be committed if it were sought to pass judgement against free love by invoking sentiments of chastity, decency and modesty.

---

* Chapter 2, §§101 (4 and 5), 108, 117.
† Cf. *Systèmes*, p. 128 above; *Treatise*, §§401 and 843–4, pp. 207, 216 below; and *Trasformazione*, p. 300 below.

In a society organised in a certain way and in which exist certain sentiments, A, it is reasonable to maintain that a thing, B, which is contrary to these sentiments may be harmful. But since experience teaches us that there exist societies which are organised in a different way, there may exist in one of such societies certain sentiments, C, which are favourable to B, and B therefore may be useful to such a society. Consequently, if it proposed to establish B in order to pass from the first form of social system to the second, it can no longer be a valid objection to B that it is contrary to the sentiments A which are associated with the first form. The universal consensus of men, assuming hypothetically that it could ever be known, would in no way alter this conclusion, for the universal consensus of yesterday may very well differ from the universal consensus of tomorrow.

(108) The economic and social theories employed by those engaged in social struggles are not to be assessed for their objective value but mainly for their effectiveness in arousing emotions. A scientific refutation of them, however correct it might be objectively, would achieve nothing. This is not all. When it is useful to them, men can believe in a theory of which they know scarcely more than the name. This is a phenomenon observable with all religions. Most marxist socialists have not read the works of Marx. There is sure proof of this in indisputable particular cases. For example, before these works were translated into French and Italian, it is certain that French and Italian socialists who did not know German could not have read them. In fact, the French translation of the last sections of Marx's *Capital* coincided with the beginnings of marxism's decline in France. Equally, all the scientific discussions for or against free trade have had no influence, or at most only a very slight influence, on the practical question of whether free trade or protection is to be the policy in a given country.

Human beings follow their sentiments and their interests, but they like to think they follow reason. They also look for—and never fail to find—a theory which, *a posteriori*, gives a certain colour of logic to their behaviour. If this theory could be reduced scientifically to nil, the only outcome would be the substitution of another theory for the first in order to achieve the same aim. It would have a new form, but the pattern of behaviour would remain the same. Hence when it is desired to get men to act in a particular way and follow a prescribed path, the main appeal is to sentiments and interests. Very little is known as yet of the theory of these phenomena, and we cannot here go further into the question.

(117) History shows us that the governing classes have always endeavoured to speak to the people, not in the language which they believe most truly reflects reality, but in that which they believe best suits the ends they have in mind. And this is the case even in the most advanced democracies, France for example. We have here a further example, and a notable one it is, of the persistence under different forms of the same social phenomena.

3. DIFFERENTIAL ROLE OF BELIEFS IN GOVERNORS AND GOVERNED*

(42) Have sentiments an objective existence, independent of the diversity of human intellects; or are they subordinate to this diversity? It is not difficult to see that it is the second hypothesis which is correct. Even when sentiments associated with religion, morality, patriotism, etc., are in their forms of expression common to many men, individuals understand them differently. Socrates as revealed to us by Plato and the superstitious individuals depicted by Theophrastes shared the same religion, but unquestionably they understood it in different ways. . . . When we speak then of love of country, for example, we are envisaging an abstract category of sentiments which is made up of the particular sentiments existing in different individuals. And this category has no more of an objective existence than the category of mammals which is made up of several particular species of animal, these alone having real existence. Nevertheless, for the individuals composing a given society these sentiments, even if they differ to some extent from one another, do have something in common.

(43) The sentiments which belong to these different categories do not seem to be completely independent. Their dependence on one another is generally not logical, although most people, quite wrongly, imagine that it is logical. It arises from the remote common causes of these sentiments. They are to be regarded as branches stemming from the same trunk. Dependence appears between actions of the same kind; non-logical actions are jointly affected by factors sustaining or opposing them—they stand or fall together. The same is true of logical actions. A man who is influenced by sentiments of one kind will more readily be influenced by other kinds of sentiments. A man who is accustomed to employ reason in certain matters will more readily employ it in other matters.

(44) If then, following the same procedure as is involved in categorising men according to their wealth, we arrange the individuals in a society in strata according to their respective qualities of intelligence and character— that is, by putting in the upper strata those who have these qualities in the highest degree, and in the lower strata those who have one or both of these qualities only in a very small degree—we shall find that the interdependence of different sentiments is less marked as we trace them through the upper levels, and more marked the further they are traced downwards through the lower levels. We could say that in the upper levels the branches of the tree are distinct and separate, while lower down they are indistinguishable from the main body of the trunk. Human society therefore presents in space a conformation analogous to (but not identical with) its conformation in time. We know that, in primitive times, different sentiments, now completely distinct, used to form a homogeneous mass.

(45) The qualities of intelligence and character are not the only ones which exist in differentiated degrees; the same effect of differentiation is produced by many other factors. Those who command in small things or

---

* Chapter 2, §§42, 43, 44–7, 119–23.

great, from the private firm to the government of the state, in general have sentiments which are more distinct and independent than the sentiments of those who are commanded. This arises from the fact that the former must necessarily have larger views than the latter; and precisely because their view takes in a wide area, they acquire by practical experience notions which are not to be found among those whose affairs confine them to a more limited terrain.

(46) This new classification we have made corresponds to some extent to the classification of individuals according to intelligence and character, and to some extent also to the classification according to wealth. But these different categories also differ to some extent. First: it is noticeable that in the upper strata there are descending elements, and in the lower ascending elements. Secondly: there are individuals belonging to the intellectual aristocracy who do not use their talents to acquire wealth or material benefits, but devote themselves to art, literature or science; there are the leisured, the idle and the useless who expend their intelligence and energy in recreation, sport and so forth. Thirdly: there are any number of circumstances which may put men with the same qualities of intelligence and character in different positions in the social hierarchy.

(47) There is yet another analogy with what occurs in time: it is noticeable that the faculty of abstraction grows more marked as the phenomenon is traced from the lower to the upper levels of the social hierarchy. It is only in the upper strata that we find different types of behaviour and action embodied in general principles. And the appearance of these principles reveals the contradictions which may exist among them, contradictions which are less marked in specific cases where these principles are less clearly developed.

(48) The human mind is so constituted that in times of ardent faith it discovers no contradiction between its ideas about religion and other ideas it has about morality or the facts of experience; these different ideas, although sometimes completely opposed, can coexist in the same mind. But when the fervour of faith diminishes—or even when, in passing from the lower to the upper strata in the same society, the different kinds of sentiments become more independent—this coexistence of contradictory ideas becomes distasteful and painful. In the minds of the individuals concerned an effort is made to remove it by suppressing the contradictions which only now are apparent to them. . . .

(119) The lower one descends in the social structure, the more does misoneism* appear to predominate, and the more one finds men refusing to act out of any other consideration than their own direct and immediate interests. It is from this level that the upper classes, in modern societies no less than in ancient Rome, draw support in order to govern. But this situation cannot last long, for the lower classes finally come to a better appreciation of their personal interests and turn against those who exploited their ignorance.

(120) This phenomenon can be clearly observed in modern England.

---

* Hatred of the new.

The Tory party joined in the movement to extend the suffrage even further because it wanted to draw on the lower classes for support in getting control of government, and it has rewarded its allies by measures which have been very aptly called 'Tory socialism'. And now the Whigs, who formerly upheld liberal principles, are in competition with the Tories to win the good favour of the plebs. They seek an alliance with the socialists and are going far beyond the modest measures of Tory socialism in 'doing good' for the people. The two parties are fighting it out to see which shall prostrate itself the more humbly at the feet of the Man of the People. Each strives to outdo the other in flattering him. This is pursued down to the minutest detail. When the time comes for contesting elections, the candidates are not ashamed to send out their wives and daughters to canvass voters. The unexpected novelty of this entrances the Man of the People, overcome by so much solicitude and goodwill. But in the long run this sort of thing ends by arousing revulsion in those who come to see only too clearly the motives actuating such flattery.

(121) When those in a particular social strata realise that they are simply being exploited by the upper classes, these latter descend lower in the social structure to find adherents. But it is evident that the day will come when they can go no further because there is no further to go. When the vote has been given to all men, including lunatics and criminal, when it has been extended to women and even—if they like—to children, there has to come a halt; one just cannot go any further—unless the vote is to be given to animals (and giving the vote to them would be easier than getting them to use it!).

In Germany, universal suffrage has been granted partly to counter the liberal bourgeoisie: the phenomenon is similar therefore to what has taken place in England; and in much the same way a good deal of social legislation has been enacted in the hope of weakening the support of the socialists. But this result has not been achieved, for the people have become perfectly well aware of the artifices employed to gull them. So now we find that the German upper classes are beginning to complain about universal suffrage, and some among them are looking for ways to revoke it.

(123) At the very moment when there started the democratic evolution which has developed in the course of the nineteenth century and seems likely to terminate in the twentieth, certain thinkers clearly foresaw what the outcome would inevitably be. But their predictions, now when they are being realised, are forgotten in our movement towards that point when finally the man belonging to the very lowest social strata will grasp and give effect to the logical observation: 'If the arbitrary expression of my will is the principle of the legal order of society, my pleasure and satisfaction can also be the principle regulating the distribution of wealth.'

But history will not halt at the present stage of evolution. If life in the future is not to be wholly different in character from life in the past, the existing evolutionary process will be succeeded by a development in the contrary direction.

4. CIRCULATION OF ELITES; SPOLIATION

(i) Notion of an elite*

(102) Human society is not homogeneous; it is made up of elements which differ to a greater or lesser degree, not only in respect to very obvious characteristics—like sex, age, physical strength, health, etc.—but also in respect to less obvious but no less important characteristics—like intellectual and moral qualities, energy, courage, etc. The assertion that men are objectively equal is so patently absurd that it is not worth refuting. On the other hand, the subjective idea of human equality is a fact of great importance and one which has a powerful influence in determining the changes which occur in society.

(103) Just as one can distinguish the rich and the poor in a society, even though incomes may show an almost imperceptible increase as one traces them upwards from the very lowest to the very highest, so one can distinguish the elite in a society—the aristocratic groups (in the etymological sense of the word, i.e., 'best')—and the commonalty. But it must always be remembered that these groups imperceptibly merge into one another.

The notion of an elite is governed by the qualities which are looked for in it. There can be an aristocracy of saints or an aristocracy of brigands, an aristocracy of the learned, an aristocracy of the criminal and so on. The totality of qualities promoting the well-being and domination of a class in society constitutes something which we will call simply *the elite.*

This elite exists in all societies and governs them even in cases where the regime in appearance is highly democratic. In conformity with a law which is of great importance and is the principal explanation of many social and historical factors, these aristocracies do not last but are continually renewed. This phenomenon may be called *the circulation of elites.* ...

(ii) Social conflicts†

(104) Let us suppose there is a society in which a dominant section, A, and a subject section, B, are hostile to one another. Both could appear as they really are. But more often than not it will be the case that the dominant group will want to appear to be acting for the common good, hoping thus to reduce the opposition of the subject group. This latter, on the other hand, will frankly stake its claim to the advantages it is seeking.

The situation is similar when the two sections are of different nationalities; for example, English and Irish, Russians and Poles. The phenomenon becomes more complex in a society which has a national homogeneity or—which amounts to the same thing—is considered to have such homogeneity by its members.

In such a society, there emerges between the two hostile sections, A and B, a third section, C, which has links with both and may be found sometimes on one side and sometimes on the other. Eventually section A

---

* Chapter 2, §§102–3.   † Chapter 2, §§104–7.

splits into two groups: one group—which we will call A^1—has still enough strength to defend its portion of authority; the other group—A^2—consists of degenerate individuals, weak in intelligence and will: in our day they are called *humanitarians*. Similarly, section B splits in two. One group—B^1—constitutes the new nascent aristocracy; it receives elements from A who, out of greed and ambition, betray their own class and put themselves at the head of its adversaries. The other group of B—B^2—comprises the common mass which forms the largest section in human society.

(105) Objectively, the struggle is simply a matter of the B^1 group's desire to take the place of the A^1 group; everything else is subordinate and secondary.

In this battle, the leaders—the A^1 and the B^1—need soldiers, and each of them looks around to find them. The A^1 try to get it believed that they are working for the common good, but in the given circumstances this is a two-edged sword. For if, by this device, the A^1 manage to reduce the hostility of the B^2, it has at the same time the effect of diminishing the inner strength of the A^2, who come to accept as true (the concern of the A section for the common good) what is no more than pure fiction, this being the sole point of the device. In the long run, it may occur that, while the B^2 come to believe less and less in the catchwords of the A^1, the A^2 come to adopt them more and more as their working rule. In this case, the device of the A^1 turns against them and ultimately does them more harm than good. This can be observed at the present time in the relations of the bourgeoisie and the masses in certain countries.

(106) As for the B^1: they come forward as the defenders of the B^2: nay more, as the exponents of measures of advantage to all citizens. In this way the dispute which objectively is a struggle for domination between the A^1 and the B^1 subjectively takes on the form of a struggle for liberty, justice, right, equality and such like. And it is in this form that it is recorded by history. The advantage of this approach for the B^1 is that it attracts to its cause not only the B^2 but also some of the C section, together with the majority of the A^2 group.

Suppose that the new elite were clearly and simply to announce its intentions: that is, to supplant the old elite. Nobody would support it. It would be defeated before the battle. Instead, it gives the impression of seeking nothing for itself, being well aware that, without having to demand it in advance, it will get what it wants as a result of its victory. The new elite asserts that it is fighting simply and solely to achieve equality between the B section and the A section in society, as a matter of principle. With the aid of this fiction it wins the favour, or at least the benevolent neutrality, of the intermediary C section, which would not acquiesce in the particular-ist aims of the new aristocracy if these were made clear at the start. The new elite not only has with it the greater part of the people, it also gains the support of the degenerate element in the old elite. It should be noted that this latter group, albeit degenerate, is always superior to the common mass. The A^2 are superior to the B^2 and they have, moreover, the money necessary for meeting the expenses of the war. It is almost invariably the case that revolutions are the work, not of the masses, but of the aristocracy and notably of the decadent element in the aristocracy. This can be seen in history, from the time of Pericles up to the period of the first French revolution. And today we see that an element in the bourgeoisie is giving strong support to socialism, the leaders of which, moreover, are of bourgeois origin. Elites commonly end up by committing suicide.

The importance, subjectively, of the concept of the equality of mankind will now be clearly apparent: an importance it wholly lacks when considered objectively. This concept is the means commonly employed, especially in our own times, for getting rid of one aristocracy and replacing it with another.

(107) The degenerate element in the elite, the A^2, is the real victim of the deception, and it is made to go where it would not. The mass of the people, the B^2, often end up by gaining something, either during the conflict or when it has a change of masters. The elite of the old aristocracy, the A^1, is not deceived: it succumbs to force. The new aristocracy is victorious.

The work of the humanitarians in eighteenth-century France paved the way for the slaughter of the Terror. The work of liberals in the first half of the nineteenth century paved the way for that era of demagogic oppression which is now dawning. Those who demanded the equality of all citizens before the law certainly did not envisage the privileges the masses now enjoy. The old special jurisdictions have been suppressed, but the same thing in a new form is being instituted: a system of arbitration which operates always in favour of the workers. Those who demanded the freedom to strike did not imagine that this freedom, for the strikers, would consist of beating up workers who want to continue working, and of burning down factories with impunity. Those who sought equal taxation to help the poor did not imagine that it would lead to progressive taxation at the expense of the rich, and to a system in which taxes are voted by those who do not pay them—a system of such a kind as to encourage people to advance unblushingly the following style of argument: 'Such-and-such tax only hits rich people, and it will go to meet expenditure of benefit only to the less fortunate; it will be sure to find favour with the majority of the electors.'

The ingenuous people who, in some countries, have disorganised the army in their obsession with high-sounding phrases about justice and equality, become astounded and indignant at the growth of anti-militarism, and yet they are the begetters of it. They have not the wit to realise that as a man sows so shall he reap.

The great error of the present age is of believing that men can be governed by pure reasoning, without resort to force. Yet force is the foundation of all social organisation. It is interesting to note that the antipathy of the contemporary bourgeoisie to force results in giving a free hand to violence. Criminals and rioters, their impunity assured, do more or less as they like. The most peaceable people form combinations and have recourse to threats and violence, compelled thereto by governments which leave open to them no other way of defending their interests.

The humanitarian religion will very probably disappear when its work of social dissolution is accomplished and when a new elite has arisen from the ruins of the old. This religion, which has nothing more to it than the naïve imperception of a bourgeoisie in decadence, will be of no further use

from the day when the enemies of the bourgeoisie become strong enough
not to need to hide their hand any more. The best among them have already
reached this stage. Syndicalism is here and now giving us an insight into
what is likely to be the strength and dignity of the new elite. One of the
most remarkable works of our epoch is Georges Sorel's *Réflexions sur la
violence*. In its utter rejection of the meaningless declamations of humanitarianism and its entry into the realm of scientific reality, it anticipates the
future.

(iii) *Circulation and selection of elites**

(18) The surface A–K–B–C of this figure gives us an image of society. The
external form varies hardly at all, but internally there is constant movement. As certain individuals rise to upper levels,

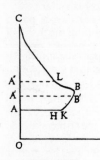

Figure 10

others descend. Those who fall down to A–H disappear, for at this level certain elements in the social
structure are eliminated. Strange to say—yet such is
the case—this same phenomenon occurs in the upper
levels. Experience shows that aristocracies do not
last. There are many reasons for this, and we know
only a little about them; but there is no doubt of the
reality of this phenomenon.

(19) We have first a section A–H–K–B′–A′ in
which, incomes being extremely low, the individuals
in this section, good, bad or indifferent, cannot subsist. Here selection operates only to a very small
extent, for poverty crushes and destroys the good
elements as well as the bad. Next, we have the section A′–B′–B–L–A″ in which
selection operates with maximum intensity. Incomes are not yet so high as
to preserve all the elements in the section irrespective of whether they are
fitted for the struggle of life or not, nor yet so low as to depress the best
elements. In this section, child-mortality is considerable and is probably
a powerful factor in selection. This is the crucible in which are moulded
the future aristocracies. . . . It is from this section that elements emerge to
rise up to the upper section A″–L–C. Once arrived there, their posterity
degenerates. The section A″–L–C subsists thanks only to incomers from the
lower section. As we have already said, the reasons for this are manifold
and little understood. It may be that one of the main factors operating
here is the absence of selection. Incomes are so large that they allow the
survival of the weak, the ill-adapted, the incompetent and the defective.

The lines A′–B′ and A″–L are indicated only to give clarity to the argument; they have no real existence. The boundaries of the sections cannot be
indicated by fixed lines, for the elements they frame pass by degrees from
one section to another.

(20) The inferior elements in the section A′–B′–L–A″ fall down into the
section A–H–B′–A′ where they are eliminated. If this section should disappear, and if no other method could be found to perform the same

* **Chapter 7, §§18–21, 97–100.**

function of elimination, inferior elements would contaminate the section A′–B′–L–A″, which would thereby be less able to produce superior elements to pass up into section A″–L–C, and the whole society would go into decadence. This decadence would be all the more rapid if serious obstacles were to be put in the way of the operation of selection in section A′–B′–L–A″. The future will show our descendants whether or not such will be the effects of the humanitarian measures of our epoch.

(21) Society is harmed not only by the accumulation of inferior elements in upper strata but also by the accumulation in lower strata of superior elements which are prevented from rising. If at one and the same time the upper strata are filled with inferior elements and the lower strata with superior elements, the social equilibrium becomes highly unstable and a violent revolution is imminent. In a certain sense, the social body is comparable to the human body which perishes very quickly if it cannot eliminate toxic elements.

(97) As we have already pointed out [see above p. 155], society has the appearance of a heterogeneous mass with a hierarchic organisation. This hierarchy always exists, save perhaps among very primitive peoples who live in dispersed units like animals. It follows from this that a community is always governed by a small number of men, by an *elite*, even when it seems to have an absolutely democratic character. Evidence for this exists from the very earliest times. In Athenian democracy there were the demagogues, i.e., the 'leaders of the people' whom Aristophanes depicts in his *Knights* as making themselves the masters of a stupid people. In our own day, the democracies in France, England, the United States and so forth are, in fact, governed by a handful of politicians. The same is true of absolute monarchies; except in very rare cases where the monarch is a genius of the first order, they also are governed by an elite, often in the form of a bureaucracy.

(98) One could conceive of a society in which the hierarchy were stable, but this would not be a real society. In all human societies, even in those organised into castes, the hierarchy is eventually modified. The main difference between societies lies in the time taken for modifications to occur; in some the change may be more or less slow, in others more or less rapid. . . .

(99) All species of living beings degenerate without the operation of selection. The human race cannot escape this law. Humanitarians may be able to close their eyes to this truth, deliberately ignoring it, but this can in no way alter the facts. In every race reject-elements are produced which must be eliminated by selection. The grief and suffering caused by this are the price which has to be paid for improvement of the race. This is one of the many cases in which the good of the individual is in opposition to the good of the species. Certain forms of selection may disappear, but they must be replaced by other forms if the race is not to degenerate. There are some people at the present time who think that from now on the human race can dispense with war as a form of selection. They could be right, but equally they could be wrong. What is certain is that they provide no solid proof for their belief—we cannot consider as proofs declamations against the evils entailed by war and the sufferings it inflicts on human beings.

(100) There is another very important factor ... which is closely related to very many social facts and partly conditions them: the production of wealth—or perhaps we should say, of capital—per head of the population. This proportion is an index-mark of civilisation: where it is greatest there civilisation is most highly developed. We must note, however, that we are obliged to estimate wealth in terms of monetary values, and there is nothing fixed about monetary units. Consequently we are able to compute only in a roughly approximate way the wealth per head in different societies at different times.

A great many people believe that new social forms are determined much more by variations in the distribution of wealth than by variations in the average amount of wealth per head. This opinion is utterly mistaken. ... Changes in the distribution of wealth are of little importance; what really matters are variations in the average amount per head, and these may be very important indeed.

(iv) Interdependence of social factors*

(101) We have just referred to four kinds of factors: the social hierarchy; the succession of aristocracies; selection; and the proportion of wealth or capital per head. These factors are by far the most important in determining the character of society—that is to say, of other social facts. But in reality what is involved here is not a relationship of cause and effect. The first factors act upon the second, but these latter in their turn react upon the former; in short, we have to deal with a relationship of interdependence.

(103) Matters such as the maximum social utility, the succession of aristocracies and selection are mainly quantitative in their relevance to the social hierarchy. Human societies cannot exist without a hierarchy, but it would be a grave mistake to conclude from this that their prosperity increases in proportion to the rigidity of the hierarchy. Equally, the changing of aristocracies is advantageous to society, yet we cannot discount the advantages also of a certain stability. Selection should operate within such limits as ensure advantage to the species without excessive sufferings for individuals. ...

(104) One could envisage a human society in which each individual behaved each day independently of the past; the faculty of change or mutation in this case would be very great. But in absolute terms this state of things is not possible, because it is impossible for an individual not to be dependent, to some degree at least, on his own past behaviour and on the circumstances in which he has lived, if only because of the experience he has acquired thereby. ...

(105) At the other extreme, we can envisage a society in which each person has his role assigned to him from birth to death and from which he cannot depart. In such a case there would be a very high degree of stability: society would be crystallised. But this extreme case, like the other, has no existence in reality, although societies with a caste organisation to a greater or lesser extent come near to it.

---

* Chapter 7, §§101, 103–11.

(106) Societies as they have existed and still exist present a wide variety of intermediary types. In modern European societies the factor of stability is provided by private property and inheritance; the factor of mutability and selection derives from the opportunity all individuals have to rise in the social hierarchy as far as they have the capacity to do so. It is true, of course, that there are no grounds for assuming that this state of affairs is perfect or that it is bound to continue indefinitely. If a certain type of property—capital, for example—could be effectively abolished, and if inheritance could be partly or entirely suppressed, then the factor of stability would be considerably weakened and the factor of mutability and selection correspondingly strengthened. It cannot be decided *a priori* whether this would be advantageous or detrimental to society.

(107) Starting from the premise that it has been advantageous in the past to weaken one of these two factors and strengthen the other, the conclusion is drawn that it will be equally advantageous in the future to do likewise. But this argument is groundless because in all quantitative problems of this kind there is a maximum. To advance this argument is like saying that, since the germination of a seed is fostered when the temperature rises from 6°C. to 20°C., it would be fostered all the more if it rose to 100°C. (108) The conclusion drawn from this premise is invalid because movements occurring in societies are not all constant in the same direction; in general they are oscillatory.

(109) The advantages of mutability as a causatory factor of selection, and the disadvantages of stability both depend to a great extent on the fact that aristocracies do not last. Moreover, in view of the misoneism inherent in man and the reluctance of human beings to exert themselves too much, it is a good thing that the best of them should be stimulated by competition with those who are less capable than they; so that even the mere possibility of change has a distinct utility. On the other hand, human beings find excessive change painful; it discourages them and reduces their efforts to a minimum. An individual whose situation is not as good as another's naturally desires change; but if he succeeds in making a change for the better, he will strongly desire to conserve what he has acquired and stabilise his condition. Human societies have a very strong tendency to impart a certain rigidity to any new social organisation and to crystallise themselves in any new form. Hence it often happens that the passage from one form to another is not by continuous movement but by leaps and jerks. This is observable in all forms of human activity; for example, in language, in law and so forth. No living language is immutable. On the other hand, a language consisting entirely of neologisms would be incomprehensible. A happy medium is necessary. The introduction of neologisms in a language is not uniformly continuous; it occurs at intervals on the authority of famous writers or of some literary institution like the Académie Française or the Accademia della Crusca in Italy. Similar phenomena are to be found in matters of law. It is not only in countries where the law is codified that changes lead to a rigid new system; this happens even in countries where one would think that the process of lawmaking would be much more flexible than it actually is.

(110) In social economics, mutability may be expressed in a variety of

forms and these may partially be replaced by others. Mutability could act in contradiction to selection, but here we shall only consider it as an auxiliary of selection. When active, energetic and intelligent elements accumulate in the lower strata of society, while in contrast the upper strata contain too high a proportion of degenerate elements, a revolution breaks out which replaces one aristocracy by another. The new social structure soon takes on a rigid form, and it will eventually be broken up by a similar revolution.

Instead of revolution there may be infiltration whereby choice elements, the people of greater aptitude, rise up in the social structure while elements affected by decay fall down to lower levels. This movement is almost always at work, but it may vary in intensity. It is this variation in intensity which determines whether or not decadent elements accumulate in the upper strata or superior elements in the lower.

(111) For the movement to be sufficiently pronounced to militate against accumulation it is not enough that the law and custom should allow it and refrain from putting obstacles of any kind in its way (like castes, for example). It is also necessary that circumstances should be such as to enable the movement to develop. For example, in a bellicose society, it is not enough for law and custom to allow the ordinary soldier to become a general; there has to be war to provide the opportunity. In commercial and industrial societies, it is not enough for law and custom to allow the poorest to become rich and attain the highest pinnacles of the state; there has to be a commercial and industrial development of sufficient scale to make this a real possibility for an appreciable number of citizens.

(v) Social stability and spoliation*

(112) Measures which, directly or indirectly, reduce debts impair the factor of stability, and in consequence indirectly strengthen the factor of mutability and selection. The same effect is produced by anything which generally leads to price-increases, but only for as long as this increase lasts. If, for example, all prices double, the economic equilibrium sooner or later ends up by being identical with what it was formerly. But in the passage from one state to another, debts diminish and mutability and selection are encouraged. Alterations in the value of money, increases in the quantities of precious metals (like those occurring after the discovery of America, for example), issues of paper-currency, customs protection, trade unions obtaining salary increases, and so on: factors like these in part have the effect of encouraging mutability and selection. But they have other effects also, and it remains to be seen in each particular case whether the damage caused by these effects is not greater than the advantage which flows from them.

(113) In Athens after Solon's reform, there was no longer any need to have recourse to a reduction of debts; money underwent no change in value and nothing else occurred to raise prices. The main reason for this

---

* Chapter 7, §§112–16.

must be sought for in the intense commercial activity of Athens which of itself was sufficient to ensure the circulation of aristocracies.

(114) From the days of classical antiquity up to our own times, we observe among the peoples of Europe a series of revolutions, of legislative measures, of intentional or accidental factors which all combine to strengthen the factor of mutability and selection. It can with a high degree of probability be concluded that the factor of stability, or even of mutability contrary to selection, was at one time extremely strong and therefore by reaction produced elements tending to weaken it. A different conclusion would very likely have to be drawn for other societies. The need to produce elements favourable to selection is also related to the proportion of superior elements developed in the lower strata. It may be that the greater stability of certain oriental peoples derives, to some extent at least, from the fact that this proportion is smaller among them than among western peoples.

(115) If in western countries the factor of stability were exclusively the product of the institution of private property and inheritance, this would be very strong evidence in arguing for the necessity of reducing, or even suppressing, private property. It is odd that the socialists have not perceived the support that could be brought to their theories by considering matters in this way.

But the factor of stability which conflicts with change by selection is far from being, in our societies, exclusively the consequence of the institution of private property. Laws and custom have divided men into classes, and even where these classes have disappeared, as among modern democratic peoples, wealth brings with it advantages which enable certain individuals to repel competitors. In the United States, politicians and judges frequently offer themselves to the highest bidder. In France, the Panama affair and similar scandals have shown that European democracy, from this point of view, does not differ essentially from American democracy. In general, from the earliest times to our own day, the upper classes of society have made use of political power to despoil the poorer classes. In some democratic countries, a diametrically opposed phenomenon now seems indeed to have emerged. There is no record anywhere of the existence of a situation, over any appreciable length of time, in which the government remains neutral and gives no help either to the upper classes' spoliation of the poor or to the poorer classes' spoliation of the rich. We cannot therefore decide empirically whether the considerable strength of the factor of stability has its origin in the institution of private property or in political oppression by the upper classes. In order to draw correct conclusions, one would have to be able to separate these two species of facts and study their effects separately.

(116) So far we have examined facts objectively. But they are revealed in quite a different way to the awareness and understanding of men. We have shown earlier how the circulation of elites is manifested subjectively and we cannot here linger over this point. In general, human beings are induced to formulate their particular claims as general claims. A new aristocracy which seeks to take the place of an older one as a rule declares war, not in its own name, but in the name of the greatest number. A rising aristocracy always wears the mask of democracy.

The state of mind produced by the accumulation of superior elements in the lower strata and of inferior elements in the upper, is often revealed in religious, ethical, political and pseudo-scientific theories about the equality of men. It is, paradoxically, precisely the inequality of men which prompts them to proclaim their equality.

Part Two
The Treatise

Trattato di Sociologia Generale

Treatise on General Sociology

I

Methodological Preliminaries

1. THE METHOD

(i) Definition of sociology*

(1) Human society is the object of many studies. Some of these are specialised; for example, the studies dealing with law, history, political economy, religious history and so forth. There is also a group of studies of society which embraces categories which do not as yet have a distinct form and which, in synthesis with other studies which have already achieved a defined form, are directed to the study of human society in general. This group of studies may be termed *sociology*.

(ii) Sociological theories as scientific material: their classification†

(7) In a given community, there are in circulation propositions, maxims and received opinions, of a descriptive or perceptive kind; for example: 'youth is rash'; 'do not covet another man's property or wife'; 'be wise and save if you would avoid poverty later on'; 'love your neighbour as yourself'. Propositions such as these, when combined in a logical or pseudo-logical connection and embodied in various kinds of explanatory accounts, constitute theories. They can be of various types: theological, cosmological, metaphysical and so on. All these are experimental facts‡ if examined from

---

* Chapter I, §1. The arabic numbers in curved brackets refer to the section numbers of the original edition of 1916.

† Chapter I, §§7, 8, 12, 13.

‡ Cf. *Fatti e Teorie*, in which Pareto republished his article, 'Experimental Economics', *Giornale degli Economisti*, July 1918:

(p. 126) 'The *history of doctrines* is, like all historical studies, useful to the understanding of the relations between the things which constitute the material of history. It is desirable that such a history should be written only by those

without, avoiding preoccupation with their intrinsic merit as being derived
from faith. And it is as experimental facts that we must study and understand them.

(8) Such a study is very useful for sociology since a great many of these
propositions and theories embody the image of social behaviour. Very
often it is thanks to them alone that we can appreciate the forces which are
operating on and in society, i.e., the dispositions and inclinations of human
beings.

At the start, we must try to classify propositions and theories; this is
wellnigh indispensable for the closer understanding of a large number of
varied subjects. To avoid constant repetition of the terms 'propositions'
and 'theories', we shall in what follows speak only of 'theories'. Unless a
comment is made specifically to the contrary, it is to be assumed throughout that what is said of theories applies equally to propositions.

(12) Let us then try to classify these theories, employing the same
precise methods we would employ if we were classifying rocks, plants and
insects. We see immediately that a theory is not a homogeneous entity

---

who know about such subjects. It is rather ridiculous that most of the history of
economics should be the work of people who are ignorant of economic science.
No one without any knowledge of chemistry, astronomy or physiology would
dream of writing the history of these sciences. Yet there are people who write
about the history of *labour*, of *money*, or *protection* and of economic matters in
general, and who have very little idea, if any at all, of what they are writing
about.'

(pp. 137–8) 'How useful can the history of theories be in constructing a
strictly experimental theory? It can be useful for theories which have an
asymptote; for example, mathematics, astronomy, physics, etc. But its usefulness is limited, very limited indeed, for those theories which have no asymptote,
as is the case with many economic theories. All the same, theories are facts. The
history of these facts is the basis of a theory of them, that is to say, of a theory
of theories. Such theories of theories are fully discussed in the *Treatise*.

'For a century or more, men have been engaged in saying the same things
about fiscal protection and free trade, and it is quite useless to read the greater
part of these writings in the expectation of acquiring knowledge of the experimental effects of protectionism and free trade. But it nevertheless is useful if one
wishes to study a particular case of derivation, to make a theory of these
theories. For one will thereby perceive that there is nothing special about them;
they simply express sentiments and interests. And it is precisely because these
sentiments and interests are enduring factors that the theories attached to both
of these opposing poles of protectionism and free trade are also enduring. If the
sentiments and interests were still operative which prompted the Athenians to
believe that the sun was a god, or the Holy Office to believe that the earth did
not move, then any new Anaxagoras of Galileo would still be condemned.
Happily for logico-experimental astronomy, modern theology is not concerned
about the movements of the stars, while the "speculators" and their adherents
have something more profitable to occupy their attention than thinking about
the movements of the sun. The contest between protection and free trade is only
an episode in the contest between rentiers and speculators. One cannot properly
understand the one conflict without an understanding of the other. And indeed,
clearly to understand the rentier-speculator conflict entails even more general
considerations of the social system.'

like the chemist's 'element'. It is more like a lump of rock in whose composition are several elements. A theory contains descriptive elements and axiomatic assertions together with concrete or abstract, real or imaginary elements. This whole complex is to be understood as constituting the material of theory. There are, moreover, logical or pseudo-logical modes of reasoning, appeals to sentiments,* elaborations of feelings and passions, the intervention of ethical, religious and similar elements. All this conditions the way in which the materials are put to work to build up the structure called 'theory'.

(13) In this way, then, a structure is built; the theory exists; it is now one of the matters for us to classify. We can consider these matters under various aspects.

(a) *Objective Aspect.* A theory can be considered independently of its author and of its acceptor—that is, objectively. But note that no metaphysical meaning is to be attached to this term in the sense in which we employ it here. To take account of all the possible combinations between the nature of the material and of the nexus linking the various elements in this material, the following classes and subclasses are to be distinguished:

OBJECTIVE CLASSIFICATION OF THEORY-MATERIAL

Class I   Experimental Material

    (Ia) Logical nexus
    (Ib) Non-logical nexus

Class II   Non-experimental Material

    (IIa) Logical nexus
    (IIb) Non-logical nexus

The subclasses (Ib) and (IIb) comprise logical sophistries, artful modes of reasoning intended to deceive others. For the purposes of this present enquiry, these are on the whole of lesser importance than the subclasses (Ia) and (IIa).

Subclass (Ia) embraces all the experimental sciences. We propose to term it the *logico-experimental* subclass. Two varieties are distinguishable in this subclass (Ia):

(Ia 1) This comprises the strictly pure type of the logico-experimental, where the material is experimental and the nexus logical. The abstractions and general principles employed here are drawn exclusively from experience and are subordinated to it.

(Ia 2) This represents a deviation from (Ia) and approaches near to Class II. The material here is still explicitly experimental and nexus is logical. But the abstractions and general principles assume, explicitly or implicitly, a significance which transcends experience.

---

* As employed by Pareto, the word 'sentimenti' carries a wider range of meaning than 'sentiments' in modern English usage. It signifies not only 'feelings', but also 'attitudes' and 'opinions'.

This could be regarded as a transitional type. Others like it could be considered but they are not so important as this one.

Like every other classification one could make, the one outlined above is governed by our knowledge and understanding. One man will regard as experimental certain elements which another will put into Class II. Someone who believes he is using logic, and is mistaken therein, will include among logical propositions a proposition which someone else, who is aware of the error, will place in the non-logical category.

It should be noted that the classification given here is of types of theory. In reality, a particular theory may be a mixture of these types; that is to say, a given theory may well contain experimental and non-experimental elements, logical and non-logical elements.

(b) *Subjective Aspect.* As we have noted, theories can be considered in relation to their author and to their acceptor. They are therefore to be considered under the following subjective aspects:

A. *Reasons and causes for a given individual's producing a given theory.* Why should a given individual assert that x equals Y? Alternatively, if he asserts this, why does he do so?

B. *Reasons and causes for a given individual's accepting a given theory.* Why should a given individual accept the assertion that x equals Y? Alternatively, if he accepts that assertion, why does he do so?

Enquiries such as these extend from separate individuals to embrace groups and communities.

(c) *Aspect of Utility.* It is important for our enquiry to avoid confusing 'theory' with 'state of mind' and the sentiments and attitudes it reveals. Some people produce a theory because they have certain sentiments and attitudes, and then this theory in turn works on these people or on others to produce, strengthen or modify certain sentiments and attitudes.

CLASSIFICATION ACCORDING TO UTILITY

Class I   Advantage or disadvantage of sentiments revealed by a theory

(Ia) For the theory's author
(Ib) For the theory's acceptor

Class II   Advantage or disadvantage of a given theory

(IIa) For the theory's author
(IIb) For the theory's acceptor

These considerations also apply to groups and communities as well as to separate individuals.

We can therefore say that it will be our purpose to consider propositions and theories under the classification of the *objective* and the *subjective* aspects and of the aspect of *social or individual utility*. But for this purpose, the meaning of such terms is not to be derived from their etymological definition or from their common usage, but exclusively from the definitions given in the text.

(iii) Dogmatic and experimental sociology*

(6) Up to the present time, sociology has almost always been presented dogmatically. Let us not be deceived by Comte's attaching the label *Positive* to his philosophy. His sociology is fully as dogmatic as Bossuet's in the *Discours sur l'histoire universelle*. They are different religions, but religions they are still. The same may be said of the works of Spencer, de Graaf, Letourneau and of very many other writers.

Belief by its very nature is exclusive. The man who believes he possesses the absolute truth cannot concede that there are any other truths in the world. Hence the fervent christian and the pugnacious 'free-thinker' are, and must be, equally intolerant. To those who have the faith, one way alone is good; all other ways are bad. The mohammedan will not swear on the Gospel, nor the christian on the Koran. But the man who has no faith at all will swear on either or both, and even on Rousseau's *Social Contract* if that gives any satisfaction to the humanistic faithful. Nor would he even scruple to swear on the *Decameron*, if only to relish the scowl he would get from Sénateur René Bérenger and the adepts in that gentleman's religion of anti-pornography.

This does not imply that sociological works whose starting points are certain dogmatic principles are to be considered useless, no more than the geometric systems of Lobachefsky and Riemann are in any way to be considered useless. The only thing we ask of such sociologies is that they use as much as possible clear and strict premises and arguments.

We have 'humanitarian' sociologies in plenty: almost all that are now being published are of this kind. We suffer from no lack of metaphysical sociologies, among which are to be included all the 'positivist' and human-itarian essays in this field. In small numbers come the christian sociologies, catholic and protestant. Without seeking in any way to denigrate these sociologies, our intention here is to expound an exclusively experimental sociology—experimental in the same sense as chemistry, physics and other similar sciences. In what follows, therefore, we intend to take experience and observation as sole guides. For the sake of brevity, we shall speak only of experience.† When we say that a thing is revealed by experience, we imply 'and by observation'; and when we speak of experimental sciences, we imply 'and of observational sciences', and so forth.

(67) Whether the principles employed instead of experience and observation be theological, metaphysical or pseudo-experimental, may in certain respects be a question of great importance. But it is of no import-ance so far as concerns the logico-experimental sciences which we are now considering. Saint Augustine denies the existence of the Antipodes because

---

* Chapter I, §§6, 67–72, 76.
† The Italian word *esperienza* connotes both 'experience' and 'experiment'. Save in cases where the context clearly requires the latter, the word throughout has been rendered as 'experience'.

Holy Scripture makes no mention of them. The Fathers of the Church, generally speaking, make the sacred texts the criteria of all truth, even of experimental truth. The metaphysicists hold them in scorn and substitute other principles in the place of theological principles; yet these are equally outside experience. Scientists after Newton, forgetting that in his wisdom he had asserted only that the heavenly bodies moved as if by attraction according to a certain law, saw in this hypothesis an absolute principle, discovered by human genius, verified by experience, and to which all creation must for ever adhere. But in recent years, the principles of mechanics have been examined with critical severity and the conclusion has been reached that the only things which remain certain are the observed facts and the equations embodying them. Poincaré justly remarks that, in so far as certain phenomena admit of a mechanical explanation, they also admit of an infinite number of other explanations.

(68) All the natural sciences—some more, some less—are little by little approaching closer to the logico-experimental type (Ia 1). And this study in sociology, it must be made clear, is similarly directed. The aim is to bring sociology into conformity with what we have called the pure experimental type, which consists only of experimental material and the logical nexus.

(69) The procedure to be followed in this work therefore involves the following considerations.

1. We do not propose to concern ourselves at all with the intrinsic 'truth' of any religion, faith, metaphysical or moral belief whatever—not because of any scornful disregard for these things, but simply because they are outside the limits in which we choose to work. Religions, beliefs and the like will only be considered externally in as much as they are social facts, and entirely apart from their intrinsic merits. A proposition like 'A *must* equal B by grace of some principle superior to experience' will therefore not come within our examination. But we shall examine how such a belief originates and grows and what its relations are with other social facts.

2. Our field of work is therefore exclusively that of experience and observation. These terms are used in the same sense which they bear in the natural sciences—astronomy, chemistry, physics and the like. They are not at all to be taken as signifying what others mean by terms such as *inner experience* or *christian experience*: terms which revive, with hardly any change of name, the 'introspection' of the old schools of metaphysics. Such introspection or personal experience is to be considered by us only as an external fact, to be studied as a social fact and in no other way.

3. Just as we make no incursion into anyone else's field, so we require that there should be no incursion into our field. To oppose experience to principles which transcend experience can only be regarded as vain and foolish. But equally we reject the lordship of those principles over experience.

4. To arrive at theories we shall proceed from facts and constantly endeavour to stray as little as possible from the facts. We do not know what may be the *essences* of things, nor are we concerned about this since such an enquiry would take us outside our determined field. What we are looking for are the uniformities which facts present to us. These

uniformities we shall certainly call laws, yet it is understood that the facts are not subordinated to the laws, but rather the laws to the facts. The laws are not *necessary*; they are hypotheses which serve to epitomise a more or less extensive number of facts, and are valuable as hypotheses only for as long as they are not replaced by other and better hypotheses.

5. All our enquiry then is contingent and relative, offering conclusions which are only more or less probable, and at the best highly probable. The space in which we live does indeed appear to be three-dimensional. But if someone were to say that one day the sun would convey us with all its planets into a four-dimensional space, we would neither assent nor dissent. When experimental evidence for such an assertion were shown us, we should examine it. But so long as this evidence is lacking, the question does not concern us. Each and every proposition affirmed by us, not excluding propositions of pure logic, must be understood as being put forward subject to the condition: *within the limits of time and experience as known to us.*

6. Our reasoning is based exclusively on things, not on the sentiments aroused in us by the names of things. Such sentiments are here studied solely as external facts. Hence, for example, we refuse to discuss whether an act is *just* or *unjust, moral* or *immoral*, unless it has first been made quite clear to what things it is intended that these terms are to refer. We shall, of course, study as an external, objective fact what men of a given country, time and social class meant when they asserted that A was a just and moral act. We shall see what motivated them and how major motives often have operated all unknown to the men who were being influenced by them. We shall seek to understand the relations between these and other social facts. We reject arguments which use terms lacking precision, because from imprecise premises can only be drawn imprecise conclusions. But we shall study such arguments as social facts. And we shall seek for the solution of one curious problem in particular: the problem of understanding how it is that, from premises which are entirely remote from reality, conclusions are drawn which in effect are not too far removed from reality.

7. We look for the proofs of our propositions in experience and observation alone, with the logical inferences they entail, excluding all proofs by accord of sentiments, by inner persuasion or by dictate of conscience.

8. To this end, we shall only use expressions which correspond to things, taking the most painstaking care to give them as precise a meaning as possible.

9. Our procedure will be by *successive approximations*; that is to say, we shall first consider the phenomenon in its full complex, deliberately passing over the particular details; these we shall later take note of in the successive approximation.

(70) We do not in the least mean to assert that the method we are using is *better* than others. This cannot be so, for the term 'better' in this case has no meaning. No comparison is possible between theories which are entirely contingent and those which admit of the absolute. They are heterogeneous things, incommensurable with one another because of

different kinds, and remaining always separate. If any one wishes to derive a sociology from certain metaphysical or theological principles, or—as many desire at the present time—from principles of 'democratic progress', we shall have no contention with him, and certainly we shall not gainsay his work. Battle will only become inevitable if, in the name of these principles, some conclusion or other is enjoined on us which falls within the domain of experience and observation. When Saint Augustine—to revert to the example already cited—affirms that the sacred texts are inspired by God, we have nothing to object against in this statement (which, for one thing, we do not altogether understand). But when from those texts he seeks to find proof for his assertion that the Antipodes do not exist, we cannot accept his arguments as worthy of serious attention, for questions such as this belong to the domain of experience and observation.

(71) We are working in a restricted field, the bounds of which are set by experience and observation. This is not to deny that there are other fields for working in. But we have no wish to enter them. The end we have set for ourselves is to discover theories which embody the facts of experience and observation. In this study we therefore refuse to go beyond this purpose. Those who are diffident about proceeding in this way, who want to travel out of the logico-experimental field, should seek other company and leave ours, which is not suited to them.

(72) We differ completely from many of those who follow a path analogous to our own in that we certainly do not deny the social utility of theories different from our own. Indeed, in certain cases we believe such theories can be most useful. *The equating of the social utility of a theory with its experimental truth is precisely one of those a priori principles which we reject.* Are these two things—social utility and experimental truth—always conjoined, or are they not? The observation of facts alone can give the answer to this question. In what follows, evidence will be produced to show that, in certain cases, these two things can be entirely unconnected and unrelated.*

(76) To persuade others in matters of experimental science requires mainly—and better still, exclusively—the expounding of facts and of logical deductions from facts. But to persuade others in matters of what is still called *social science* entails mainly an appeal to sentiments, supplemented by considerations of facts and of logical deductions from them. Indeed, the 'social scientist' so-called *has* to work in this manner since, if he were to omit considerations of sentiment, he would convince very few people and perhaps get no hearing at all. If, instead, he can skilfully play upon sentiments, his arguments will be deemed eloquent.

(iv) *Dogmatic and scientific principles*†

(4) A writer can present the principles he intends to observe in two quite

---

* Cf. *Trasformazione della Democrazia*, p. 12: 'Scepticism produces theory, faith stimulates activity, and it is creative action which constitutes practical life. Ideal aims can at one and the same time be absurd and highly useful to society.' (See below, p. 300.)

† Chapter I, §§4, 5, 53, 54, 56, 58–62.

distinct ways. In the first place, he may wish to have those principles accepted as self-evident, demonstrated truths; in which case all their logical inferences will also be held to be evident and demonstrated. Alternatively, he may put forward his principles simply as an indication of one course among the many which could be followed; in which case, each logical conclusion from them is in no way demonstrated in concrete reality, but is merely hypothetical just as the premises from which it is drawn are hypothetical. It is therefore very often advisable to abstain from drawing such inferences, keeping the argument clear of this deductive element and allowing the commentary and discussion to be shaped directly by the facts.

To cite an example of what we mean: Let us suppose that someone is propounding to you the euclidian postulate as a *theorem*. You must immediately take issue on this point, for if you concede the theorem, the whole of euclidian geometry is thereby proved and you can make no further demur against any part of it. But let us suppose instead that the postulate is proposed to you as an *hypothesis*. In this case you do not have to argue the point, but simply allow the geometrician to draw out its logical consequences. If these agree with concrete reality, you will accept them; if not, you will reject them. Your freedom of choice is not shackled by a forestalling concession. There are other, non-euclidian systems of geometry; by receiving the euclidian postulate as an hypothesis, you can still study these other systems without in any way hampering your real freedom of choice. If geometricians felt they were bound to decide, before proceeding in their studies, whether or not the postulate of Euclid corresponds to concrete reality, there would be no geometry whatever in existence today.

This observation is of general application. All the sciences have advanced when students, instead of quarrelling over first principles, have discussed effects and results. Celestial mechanics is based on the hypothesis of a law of universal attraction, of gravitation. It is now suspected that the attraction may be something different from what used to be thought. But even if this doubt were to be substantiated by new and better observations, the achievements of celestial mechanics would still remain, and it would only be necessary for us to make revisions and additions.

(5) Instructed by experience, our endeavour is to apply to the study of sociology the methods which have been so useful in the study of the other sciences. Hence we do not put forward any dogma whatever as a premise of our enquiry. Our principles of procedure are set forth only as an indication of the course which, among the many that could be chosen, we choose to follow. This means that those who join with us in our purpose do not in the least renounce following other ways.

From the first page of a geometric treatise, it is incumbent on the author to inform the reader if he is going to expound euclidian geometry or instead, for example, the system of Lobachefsky. But this is simply a preliminary notification; and if he does expound the system of Lobachefsky, this in no way implies that he denies the value of other systems of geometry. In this sense and in no other should be understood the declaration we make of our principles.

(53) Let us suppose that a certain number of facts are given. There is no single solution to the problem of deriving a theory from these facts.

Various theories are possible which can equally well satisfy the data of the problem, and the choice of a particular one of these possible theories may sometimes be influenced by subjective motives, like the preference most people have for simple explanations.

(54) In logico-experimental theories type (Ia), principles are no more than certain abstract propositions in which are epitomised the characteristics common to many facts. These principles are dependent on the facts; the facts are not dependent on the principles, for these latter are governed by the facts and not *vice versa*. They are accepted hypothetically only so much and so far as they are in accord with the facts. They are rejected as soon as they disagree with the facts.

(56) On the other hand, scattered about in non-logico-experimental theories we find principles which are admitted *a priori* and independently of experience, over which they claim supremacy. In this class of theory, principles are not dependent on the facts; it is the other way about. They govern the facts, are not governed by them. They are accepted without any heed to the facts which *must* of necessity be in accord with the inferences drawn from the principles. Where the facts appear to be in conflict with the principles, various methods of reasoning are tried until one is hit on which is capable of re-establishing that accord, which thus can never vanish away.

(58) In non-logico-experimental theories, the subordination of facts to principles shows itself in various ways:

1. People are so certain of the principles with which they start that they take no trouble to ascertain if their implications and conclusions are in accord with experience. Such accord must exist, and experience as a mere handmaid cannot, must not rebel against its mistress. This is especially the case when logico-experimental propositions type (Ia) try to invade the domain usurped by non-logico-experimental theories.

2. Once the invasion is made, experimental sciences gain ground to the point where they are liberated from servitude. They are conceded a measure of autonomy; they are permitted to verify the inferences drawn from general principles. But it is firmly maintained that their role is always to confirm these principles. If it appears that such is not their tendency, then recourse is had to casuistry in order to re-establish the desired accord between general principles and experience.

3. When finally even this method of maintaining the supremacy of general principles proves a broken reed, the upholders of the supremacy resign themselves to allowing the experimental sciences to enjoy the independence they have won for themselves. But now it is asserted that the domain of the experimental sciences is something inferior, being concerned purely with the relative and the particular, whereas philosophical principles have to do with the absolute and the universal.

(59) In using hypotheses, one does not desert the experimental field, nor hence the domain of logico-experimental theories, provided these hypotheses are employed only as a means of investigating consequences which are always submitted to verification by experience. It is altogether otherwise if these hypotheses are employed as instruments of proof, without reference to experimental verification. For example, in accepting the hypothesis of universal gravitation, we are not led outside the experimental field if, as is

the rule in modern celestial mechanics, we understand that its implications are always to be subject to the test of observation. Conversely, we should certainly be abandoning the experimental domain if we asserted that universal gravitation is an *essential property of matter*, and that therefore the movements of the stars must *necessarily* proceed according to the inferences of this hypothesis. This was not understood by those who, like Comte, sought to exclude from the domain of scientific enquiry the hypothesis of luminous ether. This and similar hypotheses are not to be judged intrinsically, as possessing an inherent validity, but extrinsically, as non-inherent and operating from without. They are to be examined to discover whether, and at what point, their inferences are in agreement with the facts.

(60) When very many inferences from a hypothesis have been verified by experience, it becomes highly probable that a new inference will also be verifiable. In this case, the two types of hypothesis noted above [§§55 and 56] tend to blend, and in practice the new inference is made and accepted without being verified. This explains how it comes about that in the minds of many people there is a confusion between hypotheses which are subject to experience and those which predominate over experience. At the same time, there are cases in practice where the inferences of certain hypotheses may be accepted without fail. For example: at the present time, some of the principles of pure mechanics are in question, at least so far as concern speeds very much greater than those which can be practically observed. Yet it is clear that the engineer constructing machines is able, without the least risk of error, to continue to accept these questionable principles, since the speeds of the component parts of his machines are assuredly much slower than the velocities which are now making it necessary to revise the principles of dynamics.

(61) In pure economics, the hypothesis of ophelimity* remains an experimental hypothesis if its inferences have to be verified by facts. If it should cease to depend on facts, it would no longer be an experimental theory. Walras did not appreciate this when propounding his theory of *exchange-value*. If the validity of the hypothesis of ophelimity is impugned,

---

* Ophelimity, from the Greek ὠφέλιμος. Cf. §2271 of the *Treatise*: 'The concept of "needs" is altogether undefinable and cannot therefore be used as a premise for strict reasoning. Economists came up against this kind of difficulty and were unable to surmount it save by making a distinction between an *objective* utility, which they refrained from defining, and a *subjective* utility (ophelimity) which they studied as providing the only basis for determining the economic equilibrium. But that was not all: they were forced to admit, in the first place, that the individual is the sole judge of the question as to whether or not the subjective utility exists; and, secondly, that he is the sole judge of the extent and intensity of this utility. All this could have meaning for a community only if it were possible to consider the community as a single person, with unity of sensation, consciousness and thinking. But as this hypothesis is irreconcilable with the facts, so the deductions drawn from it are also irreconcilable with the facts. The concept of collective "needs" is used as a method for artificially removing the difficulties which arise from the necessity—in recognition of reality—of considering the various sorts of *utility*.' See also *Cours*, pp. 97–103 above.

as it is possible to do by observing the curves of indifference and by other similar means, the necessity disappears of experimentally verifying the inferences of the hypothesis, for it has faded into insignificance.

(62) Similarly, the hypothesis of *value* remains experimental if *value* is thought of as something begetting inferences which are experimentally verifiable. It cease to be experimental when it is thought of as a metaphysical entity superior to experimental verification.

(v) Believers' truth and experimental truth*

(26) For those with a 'living faith', the various characteristics of theories indicated in §13 [p. 169 above] often amount to one only. What the believer wants to know—and nothing else—is whether the proposition is true or not. What precisely does this term *true* signify? No one knows, and the 'believer' least of all. The term's meaning seems generally to be based on what is conformant to the believer's feelings and opinions. But this appears to be so only to those who judge the belief externally. The believer certainly does not accept this interpretation; he rejects the argument (and considers it almost an affront to imply it) that a belief which he regards as absolutely *true* may have such a subjective character. He therefore refuses to detach the term *true* from the meaning he gives it, and he will roundly deny the validity of experimental truth, which is 'inferior' to *his* truth. . . .

(43) In matters of proof, experience is impotent against faith, and equally faith is powerless against experience, provided each remains in its own sphere. John, let us say, is a non-believer and denies that God created heaven and earth. If you bring against him the authority of the Bible, you will be ploughing the sands for John will deny the authority of the Bible. Thus your argument falls to the ground. It is quite pointless to have recourse to the authority of *christian experience* as a substitute for the authority of the Bible, for he will assuredly retort that *his* experience in no way leads him to accept your contention. If you retaliate by saying that his experience is not christian experience, you are simply giving a copybook example of arguing in a circle, for it is certain that, if christian experience is the only experience that sustains certain conclusions—*your* conclusions—then all you are saying is that these conclusions can incontestably be deduced from christian experience. But that gets us nowhere.

(44) If you affirm a logico-experimental proposition, it is possible for you to put your antagonist in the dilemma either of accepting your proposition as true or of denying any belief in experience and logic. If your opponent follows the latter course, he is taking up the same position as John, and the upshot will be that you can have no way of persuading him. (45) We perceive therefore that—always excepting sophistries or deceitful tricks of arguing—in this matter of proofs the difference between theories which are logico-experimental (Ia) and those which are not, lies mainly in the fact that it is much harder in our western society at the present time to find people who deny belief in experience and logic than it is to find people who deny belief in the Koran, the Gospel, in various kinds of experience

---

* Chapter I, §§26, 43–46, 48–50, 98.

such as christian, personal, humanitarian, rational experience: what you will—in the categorical imperative, in the dogmas of positivism, national-ism, pacifism and innumerable other things of this sort. In dealing with other times and other societies the position may be different.

(46) We must take care to avoid the error—which a certain materialist metaphysic makes—of attributing to logic and experience a greater power and dignity than that allowable to dogmas accepted by sentiment. Our aim is analysis, not comparison, and even less is it to stand in judgement over the merit and demerits of these various different approaches to fact and theory.

(48) The extreme case of the man who rejects belief in any logical reasoning, in any proof from experience, is very rare. By various devices, logico-experimental considerations can be left unmentioned, ignored or pushed aside, but it is hard to find any one who really fights them as enemies. What one almost always finds is that people try to demonstrate theories which are not experimental or objective by means of pseudo-logical and pseudo-experimental proofs.

(49) All religions have proofs of this kind, to which are readily added proofs of individual and social utility. And when one religion replaces another, it wishes it to be believed that its experimental proofs are better than those which can be mustered by the vanquished religion. The christian miracles were certainly more convincing than the pagan miracles, and today the 'scientific' proofs of *solidarism* and *humanitarianism* are incontestably better than the christian miracles. But to any one who studies such facts without the support of faith, they do not appear to be very different, and he will assign to them precisely the same scientific value: zero. We are required to believe that 'when thundered the Punic fury from the Thrasimene', the Roman defeat was caused by the consul Flaminius' crass neglect of the omens sent by the gods. The consul had fallen from his horse before the statue of Jovius Stator; the sacred chickens had refused their feed; and finally the legionary standard could not be pulled out of the ground where it had been set up. It will be taken for certain—but I do not know whether more or less certain—that the victory of the crusaders at Antioch was owed to divine protection in the shape of the Holy Lance. Furthermore, it is certain—nay, it is beyond all peradventure because affirmed by a better and more recent religion—that Lewis XVI of France lost throne and life solely because he did not have as much love as was fitting for the dear, good people. The humanitarian god of democracy never lets such offences go unpunished.

(50) Experimental science, it must be noted, has no dogma—not even the dogma that experimental facts can be revealed only by experiment and, observation. If the contrary were observed, experimental science would accept the fact as it accepts every other fact of observation. And indeed it greatly welcomes the proposition that *discovery* at times may be assisted by non-experimental principles; it does so because such a proposition is in accord with the results of experience. But so far as demonstration is con-cerned, the history of human knowledge clearly makes it plain that all attempts to explain natural facts have continually failed when based on propositions derived from religious or metaphysical principles. Enquiries

of this kind are now entirely abandoned in astronomy, geology, physiology and all other similar sciences. If then traces of them remain in sociology and in its branches of law, political economy, ethics and so on, this is only because these studies have not yet attained to a strictly scientific status.

(98) Some people assert that a 'miracle' is impossible because it would be going flat against the recognised constancy of natural laws. But this is no more than to offer as proof of an assertion the assertion itself—which is simply to argue in a circle. If a miracle could be proved, this would of itself invalidate the constancy of natural laws. The nub of the question lies wholly in the proof of the fact. Of course, it is understood that such a proof has to satisfy criteria which become all the more severe the further we are carried outside the circuit of known facts. If it should be asserted that one day the sun will convey its planetary system to a region where the laws of chemistry, physics and mechanics will be different from the laws we know of at present, we would have no objection to make against the truth or falseness of the assertion, but we should remind its promulgator that there rests on him the onus of proving it.

(vi) *Metaphysical science and experimental science**

(19) The metaphysicians in general call *science*† the knowledge of the essence of things, of prime causes. If we accepted this definition, we would have to concede that this present enquiry of ours is in no way scientific, for not only are we abstaining from indicating *essences* and *prime causes*:

---

* Chapter I, §§19, 20.

† In a passage in the *Transformazione della Democrazia* (p. 25), not included in the extracts in Part Three below, Pareto illustrates the differences between metaphysical and experimental concepts of science thus: 'Metaphysics starts from the experimental method and then descends to real facts, whereas the experimental method starts from the real facts and then moves forward to determine their common properties. These we can certainly call abstractions, but experimental abstraction has nothing in common with metaphysical abstraction. We make this point because there are many writers who, in ignorance of the experimental method, confuse these two types of abstraction. The series of experimental abstractions is infinite. Every general principle can be made dependent on another principle even more general, and so on without limit. But constant following of this procedure is not always to be recommended; it can be appropriate at times, but not at other times. It is desirable to avoid going beyond the confines of present experience and the consequent risk of wandering about in an imaginary vacuum. Newton did well to stop at universal gravitation; modern scientists do well in seeking to go further than Newton, and future scientists will find it possible to go even further than the modern. It is of paramount importance to know how and when to limit one's researches. Those of Newton's successors who limited themselves to studying the inferences of the principle of universal gravitation did very valuable work. Their work would have been useless and indeed harmful for science had they tried to discover the *essence* of gravity—as useless and detrimental as is the work of certain economists of the present day in their vain speculations about value ... [therein showing that they] know nothing of the experimental method.'

we do not even know what these terms mean. Vera says*: 'The notion of science and the notion of absolute science are inseparable. . . . Now if there is an absolute science, it can be none other than philosophy. Thus philosophy is the common foundation of all the sciences and is, so to say, the common intelligence of all intelligences.' We want to have nothing to do with such a science or with those other high-sounding things that go with it, according to Vera. 'The absolute or the essence, and unity or the necessary relations of beings, these are the two prime conditions of science.' Both of these will be found wanting in our enquiry. We do not even know what they mean. What we seek are the relationships of things within the limits of space and time known to us and as revealed to us by experiment and observation. '. . . The science which knows the absolute,' Vera continues, 'and understands the inner reason of things, knows also how and why events and beings are engendered; moreover, it not only knows this, but in a certain way engenders them itself through its very grasp of the absolute. . . . A science of the absolute which subsisted apart from the absolute, and hence failed to realise its real inner nature, would not be a science of the absolute or, to be correct, a science at all.'

(20) Admirable! We can at least agree with Vera on this. If science must be what he defines as science—in terms as impressive as they are, to us, incomprehensible—then in this enquiry we are not dealing with science. We are, instead, dealing with something else, which Vera well describes in a particular case when he says: 'In general, mechanics is only a medley of experimental data and mathematical formulae.' To be still more general, one could say: a medley of experimental data and logical inferences from such data. Granting for a moment that this is *non-science*, Vera and Hegel would then be quite right in saying that the theories of Newton are not science but *non-science*. So be it: it is precisely with this *non-science* that I wish to deal, for my aim is to construct a sociological system on the model of celestial mechanics, chemistry and other similar *non-sciences* . . . (21) A reader might remark: 'Granting that, why then throughout your book are you perpetually talking about science, meaning thereby *non-science*?' . . . My reply is: If the word *science* generally had the meaning which the metaphysicists give it, then I would, in rejecting the meaning, rigorously abstain from using the word. But this is not the case. Most people call celestial mechanics, physics, chemistry and so forth *sciences*, and to call them *non-sciences* or something else like it would, I feel, be simply ridiculous. Still, if any one is not satisfied with this, let him put a *non-* in front of the words *science* and *scientific* wherever he finds them in this text, and he will see that the argument makes its point just the same because it is an argument based on things and not on words.

(vii) *The logico-experimental tribunal*†

(17) . . . If someone says: A has the property B, we have to know, before going any further in the matter, who will adjudicate the case between him

---

* Augusto Vera: *Introduction à la philosophie de Hegel*, 1855. The passages cited by Pareto occur within pp. 78–89.

† Chapter I, §17.

and someone else who says that A does *not* have the property B. If they mutually agree that objective experience should be the judge, then this latter will decide whether or not A has the property B. We have fixed our position firmly in the domain of logico-experimental science and—the reader should know this—the intention throughout this study is to keep in this domain and to refuse to leave it, come what may. Therefore, if the reader prefers to have a judge other than objective experience, let him proceed no further with this book—just as he would not go on with a lawsuit before a court whose credentials he disputed.

(viii) *Physical and sociological laws**

(99) For us, therefore, scientific laws are nothing other than experimental uniformities. In this respect, there is no difference whatever between the laws of political economy or sociology and the laws of the other sciences. Such differences as there are between them are of quite another kind, subsisting mainly in the varying degrees to which the effects of the various laws intertwine. Celestial mechanics is fortunate in being able to study the effects of a single law: uniformity. Now, the effects could be such as to make difficult the discovery of the uniformity inherent in them; but, by a further piece of good fortune, it so happens that the mass of the sun is much greater than the mass of the planets, so that the uniformity is revealed in a simple—though not strictly exact—form by assuming that the planets move round a fixed sun. Thus we are able to rectify the error made in the first approximation. Chemistry, physics and mechanics are likewise able in many cases to study separate laws, or at least by various means they can separate the effects of these laws. Even so, in some cases the intertwining is so complicated that it is difficult to disentangle the effects. Such cases crop up in biology, geology and especially in meteorology. It is with these latter sciences that the social sciences are most closely related.

(100) A further difference in scientific laws lies in the possibility or impossibility of separating their effects from one another by means of experiment, as distinct from observation. Certain sciences, like chemistry, physics, mechanics and biology can and do make very great use of experiment. Some sciences can employ it only sparingly; others—like the social sciences—can make little or no use of it; while yet other sciences cannot use it all, like celestial mechanics, for example—at least, so far as the movements of heavenly bodies are concerned.

(101 Neither economic and social laws nor the laws of other sciences can properly suffer exceptions. A uniformity which is not uniform can have no meaning at all. The phenomenon which is commonly called 'an exception to the law' is in reality the superimposing of another effect of another law on the effect of this first law. In this respect, all scientific laws, even the laws of mathematics, suffer exceptions. All weighty bodies on the surface of the earth tend towards the centre of the earth; but a feather stirred by the wind moves away from the centre of gravity, and a balloon filled with hydrogen rises up into the air. The main difficulty met with in

---

* Chapter I, §§99–101.

very many sciences lies precisely in finding ways for unravelling this tangled skein produced by the intertwining of many different uniformities.

2. THE PURPOSE

(i) *Logical and non-logical behaviour**

(149) Every social phenomenon can be considered under two aspects: either as it is in reality, or as it appears to the mind of one person or another. The first aspect we will call the *Objective* aspect, the second the *Subjective* aspect. Such a distinction is necessary since we cannot classify in one and the same category the operations of a chemist in his laboratory and the operations of a practitioner of magic. There is a difference between the behaviour of the Greek sailors in using their oars to drive their ship through the water, and their behaviour in offering sacrifices to Poseidon to ensure a safe and rapid voyage. In Rome, the Laws of the Twelve Tables punished any one who put a spell on the harvest; this we distinguish from burning a field of standing corn.

We must not be led astray by the names given to these two classes. In reality, both are subjective, for all human knowledge is subjective. We have to distinguish them not so much by any intrinsic differences as by the greater or lesser amount of factual knowledge which we ourselves have. We know—or think we know—that sacrifices to Poseidon can have no effect at all on the course of a voyage, and so we distinguish them from other forms of behaviour which, so far as we can tell, are capable of such an effect. If eventually we should discover that, in fact, sacrifices to Poseidon were capable of ensuring a calm sea and a prosperous voyage, we would have to alter our classification and include such sacrifices in the category of actions capable of ensuring such an end. ... All that this amounts to is that, when someone makes a classification, he does so according to the knowledge he has. One cannot imagine how it could be otherwise.

(150) There are actions, forms of behaviour, which consist of means to an end and logically connect the means with the end. And there are other actions in which this characteristic is lacking. These two kinds of behaviour are very different according as they are considered under the Objective or the Subjective aspect. Under the Subjective aspect, almost all human actions belong to the first, the logical class. For the Greek sailors, the sacrifice to Poseidon and the act of rowing were equally logical means of navigation.

To avoid prolixity which might be irksome, it will be convenient to give names to these classes of behaviour. It would perhaps be best to use terms that have no meanings in themselves, such as the letters of the alphabet. But against this it can be argued that such a procedure would impair the clarity of the argument. We must resign ourselves, therefore, to using the terms of ordinary speech. But the reader must bear firmly in mind that these terms—or their etymologies—are in no way whatever

---

* Chapter II, §§149–54, 161.

descriptive of the things they indicate. These things must be examined directly; their name is simply a sort of label, useful for indicating them as and when they are referred to.

This being made clear, let us employ the term *logical behaviour* for those actions which are logically linked to an end, not only in respect to the person performing them, but also to those other people who have more extensive knowledge: that is to say, behaviour which is subjectively and objectively logical in the sense here indicated. Other actions we shall call *non-logical*. This does not at all mean that they are *illogical*.

(151) This non-logical class is divisible into various genera, as set out in the following synoptic table of classification of logical and non-logical behaviour.

Has the behaviour a logical end?

Objectively a   *Subjectively* b

		Objectively a	Subjectively b
Class I	Logical Behaviour		
	The objective end is the same as the subjective end	YES	YES
Class II	Non-Logical Behaviour		
	The objective end is different from the subjective end		
	Subclass 1	NO	NO
	Subclass 2	NO	YES
	Subclass 3	YES	NO
	Subclass 4	YES	YES

Species of Subclasses 3 and 4

3*a*, 4*b*: The objective end would be accepted by the person concerned if he knew it;

3*b*, 4*b*: The objective end would be rejected by the person concerned if he knew it.

The end referred to here is an immediate end; consideration of an indirect, non-immediate end is excluded. The objective end is a real end, situated in the field of observation and experience; it is not an imaginary end, outside this field. On the other hand, an imaginary end may be a subjective end.

(152) Acts of logical behaviour are more numerous among civilised peoples. Activities associated with the arts and sciences—at least for the people engaged in arts and sciences—belong to this Class I. For those who are engaged in the material performance of them, those who only execute the instructions of their superiors, these acts of behaviour belong to Subclass 4 of Class II (II-4). Behaviour studied by political economy also belongs, to a very great extent, to the class of logical behaviour. We must, moreover, include in this category a certain number of military, political, legal and similar forms of behaviour.

(153) Thus induction makes us recognise how great a part in social phenomena is played by non-logical behaviour. In proceeding further in our examination of non-logical actions, we shall have occasion in this section to make only passing reference to a good many matters which will

be specifically dealt with later on in this study when we return to matters touched on here.

(154) And now, so as to understand these acts of non-logical behaviour better, let us look at a few examples. Many others will more suitably arise in illustration in later sections. Here are some examples of Class II behaviour.

Subclasses 1 and 3, which have no subjective logical end, are of very little importance for the human race. Human beings have a very marked tendency to cover their behaviour with a veneer of logic; almost all human behaviour therefore belongs to subclasses 2 and 4. Many of the things we do which are imposed on us by courtesy and custom could indeed be included in subclass 1. But most often men produce some reason or other to justify acts of behaviour of this kind, and so they must be placed in subclass 2. If we set aside the indirect motive resulting from the fact that a man who departs from common usage is censured and ill-thought of, we may find some forms of behaviour to place in subclasses 1 and 3.

Hesiod says: 'Do not urinate at the mouth of a river which flows into the sea, nor into a spring. That you must avoid. Do not defecate in these places, for it is not seemly so to do.' The precept that one should not defile the mouths of rivers belongs to subclass 1. No objective or subjective end can be perceived to behaviour which avoids such defilement. The precept that one should not defile spring-water belongs to subclass 3. It has an objective end which we today can appreciate even if Hesiod could not: to avoid the spreading of certain diseases.

It is probable that among savages and primitive peoples, there are a good many actions of subclasses 1 and 3. But travellers, intent on learning at all costs the reason for the behaviour they observe, end up by obtaining, in one way or another, some answer which moves these acts of behaviour into subclasses 2 and 4.

(161) Logical behaviour, for the most part at least, is the result of a process of reasoning. Non-logical behaviour originates mainly from a definite psychic state: sentiments, subconscious influences and so on. It is for psychology to study this psychic state. In this enquiry we accept it as a fact without seeking to go any further than that.

(ii) *Logical development of non-logical behaviour**

(180) Human beings have so strong a tendency to attach logical developments to non-logical actions that everything and anything can serve as a pretext for them to indulge in this favourite occupation. Associations of ideas and acts were probably as common at one time in Greece as they were in Rome, but in Greece most of them disappeared and sooner than was the case in Rome. Greek anthropomorphism transformed simple associations of ideas and acts into attributes of gods. . . . It may be that what is observable in the development of Greek religious ideas is simply a number of stages—rather more advanced than in the case of Rome—in the evolution from the concrete to the abstract, from the non-logical to the logical.

---

* Chapter II, §§180, 184, 207, 211, 212, 217.

(184) Let us suppose that the only instances of custom and superstition known to us are those in which the success of magical operations depends on the intervention of the Devil. We would perhaps be able to accept as true the logical interpretation and say: 'Men believe in the efficacy of magical operations because they believe in the Devil.' This inference would not be substantially modified by the knowledge that in other instances the intervention is ascribed, not to the Devil, but to some divinity or other. But it is nullified when examples are produced which are absolutely independent of any divine intervention. In such cases, we see that the substance of such phenomena consists of act; of non-logical behaviour which associate certain words, invocations, and practices with particular desired effects, and that the intervention of gods, devils, spirits and so forth is nothing more than the logical form given to these associations.

We should note that, the substance remaining intact, several forms may coexist in the same individual without his being aware of what share belongs to each. The Witch in the Second Idyll of Theocritus relies both on the intervention of the gods and on the efficacy of magical practices without clearly distinguishing how these agencies of power work. She calls on Hecate to make the philtres she has compounded more deadly than those of Circe, Medea or the golden-haired Perimede. If she had relied on Hecate alone, it would have been simpler to invoke the goddess directly for the effects desired from the philtres. When she repeats the refrain: 'Wryneck, Wry-neck, bring this man to my dwelling', she evidently envisages some occult association between the magic bird and the desired effect.

For age after age people have believed in silly stuff like this in various forms, and even today there are those who are influenced by it. The difference is that, over the last two or three centuries, the numbers of those who laugh at it as Lucian did have increased. But spiritualism, telepathy and 'Christian Science' are evidence enough to show how much power is still exerted by these and similar sentiments.

(207) In our day, we can say what we like about witches, but not about sex; and just as, once upon a time, governments used to persecute those who freely discussed the Bible—either out of a conviction that such free handling of sacred matters was an evil, or in the desire to placate those who can only be regarded in these matters as ignorant fanatics—so modern governments for similar motives take stern action against people who uninhibitedly write and speak about the sexual act. Lucretius was able to write with equal freedom on the religion of the gods and on the religion of sex.

(211) As late as the eighteenth century, witches continued to be condemned. Governments no less than the church gave way to popular prejudice, and thereby helped to strengthen this prejudice, although they were certainly not the creators of it. Indeed, far from having at the outset enforced the belief in this type of non-logical behaviour, the church on the contrary had this belief enforced on it, and so sought to give it logical interpretations. It is only later that the church comes to accept it entirely, with the corrective of these interpretations.

(212) Therefore they err who, seeing logical actions everywhere, blame catholic theology for the witchcraft trials. Such persecutions, be it noted, were as common in protestant as in catholic communities. Belief in magic

is to be found in all periods and amongst all peoples. Its interpretations are the servants, not the masters, of the thing itself.

Some writers, like Michelet in his *Sorcière*, see in feudalism the cause of witchcraft. But where was feudalism when, in Rome, the Twelve Tables singled out for condemnation the casting of spells over the harvests? Where was feudalism when men believed in the powers of the witches of Thessaly, or when Apuleius was accused of having gained by magic arts the affections of the woman he married? Instances of this sort are legion. The 'feudal' interpretation is merely a variant of the christian explanation; the only difference is that the Great Enemy has changed his name: instead of Satan he is now called Feudalism.

(217) From this survey of the question, the following characteristics can be deduced:

1. There exists a non-logical nucleus which combines in a simple form certain acts and words which have specific effects—such as a hurricane or the destruction of crops.*

2. From this nucleus, many branches of logical interpretation spread out. It is impossible not to recognise that in general these interpretations are contrived only in order to account for the fact that storms can be raised or lulled, crops destroyed or preserved. It is only very exceptionally that the opposite phenomenon is observable: that is, the case in which it is the logical theory which has led to belief in the fact. Such interpretations are not always clearly distinguishable from each other; often they intertwine so that the person adhering to them may not know exactly what role or importance is to be attributed to each.

3. Logical interpretations assume the forms which are most commonly current in the epoch in which they are evolved. They are comparable to fashions in clothes.

4. There is no direct evolution, of the kind indicated in Figure 11. Evolution occurs in the form shown in Figure 12. The pure non-logical action is not transformed into an action of logical form; it continues to subsist with the other actions deriving from it. One cannot determine how this transformation occurs by endeavouring, for example, to establish that simply from the association of acts and

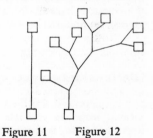

Figure 11   Figure 12

---

* In §§186–206 of the *Treatise*, Pareto examines in detail pagan and christian beliefs in the prevention and excitation of tempests and in the control, beneficial or harmful, of the weather. Here we need only cite his observation in §187: 'There are many cases in which it is believed that, by means of certain rites and actions, it is possible to raise or suppress storms. Sometimes it is not indicated exactly how the effect comes about; at other times, supposed reasons are given: the effect is held to be the theoretically explicable consequence of the operation of certain forces. In general, meteorological phenomena are considered to be dependent on certain rites and actions, either directly or indirectly, through the intervention of higher powers.'

facts (fetishism) men passed on to a theological interpretation, then to a metaphysical interpretation, and finally to a positivist interpretation. There is no such succession in time. Moreover, the interpretations which might be called fetishistic, magical, pseudo-experimental or experimental are very often mingled together in a way which makes it impossible to distinguish between them; and very probably those who accept them may be unable to distinguish them. They know that certain acts must have certain definite consequences, and they do not trouble to understand how this comes about.

5. Certainly, in the long run, the degree of intellectual maturity of people exerts an influence on the phenomenon of non-logical behaviour, but there is in this no constant correlation. The Romans did not burn witches or sorcerers, yet their scientific development was without question inferior to that of seventeenth-century Italians, Germans, French and other peoples who slaughtered witches and sorcerers in great numbers. At the end of the twelfth century and the beginning of the thirteenth, these unfortunates were not persecuted at all; yet there can be no question but that the intellectual and scientific development of that age was inferior by a long way to that of the seventeenth century.

6. It is not by the logical devices of the church, of governments or of any other institutions of authority that belief in such non-logical behaviour came to be imposed. It is the other way about: it was the non-logical behaviour which imposed on these institutions the necessity of finding logical devices to explain them. This is not to deny that, in their turn, these devices may have strengthened belief in non-logical behaviour, and even in some cases given rise to it where it did not previously exist. This last induction puts us in a position to understand how similar phenomena may have come into being, and how we may be in error when, knowing non-logical behaviour only under its logical varnish, we give to this logical varnish an importance it does not merit.

(iii) *Constant and variable factors**

(218) In all the many cases we have studied in regard to tempests,† there is a common constant factor: the belief that by certain means the weather can be influenced. Furthermore, there is a differing variable factor: the means themselves and the reasons why they are employed. The more important factor is clearly the first. When and where it exists, men have little difficulty in finding the other. It could well be, therefore, that in the determining of the form of society, factors similar to the constant factor just revealed might be of greater importance than other factors. For the present, we cannot come to any decision on this point; induction is simply making us aware of an approach which it will be advisable later to take.

As often happens with the inductive method, we have found not only the thing we were looking for but also something else which was far from our purview. We set out to discover how non-logical behaviour can assume

---

* Chapter II, §§218, 219.   † See note on page 187.

logical forms. By considering a special case in some detail, we have seen how this comes about. But more than this: we have seen how such phenomena have a constant—or almost constant—factor, and also a very variable factor. It is precisely the constant factors in phenomena which science seeks for in order to arrive at the understanding of uniformities. We shall have to make, therefore, a scientific study of these factors.

(219) Meanwhile, other inductions emerge, not as yet affirmations because they are derived from too few facts, but rather as propositions we have to verify as the scope of our enquiry is extended.

1. If for a moment we consider the facts exclusively from the logico-experimental aspect, the position of the church in regard to magic is simply insane, and all those stories about demons are ridiculously puerile. Assuming this, there are some who draw from this premise the conclusion that the religion of the church also is insane and puerile, and therefore harmful to society. Can we accept this conclusion? We must first note that the argument is valid not only for catholicism but for all other religions, indeed, for all systems of metaphysics—in fact, for everything which is not logico-experimental science. It is impossible to accept such a conclusion and to consider as insane the greater part of the lives of all human societies from remote times down to the present day. Moreover, if everything which is not logical is harmful to society and hence also to the individual, then we ought not to find instances (like those observable amongst animals,* and those which we are going to observe amongst human beings) in which—on the contrary—certain non-logical behaviour is beneficial, sometimes extremely so. The inferences being wrong, the reasoning also must be wrong. Where then is the error?

The complete syllogism would go like this: (*i*) Any doctrine whatever which has an absurd element in it is absurd: the element in church doctrine which relates to magic is absurd, therefore . . . etc. (*ii*) Any doctrine whatever which is not logico-experimental is harmful to society: the doctrine of the church is not logico-experimental, therefore . . . etc. The propositions which probably falsify this process of reasoning are: (*a*) any doctrine whatever which has an absurd element in it is absurd; and (*b*) any doctrine which is not logico-experimental is harmful to society. It behoves us therefore to examine closely these propositions to see whether or not they correspond with the facts. But to do this, we must first have a theory of doctrines and of the operation of these on individuals and on society. This is something we shall have to deal with later on in this enquiry.

2. Questions similar to those raised in regard to doctrines arise also in respect to human beings. If we consider human behaviour from the

---

* In §§155-7 of the *Treatise*, Pareto cites examples of instinctive, non-rational behaviour by animals and insects which is vital to their survival and well-being, many of which are not only highly complex but also involve provision for the future as well as for the present. 'Granting that animals do not reason, we can place almost all their so-called instinctive acts in subclass 3, and some may even belong to subclass 1. Subclass 3 is the pure type of non-logical behaviour; the study of it in animals helps to an understanding of non-logical behaviour in human beings.' He later notes (§157): '. . . even in the animal one can detect a seed of the logic that is to flower so richly in the human being.'

logico-experimental aspect, then there is no other name but imbecile for a writer who produces the staggering idiocies we find in Bodin's *Demonomania*. And if we regard such matters from the viewpoint of the good or evil done to others, then 'knave' and 'murderer' are the only suitable names to be given to the men who, influenced by such idiocies, have inflicted the bitterest sufferings on so very many of their fellow-men, hounding not a few of them to death.

But straightway we perceive that this mode of reasoning extends to the whole what in reality belongs only to the part. There are any number of examples to show that a man may be out of his senses in some things and yet levelheaded enough in other matters; dishonest in some of his dealings, honest in others. From this dichotomy arise two errors, equal in origin but different in appearances. Equally false are the following propositions:

A. Bodin has spoken utter stupidity and caused great harm to others;

B. Bodin was an intelligent and honest man; therefore what he wrot; in his *Demonomania* is sensible, and his aims and achievements are worthy.

We see from this that we cannot judge of the logico-experimental value and utility of a doctrine by facile considerations of the worth and merits of its author, but that we must instead pursue the steep and arduous path of studying doctrines directly in the facts. And so once again we are led to conclusions drawn from examination of the doctrines themselves.

(iv) Logical forms in religious and political systems*

(220) It is worthwhile to note the logical form given by the Romans to their relations with the gods. In general, the form is that of a precise and clear contract which has to be interpreted according to the rules of law. If we were to stop at this point, we should see in this merely a manifestation of what has been termed the 'legal-mindedness' of the Romans. But similar facts are to be observed amongst all peoples. Even in our day, the pious housewife who promises a few coppers to Saint Anthony of Padua if he helps her to retrieve something she has lost, is acting towards the saint exactly as the Romans acted towards their gods. What distinguishes the Romans in this respect is the abundance and precision of the details, the predominance of form over substance—in short, the force of cohesion of acts with other acts. From this we gain an insight into the psychic state of this people.

(226) The Romans dealt with the substance as it suited their convenience while at the same time strictly respecting the forms or—as it is better to say—certain associations of ideas and acts. The Athenians modified both substance and forms, whereas to the Spartans it was abhorrent to alter either. Before the battle of Marathon, the Athenians sent to Sparta for help:

---

* Chapter II, §§220, 226, 229, 230, 233, 234, 242, 244, 246.

The Spartan authorities readily promised their aid, but unfortunately it was now the ninth day of the moon; an ancient law or custom forbade them to march, in this month at least, during the last quarter before the full moon; but after the full they engaged to march without delay. Five days' delay at this critical moment might prove the utter ruin of the endangered city; yet the reason assigned seems to have been no pretence on the part of the Spartans. It was mere blind tenacity of ancient habit, which we shall find to abate, though never to disappear, as we advance in their history.*

The Athenians would have changed both substance and form. The Romans would have changed the substance while respecting the form. For example, in order to declare war, one of the *feciales* (order of Heralds) had to fling a spear into the territory of the enemy. But how could this rite be performed and war be duly declared when the enemy was Pyrrhus, whose states were far distant from Rome? Nothing easier! The Romans had a soldier of Pyrrhus as prisoner; they made him buy a small piece of ground in the Flaminian Circus, and the *fecialis* flung his spear at that. Thus was formally respected the Roman people's association of ideas between the throwing of a herald's spear and a just war.

(229) Further examples could be adduced of this characteristic of the Roman mind, which is especially observable in their legal history. In all sectors of Roman law, we can perceive manifestations of a state of mind which accepts development and modifications while maintaining close regard for associations of ideas. Traces of it are to be seen in the system of the *legis actio* and also in the formulary system, and it is altogether paramount in the sector of the so-called legal fictions. These are to be found amongst all peoples at certain stages of their history, but the extent of the development and long survival of legal fictions are remarkable in the case of ancient Rome, as they are in the case of modern England. [Cf. §244 overleaf.]

(230) In political life we find similar manifestations of the same phenomena. By an evolution common to the majority of the Greek and Latin city-states, the king was superseded by new magistrates in Athens, Sparta and Rome. But in Athens both substance and form were completely changed; in Sparta the change was much less marked in both respects; while in Rome the changes were more marked in the substance than in the form. To preserve certain associations of ideas, the sacerdotal functions of the king pass, in Athens, to the archon-king, in Rome to the *rex sacrorum*; but neither of these officials has political importance. In Rome, the kingship is transformed with the least possible alteration in the forms. The supreme magistracy becomes annual and is divided between two consuls, each of whom is able to act on his own and to veto the actions of the other. . . .

(233) At the end of his life, Caesar appeared to be desirous of escaping from this rule of preserving the forms even where the substance is changed. A people like the Athenians would not have thought this at all unreasonable, but the few Romans who at this time were still imbued with the old

---

* Grote, *History of Greece*, Vol. IV, pp. 341–2.

ideas were indignant at the disassociation of ideas and acts which Caesar was attempting. Only if the part is taken for the whole can it be said that it was the excessive honours he demanded should be paid him which brought about Caesar's fall. These honours were only one factor in a whole complex of factors which aroused the resentment of those Roman citizens who still had the psychic state of their ancestors. Augustus knew better how to respect tradition. He lies glibly and boldly when he says in the Ancyra inscription:

> In my sixth and seventh consulates, after the ending of the civil wars, I restored to the Senate and Roman People the powers which had been granted to me by universal consent, and in honour of that action a decree of the Senate gave me the name of Augustus. . . . Ever after, although I have been above all others in honours, I have had no powers greater than my colleagues.

Velleius Paterculus, who loads Augustus and Tiberius with the most fulsome praises, says that Augustus returned to the laws their former force, to the courts their former dignity, to the Senate its former majesty, and to the magistrates their former authority.

(234) Under the Empire, there are still consuls and tribunes, but they are no more than empty names. In the same way, under Augustus the *comitia* are still convoked for the election of magistrates, and—what is even more surprising—we find even in Vespasian's time a law voted by the *comitia* investing the emperor with power! On the face of it, one is tempted to think that time really must have hung very heavily on Roman hands for them to indulge in such meaningless mumbo-jumbo! . . .

(242) However, one might well ask, could a system so patently absurd from the logical point of view have existed and survived? These magistrates with equal rights, like the two consuls and the two censors; these tribunes who could control the entire juridical and political system; these *comitia* entrammelled with all the complications of the auspices; this senate without any clearly defined attributes—surely such a ramshackle machine as this could never have functioned. Yet it did function, for century after century, and it gave Rome the mastery of the whole Mediterranean world. Its final breakdown came about only because control of it fell into the hands of a new people which no longer had the *religio* of the old. Thanks to the interaction of the binding power of non-logical behaviour and of forces of innovation, Rome succeeded in reconciling order with freedom, and established a golden mean between Sparta and Athens.

(244) Among modern peoples, the English—at least, down to the end of the nineteenth century—have more than any other resembled the Romans in their psychic state.* English law is still replete with fictions.

---

* Pareto at this point in the *Treatise* appends the following footnote: 'However, all this is tending to change as a result of new customs and attitudes which seem to be on the verge of becoming entrenched in England. This reservation has to be made for, by the first decade of the twentieth century, the government of England was falling into the hands of Welsh and Irish fanatics. If this is not a temporary aberration, but is indicative of a change in the

The English political system maintains the same antiquated forms, although its substance is constantly changing. England still has a king, as in the days of the Plantagenets, the Tudors and the Stuarts; but he has less authority and power than the president of the United States. In the reign of Charles I we see a civil war fought by the King-in-Parliament against the King-in-Camp. The Romans never contrived so elaborately subtle a fiction! Even today, the ceremonial involved in the opening of Parliament is archaic to the point of comedy. Before the Commons there appears a majestic individual called the Gentleman Usher of the Black Rod, who invites them to proceed to the House of Lords to hear the Speech from the Throne. They move off thither, and listen to the Gracious Speech, later returning to their own chamber where the Speaker imparts to them, with an absolutely straight face, what they have already heard as clearly as he. Immediately a bill has to be read, as a plain matter of form, to safeguard the right of Parliament to be the first to discuss public business, without going into the reasons for its being assembled. English political organisation is adapted to the needs of the English people in the same way as the political organisation of ancient Rome was adapted to the needs of the Roman people, and all modern peoples have tried to copy the English system more or less faithfully. This organisation enabled England to emerge victorious from the napoleonic wars and has obtained for Englishmen greater liberties than the majority of European peoples have enjoyed.

(246) Every people is governed by an *elite*, by the 'choice' elements in the population. Strictly speaking, it is the psychic state of this elite we have been studying in the foregoing pages. The most one can say further is that in the cases cited the rest of the population accepted the impulse given by the elite. An elite can change with variations in the men composing it or in their descendants, or even through the infiltration of extraneous elements belonging either to the same people or to some foreign people. . . .

(v) *Rationalisation of non-logical behaviour**

(249) Our enquiries in the preceding pages have made us aware, in addition to certain incidental inductions, of the following considerations:

1. The existence and importance of non-logical behaviour. Our enquiry differs in this from many sociological theories which either scorn or neglect non-logical behaviour, or consider it of little importance. Methods of studying human behaviour in relation to the social equilibrium will vary in the degree to which one gives greater importance to logical or to non-logical actions. We have now reached the point for us to go deeper into this question.

2. Non-logical actions are usually seen and assessed from the ogical standpoint by those who perform them and by those who study

---

character of the country as a whole, then the England of the future will be very unlike the England of the past. It is to this latter, the only England we as yet know anything of, that I am referring when I speak of England in the context above.'
* Chapter III, §§249, 251, 254, 255, 260.

them with a view to formulating a theory about them. This sets us a necessary and all-important task in that our study aims at removing these 'logical' masks to reveal the things which are hidden beneath them. In this respect also our work differs from that of many theorists who halt before these masks without going further. Indeed, they do not consider them to be masks at all but believe them to be the substantial element in human behaviour. We must closely examine such theories for, if we were to find them true—if, that is to say, they are in agreement with experience—we should have to adopt a quite different method from that which is entailed by the recognition that it is the things under the masks which, in fact, constitute the substantial element.

3. The experimental truth of a theory and its social utility are different things. A theory experimentally true may be useful or harmful to society, and the same applies also to a theory which is experimentally false. Very many people deny this. . . .

4. In regard to logical and non-logical behaviour, differences arise between individuals, or—looking at things as a whole—between social classes. There are also differences between the degrees of utility which theories experimentally true or false offer for individuals and for classes. The same applies to the sentiments expressed through non-logical actions. Such differences are denied by many, and asserting their existence arouses the scorn of not a few. Hence it will be necessary for us to pursue this matter and to scrutinise carefully what the facts tell us.

(251) Our main concern will be to identify traces of non-logical behaviour in the theories and descriptions of social facts which are made by various authorities. This will enable us to get an approximate notion of the ways whereby non-logical behaviour is disguised by logical masks.

(254) To turn to cases: let us begin with those in which it is easy to recognise experimental truth beneath forms of expression which are imperfect and partly erroneous. Thence we shall proceed to examine other cases in which experimental truth is more difficult to perceive.

Here, for example, is a quotation from *La Cité Antique* by Fustel de Coulanges: 'From all these beliefs, from all these customs, all these laws, it clearly results that from the religion of the hearth human beings learned to appropriate the soil and on it based their title to it.'* But really, it is strange that domestic religion should have preceded possession of the soil. Of this pre-existence of domestic religion the author gives no proof at all. It could well be the other way about, or that religion and possession were developed together. It is clear that Fustel de Coulanges has the preconceived idea that possession must have a *cause*; assuming this, he looks for the cause and finds it in religion. Seen in this way, the act of possession becomes a logical action, derived from religion; and all religion in its turn can be logically derived from something else. Now it is a curious coincidence that the author himself gives us the means for rectifying his theory. A little earlier he had written: 'There are three things which, from the most ancient times, one finds founded and solidly established in these Greek and

---

* *La Cité Antique* (1885), p. 73; translation by Willard Small, *The Ancient City*, p. 89.

Italian communities: domestic religion, the family, the right of property—three things which were obviously related in the beginning and which seem to have been inseparable.'* How ever could the writer have failed to see that this passage is in flat contradiction with his later statement, that religion preceded possession? If three things, A, B and C are 'inseparable', then one of them—for example, A—cannot of itself produce one of the others—for example, B. For if A has produced B, it must therefore have been separate and distinct from B. We have then of necessity to make a choice between these two propositions of the same writer. If we want to keep the first, the second must go, and *vice versa*. In fact, our decisions must be to discard the proposition which puts religion and possession in a relationship of cause and effect, and maintain the proposition that puts them in a relationship of interdependence. The very facts noted by Fustel de Coulanges impose this choice on us. He writes: 'And the family, which by duty and religion remains grouped around its altar, becomes fixed to the soil like the altar itself.'† The comment comes spontaneously to mind: Yes, provided that be possible. Supposing a social situation may exist in which the family cannot settle permanently on the soil, then it is the religion which will have to be modified. It is clear that in this field of human affairs there has been a series of actions and reactions, and it is not possible for us to say how things were at the outset. The fact surely is that it has somehow come about that certain peoples have lived in family groups fixed to the soil, and this has produced as its manifestation a certain form of religion. This religion in its turn has served to promote the continued existence of families separate and fixed to the soil.

(255) This particular case we are considering exemplifies a very common error: that of substituting relationships of cause and effect for relationships of interdependence. A further error arises from this misprision: that of including in the category of logical behaviour the effect which, erroneously, is thought to be a logical outcome of the cause.

(260) The logical interpretation of non-logical behaviour becomes in its turn a 'cause' of logical, and sometimes even of non-logical, behaviour. All this has to be taken into account in order to determine the social equilibrium. From this point of view, the interpretation of the average man is generally of greater importance than that of the theorising intellectual. So far as the social equilibrium is concerned, it is much more important to know what ordinary people understand by 'virtue' than to know what philosophers think about it.

(vi) *Reasons for minimising non-logical behaviour*‡

(261) Of course, it is a fact that very few writers entirely neglect to take account of non-logical behaviour. But with most of them, such behaviour is considered only in relation to certain natural inclinations which one must, willy-nilly, recognise as existing in men. But the eclipse of logical

---

* *Op. cit.*, p. 63; Small, p. 78.   † *Op. cit.*, p. 64; Small, p. 79.
‡ Chapter III, §§261–5, 270–82, 300, 304, 305.

interpretations is only temporary; driven out on one side, they return by another. The significance of these natural inclinations is minimised, and then it is assumed that from them men draw logical inferences and act according to these inferences.

(262) Such is the general situation. But in the particular, theorists have a further and very powerful motive for replacing non-logical by logical behaviour. If we suppose that certain actions are logical, it then becomes much more easy to embody these in a theory than if they were non-logical. There is, in the mind of each of us, an instrument for making logical inferences. This is all we need; nothing else is necessary. On the other hand, it is quite the reverse when dealing with non-logical actions, for these require close observation of many facts, and far-reaching researches in space and time. The strictest vigilance must be maintained lest imperfect evidence leads us to erroneous conclusions. In short, if we intend to formulate a theory to take account of non-logical behaviour, we are of necessity involved in a long and arduous task for we have to discover outside ourselves, outside our own reasoning and personal experience, the material of enquiry—material which, in the case of logical behaviour, our mind provides us with by the help of logic alone.

(263) If political economy as a study has progressed further than sociology, this is to a large extent due to the fact that its concern is with logical actions. It would indeed have been from the outset an admirably constituted science had it not come up against a serious obstacle, namely, that the phenomena studied were interdependent, whereas the people engaged in the study were incapable of employing the one method which alone, as we have noted, is valid in dealing with the factor of interdependence. This obstacle was partly removed when mathematics began to be applied to the study of economic phenomena. In this way a genuine science was evolved—mathematical economics—which can now claim to be on the same level as the other natural sciences.

(264) Other motives also operate to drive theorists from the field of non-logical behaviour and induce them to return to the pastures of logical behaviour. Most intellectuals and scholars do not confine themselves to the study of what is: they desire to know, and especially to make others know, what *ought* to be. In undertaking this task, they take logic for their sovereign. And so, when they have arrived at the point where the existence of non-logical behaviour is clearly recognisable, instead of pursuing the path on which they have put the first foot, they withdraw, turn aside and, as if forgetful or ignorant of non-logical actions, they march along the well-worn highway that leads to logical actions.

(265) Similarly, many theorists eliminate non-logical actions by considering them, although they do not usually say this explicitly, as things reprehensible or at least irrelevant which ought to have no part in a well ordered society. They are, for example, regarded as *superstitions* which must be unmasked by the use of reason. Of course, in practice, no one proceeds from the assumption that a man's physical and moral make-up plays no part at all in determining his actions. But nonetheless the theorist maintains that man *ought* to be moved by reason alone, and so he deliberately closes his eyes to what the daily practices of life teach us.

(270) We will now examine concrete examples of the arguments of various writers.

Aristotle begins his *Politics* thus: 'Seeing that every State is a sort of association and every association is formed for the attainment of some Good—for some presumed Good is the end of all action—it is evident that, as some Good is the object of all associations, so in the highest degree is the supreme Good the object of that association which is supreme and embraces all the rest, in other words, of the State or political association.' [*Politics*, I, 1, 1.]* Here we are entirely in the domain of logical behaviour. By deliberate will and with the aim of achieving a certain good, men have instituted the society which is called *polis*. It would seem from this that Aristotle cannot fail to entrammel himself in the absurdities of the 'social contract'. But in fact this is not the case: he very soon goes off on another tack. The principle laid down in his first paragraph will be used by him to discover what, in the city's character and composition, *ought* to be rather than what is.

(271) Scarcely has he enunciated his principle of an association whose final cause is some good than he puts it aside and gives us another explanation of the origin of society. He notes first the necessity of sexual union, and rightly observes that this does not come about by deliberate choice. Clearly he is now in the domain of non-logical behaviour. He continues: 'There are some persons qualified intellectually to form projects, and these are natural rulers or natural masters; while there are others qualified physically to carry them out, and these are subjects or natural slaves.' [I, 2, 4.] Amongst the Greeks, Nature has differentiated the woman from the slave; not so among the Barbarians, because amongst them Nature has not created beings of the commanding kind. We are now wholly in the domain of non-logical behaviour, and Aristotle moves further into it when he goes on to say that the two associations, master and slave, husband and wife, are the foundation of the family; that the village is made up of many families; that many villages constitute a city; and that, as he concludes explicitly, 'the simple associations, the household and the village, have a natural existence, and so has the State in all cases, for in the State they attain complete development'. The existence of non-logical behaviour could not possibly be more clearly affirmed.

(272) Yet if the State derives from Nature, it does not therefore derive from the deliberate will of its citizens, whom he earlier described as associating themselves with the aim of a certain Good! There is a clear contradiction between his first principle and the conclusion he eventually arrives at. Exactly how Aristotle could have fallen into this contradiction we cannot know, but if you want to trace the outline of the probable thought-process between the first principle and the conclusion, you could proceed thus: first concentrate exclusively on the concept of 'city' or 'state'. This will readily lead you to the concept of 'association', which in turn will give rise to the concept of association by *deliberate intention*. This will bring you to Aristotle's first principle. Next, think of the very many factors that

---

* Citations from Aristotle are taken from J. E. C. Welldon's version (1883), based on Bekker's text and ordering of the Books.

can be seen to exist in a city or state; this will entail concepts of the family, of master and servant, and so forth. Such concepts will not appear to owe anything to deliberate intention; they will, on the contrary, suggest the idea of something which develops *naturally*. And so you will arrive at Aristotle's second position.

(273) Even so, the contradiction is still there. What does Aristotle do about it? He gets round the difficulty by metaphysics, which never refuses its help in such desperate cases. Having recognised the existence of non-logical behaviour, he says: 'We see then that the State is a natural institution and also that it is prior to the individual. . . . Now the impulse to political association is innate in all men. Nevertheless, the author of the first association, whoever he was, was a great benefactor of human kind.' [I, 2, 13.] So there is an inclination to association which is implanted in human beings by Nature, and yet it is nevertheless necessary that an individual should institute the state! A logical action is superimposed on a non-logical action. All praise then to the noble Lady, Nature, who can so opportunely rescue philosophers from the pit they have digged for themselves!

(274) In using his famous theory of natural servitude to differentiate between Barbarians and Greeks, Aristotle has recourse to a concept of non-logical behaviour. This cannot be avoided, for clearly—logic being the same thing for Barbarians as for Greeks—there could be no difference between these nations if all actions were logical. But this is not all. Like the good observer he is, Aristotle notes that even among the citizens of the *polis* there are differences. Discussing forms of democracy, he says: 'As the agricultural population is best, it is only possible to realise the best Democracy where the people live by agriculture or grazing.' [VI, 2, 1; Bekker's text VII, 4.] And again: 'Next to an agricultural people, the best population is one consisting of graziers who depend for their living on livestock. . . . The other populations of which the remaining forms of Democracy are composed are practically a great deal lower in the scale of civilisation than these.' [I, 2, 7; Bekker's text VII, 4.] To Aristotle then there are two clearly distinguished classes of citizens. He comes near to providing a point of departure for economic determinism. But there is no reason for us to stop where Aristotle stops; if we go beyond this point we perceive that in general the behaviour of men depends on their inclinations and their occupations.

Cicero gave the ancestors of the Roman of his own day the credit of knowing that: 'The character and habits of men are not so much the creation of race and breeding as of those things which, from the nature of the place they inhabit, provide food and life and thereby condition modes and habits of living. . . .' [*De lege agraria*, II, 35, 95.]

(275) In his *Rhetoric* [II, 12, 14], Aristotle makes his celebrated analysis of the characters of men by age, classifying the traits of youth, maturity and old age. He pushes the analysis even further [II, 12, 17] and examines the effects on habits and customs of noble birth, wealth and power. All this he does admirably. But it is clear that, in employing such a method, Aristotle has entered the domain of non-logical behaviour. (276) We must also note in Aristotle a concept of evolution. In the *Politics* [II, 5, 12], he

observes that the ancestors of the Greeks probably resembled closely the vulgar and ignorant types of men among his own contemporaries.

(277) If he had continued further along the path on which he had made such commendable first steps, it is very likely that we would have had a scientific sociology as early as Aristotle's day. Why did he not take the necessary further steps? Of the many reasons possible, it is probable that a good deal of influence was exerted by a particular motive: that desire for immediate practical applications which, being premature, at all times obstructs the progress of science. Nor can we exclude that passion for preaching to people about what they ought to do—an utterly fruitless activity—instead of investigating what they actually do. His *Natural History* avoids these misleading influences and it is almost certainly because of this that it is scientifically so superior to the *Politics*.

(278) It may seem strange that a dreamer like Plato should adumbrate a concept of non-logical behaviour; yet such in fact is the case. This concept comes to light in the reasons he advances to justify establishing his republic far from the seacoast. Life by or near the sea may initially be pleasant but, Plato argues, it can only finish by being bitter and harmful for a community because 'the maritime city, by filling itself with commerce and traffic, produces unreliable and unstable habits and deceitful minds'. [*Laws*, IV.] The non-logical element is further detectable in Plato's well-known fable of the races of men. The gods who created the human race put gold into the composition of the guardians of the republic, silver in the warriors, and iron in the farmers and those who do hard work of various kinds. Plato has, moreover, a faint notion of the 'circulation of elites'. He is aware that an individual of the race of silver may well be born of the race of gold, and *vice versa*, and that the other races can produce offspring of a 'metal' different from the race they are born into. [*Republic*, III, 21, 415A.]

(279) A thinker who accepted this and sought to observe scientific principles of enquiry would be concerned to find out what might be the characteristics and the possible evolution of a society made up of different races or types of men in which the respective traits of each group are not consistently and exactly reproduced from generation to generation, and between which there is the possibility of intermingling or 'circulation'. He would thereby aim at formulating a 'science of society'. But not Plato: he has a very different purpose in mind. He is little concerned with what is; all his intellectual effort is devoted to discovering what *ought* to be. And so non-logical behaviour disappears from his purview, and his imaginative bent is indulged by the invention of logical actions in great numbers. Thus we find him instituting, with effortless ease, a magistracy charged with the task of fitting into their proper station in life those who are born into a particular race but who have characteristics different from their parents. Thus he ordains laws for maintaining or modifying manners and morals; and thus, in short, he abandons the modest domain of science in order to ascend to the sublime realms of creation.

(280) The controversies over the question: 'Can virtue be taught?' also reveal a distant notion of non-logical behaviour. From what we can discover from the documentary evidence, it would seem that Socrates considered 'virtue' to be a 'science'; we therefore find he leaves little room in

his system for non-logical behaviour. His extreme position is abandoned by Plato and Aristotle, who maintain that a certain natural inclination is necessary to 'virtue'. But the assumption that such a natural inclination exists takes them back to the domain of logic, where their concern is to deduce logical inferences from inclinations which govern human behaviour. This sort of controversy has points in common with the much later disputes about 'efficient' and 'non-efficient' grace.

(281) The line of argument taken by Plato and Aristotle in the discussion of the teaching of 'virtue' is general in character. It ascribes a role to non-logical behaviour, for it would be absurd to deny its existence. But what is given with one hand is taken away by the other; the logical implications of inclinations are fastened on and are divided into 'good' and 'bad' inclinations. This treatment of the problem, in which the existence of certain inclinations has perforce to be admitted, contrives a way for preserving only those non-logical actions which conform to the logical system and for eliminating all others.

(282) Aquinas similarly exercises his skill in contriving to reconcile the necessity of admitting certain non-logical inclinations with his motivating desideratum of establishing the effective empire of reason, and to reconcile the factor of determinism inherent in non-logical behaviour with the doctrine of free will implicit in logical behaviour. He says: 'Virtue is a good quality or disposition of the soul; it is not corruptible to evil uses, and by it and through it a man lives righteously; God produces it in us independently of ourselves.'* By defining it as a 'disposition of the soul, produced in us by God and in no way by ourselves, Aquinas is enlisting 'virtue' in the ranks of non-logical factors. But, for Aquinian theory, this very intervention of God removes the element of uncertainty as to the purpose of non-logical actions, for they become logical in relation to the mind of God. They are therefore logical for the theologians who have the exceeding good fortune to know the divine mind. Others to the same purpose make use of Nature, and always with the self-same result. Human beings act according to certain inclinations; this is granted. But even this minimal acknowledgement of non-logical factors is made to disappear by intellectual sleight-of-hand, since it is contended that men are endowed with these inclinations by an entity (God, Nature or something akin) which operates logically. It therefore follows that—albeit those who, in performing actions according to these inclinations, may sometimes be under the impression that their behaviour is non-logical—those who know the mind or the logical processes of the aforesaid entity know also that all actions are logical. It goes without saying that all philosophers, sociologists and the like have the privilege of knowing this entity intimately.

(300) In some writers, the element of non-logical behaviour disappears entirely, or at the most it is only considered as the exceptional element, the 'bad' element. For these, logic alone is the agent of human progress. It is synonymous with 'good', just as all that is not logical is synonymous with 'evil'. But let us not be led astray by this word 'logic'. Belief in logic has nothing to do with logico-experimental science. The cult

---

* *Summa*, Ia, IIae, qu. 55, *art.* 4; *Opera*, Vol. VI, p. 353.

of reason can be on the same level with any other religious cult, not excluding fetishism.

(304) . . . The worship of 'Reason', 'Truth', 'Progress' and other similar entities is to be classed as non-logical behaviour, as are all cults. This form of worship was born and has continued to flourish for the purpose of combating other cults, just as in Graeco-Roman society oriental cults emerged out of the opposition to polytheistic cults. . . . Similarly, towards the end of the eighteenth century and at the beginning of the nineteenth, a common trend of non-logical behaviour gains expression in the theism of the *philosophes*, the sentimental maunderings of Rousseau, the cult of 'Reason' and of the 'Supreme Being', the vogue for the Number Ten in the First Republic, theo-philanthropy (of which Comte's 'positivist' religion is simply an offshoot), the religion of Saint-Simon, the religion of pacifism, and other religions which still have devotees in our own day.

These considerations belong to a much more extensive order, properly relating to the *subjective aspect* of theories referred to in §13. [See above page 169.] In other words, we have to ask generally why and how individuals produce and accept certain theories. In particular, having now determined one reason why—namely, to give a logical character to behaviour which is not logical—we have to ask by what means this purpose is attained. From the *objective viewpoint*, the error in the arguments dealt with in the foregoing pages lies in their giving an *a priori* answer to the question why men say or accept that x=y, and in supposing that a theory needs only to be in accord with the facts for it to be advantageous to society. This error is usually augmented by the further error of considering facts, not as they are in reality, but as they are depicted by the heated fancy of those advancing the theory.

(305) The induction so far followed has brought us to realise, in certain particular cases, that there exists a tendency to eliminate considerations of non-logical behaviour: considerations which nevertheless force themselves on the awareness of anyone who undertakes to study human societies. It has also shown us that this tendency is of no small importance. We have now to study the tendency in general terms. Later on [see below page 238 *et seq.*] we shall have to broach an even more general subject: the variable arguments to which human beings are prone when prompted by certain sentiments of theirs and by their passion for giving a logical varnish to non-logical behaviour. This inductive method we have been following raises the particular problem in advance of the general problem. This has the drawback of obliging us to keep harking back to matters which have previously been touched on. But it has, on the other hand, the advantage of making the subject-matter we are dealing with more clear and manageable.

*(vii) Methods of eliminating non-logical behaviour**

(306) Let us now examine the ways whereby actions of non-logical behaviour are eliminated so as to leave logical actions alone masters of the field. . . .

---

* Chapter III, §§306, 307, 309, 312, 321, 333–5, 337, 338, 340, 341, 347–51, 353.

Class a	*The causes of non-logical actions are supposed to be devoid of any objective reality*
Subclasses	
I	They are entirely disregarded
II	They are regarded as absurd prejudices
III	They are regarded as tricks to deceive

Class b	*The causes of non-logical actions are supposed to have varying degrees of objective reality*
Subclasses	
I	They are considered to be completely and directly real

      I*a*: precepts with sanctions in part imaginary
      I*b*: intervention of a personal god or a personified abstraction
      I*c*: the same intervention, supplemented by legends and logical inferences
      I*d*: reality is ascribed to a metaphysical entity
      I*e*: what is real is taken to be an implicit accord between the causes of non-logical behaviour and certain sentiments

    II They are held to have no complete or direct objective reality. This is sought for indirectly in facts which are held to be incorrectly observed or understood
      II*a*: it is assumed that human beings make imperfect observations, drawing inferences from them logically
      II*b*: a myth is regarded as the reflection of an historical reality which is concealed in various ways, or else as a simple imitation of another myth
      II*c*: a myth is taken to consist of two elements—an historical fact and an imaginary accretion
    III They are held to be mere allegories

Class c	*It is assumed that non-logical actions have no favourable influence on 'Progress', or indeed that they are inimical to it*

Class A

Subclass I: *Non-logical actions are entirely disregarded.* (307). . . . This method often amounts to regarding beliefs as non-logical behaviour to be accepted for what they are without any attempt to explain them—the problem merely being to discover the relationship in which they stand towards other social facts. This, overtly or covertly, is the attitude of many political leaders.

Subclass II: *They are regarded as absurd prejudices.* (309) Simply the forms of non-logical behaviour may be considered and—found irrational—be judged as absurd prejudices, at the most meriting attention, pathologically, as veritable maladies of the human race. . . . This is especially the attitude of writers on religion, and most of all of writers on forms of worship. It is also the attitude of our contemporary anti-clericals towards the christian religion.

Subclass III: *They are regarded as tricks to deceive.* (312) . . . It may be asserted that the carrying out of certain actions of non-logical behaviour is the work of people who seek some personal advantage or some advantage for the state. . . . Polybius speaks of the religion of the Romans as originating in deliberate artifice: 'I believe this religion was established with an eye to the masses.'

Class B

Subclass I. Varieties: I*a*: *Precepts with sanctions in part imaginary.* (321) This variety consists of interpretations obtained by some adjunct or other to the simple type of sanctionless precept or taboo. I*b*: *Intervention of a personal god or a personified abstraction.* (333) When the Greeks said that 'strangers and beggars come from Zeus', they were merely expressing their inclination to hospitality towards visitors. Zeus was brought in only to give a logical veneer to the precept. I*c*: *The same intervention supplemented by legends and logical inferences.* (334) . . . To this variety belong the interpretations of the patristic writers of the christian church who termed the pagan gods demons. I*d*: *Reality is ascribed to a metaphysical entity.* (335) Here reality is ascribed, not to a personal god or to a personification, but to metaphysical abstractions such as 'the true', 'the beautiful', 'the good', 'the honest', 'virtue', 'morality', 'natural law', 'humanity', 'solidarity', 'progress', or their opposite abstractions. These enjoin or forbid certain actions, and the actions become logical consequences of the abstraction. I*e*: *What is real is taken to be an implicit accord between the causes of non-logical behaviour and certain sentiments.* (337) . . . Thus, to certain neo-christians, the reality of Jesus amounts to an accord between their conception of Him and certain of their sentiments. They . . . deny the divine nature of Christ and do not seem to be much concerned about His historical reality. They are content to assert that Christ is the most perfect type of humanity, which is to say that their notions of Him happen to coincide with what their sentiments hold to be the most perfect type of human being . . . and end with the assertion that 'religion is a way of life'. (338) . . . They might appear to be approximating to the concept of non-logical behaviour, but they are still fundamentally at variance with it for they are not thinking of what is but of what ought to be. . . .

Subclass II. Varieties: II*a*: *It is assumed that human beings make imperfect observations and draw inferences from them logically.* (340) This method of reasoning seeks to impute to the premises a logico-experimental inadequacy which is indisputable. Certain assertions are clearly in contradiction with logico-experimental knowledge. The contradiction may be held to arise because the reasoning behind the conclusions is not logical . . . or else the reasoning may be held to be logical but that its premises are inconsistent with experimental knowledge, so leading to conclusions where the contradiction is likewise apparent. . . . The importance of non-logical behaviour is minimised and may even be eliminated. . . . It is assumed that people draw inferences from observations of fact which underlie certain phenomena, reasoning very much as an intellectual would reason. . . . (341) Concepts of this kind are present to a greater or lesser degree in almost all theories of the 'origins' of social phenomena, such as 'religion', 'morality', 'law', and the like. The existence of non-logical behaviour has to be admitted, but it is relegated as far back into the past as possible. II*b*: *Myth is regarded as the reflection of an historical reality concealed in various ways, or as the simple imitation of another myth.* (347) In this variety it is assumed —origins and evolution being discarded—that every myth is the distorted reflection of something real. Such were the so-called euhemeristic theories about the origin of the gods. . . . (348) Anything in a myth which needs to be changed can be arbitrarily altered to produce an explanation which is real. . . . For example, in Dante's *Inferno* Paolo and Francesca are buffeted by the infernal whirlwind. This latter can be interpreted as a symbol of the carnal passion which swept the two lovers to their doom. . . . (349) With this variety we may class those theories which explain the non-logical behaviour observable in a given society as an imitation of non-logical behaviour prevalent in other societies. . . . II*c*: *Myth is taken to consist of two elements—an historical fact and an imaginary accretion.* (350) Here there is a closer approach to reality. In every myth the legend is assumed to have a hard core of historical fact covered over by an accretion of fiction. Remove the accretion and beneath may be found the hard core of fact. . . . Until recently the legends of Graeco-Roman antiquity were treated in this way. The variety B-II*b* is often an extreme form of this variety B-II*c*. If any historical element in a myth is reduced to a minimum until it finally disappears, we have the B-II*b* variety.

Subclass III: *The causes of non-logical behaviour are held to be mere allegories.* (351) Such behaviour is held to be logical in reality, seeming to be non-logical only because the allegories are taken literally. A further assumption puts the source of such errors in language by an allegorical interpretation. For example, Max Müller says* that 'there are many myths in Hesiod, of later origin, where we have only to replace a full verb by an auxiliary in order to change mythical into logical language . . . and . . . (translate) the language of Hesiod . . . into modern thought and speech'. . . . Müller's disciples went even further than their master, and the solar myth became a convenient and universal explanation for every conceivable legend.

Class C
It is assumed that actions of non-logical behaviour have no favourable influence on 'progress', or indeed that they are inimical to it; hence they are to be eliminated from any enquiry which aims solely to promote 'progress'. (353) Strictly speaking, in this class non-logical actions are not interpreted so as to make them logical; rather they are eliminated so that only logical actions remain. This is, in fact, to reduce all behaviour to logic. Opinions such as these are widely current in our day, and are an article of faith for a great many people who worship at the shrine of a potent divinity called 'Science'. A good many humanitarians are of the same persuasion.

---

* *Chips from a German Workshop*, (1867–75), Vol. II, p. 64.

(viii) Theories transcending experience*

(368) . . . Of great interest and importance for sociology are the phenomena which in common language are called 'religion', 'morality', and 'law'. For centuries men have disputed over these terms and they are still no nearer to agreeing on their meaning. Very many definitions have been attempted, but since these do not concur, the result is that the same word is used to indicate quite different things. This is a great help in not coming to a common understanding! Why is this? Do we have in our turn to attempt a new definition to add to the great number already advanced? Or is it perhaps advisable to try in some other way to understand the character of these phenomena?

(376) . . . Each man is firmly convinced that *his* religion, *his* morality, *his* idea of law, are the true types. But he has no means of persuading another man that this is so, for he can neither call in the aid of experience in general nor of that special kind of experience which is provided by logical reasoning. In a difference of opinion between two chemists, there is a judge: experience, scientific experiment. But in a difference of opinion between a christian and a mohemmedan, who is the judge? No one. [Cf. above, pages 181–2.]

(377) . . . There are people in our day who have believed it possible to evade this dilemma by eliminating the element of the supernatural. They conceive that it is this element alone which is responsible for the obvious divergency of opinion. But they deceive themselves in thinking thus, just as in the past the various christian sects deceived themselves in thinking that their divergencies arose only from differences of interpretation of Holy Writ, which in itself was beyond discussion or dispute.

(398) The difficulties encountered by those who are put to the test of defining law or morality are certainly not less than the difficulties which . . . confront those who attempt to define religion.† So far, it has not even been possible to find a method for distinguishing law from morality. At one extreme we have a definition which is crudely empirical. We are told that law consists of norms the sanction of which lies in the injunctions of

---

* Chapter IV, §§368, 376, 377, 398–408, 442, 445.

† At §§371–97, Pareto examines definitions of 'religion' by various writers, and concludes that no satisfactory definition exists because disputants in the question pose definitions which are of a fundamentally different character. The debate is barren because (§382) 'If one sets out to define what is the "true" or the "type" or the "ultimate" religion, clearly one cannot allow the definition to be entrusted to one's adversary since the term contains a thesis. It asserts that the thing defined corresponds to the truth, the type, the ultimate. Whereas . . . physicists or chemists never dream of quarrelling over the names to be given to things like "X-rays" or "radium" . . . an enormous amount of fruitless effort is devoted to debating the definition to be given to religion. . . . (390) . . . [River water, for example, can be chemically analysed] but how are we to *analyse* religions and *weigh* the elements in them? . . . (396) The only possible conclusion is that . . . the terms of ordinary language do not allow of rigorous classification. . . . The natural sciences were not developed by studying and classifying the terms of ordinary language, but by studying and classifying facts. Our aim is to try to do the same for sociology.'

public authority, and that morality consists of norms imposed only by conscience. Such a definition is excellent for the practical purposes of lawyers and judges, but it has not the least scientific value since it adopts as its criteria factors which are accidental and changeable. It is akin to making the colour of the feathers the criterion for classifying birds. An action passes from law to morality or *vice versa* according to the will or the caprice of the legislator. This classification may tell us a great deal about such will or caprice, but nothing about the intrinsic character of the action. Moreover, this classification becomes useless when, as has been the case in the past, the public authority does not intervene to sustain or impose private law. In modern civilised countries, there is a body of written legislation and it is therefore easy to know whether or not a given act is regulated by the law. It is true that the definition referred to above is experimental, clear and precise; but it is of little value since it does not classify the things we want to consider.

(399) Furthermore, when people try to study these matters intrinsically, they generally tend to look for the essences of them, and so little by little the domain of experience is abandoned and they go wandering off into cloudy metaphysics, eventually finishing at the opposite extreme to the empirical and all objective reality disappears.

(400) There are some who have the candour to confess it. Take, for example, these words of Adolf Franck: 'The idea of law, considered in itself, independently of the applications of which it is susceptible, and of the laws more or less just which have been made in its name, is a simple, absolute idea of reason and it is therefore beyond any logical definition.'* Splendid! Here it is openly recognised that this concept belongs to a category related to non-logical behaviour. If we cannot bring into service some other theory—like that of *innate ideas*—we must admit that such a concept does vary according to time, place and individuals. If we deny that this is the case, we must then ascribe objective existence to these 'simple ideas', just as objective existence once upon a time was attributed to the gods of Olympus. There are some people who try to disguise the departure from reality by ingenious subtleties; this is the usual practice of those who seek to spread a logical veneer over acts of non-logical behaviour.

(401) Another good example of utterly imprecise discussions is provided by the theories about 'Natural Law' (*jus naturale*) and 'Law of Nations' (*jus gentium*). Many thinkers have with greater or lesser vagueness expressed their sentiments under these terms, and then have bent their energies to relate their sentiments to the practical ends they desire to achieve. As is generally the case, they have derived great advantage in this enterprise from the employment of imprecise words which correspond, not to things, but only to sentiments. We are now going to examine such ways of reasoning strictly in the light of the correspondence they may or may not have with experimental reality. However, it behoves us not to carry into another field the conclusions we arrive at in this examination. Any experimental validity they may have is independent of any question of social utility. It can well be that a theory may have social utility in certain cases

---

* *Dictionnaire des Sciences philosophiques* (2nd ed. 1875); article on 'Droit'.

and at certain times without having any correspondence with experimental reality.* Natural Law is simply that law which seems best to those who use the term. But simple plain-speaking like this is ruled out of court; the case has to be put with a certain subtlety, with a gloss of reasoning.

(402) The advocates of Natural Law rebut objections against their case thus: to the question, 'Why must I accept your opinion in favour of Natural Law?', they reply, 'Because it is consonant with reason'. 'But I also use reason and yet I think differently from you.' 'Yes, but my reason is *right* reason.' 'Indeed; how is it then that so few of you have this opinion?' 'We are not a few by any means; our opinion has *universal consensus*.' 'Really? Yet there are other people who think differently.' 'All right, let us say then the consensus of the good and the wise.' 'I see; then it is you, the good and the wise, who invented this Natural Law?' 'Oh no, indeed; it was given us by Nature, by God.'

(403) The working materials of the supporters of Natural Law are, in the main, Right Reason (with its appendages, such as rational nature, state of nature, conformity with nature), the Universal Consensus—or the consensus of some distinguished group of men—and the Divine Will.

(404) Two questions are particularly relevant: who is the author of Natural Law?; and, How is it revealed to us? God may be the author of Natural Law directly by means of the agencies Right Reason or Nature. Nature may be the author of Natural Law directly, or—for preference— indirectly through its implanting in the human mind the seed of Natural Law (or simply of *positive law*). It is then revealed by Right Reason, or by observing general opinion or the opinion of the best qualified people. Some writers then engage in speculations about what 'man in a state of nature' may be like. This 'man' has never been encountered, it is true; but our metaphysical friends know him so intimately that from this state of nature —so well known to them, to the rest of us entirely unknown—they derive their knowledge of matters which the rest of us have before our eyes and might therefore know directly. Finally, Right Reason can ordain Natural Law by its own independent authority.

(405) Natural Law may be revealed to us directly by God through the Scriptures inspired by Him, but this is rare. The direct observation of the consensus of all men, or of some men, may also reveal Natural Law directly. But in practice this method is rarely if ever adopted. It is generally held that the revelation of Natural Law is properly the function of Right Reason, either of itself or else as the creation of Nature or of God, or as deriving from Universal Consensus or from some more limited consensus.

(406) It is on the whole generally asserted, in substance, that the concept of Natural Law exists in the human mind. Often there is added an indication of the source of this concept, together with further recourse to the Universal Consensus or to the consensus of the best qualified men. As a rule, almost all these materials are put to work together because the object in view is best promoted by making use of the greatest possible number of sentiments. The various modes of revelation of Natural Law are

---

* Cf. *Systèmes*, p. 128 above; *Manuel*, p. 150 above; *Treatise*, §§843–4, p. 218 below; and *Trasformazione*, p. 300 below.

also declared to be in agreement with one another, precisely for the same reason: to marshall every possible contribution to bolstering up the argument.

(407) The subjective argument by accord of sentiments seems to be as follows: The mind intuitively perceives that existing laws are not an arbitrary, or even a wholly logical, product, that there is in them a substratum which is not affected by will or intention but exists intrinsically. This induction is in agreement with the facts and should properly be formulated thus: There are certain activating causes of non-logical behaviour from which men derive their laws. These activating causes—or *Residues**—relate to the conditions under which men live and change with those conditions.

(408) But this form of the argument, which exposes the relative, subjective and non-logical character of the activating causes, is repugnant to metaphysicists and theologians and even to a good many run-of-the-mill students of social matters. They seek the absolute, the objective, the logical, and they can always find what they are looking for by using indeterminate words and defective reasonings (or *Derivations*). In this particular case, the proponents of Natural Law seek the absolute and the objective in the consensus of many or of all men; in conformity with nature; in the Divine Will. All these things, or some of them, they esteem as the highest and the best, hence they must be in accord with that other thing which is of the highest and the best: Natural Law. And that noble thing, Logic, must provide us with the nexus uniting all these perfections. In such theories, beneath the disguising surface matter, there always escapes a glint of a concept of a contrast beneath something which is constant and good (Natural Law) and something else which is variable and not so good (positive law); and it is mainly this contrast which sustains these theories and the belief of their adherents in them.

(442) All these definitions, and others like them, have the following characteristics:

1. They use indeterminate words which arouse certain sentiments, but do not correspond to anything precise.
2. They define the unknown by the unknown.
3. They mix definitions with theorems which are not proved.
4. Their aim, in substance, is to play upon sentiments as much as possible in order to lead other people to a predetermined conclusion.

(445) If we attend only to the forms, all these disquisitions on Natural Law seem a heap of rubbish. But if, instead, we disregard the forms and look to see what it is they cover up, we find sentiments and inclinations which have a powerful influence in determining the composition and character of society, and which therefore merit the closest study. The demonstrations given in such forms are neither to be accepted because they are in accord with certain sentiments, nor yet rejected because they manifestly conflict with logic and experience. They are to be considered as non-existent. We

---

* See below p. 216 *et seq.*

should, rather, concentrate on the matter they hide and examine this directly, closely observing its intrinsic characteristics. Thus once again our induction leads us to separate doctrines, as we find them formulated, into two parts—one of which, we perceive, is much more important than the other. In pursuing our enquiry, we must, therefore, try to separate these two parts. Having done this we must not linger to argue that a certain position is inconclusive, foolish or absurd, but investigate whether or not it may manifest sentiments which are useful to society and in a form which is useful for persuading many people who would not be amenable to the best logico-experimental arguments. For the moment it suffices to have perceived this path opening before us; to tread it is a task reserved for us later on in this work.

(ix) Pseudo-scientific theories*

(523) If we seek to arrange theories according to the character of their demonstrations, we must distinguish two types. In one, the nexus consists solely of the logical implications of facts; in the other, there is something additional which transcends experience: a concept of necessity, duty or the like. Finally, to complete the matter, we must also consider propositions in which the logical nexus is reduced to little or nothing, and which are simply descriptions or narrations. We obtain thereby the following three classes:

1. Descriptive propositions.
2. Propositions asserting experimental uniformities.
3. Propositions which either add something to experimental uniformities or ignore them.

(524) Scientific theories consist of propositions of classes 1 and 2. Sometimes propositions of class 3 are appended; these may be harmless if the non-experimental adjunct is superfluous, but they are capable of damaging the scientific character of the theory if the non-experimental adjunct influences its conclusions. Sociological theories and many economic theories up to the present time have freely made use of propositions of class 3 which have had this damaging influence on conclusions. Such propositions must be excluded if we wish to have a sociology and an economic theory which bear the stamp of genuinely logico-experimental sciences. . . .

(797) We can now assess the results so far of following the inductive method. Not only has it confirmed the extent and importance of non-logical actions, as noted earlier [see above, pages 184–93]; it has in addition shown us that these actions constitute the basis of many theories which otherwise, judged superficially, would seem to be exclusive products of logic.

(798) The . . . examination . . . of certain theories . . . leads us to recognise that theories in the concrete may be divided into at least two elements, one of which is much more constant than the other. To avoid as much as possible the dangers of reasoning on words rather than on things, we shall at the outset use letters of the alphabet to designate the things we

---

* Chapter V, §§ 523, 524, 797–802, 804, 815, 817–21, 825–32.

are dealing with, postponing the use of descriptive terms until a later section [see below 'Constants and Variables', page 215 *et seq.*]. Accordingly, in concrete theories—which we designate as (*c*)—we identify, besides factual data, two principal elements or parts: a fundamental element or part, which we shall designate as (*a*); and a contingent element or part, generally rather variable, which we shall designate as (*b*).

The element (*a*) directly corresponds to non-logical behaviour; it is the expression of certain sentiments. The element (*b*) is the manifestation of the human need for logic. It also partially corresponds to sentiments, to non-logical behaviour, but it invests them with logical or pseudo-logical reasonings. The element (*a*) is the *principle*, or activating cause, which exists in the human mind; the element (*b*) represents the explanations of that principle or cause, and the deductions drawn from it.

(799) There is, for example, a psychic state—which can be termed a principle, or a sentiment, or what you will—in virtue of which certain numbers seem worthy of veneration. This is the main element (*a*) in the phenomenon we describe later as the mysterious association of names with things. But the human mind is not content with associating sentiments of veneration with numbers; it also wishes to 'explain' how this comes about, to 'demonstrate' that the behaviour resulting from this psychic state is prompted by the force of logic. So the element (*b*) is brought into play, begetting various 'explanations', 'demonstrations' as to why certain numbers are sacred. There is in man a sentiment which militates against the sudden abandonment of old beliefs. . . . But he seeks to justify, explain, demonstrate his attitude, and so an element (*b*) comes into play which, in one way or another, preserves the letter of these beliefs while altering the substance.

(800) The principal element of the phenomenon is clearly that to which the human being is most strongly attached. Hence this, the element (*a*), is of the greatest importance for our investigation of the social equilibrium. (801) But the element (*b*), albeit secondary, also has an effect on the social equilibrium. Sometimes this effect may be so slight that it can be reckoned as equivalent to zero: as, for example, when the perfection of the number six is justified by saying that it is the sum of its aliquot parts. But the effect can also be very considerable: as, for example, when the Inquisition sent to the stake people who had fallen into error in their theological calculations. (802) The element (*b*) is made up . . . of sentiments and logical inferences in variable proportions. It behoves us to note that, in social matters, its persuasive force usually depends mainly on sentiments rather than on logical deduction, this latter being accepted chiefly in so far as it is in accord with sentiments. . . .

(804) In theories (*c*) which transcend experience or are pseudo-experimental, writers rarely distinguish with sufficient clarity the elements (*a*) and (*b*). The usual practice is for these elements to be more or less confused.

(815) . . . Language is nearly always synthetic in its ordinary usage and has regard to concrete situations; therefore it usually confuses the elements (*a*) and (*b*) which scientific analysis has to distinguish. From the practical point of view, it may be useful to deal with the elements (*a*) and (*b*)

together. If the principles (*a*) were precise and definite, then acceptance of them would entail acceptance of all their logical consequences (*b*). But since the principles or activating causes (*a*) are devoid of precision, anyone may infer whatever he chooses from them; and hence the logical deductions (*b*) are accepted only in so far as they are in accord with sentiments, these being given in this way the upper hand over logical implications.

(817) From the scientific point of view, any improvement of theory is strictly dependent on the greatest possible separation of the elements (*a*) and (*b*). This point cannot be too strongly emphasised. Art,* of course, has to study the concrete phenomenon (*c*) synthetically, and consequently does not separate the elements (*a*) and (*b*) therein finding a powerful method of persuasion since almost all human beings are in the habit of thinking synthetically and have difficulty, indeed utter inability, in understanding scientific analysis. But anyone wishing to construct a scientific theory cannot dispense with such an analysis. All this is very difficult to bring home to people who are unaccustomed to scientific reasoning, or who dispense with it when dealing with matters pertaining to sociology. They have an obstinate desire to consider phenomena synthetically.

(818) When, therefore, an author is read with a view to making a scientific assessment of his theories, it is first of all necessary to do something he almost certainly has never done: distinguish the elements (*a*) and (*b*). In general, it is necessary in every theory carefully to separate the premises—i.e. principles, postulates, sentiments—from the inferences drawn from them. (819) In theories which add something to experience, we must realise that very often the premises are at least partially implicit: that is to say, the element (*a*) is not indicated, or is not fully indicated. If we want to know what it is, we have to look for it. . . .

(820) From the logico-experimental point of view, the fact that in such cases the premises are implicit—even if only partially so—may give rise to very serious errors. The mere fact of declaring premises prompts enquiry into whether and to what extent they are to be accepted; whereas if the premises remain implicit, one accepts them without being aware of what this involves; they are thought too definite and exact while all along they are so far from being so that one would be hard put to it to find any meaning at all in them.

(821) Often writers keep entirely silent about those of their premises which are alien to experience; and often also, when they do declare them, they try to associate them with scientific conclusions based on experience.

There is a fascinating example of this in the theory which Rousseau advances in the preface to his *Discours sur l'origine et les fondements de l'inégalité parmis les hommes*. 'Let us therefore begin', he says, 'by setting aside all facts, for they have no bearing on the question. The investigations we may undertake in this matter must not be regarded as historical truths, but simply as hypothetical and contingent reasonings, more pertinent to elucidating the nature of things than to showing their actual origin, and in this similar to the reasonings which our physicists are making every day

---

* 'Art' is used here in the sense of skills deployed to appeal to human feelings and perceptions.

about the formation of the world.' So Rousseau intends to conduct an experimental enquiry. But the experience on which it is based is of a special kind—akin to what we today would call 'religious experience'—which has nothing to do with the experience of the physical sciences, for all that he tries to associate this experience with his own, thereby revealing only his colossal ignorance. He continues: 'Religion ordains us to believe that, as men were removed by God Himself from the state of nature immediately after the Creation, they are unequal because God has willed them to be so; but religion does not forbid us from making conjectures, drawn solely from the nature of man and the creatures around him (*here comes in Rousseau's pseudo-experience*), about what the human race might have become if it had been left to itself. This is the question before me and which I propose to examine in this essay. Since my subject concerns mankind in general (*an abstraction designed to cast off experience after the pretence made of accepting it*), I shall try to employ a language suitable for all nations (*some of which were absolutely unknown to this wily rhetorician*), or rather, forgetting times and places, and thinking only of the human beings I am addressing, I shall imagine myself as speaking in the Lyceum at Athens with men like Plato and Xenocrates for judges and the human race for audience.' So he goes prating on, and discovers, starting from the 'nature' of things, how things *must* have been, and all this without being put to the trouble of verifying his fine theories by facts, since at the outset he stated that he was setting them aside. Be it remembered that there are still many, many people who admire such meaningless drivel; this is why it has to be taken into account if one intends to study human society.

(825) Pure economics has the advantage of being able to draw its deductions from very few experimental principles; and it employs logic so strictly that it is able to give to its reasonings a mathematical form—reasonings which have the further very great advantage of enabling pure economics to deal with quantities. The science of juridical theories also enjoys the advantage of requiring few principles; but it does not have the advantage of being able to deal with quantities. The lack of this same advantage still remains a stumbling-block for sociology; but we can, at the least, get over the hurdle set up by the intrusion of element (*a*) into element (*b*). (826) In general terms, certain principles (*a*) may be arbitrarily assumed; provided they are precise, a body of doctrine (*c*) may be derivable from them. But it is clear that, if the principles (*a*) have no connection with reality, the part (*c*) will have no bearing on concrete cases. When one seeks to constitute a science, it is important, therefore, judiciously to select the principles (*a*) in such a way as to keep as close as possible to reality, bearing in mind, of course, that no theory (*c*) can ever represent reality in all its details. (827) Other sociological theories have tried to construct a strictly scientific body of doctrine, but unfortunately they have fallen short of their aim because the principles from which the theoretical inferences were drawn were too far removed from experience.

(828) One of such theories is 'social darwinism'. If it be granted that the institutions of a society are always—excepting temporary oscillations—those best suited to the circumstances of that society, and that societies which do not possess such institutions eventually disappear, then we get a

principle susceptible of important logical developments and capable of constituting a science. The attempt to create a social science on this basis was made in the nineteenth century and for a time there were grounds for hoping that at last there would be a scientific theory (c) of sociology, since some of the inferences (b) were verified by the facts. But the sociological doctrine developed on this basis declined with its originating doctrine: the darwinian theory of the origin of species. It was realised that its explanations of facts were too often simply verbal. Every form of social organisation or of living creatures had to be explained by its utility, and to do this recourse was made to arbitrary and imaginary utilities. Without realising it, the advocates of this theory were returning to the old theory of final causes. Social darwinism still remains a fairly well-constructed body of doctrine (c), but it requires considerable modification for it to be reconciled with the facts. It does not determine the form of institutions; it simply determines the limits beyond which these cannot go.

(829) Another such theory is 'historical materialism', or 'economic determinism'. If it be understood in the sense that the economic state of a society entirely determines all other social phenomena within it, this affords a principle (a) from which a great body of inferences can be drawn in such a way as to constitute a scientific doctrine. The theory of historical materialism, of the economic interpretation of history, was a notable scientific advance in social theory, for it served to elucidate the contingent character of certain phenomena, such as morals and religion, to which many authorities ascribed—as they still do—an absolute character. Moreover, it unquestionably embodies an element of truth: the interdependence of economic and other social factors. Its error . . . lies in having made of this interdependence a relationship of cause and effect.

(830) An incidental circumstance helped to aggravate the error. Historical materialism was coupled with another theory, that of the 'class struggle', with which it need have had no connection. Moreover, the classes—by an audacious dichotomy—were reduced to two. Thereby the domain of science was progressively abandoned in favour of excursions into the domain of romance. Sociology became a very easy science for the historical materialists. Why waste time and energy in discovering the relationships between facts, their uniformities? Whatever history reveals— any fact recorded, any institution described, any political, moral or religious system exemplified—all has its sole cause in the 'exploitation of the proletariat' by the 'bourgeoisie' and in the resistance of the 'proletariat' to this exploitation. If the facts were in accord with such conclusions, we should have a science as perfect as any other human science, nay more so. Unfortunately, the theory and the facts go in entirely different directions.

(831) Yet another theory is that of 'limits', which might be called the spencerian theory if one could subtract the numerous metaphysical accretions in the writings of Herbert Spencer's school. It assumes, as its principle (a), that all social institutions tend towards a limit and are like a curve which has an asymptote. If the curve is known, the asymptote can be determined. If the historical evolution of an institution is known, its limit can be determined; indeed, its limit can be determined more easily than in the simpler problem of the mathematical determination of asymptotes. In

the latter case, knowledge of a few points on the curve is not enough: we must have its equation—that is, we must know its intrinsic character. On the other hand, in regard to an institution it is possible—or rather, it is believed to be possible—from a few points on the graph representing it to determine the limit *ipso facto*.

(832) This principle (*a*) is susceptible of scientific deductions (*b*), and so yields an extensive body of doctrine which may be studied in Spencer's *Principles of Sociology* and other works by him and his disciples. This doctrine—provided always that we eliminate the metaphysical elements in it—brings us close to the experimental method for, after all, its conclusions are derived from facts. But unfortunately, facts are not the only things involved; there intrude both the principle that institutions have a limit and also another principle which holds that the limit can be determined if a few successive stages of the institution are known. Furthermore, by a coincidence which would be strange indeed if it were truly fortuitous, the limit which a writer of this school assumes to be determined strictly by his facts turns out to be identical to the limit to which his sentiments incline him. If he is a pacifist, like Spencer, the facts obligingly reveal to him that the limit to which human societies are moving is that of universal peace. If he is a democrat, there is no doubt but that the limit will be the complete triumph of democracy; if a collectivist, the limit will be the triumph of collectivism, and so on. Hence a suspicion arises in our mind and grows stronger: are the facts serving merely to conceal more potent motives of persuasion? But in any case the reasoning of these positivists in no way corresponds to the facts, and this vitiates all the inferences they draw. Finally, their theories labour under the disadvantage (which might yet in time be redressed) of the fact that we are far from possessing the historical information which strictly would be essential for the use of this method.

II

Constants and Variables

1. CONCEPT OF RESIDUES AND DERIVATIONS

(i) Definitions*

(842) ... Realising that social phenomena in the concrete are complex, we perceived that it would be helpful to divide them into at least two elements, distinguishing logical from non-logical behaviour. We gained thereby an initial idea of the nature of non-logical actions and of their importance in human society. But then comes the question: If non-logical behaviour plays such an important part in social phenomena, how is it that up to the present time so little attention has been given it? In seeking the answer to this we found that almost all writers on social or political questions have indeed perceived it—or at least caught a glimpse of it—wherefore many elements in the theory we are developing are to be found scattered about in such studies, although often so as to be barely recognisable.

(843) We saw the answer to the question to lie in the fact that all these writers were governed by ideas to which they explicitly attached a supreme importance: ideas on religion, morality, law and the like, about which men have disputed for centuries. If implicitly they recognised non-logical factors, explicitly they exalted logical actions, and most of them considered logical actions to be the only ones worth taking account of in social phenomena. It was therefore incumbent on us to see what truth there was in such theories, and to decide whether to keep to the same path we had been following, or to abandon it. We then went on to study these various ways of evaluating social phenomena; and we realised that from the logico-experimental viewpoint they were absolutely lacking in precision and devoid of any strict accord with the facts. On the other hand, we could not deny their great importance in history and in determining the social

---

* Chapter VI, §§842–6, 866–70, 875.

equilibrium. This realisation gave strength to an idea which had already come to mind and which will acquire greater and greater importance as our enquiry develops, namely, that there is a clear distinction between the experimental 'truth' of certain theories and their social 'utility'—these being two things which are not only quite different from one another but may be, and often are, in direct contradiction. (844) The separation of experimental 'truth' from social 'utility' is as important as the distinction between logical and non-logical behaviour.* By following the inductive method we have been made aware that it is the failure to make this separation which has vitiated most social theories from the scientific viewpoint.

(845) We then studied these theories a little more closely and we saw how and why they fell into error, and also how and why—erroneous though they be—they have had, and still do have, such great esteem. Continuing with our enquiry—analysing and distinguishing—we came upon a distinction which is certainly as important as the others we have made: the distinction between a constant, instinctive and non-logical element (*a*), and a deductive element (*b*) the purpose of which is to explain, justify and demonstrate the constant element.

(846) Arrived at this point thanks to the inductive method, we now have the elements of a theory. Our task now is to constitute it; that is to say, we must now dispense with the inductive and employ the deductive method and see what emerges from the principles we have found, or think we have found. We shall then compare these inferences with the facts; if they are in accord, we shall maintain our theory; if not, we shall abandon it.

(866) Catholics regard Friday as a day of evil omen because, they say, of the Crucifixion. If this were all we knew of the matter, it would be difficult to determine which of these two factors—the evil omen or the Crucifixion—was the principal and which the subsidiary factor. But there is a great deal of evidence similar to this; for example, the Roman *dies atri* or *vitiosi*, days of evil omen. Such a day was the eighteenth of July, the anniversary of the Roman defeat in 390 BC by Brennus and his Gauls at the battle of the Allia. This is one kind of (*a*): the feeling that the day which calls to mind some dire event is a day of evil omen. But there is more to it than this. The Greeks and Romans recognised days of good and bad omen independently of the special reasons of the sort here referred to. There is therefore a class of (*a*) which includes the foregoing type and has to do with an impulse to combine days—and other things too—with good or evil omen. (867) Examples such as these help us to determine how a composite phenomenon (*c*) may be broken down into (*a*) elements and (*b*) elements. . . .

(868) . . . It is now advisable to give descriptive terms to the things we have been calling (*a*), (*b*) and (*c*), since continuing to refer to them by alphabetical letters may hamper and obscure the discussion. For this, and for no other reason, let us term the things (*a*) *Residues*, the things (*b*) *Derivations*, and the things (*c*) *Derivates*. But we must all the time bear in

---

* Cf. *Systèmes*, p. 128 above; *Manuel*, p. 150 above; *Treatise*, §401, p. 207 above; and *Transformazione*, p. 300 below.

mind that nothing—absolutely nothing—is to be inferred from the proper meanings, the etymologies, of these words. Their meaning is exclusively confined to the things (*a*), (*b*) and (*c*). (869) . . . The residues (*a*) constitute an amalgam of many facts which we must classify according to the analogies we find in them. Thus we shall deal with classes, subclasses and species. The same will apply to the derivations (*c*).

(870) Residues correspond to certain human instincts; they are therefore usually deficient in precision and strict delimitation. . . . (875) We must guard against confusing residues (*a*) with the sentiments or instincts to which they correspond.* They are the manifestation of sentiments and instincts, in the same way as the movement of mercury in the thermometer is the manifestation of a change in the temperature. Only in an elliptical way, to shorten the argument, do we say that the residues—together with the appetites, interests etc.—play the principal role in determining the social equilibrium, just as we say that water boils at 100°c. The complete proposition would be: 'The sentiments or instincts which correspond to the residues, together with those which correspond to appetites, instincts, interests etc., play the principal role in determining the social equilibrium. Water boils when its calorific condition reaches a temperature which is indicated by 100 degrees on the scale of the centigrade thermometer.'

(ii) *Residues in sociology and roots in philology*†

(880) Residues (*a*) through derivations (*b*) produce the derivates (*c*) which are concretely observable in society. Other derivates (*d*) can exist which are not thus observable even though they are as regularly deducible from residues as (*c*). (881) This is analogous to the existence in philology of regular and irregular verbs. But in fact these terms must not be taken literally, since a verb called 'irregular' is in effect regular like any other verb. The difference between regular and irregular verbs lies in the various modes of derivation. A process of derivation applied to certain roots produces a class of verbs which are actually to be found in the language. If the same procedure be applied to other roots, it gives verbs which do not occur in the language. Conversely, a method of derivation which, when applied to this second type of roots, produces verbs which exist in the language, will produce non-existent verbs when applied to roots of the first type.

(883) We can go further; there are analogies of another kind. Modern philology is well aware that language is an organism which has developed

---

* See §1690 overleaf; and cf. also Pareto's observation at §851—not cited here: 'If the element (*a*) [i.e. the residue] corresponds to certain instincts, it is far from reflecting them all. This is obvious from the very way whereby we discovered them. We analysed specimens of thinking, on the look-out for a constant element. We may therefore have discovered only the instincts which underlay such thinking. Following this path there was no opportunity to meet instincts which were not so rationalised. Still unaccounted for would be the simple appetites, tastes, inclinations and—in social relationships—that very important class called "interests".'

† Chapter VI, §§880, 881, 883.

in conformity to its own laws. It is not an artificial creation. Only a few technical terms, like 'oxygen', 'meter', and the like, are the product of the logical creativity of scholars. They correspond to logical actions in social life. The formation of the majority of words used in common speech corresponds to actions of non-logical behaviour.*

(iii) *Residues and the search for origins*†

(885) Up to the present time, sociology for the most part has been preoccupied with investigations into the origins of social phenomena. All unknowingly to the thinkers engaged in them, these investigations have often been research into residues. Without being very precise about it, they have all along assumed that the *simple* must have preceded the *complex*; that the residue must have been anterior to the derivate. When Herbert Spencer ascribes the chronological origin of religion to the deification of human beings, he thinks he has found the residue of religious phenomena —that is, the simple phenomenon from which are derived the complex religious phenomena observable in our own day.

(886) . . . Seeking to discover in remote periods of time the residue (*a*) from which derive the phenomena (*c*) observable here and now is in fact simply trying to explain the known by the unknown. We take the contrary view: the less well known must be deduced from the better known. We must try to discover the residues (*a*) in the phenomena (*c*) which are observable at the present time, and then see if traces of (*a*) can be found in the historical evidence available to us. If thereby it should be found that (*a*) existed when (*c*) was yet unknown, it might be concluded that (*a*) is anterior to (*c*) and that, in this case, the 'origin' is part and parcel with the 'residue'. But where such proof is lacking, it is not legitimate to draw such a conclusion. (887) . . . We are not here concerned with 'origins', not because we think this an historically unimportant question—far from it—but because 'origins' are of little or no significance in respect to our enquiry into the conditions of social equilibrium. This enquiry is our main purpose, and therefore the instincts and sentiments which correspond to 'residues' assume paramount importance.

(1690)‡ To clarify the terms we are using, it should be noted that, since sentiments are manifested by residues, it will often be the case that— for the sake of brevity—we shall refer simply to 'residues', designating thereby also the sentiments they manifest. When we say that residues are among the elements which determine the social equilibrium, this statement must be translated and understood as meaning that 'the sentiments manifested by residues are among the elements which have a relationship of reciprocal determination with the social equilibrium'. Yet this statement

---

* For further discussion of the analogy between residues and language-roots, see below, p. 220 *et seq*.

† Chapter VI, §§885–7, 1690.

‡ In the *Treatise* this section occurs at a more advanced stage in the discussion, but in these extracts it is more conveniently introduced here where it helps to clarify the basis of Pareto's theory of residues.

also is elliptical and needs to be translated in its turn. We must beware of attributing an objective existence to residues or even to sentiments. What we observe in reality are human beings whose psychic state is revealed by what we call sentiments. Our proposition must therefore be translated in the following terms: 'The psychic states revealed by the sentiments expressed in residues are among the elements which have a relationship of reciprocal determination with the social equilibrium.' But even this is not enough if we want to express ourselves with the utmost precision. What are these 'psychic states'? They are abstractions. What underlies them? So we must say: 'The actions of human beings are among the elements which have a relationship of reciprocal determination with the social equilibrium. Among such actions are certain manifestations which we term "residues" and which are closely correlated with other actions, so that if we know the residues, we may in certain circumstances know the actions. Hence we shall say that residues are among the elements which have a relationship of reciprocal determination with the social equilibrium.' Derivations also manifest sentiments. They directly express the sentiments corresponding to the residues from which they originate; indirectly they express sentiments through the residues which serve for purposes of derivation. But to speak of derivations in place of the residues they express, as is customary in ordinary language, could lead to serious errors; therefore we shall refrain from doing so in all cases where any doubt about the meaning of a statement is possible.

Since the matter is very important, it behoves us to make further clarifications. We observe, for example, instances in which a hen defends its chicks, and we summarise our observation of past facts, our prediction of future facts and our supposition of a uniformity by saying that 'the hen defends its chickens', that there is in the hen a sentiment which prompts it to defend its offspring, and that this defence is the outcome of a given psychic state. Similarly, we observe various instances in which some individuals give their lives for their country. We summarise our observation of past facts, our prediction of future facts and our supposition of a uniformity relating to many individuals by saying that 'human beings—or some human beings—give their lives for their country', that there is a sentiment which prompts them to sacrifice their lives for their country, and that this sacrifice is the outcome of a given psychic state. But we also observe in human beings certain facts which are the consequence of the use of language among them: facts not observable in animals. Men, that is, express by language certain things which we connect with the facts observed when they give up their lives for their country. They say, for example, *dulce et decorum est pro patria mori*—thus expressing, we say, a certain sentiment, a certain psychic state and so on. But this is not very precise, for the axioms and propositions which we thereby regard as expressing a sentiment (or, it would be much better to say, 'a sum of sentiments'), a psychic state and so forth, are multiple and diverse. It is by separating in these and other axioms and propositions the constant element from the variable element that we have identified residues and derivations. But in so saying, we are adding something to the facts. Experimental observation tells us only that the fact that men die for their country and the fact that

they express themselves in a certain way about it, are concomitant facts.*
That this is so will be seen from the following propositions which, starting
close to reality, gradually draw further away from it.

---

* At this point in the original, Pareto inserts a long footnote elaborating
the argument. 'Between propositions D and behaviour A there may be a
direct relationship DA. This indeed is the only relationship considered by those
who reduce all social phenomena to logical behaviour. But in fact the relationship is normally different; that is to say, it derives from an origin O which is
common both to the propositions and to the behaviour. This common origin,
which generally is unknown to us, may be called a 'sentiment' or 'psychic state'
or something similar. But giving a name to an unknown thing in no way makes
it knowable to us. Again, one might assume that D represents residues and A
derivations and so repeat the foregoing observations: i.e., residues and derivations have a common origin O which is unknown. To detect the residues, we
have theoretically established a relationship AD; then, to deduce the derivations
from the residues, we have similarly established the relationship DA. But the
actual relationships are OD, OA.

'Reverting to the analogies drawn earlier between language and other social
facts, we can say that D represents roots and A the words of the language.
Following a procedure similar to that which we have followed in regard to
residues and derivations, the philologist posits a theoretical relationship AD,
therein deriving roots from words; and then in the same way he traces a
relationship DA which derives words from roots. But in practice languages have
not been formed by deriving words from roots, though admittedly it may sometimes happen—once a language is maturely formed—that grammarians or
students in other scholarly disciplines make such derivations. Generally speaking, words have been created spontaneously by the community as a whole, and
the same influences which produced them gave rise at the same time to roots;
that is to say, the influences of the relationships OA, OD were operative. Sometimes, as in the case of onomatopœic words, we can achieve a passably good
idea of the origins O of a family of words A and its roots D. But in the vast
majority of cases this origin is wholly unknown; all we know is the family of
words from which philologists extract the roots. Studies have been made of the
'origin' of languages aimed specifically at the discovery of O, but so far they
have been of no use either to grammar or to lexicography, though certainly
these sciences have profited from knowledge of roots. For example, in studies of
the Greek language, grammar and lexicography stop short at roots; this is well,
for scholars would have been unable to achieve a proper scientific basis had
they been determined to wait until they had discovered 'origins'. Similarly, in
sociology there may be cases where we get an insight, albeit remote and imperfect, of the origin O in regard both to the residues and the derivations or
behaviour A. But in the vast majority of cases, our knowledge is no greater in
kind than the philologist's. We know only the derivations or the behaviour A.
Theoretically, we infer from these the residues D and then reciprocally infer
from the residues D the derivations and behaviour A; that is to say, we direct
our thinking to the relationships AD and DA. But in effect the relationships are
OA and OD.

'Very many studies in sociology are akin to philological investigations
aimed at revealing the 'origins' of languages; that is to say, they seek to discover
the 'origins' of social phenomena. They have been of little value to science.
What we are attempting is to constitute a science of sociology, and to that end
we halt at residues just as the philologist halts at roots, the chemist at elements,
the student of celestial mechanics at gravity, and so on. As regards our forms

1. At one and the same time, there are acts of devotion to country and expressions of approval and praise for such behaviour. These expressions have a common element which we call a residue. 2. Human beings sacrifice themselves for their country and have a sentiment, manifested by residues, which prompts them to such self-sacrifice. But the term 'sentiment' is vague, and herein begins the departure from reality. Moreover, the uniformity is stated without reservations, yet some limitation is essential. Finally, objection can validly be made against the supposition that behaviour is always inspired by sentiment. 3. Instead of saying '*and* have a sentiment', the usual expression is '*because* they have a sentiment'. Now this 'because' takes us further from reality in that it indicates a relationship of cause and effect, whereas we do not know with certainty whether any such relationship exists. 4. Human beings *believe* that they have a duty to sacrifice themselves for their country, and it is said that this is *why* they perform acts of self-sacrifice. But this draws us very far indeed from reality since it assumes behaviour to be the consequence of beliefs, therein substituting logical for non-logical behaviour. This (4) is the usual mode of expression in such matters but it is all too easily misleading, even if we are aware that it is no more than a form of 1. It is legitimate to employ the mode of expression in 2 provided we bear in mind that strictly we should always consider it in relation to 1. In this enquiry we have made—and shall continue to make—abundant use of mode 2, particularly in its equivalent form of associating behaviour and residues. Equally, mode 3 is employable, but always subject to the precaution that it has to be seen in relation to 1, guarding against the danger of drawing logical inferences from the 'because' which occurs in it. Terms like 'sentiments' and 'residues' are conveniences in sociology in the same way as 'force' is a convenient term in mathematics. They may be safely employed so long as we always bear in mind the reality to which they correspond.

---

of expression: when we say elliptically that residues determine behaviour, we are substituting, in the interests of simplicity, the theoretical relationship DA for the practical relationships OA, OD. In this we proceed like the philologist when he says that a family of words A originates in a root D, or that certain tenses of verbs are *formed* from the indicative radical, certain others from the aorist radical, and so on. No one has ever understood this way of putting things as meaning that the Greeks gathered together one day to settle certain aorist roots and thence went on to derive from these radicals the aorist verb-forms. Equally, no one should give a similarly perverse interpretation to our statement that residues *determine* behaviour.

'If we had been following the deductive method, the matter dealt with in this note would have had to be part of the main text and be introduced near the beginning of this work. But in such a position it would have been difficult to grasp in view of its unfamiliarity. The deductive method is excellently suitable for the treatment of ideas and doctrines which are already to some extent familiar and understood. But in cases where the subject-matter is entirely new, the inductive method is the only one which can prepare the reader to grasp what it is all about and clearly understand it. It is for this reason that we find the inductive method employed in such treatises as the *Politics* of Aristotle the political writings of Machiavelli, the *Wealth of Nations* of Adam Smith and other similar works in all fields.'

2. RESIDUES

(i) Classification of residues*

(888) . . . It must not be overlooked that, in social phenomena, as well as the sentiments manifested by residues, there are appetites, inclinations and the like. Here our only concern is with the element which corresponds to residues. In this element often inhere many—indeed sometimes very many —simple residues, therein resembling rocks containing many simple elements which can be isolated by chemical analysis. In specific phenomena, one residue may predominate over others; consequently such phenomena may by and large be taken as representing that residue. The classification made below is objective in character, but we shall find it necessary on occasion to add some subjective considerations.†

CLASS I   INSTINCT OF COMBINATIONS

      I-a: *Combinations in general*

      I-b: *Combinations of likes and unlikes*
           I-b1: In general
           I-b2: Rare things with unusual events
           I-b3: Terrifying or awesome things with terrible things and events
           I-b4: Good things with fortunate events; and bad things with unfortunate events
           I-b5: Physical assimilation; causes linked to effects

      I-c: *Mysterious power ascribed to certain things and certain acts*
           I-c1: In general
           I-c2: Associations of names and things

      I-d: *Urge to combine residues*

      I-e: *Urge to seek logical explanations*

      I-f: *Belief in the efficacy of combinations*

CLASS II   PERSISTENCE OF AGGREGATES

      II-a: *Persistence of the relations of individuals with other individuals or places*
          II-a1: Relations with family or community
          II-a2: Relations with places
          II-a3: Relations with social classes

      II-b: *Persistence of relations between the living and the dead*

---

   * Chapter VI, §888.

   † The translation of the synoptic table given here is, with some variations, based on that set out in Homans and Curtis, *An Introduction to Pareto* (1934), p. 96. For easier reference, the Greek letters used by Pareto to distinguish subclasses have been replaced by Latin letters.

II-c: *Persistence of relations between the dead and the things they possessed in life*

II-d: *Persistence of an abstraction*

II-e: *Persistence of uniformities*

II-f: *Sentiments transformed into objective realities*

II-g: *Personification*

II-h: *Need of new abstractions*

CLASS III MANIFESTATION OF SENTIMENTS BY ACTIVITY

III-a: *By combinations*

III-b: *In religious exaltation*

CLASS IV RESIDUES OF SOCIALITY

IV-a: *Particular societies*

IV-b: *Need for uniformity*
IV-b1: Obtained by self-discipline
IV-b2: Imposed on others
IV-b3: Neophobia

IV-c: *Pity and cruelty*
IV-c1: Self-pity and pity for others
IV-c2: Instinctive repugnance to suffering in general
IV-c3: Reasoned repugnance to useless suffering

IV-d: *Self-sacrifice for others*
IV-d1: Risking one's life
IV-d2: Sharing one's goods with others

IV-e: *Sentiments of hierarchy*
IV-e1: Of superiors
IV-e2: Of inferiors
IV-e3: Need of group approval

IV-f: *Asceticism*

CLASS V INTEGRITY OF THE INDIVIDUAL AND HIS APPURTENANCES

V-a: *Sentiments opposing alterations in the social equilibrium*

V-b: *Sentiments of equality among inferiors*

V-c: *Restoration of integrity by operations on the subject of change*
V-c1: Real subjects
V-c2: Imaginary or abstract subjects

V-d: *Restoration of integrity by operations on the object of change*
V-d1: Real agents
V-d2: Imaginary or abstract agents

CLASS VI SEX RESIDUE

(ii) Epitome of residue classification*

Class I: Instinct for Combination.† (889) This class comprises the residues corresponding to the instinct for combinations which is very strong in the human species. It has been, and still is, a powerful activating cause of civilisation. There can be detected in an enormous number of phenomena— as a residue—an inclination to combine certain things with other things. The scientist in his laboratory makes combinations according to certain norms, intentions and hypotheses. These for the most part are rational, although at times he will make combinations at random. His behaviour is logical. The ignorant person also makes combinations, prompted thereto by analogies which for the most part are fantastic, puerile and absurd; and often combines by chance. For the most part his behaviour is non-logical.

I-a: Combinations in general . . . The instinct for combinations is among the greatest of the forces determining the social equilibrium; if it sometimes shows itself in ridiculous and absurd forms, this in no way lessens its importance. . . . (899) . . . Most discoveries, especially in the past, have been made . . . thanks not to logic, but to the instinct of combinations which impels human beings to link certain things and acts without a pre-determined plan. . . . They move about in the dark; sometimes they find something, more often they do not. . . . (909) . . . This is one of the most tenacious of residues. It is to be found at all times and in all societies, among the educated—even the highly educated—as well as among the ignorant; and whether people are superstitious or unsuperstitious has very little to do with the matter.

I-b: Combination of likes and unlikes. (910) Similarity or contrasts in things—irrespective of whether they are imaginary and fantastic—is a potent promoter of combinations. . . . (912) The homœopathic principle (*similia similibus curantur*) combines likes; the opposite principle (*contraria contrariis*) combines unlikes. . . .

I-b1: Generic form. (913) Residues of this general variety of subclass I-b are of common occurrence. They often occur in magic; like things and like operations are combined. . . . Unlikes also are associated, and it would seem that in many cases there are at work sentiments which foster a

---

* This epitome seeks to outline the main points and clearest examples in Pareto's long elaboration of residues (Chapter VI, §§889–1088; Chapter VII, §§1089–206; Chapter VIII, §§1207–396). For reasons of space many of his differentiations and special considerations are not included.

† The full range of meanings of *combinazione* is impossible to render by one term in English. The Italian word, when associated with individuals, connotes— in addition to the simple English meaning of 'combining'—notions such as 'dexterity', 'resourcefulness', 'imaginative originality', 'shrewd scheming', 'skullduggery'. Since 'combination' has acquired, thanks largely to Arthur Livingston's pioneer work, a technical sense *sui generis* in relation to Pareto's teaching, it is employed throughout this translation in rendering *combinazione* as Class I of the residues. Where Pareto uses the word outside the specific context of Class I residues, we have generally preferred, so as to avoid confusion, not to translate it by 'combination'; cf. 'interaction', pp. 260 *et seq.*

deliberate search for contrasts. . . . (981) There is a I-b1 residue traceable in parodies of religious rites, the object of such parodies . . . being to obtain things contrary to religion and morality. The 'black masses' offer an example. . . . (921). . . In general, it is present to a greater or lesser extent in the sentiments which move us to reason by analogy; consequently we shall encounter it again when dealing with derivations.

I-b2: *Rare things combined with unusual events.* (922) The instinctive belief that rare things and exceptional occurrences are connected with other rare things and events—or simply with things ardently desired— contributes to sustaining faith in the efficacy of combinations. . . . This belief is never, or scarcely ever, undermined by even the most frequent experience to the contrary. . . . (923) . . . A good many talismans and relics belong to this category. (924) Omens very often yield residues of the I-b2 variety. . . . (925) . . . Although christians attribute everything to God, they often cite omens without mentioning, at least explicitly, divine interven-tion, and this is so because it seems perfectly natural for rare things and unusual events to go hand in hand. . . .

I-b3: *Terrifying or awesome things combined with terrible things and events.* (929) This residue appears almost always by itself in certain situa-tions, typical of which is Sallust's account of the Catiline conspiracy. . . . Whether the story of the oath-taking be true or false, there remains the association of two terrible things: the drinking of human blood and a conspiracy to destroy the Roman Republic. This residue is seen in certain cases where human sacrifices are substituted for animal sacrifices. . . .

I-b4: *Good things combined with fortunate events, and bad things with unfortunate.* (933) For example, over a long period in Europe everything good was ascribed to the protection of the 'wisdom of the ancestors'. Today everything esteemed good is assigned to 'progress'. To have a 'modern attitude' to things means to have correct ideas and sound sense. In the past, you were praising a man when you said he had the 'old virtues'; today you praise him for being a 'modern man' or for having—to use the neologism favoured by some people—'a modern outlook'. In the past it was praiseworthy to behave 'like a christian'; nowadays you acquire merit by behaving 'humanely' or (even better) in a 'nobly humanitarian manner' —as when, for example, protecting thieves and murderers. To help one's fellow man used to be called 'charitable'; in our day it is called 'an act of humanity'. To characterise dangerous men, given over to wrong-doing, there used to be employed the terms 'heretic' and 'God-accursed'; in our day such men are labelled 'reactionaries'. Everything good is 'democratic'; everything bad is 'aristocratic'. The pontiffs of the great god Progress boiled with rage and indignation when Abdul Hamid suppressed the revolt of the Armenians, calling him the 'Bloody Sultan'. But they expended so much righteous indignation over him that they had none left when, in 1910, the 'Young Turks'—bearing aloft the sacred banner of Progress—subdued the insurgent Armenians. The maxim of such people seems to be simply: A government has the right to put down an insurrection if it has a better claim to the favour of the god Progress than those who rebel against it; otherwise it has no such right. (934) . . . The selfsame Englishmen who assert that in Russia political crimes are due exclusively to bad government are persuaded that identical crimes committed in India are due solely to criminal proclivities inherent in their subjects.

I-b5: *Physical assimilation: causes linked to effects*. (937) ... Human beings have often believed that certain substances when eaten confer something of their properties on the consumer. At times this phenomenon may be associated with a mystical communion between the individual and his totem or deity, but more often these are different things. (941) ... We should note that the fact that the sentiment manifested in this residue is operative in all forms of 'mystic communion' in no way impugns catholic doctrine or the doctrine of any other theology.... Whatever the faith may be, it can find expression only in the language of men and through the sentiments subsisting in them. To study such modes of expression in no way derogates from the things they express.

I-c: *Mysterious power ascribed to certain things and acts*. (944) This residue is found in many magical practices, in amulets, in oaths taken on certain objects, in judgements by ordeal and the like. It is also the principal element in taboos, with or without sanction. It corresponds to a sentiment whereby things and acts are invested with an occult power, often vague and inadequately explained.

I-c1: *Generic form*. (948) It is ordinarily detected under the disguise of one of its derivations. Under the influence of the need human beings feel for giving a logical colouring to their attitude (I-e), people ask: 'How do these things, these acts operate as they do?' The answer comes: 'Through the intervention of a spirit, a god, a devil.' This is no more than to say that opium induces sleep because it has a dormitive property.... (951) ... The important point is that people firmly believe they can bind one another by means of certain acts in part mysterious. The residue lies in this belief and is to be traced among all peoples from the earliest times. Even today there are countries where oaths must be sworn on the Bible or on the Gospels, and the hand laid on the holy text must be bare....

I-c2: *Mysterious associations of names and things*. (958) A name may be linked to things in two ways: either mysteriously, without any experimental reason; or because it evokes certain experimental, or even imaginary, properties of things. The first way yields this subclass; the second yields residues of aggregate-persistence (Class II) ... Whereas in experimental science names are arbitrary, there is nothing arbitrary in the association of names with things by certain mysterious links which may be abstract, experimental, pseudo-experimental, sentimental, imaginary or fantastic. (960) An excellent example of this is the so-called 'perfect number'. ... For mathematicians the term 'perfect' is simply a label signifying a number equal to the sum of its aliquots. ... It could quite as well be designated by some other name. ... But when reasoning is governed by sentiments ... the name assumes great importance; 'perfect' is the opposite of 'imperfect' ... and the term becomes an epithet for certain sentiments which certain individuals find agreeable. ...

I-d: *Urge to combine residues*. (966) Human beings often feel the need to combine certain residues existing in the mind. This is a manifestation of the synthetic tendency which is indispensable in practical life. ... (967) People as a whole dislike separating faith from experience. What they want is a completed whole devoid of discordant notes. For a long time, christians believed that the Bible contained nothing contrary to historical or scientific experience. Some of them have now abandoned this assumption so far as the natural sciences are concerned, but they retain it in regard to history. Some others have abandoned both the historical and the scientific authority of the Bible, but they retain its morality at least. Yet others endeavour to harmonise matters—if not literally, then at least allegorically—by subtle interpretations. . . . (970) Among 'intellectuals', the urge to combine residues is persistent. An amalgam is made of 'welfare', 'the good', 'the beautiful', 'the true', and some add 'the humane', 'altruism', 'solidarity'— all this forming a neat amalgam which gratifies their feelings. This amalgam, which derives from the strong inclination for combinations, may— with others like it—eventually acquire an independent existence under the influence of residues of aggregate-persistence (Class II), and may even in certain cases be personified. (971) . . . Literature satisfies the human need for combining residues, a need which is left unsatisfied by science. . . . A literary work is always more likely to influence large numbers of people than a scientific work. . . .

I-e: *Urge to seek logical explanations.* (972) . . . The need for logic is as much satisfied by pseudo-logical as by strictly logical explanations. Fundamentally people want to exercise their faculty for thinking; it matters little whether the thinking be sound or faulty. . . . (973) Those who proclaim the 'bankruptcy of science' are right in the sense that science cannot satisfy the unbounded desire of human beings for pseudo-logical explanations. Science can only relate one fact to another, and consequently there is always some fact before which it comes to a halt. But the human imagination will not halt there; it is resolved to go on to draw inferences from this final fact, seeking to know its 'cause'. If it cannot find a real cause, it invents an imaginary one. (974) We must bear in mind that, although this urge to seek for causes of any sort, whether real or imaginary, has fathered many imaginary causes, it has also led to the discovery of real causes. . . . Primitive peoples scorn the metaphysical lucubrations of civilised peoples, but equally they are strangers to scientific investigations. One can arguably assert that, without theology and metaphysics, experimental science would not exist. . . .

I-f: *Belief in the efficacy of combinations.* (976) . . . One may believe that A is necessarily linked to B. This belief may derive from experience, that is, from observation of the fact that A is always linked to B. But from this logico-experimental science deduces no more than that it is more or less probable that A will always be associated with B. . . . (980) But considering matters from the viewpoint of sentiments and residues, we find that, if the combination AB is not a fact of the laboratory but of everyday life, in the long run it engenders in the minds of people a sentiment linking A indissolubly with B, and one is hard put to it to distinguish this sentiment from one which in origin is pseudo-experimental or alien to experience. (981) When a cock is put in with the hens, these lay eggs which hatch out chickens. When a cock crows at midnight someone in the house dies. For those who reason by sentiment, these two propositions are equally certain and, indeed, equally experimental. . . .

Class II: Persistence of Aggregates.* (991) Certain combinations constitute an aggregate of closely associated elements, as in a single body, so that the aggregate comes to acquire a personality like other true entities. . . . (992) After the aggregate has been formed, an instinct very often operates which, with variable force, opposes any disintegration of the things thus closely conjoined. If disintegration cannot be avoided, this instinct tries to disguise the break-up by preserving the external features of the aggregate. Roughly speaking this instinct can be compared with mechanical inertia, and it opposes movement produced by other instincts. Herein lies the tremendous social importance of Class II residues. (999) The apotheosis of the Roman emperors, considered from the logical viewpoint, is absurd and ridiculous; but considered as a manifestation of the endurance of residues, it seems natural and reasonable. The emperor, whoever he might be, personified the empire, regular administration, justice, the *pax romana*. These sentiments did not in any way suffer a weakening because one man died and another took his place. The permanence of that aggregate was the fact: the apotheosis was one of the forms by which it was manifested.

II-a: *Persistence of the relations of individuals with other individuals or places.* (1015) This subclass has three varieties with similar and closely related characteristics so that they easily mingle and their residues compensate each other. . . .

II-a1: *Relations with family or community.* (1016) . . . In the human race, relations between young and parents produce interesting and sometimes very powerful residues. (1017) These correspond to the form of family association originating them and which they then serve to strengthen or modify. . . . (1021) Whatever the causes, among many peoples communities came to be formed. We do not know the 'origins' of these social groups. . . . [Various] explanations have been offered . . . (1022) But the . . . hypothesis which best explains the known facts is that which considers such groups as natural formations developing round a nucleus which is generally the family, with various appendages. The permanence of these communities creates or strengthens certain sentiments, and these in their turn make them more solid, more firm and durable. . . .

II-a2: *Relations with places.* (1041) These residues often intermingle with the foregoing and with II-b residues. . . . (1042) Looking at things superficially, one might think that modern patriotism is territorial since modern nations take their names from the territories they occupy. But looking more closely we perceive that the sentiment of patriotism is attached to the territorial name because this evokes a sum of sentiments: a supposed common stock, language, religion, traditions, history and so on. In reality, patriotism cannot be exactly defined, any more than can

---

* The Livingston translation renders this as 'group-persistence', a term which is as misleading as it is unwarranted. The Italian word is *aggregati*, and Pareto chose it deliberately. He was, as he often boasted, 'a nominalist of nominalists'—i.e., an extremist in denying reality to compounds of simple, atomic units. Note how in §991 here he contradistinguishes the 'aggregate' from 'other true entities'. The whole point of Class II residues is that it is they—these inbuilt attitudes or urges—which induce us to *believe* to be real entities what in fact are aggregates of atomic elements.

'religion', 'morality', 'justice'. . . . Such terms simply evoke certain amalgams of sentiments, imprecise in form and with very vague limits, which are held together by residues of aggregate-persistence.

II-a3: *Relations with social classes.* (1043) The very fact of living in a group, a community, impresses certain concepts on the mind, certain ways of thinking and acting, certain prejudices and beliefs which—as is the case with so many similar entities—endure and acquire a pseudo-objective existence. Their corresponding residues have often acquired the form of residues of family relationships. It has been supposed that social classes and even nations were so many genealogies, each having a common ancestor, real or imaginary, and even its own gods who were enemies of the gods of other communities. But this is a mere derivation, and among the civilised peoples of today it has lapsed. (1045) In Europe, the 'class struggle' propaganda of the marxists—or rather the circumstances of which it is the expression—had the effect of arousing or strengthening corresponding residues in the 'proletariat', or rather in a part of the population; whereas on the other hand the fact that 'entrepreneurs' considered it necessary not to oppose democratic sentiments but instead to use them in order to make money, weakened and destroyed certain residues of group identity among the upper classes.

II-b: *Persistence of relations between the living and the dead.* (1052) . . . Residues of this subclass are found in enormous numbers of phenomena. In some degree they are similar to II-a residues, and this explains why they are found combined with them in very many cases, such as family, caste, patriotism, religion and the like. Combined with IV-d2 residues (sharing one's goods with others), they are revealed in complex phenomena such as honouring and worshipping the dead, or feasts and sacrifices associated with funerals and commemorations.

II-c: *Persistence of relations between the dead and the things they possessed in life.* (1056) These relations . . . endure in the minds of the living after a man's death, hence the widespread custom of burying or burning with him the dead man's possessions . . . (1057) . . . Such customs are logically explained . . . as indicative of a belief in another life for the person who has died. . . . (1058) Such beliefs were indeed held, but they are derivations, that is to say they are essentially variable; what is constant throughout is the persistence of the relations between the dead person and his possessions when he was alive.

II-d: *Persistence of an abstraction.* (1065) Once an agglomeration of relations has been formed, either in the way described in §991 or in some other way, there emerges a corresponding abstraction. This may persist, and if so a new, subjective entity is created. (1066) These residues are at the root of theology and metaphysics, which could be precisely defined as agglomerations of derivations from such residues. . . .

II-e: *Persistence of uniformities.* (1068) . . . It is a common procedure to generalise a particular uniformity or even a single isolated fact. A fact is observed; it is stated in abstract terms; the abstraction persists and becomes a general rule. This is of everyday occurrence, so much so that we can assert that this kind of reasoning is characteristic of people not accustomed to scientific thinking, and even of many who are. . . . In the extreme case of abstractions superior to experience, we get metaphysical principles, 'natural' principles, 'necessary' relationships and so forth. . . .

II-f: *Sentiments transformed into objective realities.* (1069) These residues are extremely numerous. . . . They are at the root of subjective proofs obtained by reference to sentiments, and they powerfully influence the motives inspiring the production and acceptance of theories. The introspection of the metaphysicists, the christian 'inner experience' and similar ways of thinking represent the transformation of sentiments into objective realities.

II-g: *Personification.* (1070) At its first level, personification consists in giving a name to an abstraction, a uniformity, a sentiment, thus transforming these into objective individual entities. Then, step by step, the highest level is reached where the personification is complete in the shape of anthropomorphism. . . . (1073) It has often been said that socialism is a religion. Such a proposition would be absurd if made in relation with anthropomorphic derivations, for assuredly no one in our day has ever conceived of socialism in a male form, as the ancient Romans conceived of the goddess Roma in female form. But when made in relation with residues, the proposition corresponds with the facts in the sense that the sentiments which were formerly expressed in the cult of the goddess Roma or the goddess Annona are similar to those which are now expressed in faith in socialism, progress, democracy and the like.

II-h: *Need of new abstractions.* (1086) The need for abstractions persists as certain of them fall into desuetude and are dispensed with for one reason or another. New abstractions are then required to take their place. Thus popular mythologies are superseded, among the educated, by scholarly, subtle, abstruse mythologies. Ingenious theogonies are developed, speculations about the creation of the world, the original state of humanity, etc. Then a further step is taken: supernatural abstractions give way to metaphysical abstractions; studies of the 'essences' of things are undertaken, and we get lucubrations in incomprehensible language on matters even more incomprehensible. Finally to these metaphysical abstractions are added pseudo-scientific abstractions. . . . People who no longer worship the relics of saints kneel in veneration to 'solidarity'. . . . Such cases as this, where the forms change but the need of persisting abstractions endures, are innumerable.

Class III: Manifestation of Sentiments by Activity. (1089) Powerful sentiments are for the most part accompanied by certain acts which may not be directly related to these sentiments but which satisfy the need for action. The same kind of thing is to be observed in animals. On seeing a bird, a cat moves its jaws; a dog will rush about and wag its tail when it sees its master; a parrot will flap its wings, and so forth. (1091) Sentiments are strengthened by the acts which express them, and the acts may beget the sentiments even in individuals who were without them. It is a well-known psychological fact that if an emotion finds expression in a certain physical attitude, a person who puts himself in this attitude may well generate in himself the corresponding emotion. Hence the residues of this class are conjoined to emotions, sentiments and passions by a complex catena of actions and reactions. (1094) . . . Religious liturgies, contortions, dances, mutilations inflicted in delirium, are a variety of this class.

Class IV: Residues of Sociality. (1113) This class embraces residues which relate to life in society. Residues relating to discipline may also be included in this class if one accepts that the sentiments corresponding to them are strengthened by living in society. . . . All domestic animals, except the cat, when at liberty live in 'societies'. On the other hand, society is impossible without some kind of discipline; therefore the social structure and the disciplinary structure must necessarily have certain points of contact.

 IV-a: *Particular societies.* (1114) The need for particular associations . . . takes different forms—for amusement simply, for special advantage, for religious, literary, political and other purposes. . . . We must distinguish between the sentiments prompting men to join together in particular societies from the sentiments which develop within such societies. . . .

 IV-b: *Need for uniformity.* (1116) In human societies, the desired uniformity may be general among a people, but it may also vary with the different groups of individuals in this people. . . . There is not one sole centre of uniformity in a given society; there are several such centres. At times conflicts may arise between these various collectivities, each seeking to extend its own particular uniformity to others. Or there may be no such conflict, each individual being content with the uniformity of the group he belongs to and respecting the uniformities of other groups.

 IV-b1: *Obtained by self-discipline.* (1117) Imitation belongs to this variant. One individual imitates other individuals; one group or nation imitates other groups or nations; hence imitation plays an important part in social phenomena. . . . (1118) The imitation may have a purpose . . . in which case it would represent a logical action. But very often there is no . . . conscious purpose, and in such cases the imitation represents non-logical behaviour. (1119) This residue is found in its purest form in the temporary uniformities imposed by fashion. . . . (1123) . . . Members of sects imitate customs which are peculiar to their sect. . . .

 IV-b2: *Imposed on others.* (1126) As well as imitating to become like others, the human being desires other people to do as he does. An individual's departure from the accepted norm . . . creates a feeling of uneasiness in those who are associated with him. Efforts are made to remove the discrepancy between his behaviour and the norm by persuasion, more often by censure, and more often still by force. . . . (1128) The need for uniformity is not expressed with equal intensity in all directions. . . . Governments in our day confiscate periodicals displaying pictures of naked women, but allow the sale of newspapers which preach pillage, arson and the massacre of the bourgeoisie.

 IV-b3: *Neophobia.* (1130) This is a sentiment of resistance to innovations which would be likely to disturb uniformities. Extremely strong among primitive peoples, among civilised peoples it is surpassed in intensity only by the instinct of combinations (Class I residues). . . .

 IV-c: *Pity and Cruelty.* (1133) . . . It is not easy to distinguish the sentiment of pity from many others which take its form. Without question over the last hundred years or so the repression of crime has grown progressively less severe. . . . It would seem that pity for criminals is on the increase and pity for their victims on the decrease. (1134) . . . Yet it may be that pity in general is increasing, and that the murderer receives more than his victim simply because he is before us in court whereas his victim is absent. . . .

IV-c1 : *Self-pity and pity for others.* (1138) People who are unfortunate and tend to attribute their woes to the situation they live in, to 'society', incline to sympathise with all who suffer. . . . (1139) People in poor economic circumstances are persuaded that 'society' is at fault. By analogy' they take the view that the crimes of thieves and murderers are also attributable to 'society', and so criminals seem to them comrades in misfortune, worthy of their pity. 'Intellectuals' are persuaded that they are denied their due position in the social hierarchy. They envy the rich, military officers, prelates, and all others in the higher levels of society. They see the criminals and the poor as fellow victims with them of the upper class . . . and so they feel benevolence and pity for them. . . . (1141) The existence of these residues makes it probable that many of those who, seeking advantages for themselves, claim to be seeking them for 'society', are in fact acting in good faith. It may well be therefore that many who derive personal advantage from engaging in practical socialism genuinely believe that they are implementing theoretical socialism for the good of all, or at least for the greatest number.

IV-c2: *Instinctive repugnance to suffering in general.* (1142) This is a sentiment of revulsion at the sight of all suffering irrespective of whether it be useful or not. . . . (1143) Pity of this kind often animates those who condemn all forms of war. They stress the sufferings of the killed and wounded without stopping to consider the advantages which may arise therefrom. . . . This kind of pity is widely prevalent in decadent elites, and it may indeed be taken as a symptom of such decadence.

IV-c3: *Reasoned repugnance to useless suffering.* (1144) . . . The term 'useless' in this context is subjective. . . . Although in certain cases it may be possible to determine that a given thing is objectively 'useless' to society, there are very many other cases in which the matter is in doubt. . . . Yet it would be mistaken to conclude that an eventual and remote possibility of some utility or other will make the infliction of suffering beneficial. Decisions have to be taken on the basis of the greater or lesser probabilities. It would clearly be absurd to argue that it might be advantageous to kill at random a hundred people on the grounds that a future murderer might be among the hundred killed off. . . .

IV-d: *Self-sacrifice for others.* (1145) Life in society is of necessity based on a measure of reciprocal goodwill between individuals. This sentiment may be weak or strong, but it cannot be entirely absent. It is revealed both in animals and human beings in actions of mutual help and common defence—in short, by the sacrifices an individual makes for the good of others. . . . (1147) . . . The individual's behaviour is conditioned not only by his own attitudes in the matter but also—and often predominately—by the desire to win the approval or avoid the censure of others. . . .

IV-d1 : *Risking one's life.* (1148) Individuals risk or even sacrifice their lives under the prompting of a deep sentiment of sociality, or influenced by the importance they attach to the esteem of their fellows. . . . General Nogi, who led the victorious Japanese at Port Arthur, killed his wife and himself on the day of the Mikado's funeral. In this case the sacrifice of life had no direct utility, being a simple manifestation of sentiments of sociality and hierarchy (IV-e) conjoined with the aggregate-persistence of the old Samurai, associated with the desire to win the approval of all sharing such sentiments.

IV-d2: *Sharing one's goods with others.* (1149) The preceding form shades by imperceptible degrees into this less acute form in which renunciation for the benefit of others involves only certain enjoyments. . . . (1152) At first sight it might be thought that this residue is present in all individuals in the governing class who take the part of the subject class. But this is not so. . . . It is undeniable that there may feasibly be individuals of energy, knowledge and good sense who, in advocating doctrines of social solidarity, are moved by the genuine desire to share their goods with others—but examples are not easy to come by.

IV-e: *Sentiments of hierarchy.* (1153) . . . It would seem that no human society of any degree of complexity could survive without such sentiments. In societies which ostensibly proclaim equality for all individuals the hierarchy may be transformed, but there nevertheless remains a hierarchy. . . . Along with sentiments of hierarchy we may put the sentiment of deference which the individual feels for the group of which he is a member or for other groups, and his desire for their approval, praise or admiration.

IV-e1: *Sentiments of superiors.* (1155) These are sentiments of protection and benevolence, and sometimes of domination and pride. . . .

IV-e2: *Sentiments of inferiors.* (1156) These are sentiments of subordination, affection, respect and fear. They are indispensable to . . . the social order. . . . Manifestations of the sentiment of authority are very numerous and diverse. People accept the authority of those who have, or are presumed to have, some real or imaginary symbol of superiority. Hence the respect of the young for the old, of the novice for the expert; in the past, of the illiterate for the learned . . . of the commoner for the noble; in our day, of the non-union worker and a good many bourgeois for the trade unionist; of the weak for the strong (or reputed strong); of the man of one race for the man of another reputedly superior race; . . . of the subject for the sovereign; . . . of the voter for the politician . . . etc. (1157) In virtue of the persistence of abstractions, the sentiment of authority may to a greater or lesser degree be removed from the person and attached to the symbol, real or imagined, of authority. Hence the advantage for those in authority of maintaining their prestige, the semblance of superiority. The separation between person and symbol may be complete and the sentiment may be attached to inanimate objects; hence the respect many people have for the written or printed word. . . .

IV-e3: *Need of group approval.* (1161) . . . This residue sometimes covers up other residues. An individual who is regarded as being moved by a desire to win the esteem of others may also be prompted to some extent, however slight, by a desire to do the thing which merits this esteem. . . . In general . . . the approbation or censure of the group reinforces an already existing sentiment in the individual. . . .

IV-f: *Asceticism.* (1163) . . . These are sentiments which prompt an individual, without aiming at personal advantage, to inflict suffering on himself or abstain from pleasures, therein going counter to the instinct which prompts living creatures to seek agreeable things and avoid painful things. . . . (1164) . . . The constant element is the self-infliction of suffering; the variable element is the reasons given for this. (1165) The main residue appears in this constant element, but it is by no means the only residue present in it. All social phenomena are complex, mingling many residues. There is often detectable in the ascetic man the residue of pride as well as the residue of asceticism. He feels superior to the generality of mankind, and those who admire him acknowledge this superiority. Sometimes he is influenced by the religious residue, at other times by the residue of uniformity—as when he seeks to impose his asceticism on others—and yet on other occasions by the residue of a presumed utility, real or imaginary. . . .

Class V: Integrity of the Individual and his Appurtenances. (1207) This class of sentiments . . is in a sense the complement of Class IV. To defend one's own things and to endeavour to increase their quantity are two operations which often merge. Defence of the individual's integrity and development of his personalia may therefore differ very little or even be one and the same thing. That sum of sentiments called 'interests' is of the same nature as the sentiments to which the residues of the present class correspond. Sentiments of 'interests' therefore ought strictly to be included in this classification, but they are of such great intrinsic importance for the social equilibrium that it is better to consider them separately from residues.

V-a: *Sentiments opposing alterations in the social equilibrium.* (1208) This equilibrium may exist in reality or be an ideal equilibrium desired by the individual. But in either case, if it is altered or thought to be altered, the individual suffers even though he may not be directly affected by the alteration; and in some cases—though this is rare—he suffers even if getting advantage from the alteration. (1209) For example, in a people among whom slavery exists, as among the ancient Greeks, even the citizen who possesses no slaves is sensible of the harm done to the slave-owner by depriving him of his slaves. This is a reaction to an act which disturbs the social equilibrium. . . . (1210) If an existing state of social equilibrium is altered, forces come into operation which tend to re-establish it; this is precisely what equilibrium means. These forces in the main are sentiments which manifest themselves as residues of the V-a type. . . . Passively, they make us aware of the alteration in the equilibrium. Actively, they prompt us to repel, remove and counteract the causes of the alteration, thereby becoming sentiments of the V-d variety (restoration of integrity). The forces, or sentiments, which are brought into being by disturbance of the social equilibrium are almost always perceived under a special form by the individuals making up the society. It goes without saying that these individuals are wholly unaware of such forces and of the equilibrium. 'Forces' and 'equilibrium' are simply technical terms we use to describe the phenomena. The members of a society in which the equilibrium is altered feel affected in their integrity as it existed in the state of equilibrium—a disagreeable disturbance which may be painful, sometimes very painful indeed. Normally, such sensations belong to the vague categories known as *just* or *unjust*. When people say: 'That is unjust', they are in fact saying that it offends their sentiments, which relate to the state of social equilibrium they are familiar with. (1214) If this sentiment of opposition to disturbance of the social equilibrium did not exist, then every slight nascent alteration in the social equilibrium would encounter little or no resistance and could therefore go on developing with impunity to the point where it came to affect a large enough number of individuals to arouse resistance on the part of those directly concerned to avoid the evil. This is what in fact happens to a certain extent in every society, even the most civilised. But the extent to which it occurs is lessened by the intervention of the sentiment of opposition to alteration in the equilibrium, without regard to the number of individuals directly affected by it. As a result, the social equilibrium becomes much more stable; a much more energetic action develops as soon as it begins to be altered.

V-b: *Sentiments of equality among inferiors.* (1220) These sentiments are often a defence of integrity on the part of an individual belonging to a lower class and a means of raising him to a higher class. It occurs without the individual who experiences the sentiment being at all aware of the difference between his real and his apparent aims. He stresses the interests of his social class rather than his personal interests simply because this way of speaking is routine. (1221) Marked tendencies arise from the nature of this sentiment, and they may at first seem contradictory. On one hand, there is a tendency to make the largest possible number of people share in the advantages demanded by the individual for himself. On the other hand, there is a tendency to limit that number as much as possible. But the contradiction disappears as soon as we realise that the prevailing tendency is to share advantages with all those whose co-operation may be helpful in obtaining these advantages and whose involvement in the matter produces more than it costs, and to exclude all who do not help, or help so little that their involvement costs more than it produces. . . . (1222) There is another apparent contradiction. Inferiors seek to be the equal of their superiors, but they will not grant their superiors to be their equals. From the logical viewpoint, two contradictory propositions cannot be true at the same time. . . . But the contradiction disappears if one considers that the demand for equality is no more than a disguised way of demanding a privilege. . . . People advocate equality to get equality in general, then make innumerable distinctions to deny it in the particular. Equality is for everybody, but is granted only to some. (1223) . . . To people today, equality for all men is an article of faith; but this does not prevent there being in France and Italy enormous inequalities between 'union' and 'non-union' workers, between ordinary citizens and those who have the favour of deputies, senators, local political figures and such like. . . . (1224) These things are known to everybody; that is why no attention is paid to them. . . . Yet all this does not prevent people from believing in good faith that they enjoy equality. In some parts of the United States there are hotels where you cannot have your shoes polished because it is contrary to Holy Equality for one person to polish another's shoes. But the very persons who have this high theory of equality want to expel Chinese and Japanese

from the United States; are revolted at the mere idea of a Japanese child
sitting in the same classroom as their own children; will not allow a Negro
to stay at the same hotel as themselves or even travel in a railway carriage
which has the honour of conveying them. . . . (1227) The sentiment which,
very improperly, bears the name of equality is lively, active and powerful
precisely because it is not in fact concerned with equality or at all related
to any such abstraction—as some naive 'intellectuals' still believe—but
because it is related to the direct interests of persons who seek to free themselves from certain inequalities which operate against them, and to set up
new inequalities in their favour. This last is their principal concern.

V-c: *Restoration of integrity by operations on the subject of change*
(1229) This subclass includes the purifications widely practised in ancient
societies and still in use among primitive and barbarous peoples. Although
they have completely or almost completely disappeared in contemporary
western societies . . . they provide valuable examples of the way in which
residues operate and germinate into derivations. . . . (1240) . . . The sentiment of integrity is among the most powerful at work in human beings,
having its roots in the instinct of self-preservation. . . . (1248) Ordinarily
concepts of alteration of integrity depend directly upon sentiments and
have only an indirect relation to utilities of individuals and societies; and
indeed when they have such it is by way of sentiments. . . .

V-d: *Restoration of integrity by operations on the object of change*.
(1312) There is in men and animals a sentiment which prompts them to
hurt those who have hurt them, to return evil for evil. Unless and until this
is done, the subject of the injury feels a sense of discomfort, as if something
were amiss with him. His integrity has been altered and is not restored to
its original state unless he performs certain operations directed towards the
aggressor. Duels and vendettas are governed by sentiments of this kind.

V-d1: *Real agents*. (1313) This is the most important variety. . . .
Residues of this kind often merge with residues of social equilibrium (V-a).
Among contemporary civilised peoples, if a citizen of one country is
harmed in a foreign country, his government often seeks compensation.
This is a simple logical act. But many people are moved to approve of this
kind of reaction under the influence of that same sentiment which in the
past made vengeance a duty. . . . (1317) A person who is excluded from a
group sees his integrity altered by this, and he may feel the alteration so
strongly that the exclusion becomes a very heavy penalty. Even if he is not
actually excluded, the mere declaration that his integrity no longer exists
may be equivalent to a penalty inflicted by force.

V-d2: *Imaginary and abstract agents*. (1320) This residue appears
clearly in cases where people show resentment against their fetish, against
some saint, spiritual being or god. . . .

Class VI: Sex Residue. (1324) Sexual appetite as such, though powerfully
active in human beings, does not concern us here. . . . We are interested in
it only as it affects, as a residue, theories and ways of thinking. In general,
this residue and the sentiments it derives from are encountered in enormous
numbers of phenomena, but they are often disguised, especially among
modern peoples. (1325) . . . For our morality-mongers of today, all love out

of wedlock is illicit; for the Romans some forms were legitimate, others illegitimate. If the Romans were less tolerant of adultery in married women than sex-reformers are today, they did not have sectarians fuming with indignation at affairs with freed women. They were influenced, not by sex residues, but by considerations of state utility. . . . (1326) Among western races, three abstinence taboos have persisted for centuries: . . . abstinence from meat; abstinence from wine; and abstinence from everything to do with sex. . . . (1328) Religious exaltation is sometimes involved in the three taboos. . . . The sex taboo has a consistent identification with religious exaltation from antiquity down to our own day. (1329) . . . The sex taboo is one of the many cases in which sentiments are so strong as to make substance virtually constant, admitting only of changes in forms. The contrast is so great that we may venture the paradox of saying that immorality is greatest precisely where it is most severely condemned by morality and law. . . . (1330) . . . The very countries which are most exercised about purity reveal the worst cases of obscenities. . . . The residue is constant; if checked in its natural forms, it assumes other forms. . . . (1331) The sex residue is present not only in thoughts anticipating or recollecting sexual congress but also in mental attitudes which show censure, revulsion or hatred towards matters of sex. . . . (1332) It may be present in relations which are quite innocent or chaste, and it is a great error to assume that wherever it is present there are necessarily involved relations of a physical kind. . . . (1335) . . . The sex residues are manifested in phenomena which are similar to those termed 'religious'; they may therefore be properly classified as a whole with religious phenomena. Like other religions, the sex religion has its dogmas, believers, heretics and atheists. . . . (1338) Among ancient peoples and primitive peoples today, the sex organs and sexual acts are simply part of a general fetishism. For us moderns . . . though other fetishisms have disappeared or become weak, the sex fetishism endures. . . . (1351) . . . In many christian countries, it is possible to blaspheme Christ as much as one pleases, and no court of law will effectively intervene. But the courts will deal swiftly with anyone exhibiting an obscene postcard. . . . (1396) If we consider, on the one hand, the immense power of the church . . . and, on the other, the insignificance of the results achieved in suppressing sexual immorality, we gain some idea of the tremendous strength of the sex residue, and realise how ridiculous are these pygmies of our day who imagine they can repress it.

3. DERIVATIONS

(i) Classification of derivations*

CLASS I   ASSERTION

     Ia: Assertion of facts, experimental or imaginary

---

* Chapter IX, §1419. Save for the replacement of Greek by Latin letters, this classification is taken from *The Mind and Society*, Vol. III, p. 899, the 4-volume translation of the *Treatise* by Arthur Livingston and Andrew Bongiorno. For a specific application of Pareto's theory of derivations, see *Fatti e Teorie*, pp. 287–98 below, pp. 287 *et seq*.

Ib: Assertions of sentiments
Ic: Mixtures of fact and sentiment

CLASS II AUTHORITY

IIa: Of one individual or a number of individuals
IIb: Of tradition, usage and custom
IIc: Of divine beings or personifications

CLASS III ACCORD WITH SENTIMENTS OR PRINCIPLES

IIIa: Accord with sentiments
IIIb: Accord with individual interest
IIIc: Accord with collective interest
IIId: Accord with juridical entities
IIIe: Accord with metaphysical entities
IIIf: Accord with supernatural entities

CLASS IV VERBAL PROOFS

IVa: Indefinite terms designating real things; indefinite things corresponding to terms
IVb: Terms designating things and arousing incidental sentiments, or incidental sentiments determining choice of terms
IVc: Terms with numbers of meanings, and different things designated by single terms
IVd: Metaphors, allegories, analogies
IVe: Vague, indefinite terms corresponding to nothing concrete

(ii) Epitome of types of derivations*

Class I: Assertions. (1420) This class comprises simple relations, assertions of fact and assertions of accord of sentiments. They are not represented as such, but in absolute, dogmatic and axiomatic ways. Assertions may be simple accounts or indications of experimental uniformities; but often they are presented in such a way that it is not certain what they are expressing: experimental facts simply, or sentiments, or a mixture of facts and sentiments. However there are many cases in which, with a reasonable amount of probability, one can manage to discover their composition. Take for example the collection of maxims of Publilius Syrus. The first four of them belong to Ia of our classification. 'We men are all equally near to death'; 'Expect from another what you have done to another'; 'Assuage with tears the anger of those who love you'; 'In quarrelling with a drunkard, you contend with an absent man'. Then follows a maxim of the Ib type: 'It is better to receive than to inflict a wrong.' And after this come four more maxims of the first type and then again one of the second type: 'He is an adulterer who makes overpassionate love to his wife.' And finally there is a maxim of type Ic: 'We all ask, is he rich? None of us asks, is he

* The examples cited here are taken from representative sections in Pareto's long analysis and discussion (Chapter IX, §§ 1470–542; Chapter X, §§ 1543–1686).

good?' In this there is the assertion of a fact (Ia) and a reproof of that fact (Ib). Consider also the maxims of Menander. 'It is delightful to garner everything in its season'; this is a maxim of the Ia type. 'To do nothing or learn nothing is base' belongs to the Ib type. 'Silence becomes all women like a jewel' is of the Ic type.

Class II: *Authority*. (1434) Here we have a mode of proof and a mode of persuasion. . . . Our special concern here is with authority as a mode of persuasion. The various subclasses of Class II are, after assertions, the simplest of derivations. . . .

IIa: *Authority of one individual or a number of individuals*. (1435) The extreme case is that of strictly logical derivations. It is clear that, in a given matter, the opinion of someone who is thoroughly conversant with it is much more likely to be verified by experience than the opinion of someone who is ignorant in the matter or not very conversant with it. This is a purely logico-experimental instance and it need not detain us. But there are other kinds of derivations in which the individual's claim to authority is not experimental, but can be assumed to derive from misleading evidence or be wholly fictitious. In the case which is the least remote from the logico-experimental, the basis for the presumption of authority may or may not be sound since what is involved is a question of greater or lesser probability. Next to this we may put the case where the individual's competence to exercise authority is extended, through sentiments of aggregate-persistence, beyond the limits of what is experimentally valid. The well-known maxim: *Sutor, ne ultra crepidam*, 'Cobbler, stick to your last', is applicable to a situation which is of all times and all places. (1436) Because he is an outstanding politician, Theodore Roosevelt thinks he also knows history and sets himself up to lecture in Berlin, making a marvellous demonstration of his total ignorance of Greek and Roman history. The university once honoured by the teaching of Mommsen awards him the degree of *doctor honoris causa*. He alights on the discovery—wonder of wonders—that the saying *si vis pacem para bellum* has George Washington as author; and he is made a foreign member of the Academy of Moral and Political Sciences in Paris. It is without question that he is a skilled practitioner in electoral manipulations, knows all about 'booming' himself and his ideas and is, moreover, not uninstructed in the subtleties of hunting the white rhinoceros. But how does all this make him competent to give advice to the English on the governance of Egypt, or to the French on the number of children they should have? . . .

IIb: *Authority of tradition, usage and custom*. (1447) This authority may be verbal, written, anonymous, of a real or a legendary person. In such derivations an important part is played by the residues of aggregate-persistence. It is due to these residues that the 'wisdom of the ancestors' in past times, and the 'traditions of the party' in the present day, acquire an independent existence of their own. Derivations by authority of tradition are very numerous. . . . (1450) As we have frequently noted, derivations are for the most part flexible. Derivations by tradition possess the characteristic of flexibility to a very high degree. Where a book is the basis of tradition, for example, one can get out of it anything one pleases. The Greeks found everything in Homer, likewise the later Romans and medieval Christendom in Virgil; while Italians are able to find all sorts of things in Dante. This is even more remarkably so in the case of the Bible. It would be hard to say what has *not* been found therein. An enormous number and variety of doctrines have been extracted from the Scriptures, which have afforded proofs for and against with equal facility.

IIc: *Authority of divine beings or personifications.* (1458) If one attends only to the substance, derivations of this sort would properly be included in the preceding classification since, to be precise, the will of a divine being or of a personification can only be made known through human beings and traditions. But if form is given due regard, supernatural intervention is important enough to merit a distinct classification. In derivations of this subclass we can detect three varieties. 1. The 'revealed' will of the deity may be obeyed simply out of reverence for the deity. . . . 2. The divine will may be obeyed out of fear of punishment. . . . 3. An individual may pay heed to the divine will out of love for the deity because he wishes to act in accord with the sentiments the deity is supposed to feel, or because he believes that, regardless of the consequences, it is good, praiseworthy and plain duty to conform to the will of the deity. These two last varieties could properly be included in Class III: accord with individual (IIIb) or collective interest (IIIc), and accord with supernatural entities (IIIf). . . . (1460) In all these three varieties, it is important to note the ways in which the divine will is supposed to be known. With a few exceptions, they are generally simple in the first two varieties, and much more complex in the third. . . . (1463) Sometimes the complex derivation ends by taking on an independent value, constituting of itself a residue or else a simple derivation of the IIc subclass. This often occurs in the case of abstractions which are deified but not personified, and hence cannot be too explicitly attributable to a personal will; and an 'imperative' of some kind or other has to suffice. . . .

Class III: *Accord with Sentiments or Principles.* (1464) This accord is sometimes regarded as representing an accord with the sentiments of all men, of the majority, of all worthy men and so forth, but it is often only an accord with the sentiments of those who devise or accept the derivation. . . . (1470) . . . For centuries 'the universal consensus' enjoyed a great deal of importance as a demonstration of the existence of gods or God. As we have already seen [p. 207 above], the demonstration is essayed by affirming that God has implanted a certain concept in the human mind, and the mind then reveals the concept to us; or conversely, the existence of God is deduced by arguing from this concept's existence in the human mind and in virtue of a metaphysical principle. 'Greeks and barbarians all recognise the existence of gods', says Sextus Empiricus. In the same vein argues Maximus of Tyre; he begins by noting that there is an extreme variety of opinions on the nature of God and of 'good' and 'evil', 'base' and 'worthy'. But howsoever great the discord among these opinions, all men agree that there is one God, entire, sovereign and father of all, with whom are associated other gods, his children and companions. 'So say the Greek and the Barbarian, so the Continental and the Islander, so the wise and ignorant alike.' This is a splendid example of a writer's making objective his own subjective theory. Yet a good many people even at the time he wrote were far from sharing Maximus of Tyre's view of the matter. (1471) He seeks to deal with the objection usually made against this mode of arguing, i.e., that from this 'all' who are said to have certain opinions there must be excepted an appreciable number of people who do not hold such views. He rebuts this general objection by a general device of derivation: he excludes such people entirely from the ranks of those whose opinions deserve consideration. Those who do not concur with him in this matter are worthless wretches, and manifestly therefore all who are not worthless creatures think as he does. 'Even if in the course of time there have been two or three abject and stupid atheists, neither seeing nor hearing aright, eunuch-souls, foolish, sterile and useless, lions without courage, bulls without horns, birds without wings—yet even from these you will learn of the divine.' Such vilifying of one's adversaries is worthless from the logico-experimental viewpoint, but it can be worth a good deal from the viewpoint of sentiments.

Class IV: Verbal Proofs. (1543) This class comprises verbal derivations obtained through the use of terms the meaning of which is indeterminate, doubtful and equivocal and which do not correspond to reality. If this classification were to be understood in a very broad sense, it would be capable of including almost all the derivations which do not conform to reality—which is to say all derivations; and there would therefore be no point in distinguishing derivations of Class IV from all the others. Hence we have to restrict its definition to the cases in which the verbal character of the derivation is very conspicuous and predominant over other features. Logical sophistries can properly be included in this class in so far as their purely formal element serves to satisfy the need men feel for logical arguments (residues II-e). But this element is almost always secondary; it does not condition the judgement of those who accept the derivation, for this is governed by an element of much greater importance, namely, the sentiments evoked by the argument. These logical sophistries usually deceive only those who are already disposed to be deceived. Or rather one should say that there is in truth no deception at all since, between the author of the argument and those who accept it, there is at the outset a mutual sympathy based on an accord of sentiments. The logical sophistry is simply added for good measure to improve the appearance of this pre-existing accord.

(1554) The fate which has befallen the term 'liberty' is comical enough. In many cases it now signifies precisely the opposite of what it used to mean fifty years ago. But the sentiments it arouses are the same in that the word still has a connotation which is agreeable to those who hear it. If John puts Edward in chains, it is 'liberty' for Edward to strike off those chains. But if in his turn Edward puts the gyves on John, this for Edward will equally be 'liberty'. In both cases the term 'liberty' is associated in the mind of Edward with something agreeable. Half a century ago in England, the name of 'Liberal party' was given to the party which sought as much as possible to reduce restrictions which deprived the individual of the power to dispose of his person and his property as he wished. Today the party called 'Liberal' is the one which is seeking to increase the number of these restrictions. The Liberal party used to be in favour of reducing taxes; nowadays it is all for increasing them. In France and Italy, the 'liberals' of other days insistently demanded for the individual the right to work as much as he pleased, and they inveighed bitterly against the 'tyranny of kings and priests' which compelled people to be idle on feast days in the church calendar. In France during the period of the Restoration, there was a war to the death over this question between the 'liberals' and the government. Who can forget the fine, vigorous writings of Courier on this subject? As late as 1856, the fear of compulsory Sunday rest prompted the Senate of the Empire, submissive and tame creature though it was, to resistance—a strong feeling will make even a lamb rebel. . . . But now all is changed. 'Liberal' doctrine seeks to impose the 'day of rest' on Sunday; only now, to satisfy the anticlericals, it rejoices in the name of *le repos hebdomadaire*. 'Ultra-liberals' are demanding that state inspectors be empowered to prevent citizens from working on this day in the privacy of their own homes. To justify this, they have recourse to a residue* of 'enforced uniformity' (IV-b2). They argue that to allow an individual to work on certain days infringes the liberty of those who do not want to work on these days, and hence it is right to reason that the day of rest is imposed by law in the name of liberty. The metaphysicists among them add that thus 'the state creates liberty'. The employment of the term 'liberty' in this derivation entails three different meanings. 1. It has an indefinite sense relating to an abstract personification. 2. It has a definite sense relating to the faculty of acting or not acting. This second meaning has two separate aspects: 2a. a particular individual's faculty of acting or not acting; 2b. the faculty of individuals other than the particular individual of acting or not acting. These two faculties come into conflict, and a measure which safeguards one may impair the other. The derivations make use of this triple signification of 'liberty' to attribute to the first sense of the term what is valid only for one of the other two senses. Sometimes this verbal trickery is disguised by adding some sort of epithet to 'liberty' in its first sense. The derivation we are at present examining charges the first sense of 'liberty' with the signification the term bears in 2b, for it is asserting that compulsory Sunday-closing 'protects' liberty. But one could just as reasonably attribute to 1. the meaning of the term in 2a, and contend that Sunday-closing is an infringement of liberty. The practical conflict is not resolved at all by either of these derivations but only by examining whether, for the desired end in view, it is better that 2a should prevail over 2b or *vice versa*. In this case, we would pass from derivations to logico-experimental reasoning.

(1557) The term 'solidarity' affords an example of the direct use of the kind of derivation we are at present discussing. The 'solidarists' themselves confess that the term is employed in widely different senses. A propos of this, Croiset says in the preface to Bourgeois' *Essai d'une philosophie de la solidarité* [1902]: 'Everybody is using the term, and because of its general currency people all too easily forget to ask themselves what it means. If we

---

* Pareto writes 'derivazione', but this translation follows Livingston in regarding this as a slip of the pen for 'residuo'.

look into the matter it is readily seen that the term is applied to very different things. There is, first, a *de facto* solidarity which is simply the mutual interdependence of diverse associated elements. In law, for example, there is "solidarity" between joint debtors, each one of whom is held liable for the debt of all. In biology, "solidarity" is said to subsist between the parts of an organism when modifications effected in one part have a counteraction on the others.' Here Croiset makes the mistake of running together two very different things. A man is condemned to have his hand cut off; if there were 'solidarity' in the legal definition of the term between his two arms, in the sense that they are equally liable for the common debt, half a hand would have to be cut off each arm. Instead, only one of the arms pays the common debt; hence they have no solidarity in the legal sense, even though they may share a relationship of solidarity, according to Croiset, as 'parts of the same organism'. He then very ingeniously explains the reason for the prestige and prevalence of this term 'solidarity', attributing it to the fact that, in substance, it is indefinite enough for everyone to make it mean whatever is desired. His observation on this point is sound and is generally valid for derivations which contain ambiguous and vague terms. This is why such terms are so good for derivations and so bad for scientific reasoning. To stir up sentiments and disguise reality, it behoves that terms should not be precise; on the other hand, when the intention is to find out the relationships between facts, they need to be as precise as possible. The preachers of 'solidarity' show great shrewdness, therefore, in their use of vague language. But, even if other evidence were lacking, this would of itself show up the emptiness of their claim to be offering us scientific arguments.

(iii) *Principle of 'compensation'**

(1718) For a given society, the following scale of variations may be established, variations which increase from the first category to the last: 1. classes of residues; 2. subclasses of these; 3. derivations. The diagram shown here (Figure 13) will perhaps make it easier to understand the

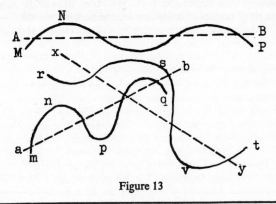

Figure 13

---

* Chapter XI, §§1718, 1719.

relationships between classes and subclasses of residues. The movement in time of a class of residues is represented by the undulating curve MNP. Certain subclasses are represented by the curves—also undulatory—*mnpq, rsvt*. The variations in the fluctuations of the class are less extensive than those of many of its subclasses. The mean movement of the class is represented by the line AB; it is shown here, simply for example's sake, as being one of overall increase. The corresponding movement in the subclasses, some of which are increasing, others diminishing, is represented by the lines *ab, xy*. The variation indicated by AB is much less extensive than that of some of the subclasses. All told, there is a certain compensation between the subclasses of residues, and it is this which puts limits, for the class as a whole, on both the variations represented by AB and the amplitude of the fluctuations of the curve MNP.

This undulatory movement gives rise to difficulties, which may be serious, for the study of social phenomena as a whole when one seeks to assess the general movement of a residue as distinct from occasional, temporary or incidental variations. For example, a comparison of the position *r* with the position *s* with the aim of deducing the general movement of the residue would lead to the conclusion that the residue was increasing in intensity. But the line *xy* shows that, on average and in general, its intensity is diminishing. Similarly, a comparison of the position *s* with the position *v* would prompt the deduction that the residue was diminishing in intensity much more rapidly than is actually the case, on average and in general, as shown by the line *xy*. Such difficulties can be eliminated if the phenomenon is measurable and if there are available observations of it over long periods of time; by interpolation it is possible to determine the line *xy*, around which the variations in the phenomenon move, and thereby to comprehend the mean, general movement. But it is much more difficult to determine this movement if accurate measurements of the phenomenon are unavailable or unobtainable, for in this case we are obliged to put in the stead of accurate mathematical evaluation an estimate in which arbitrary assumptions, individual impressions, and perhaps even whims and fancies, play a more or less important part. We must, therefore, submit such estimates to strict critical examination and neglect no possible verification.

(1719) Between the various classes of residues there is little or no compensation. . . .

(iv) Derivations, sentiments and social measures*

(1843) . . . The art of government lies in finding ways to take advantage of . . . sentiments, not in wasting one's energies in futile efforts to destroy them—the sole effect of which, frequently, is simply to strengthen them. The man who can escape the blind domination of his own sentiments is in a position to make use of the sentiments of other people for his own ends. . . .

(1864) . . . Legislation can be made to work in practice only by influencing interests and sentiments; and it must be stressed that the derivations which will have to be used for this purpose differ entirely from the logico-experimental reasonings employed in determining what legislative

* Chapter XI, §§1843, 1864-8.

measure is best adapted to a given end. As we can see from history, quite inane reasons have often been advanced in justification of social measures. Frequently legislators have aimed at one objective and attained another. In the few cases where those in government have achieved their objective, they have won the support of the public by appearing to aim at a different objective and by leading it on with arguments of a kind it can understand, i.e., with arguments which are childishly inadequate from the logico-experimental viewpoint. Moreover, in the case where the legislator aiming at a certain objective is able to influence interests and sentiments by modifying them, it can easily happen that this modification may produce, as well as the effects desired, other effects which are far from being those envisaged; hence both kinds of effects have to be considered and an insight gained into what in the end will be their social utility *in toto*. This is akin to the problem which has to be solved by applied mechanics in the construction of a machine. The machine converts part of the energy into a desired effect and part it wastes. The part effectively used is often very small in comparison with the part wasted. (1865) Similarly, social measures have, in general, some effects which are useful and others which are useless or harmful; but if one wants the first, one must of necessity accept the second. It must be stressed that, not only direct effects—such as we are now dealing with, but indirect effects also have to be considered. We deal with indirect effects later. [See pp. 253 *et seq, cf.* also pp. 261 *et seq.*]

(1866) When the engineer has found the best machine, he has little difficulty in getting it accepted; and though not rejecting derivations altogether, he can in the main make use of logico-experimental arguments. It is quite otherwise for the statesman for whom, on the contrary, derivations are the main agency; for him logico-experimental arguments can only be secondary and exceptional. Since the choice of a machine is primarily a logical act, there is no impediment in showing that a steam-engine, for example, converts only a small part of the heat produced in its fire-box into useful energy. . . . But if the choice of a machine were mainly a non-logical act, if sentiment played an important part in this choice, then it could well be that considerable advantage would accrue from advancing an absurd theory—for example, one which asserted that the steam-engine wastes not the smallest particle of the energy generated. To get a machine accepted, there has to be someone concerned with promoting it. For a social measure this is even more the case; indeed for it to gain approval it is absolutely essential that it have a strong promoter. In both cases individual interest is a powerful factor; but where social measures are concerned, much the most powerful promoter is sentiment, especially if the sentiment is heightened and takes on a religious form. It is all the better if it expresses itself in enthusiastic derivations, soaring above cold realities and in sharp contrast to the sceptical reasoning of the logico-experimental sciences. Even so, these sciences are enjoying some favour at the present time in so far as the common man accepts them as derivations. The progress made in the logico-experimental sciences has created a sentiment of reverence for them, and this sentiment has to be satisfied. This, however, is not difficult, for the common man is satisfied with a remote, a very remote, semblance of a logico-experimental element in derivations.

(1867) What we have just said with regard to the sentiments manifested by derivations could be simplified by saying that enthusiastic derivations are more likely to determine human behaviour than cold reasoning. This elliptical way of stating the matter can be accepted provided it is understood that what is involved here are not derivations but rather the sentiments they manifest.

(1868) The fact that human behaviour is strongly influenced by sentiments in the form of derivations which go beyond experience and reality, explains a phenomenon which has been well observed and elucidated by Georges Sorel, namely, that influential social doctrines (it would be more exact to say the sentiments manifested by social doctrines) take the form of myths. . . . The social value of such doctrines (or of the sentiments they express) is not to be judged extrinsically by their mythical form, which is only their mode of action, but intrinsically by the results they achieve.

(v) Ideal aims and social facts*

(1869) . . . The diagram here is very crude . : . but it will clarify the argument. . . . Disregarding cases where people, though believing they are

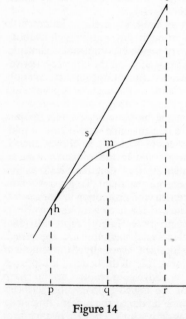

Figure 14

going in a particular direction, are in fact going in another, we will take cases where to some extent at least they are going in the desired direction. Let us suppose an individual finds himself at *h* where he enjoys a certain utility which we represent by the index *ph*, and that it is desired to induce him to move forward to *m* where he will enjoy a greater utility, *qm*. To put the matter to him just like that would be unlikely to stimulate him to action. He will be much more readily aroused if instead his eyes are raised to point т, placed far beyond the curve *hm* on the tangent *h*т, where he would enjoy a prodigious, although wholly fantastic, utility, *r*т. . . . Seeking т, the individual moves toward it but, impeded by practical considerations of all kinds, he cannot follow the tangent *h*т all the way. He is forced to follow the curve *hm*, ending up at *m*—to which he would never have arrived had he not been induced to aim for т. (1870) . . . The index *r*т is, in fact, arbitrary and has no relation to the real index *mq*, save

---

* Chapter XI, §§1869–71, 1874, 1875.

that movement towards both T and *m* extends the index which at the out-set had the value *ph*. Moreover, it matters not at all that T should be imaginary and unreal provided that *m* is concrete and real.

(1871) . . . But the human being is a logical animal, and wants to know *why* he is moving in the direction *hm*. Hence those whose instincts, interests or other similar motivations prompt them to take the line *hm* put their imaginative faculties to work and exalt T as the great purpose and end. Through the persistence of aggregates the imaginary concept of T acquires among them the strength of a sentiment and urges them, independently of other causes, along the curve *hm*. It comes to exert the same influence on other individuals who acquire this sentiment from the society in which they live—people who otherwise would have no motives, or only insignificant ones, for following this course. The imaginary objective T is simply an explanation; as such it satisfies the desire for logical or pseudo-logical reasoning, but it has little or no effect on how human beings act. As an explanation it has the same limited value as derivations in regard to logico-experimental reasoning.

(1874) . . . If we consider the phenomena as a whole, it is immediately clear that—albeit within narrow limits—acts which have ideal ends T, or which are undertaken as if they had—must also in many cases achieve a measure of individual and social utility, that is, reaching a point *m* where the indices of utility increase. In fact, in our own day non-logical actions are still very numerous and important; they were even more so in the past. The ideal end T, which is both the aim and the promoter of such actions, finds expression in theological, metaphysical and similar derivations, while the practical objective of human beings is the well-being and prosperity of themselves and their societies. If the ideal and the practical ends invariably were divergent, if those aiming at the first never achieved the second, societies which set great store by achieving an ideal end could not possibly have subsisted and prospered. . . . If, in striving for an ideal end, people had always suffered a loss in individual and social utility, history would have to show human societies as being in a continuous decline. Such has not been the case. . . . (1875) On the other hand, if history shows cases in which people aiming at imaginary ends have frequently achieved practical advantages, it does not by any means follow that this is invariably the case. . . .

4. RESIDUES AND ELITES

*Social heterogeneity and circulation of elites**

(2025) . . . Whatever certain theorists may like to think, human society in fact is not a homogeneous thing, and individuals are physically, morally and intellectually different. We must take account of this, since our concern is with things as they are. We must also take account of another fact: the social classes are not entirely distinct, even in those countries where a caste system operates; moreover, in modern civilised countries circulation among

---

* Chapter XI, §§2025, 2027, 2028, 2031–4, 2041, 2042, 2044, 2053–9.

the various classes is very rapid indeed. It is impossible for us here to consider the full implications of this question of the diversity of all the very numerous social groups and of the innumerable ways in which they mingle . . . We shall consider the problem only in relation to the social equilibrium, and try to limit as far as possible the number of groups and modes of circulation by collocating the phenomena which by and large share resemblances.

(2027) Let us suppose that in every branch of human activity an index or grade can be assigned to each individual as an indication of his capacity, in much the same way that marks are awarded for the various subjects in a school examination. Thus, we will award 10 to the highest calibre of professional man (doctor, lawyer or the like), and 1 to his colleague who fails to get a patient or a client, awarding 0 to the absolute dolt. To the man who has earned millions—no matter what means he has employed therein, fair or foul—we will likewise give 10. To the earner of thousands we will give 6, assigning 1 to the man who just manages to keep body and soul together, and 0 to him who ends up in the workhouse. The 'political woman', like Aspasia, Mme de Maintenon or La Pompadour, who contrives to captivate a man of power and plays a part in his work as a public figure, will be rated high—something like 8 or 9. The doxy who only satisfies the senses of such a man without exercising any influence at all on public affairs will rate 0. The clever swindler who can pull the wool over people's eyes without falling foul of the law will be rated at 8, 9 or 10 according to the number of dupes he catches in his net and the amount of money he squeezes out of them. The wretched pilferer who snaffles the cutlery in a restaurant and bumps redhanded into the nearest policemen will be rated at 1. To a poet like Carducci we will give 8 or 9 according to our tastes; to a tedious poetaster whose sonnets people avoid like the plague we will give 0. With the chess player we can employ more precise indices, assessing the number and kinds of matches he wins. And so on for all branches of human activity.

(2028) We are considering here, it must be noted, an actual not a potential state of affairs. If someone goes in for an English language examination and says: 'I don't know English because I haven't chosen to learn it; but I could know it very well if I wanted to', the examiner will assuredly reply: 'The whys and wherefores of your not knowing English mean nothing to me; you don't know it and so you get 0.' Likewise, if we should be told: 'This man here does not steal, not indeed because he couldn't be a very good thief, but because he is a gentleman', we should answer: 'Very well, we give him full marks for being a gentleman, but as a thief he rates zero.'

(2031) Let us therefore make a class for those people who have the highest indices in their branch of activity, and give to this class the name of *elite*. (2032) It will help our investigations into the social equilibrium if we distinguish two further classes within this main class of the elite: the governing elite and the non-governing elite. The first elite class includes those who directly or indirectly play a significant part in government and in political life; the second comprises the rest of the elite personnel, those who have no significant role in government and politics. (2033) For example . . . the mistresses of absolute monarchs, through their beauty or intelligence, have often been members of the elite, but most of them have played no significant role in political affairs—only that handful of them who possessed, in addition to beauty and intelligence, the special talents required by politics.

(2034) We have therefore two strata in the population: 1. the lower stratum, the non-elite class—for the moment we are not concerned with the influence this class may exert on government; and 2. the upper stratum, the elite class, which is subdivided into: (a) the governing, political elite; (b) the non-governing, non-political elite. (2041) . . . Those who pass from one group to another generally carry over with them into their new group certain sentiments, inclinations and attitudes acquired by them in the group they come from. (2042) In the particular case where only two groups are being considered—the elite and the non-elite—this phenomenon of movement between groups is termed 'the circulation of elites'.

(2044) The rapidity of this circulation has to be considered not only absolutely but also in relation to 'supply and demand'. For example, a country which is always at peace needs few soldiers and therefore few military leaders in its governing class. The supply of these may well be greatly in excess of the demand. But if the country becomes involved in a state of continuous warfare, it will need many soldiers, and the production of them, though remaining at the same rate as before, may well be insufficient to the need. We note in passing that this has been one of the causes of the destruction of many aristocracies.

(2053) Aristocracies do not last. Whatever be the reason, it is incontestable that, after a certain time, they disappear. History is a graveyard of aristocracies. The Athenian citizenry was an aristocracy in respect to the rest of the city's population: resident aliens and slaves. It disappeared without leaving any descendants. The various Roman aristocracies disappeared in due course, likewise the barbarian aristocracies which supplanted the Roman rulers. Where in France are the descendants of the conquering Franks? The genealogies of the English peerage have been very exactly recorded; only a few, a very few, families remain which can claim descent from the companions of William the Conqueror; all the others have disappeared. In Germany, the present aristocracy consists for the most part of descendants of the vassals of the old lords. Since the Middle Ages, the population of Europe has increased enormously. If one thing more than any other is certain it is that the aristocracies have not increased in proportion.

(2054) Aristocracies decay not only in number but also in quality, in the sense that their energy diminishes and there is a debilitating alteration in the proportion of the residues which originally favoured their capture and retention of power. . . . The governing class is renovated not only in number but also—and this is more important—in quality, by recruiting to it families rising from the lower classes, bringing with them the energy and proportions of the residues necessary for maintaining them in power. It is renovated also by the loss of its more degenerate elements.

(2055) If one of these essential components decays or—worse still—if both energy and residues peter out, then the governing class topples into ruin, often dragging the whole nation with it. The accumulation of superior elements in the lower classes and, conversely, of inferior elements in the upper classes, is a potent cause of disturbance in the social equilibrium. If human aristocracies were like pedigree breeds of animals and could reproduce themselves over long periods, perpetuating more or less the same characteristics, the history of the human race would be entirely different from history as we know it.

(2056) By the circulation of elites, the governing elite is in a state of continuous and slow transformation. It flows like a river, and what it is today is different from what it was yesterday. Every so often, there are sudden and violent disturbances. The river floods and breaks its banks. Then, afterwards, the new governing elite resumes again the slow process of self-transformation. The river returns to its bed and once more flows freely on. (2057) Revolutions occur because—either through a slowing down in the circulation of elites or from other causes—the upper strata accumulate decadent elements which no longer retain the residues appropriate to the maintenance of power and which shrink from the use of force; while among the lower strata, elements of superior quality are increasing which do possess the residues suitable for governing and are prepared to use force. (2058) In revolutions individuals of the lower strata are generally led by individuals from the upper strata because these latter possess the intellectual qualities needful for devising strategy and tactics; the combative residues they lack are provided by individuals from the lower strata.

(2059) Violent changes occur erratically, by fits and starts; hence effect does not immediately follow cause. A governing class or a nation which has for a long time maintained itself by force and has grown very rich may still subsist for a period without using force, buying peace from its adversaries, making payment not only in gold but also by sacrificing the honour and respect it had previously enjoyed and which, in a sense, constitute a capital asset. Initially, power is maintained by concessions, and so the error is fostered of thinking that this sort of policy can be pursued indefinitely. Thus the Roman empire in its decadence bought peace from the barbarians by money and honours. Thus Lewis XVI of France, prodigally consuming in a very short time an ancestral birthright of love, respect and almost religious reverence for the monarchy, succeeded by perpetual concessions in becoming the King of the Revolution. Thus the English aristocracy contrived to prolong its power into the second half of the nineteenth century, right up to the last moment before its deathknell was rung by parliament in the early years of the twentieth century.

III

The Form of the Social System and Its Equilibrium

1. THE SOCIAL SYSTEM

(i) Its elements*

(2060) The form of society is determined by all the elements acting upon it, and in turn it reacts upon them. There is therefore a reciprocal determination. Among these elements we can distinguish the following categories: 1. Soil, climate, flora and fauna, geological, mineralogical and similar conditions; 2. Elements external *in space* to a given society at a given time, such as the influence of other societies; and elements external *in time*—the effects of conditions previously obtaining in the society; 3. Internal elements, principal among which are race, residues (or rather the sentiments they manifest), inclinations, interests, capacities for reason and observation, the state of knowledge, and so forth. Derivations are also to be included among such elements.

(2061) These elements are not independent; they are for the most part interdependent.... (2066) Whether the elements we are considering be few or many, we can assume that they constitute a system which we may call 'the social system'. We propose to study the nature and properties of this system....

(ii) Organisation of the social system†

(2073) ... The analogy between economics and sociology is close enough for the states of the economic system to be considered as particular cases of the general states of the sociological system.

(2079) But, whereas the economic system is composed of certain

---

* Chapter XII, §§2060, 2061, 2066.   † Chapter XII, §§2073, 2079–81.

molecules put in motion by tastes and limited by obstacles to the acquisition of economic desiderata, the social system is much more complex. If we are to avoid serious errors in seeking to simplify it as much as possible, we must at least think of it as being composed of certain molecules—embodying residues, derivations, interests and inclinations—which, subject to numerous limitations, perform logical and non-logical actions. In the economic system, the non-logical element is entirely relegated to tastes and is disregarded since tastes are taken as data of fact. It might be asked if the same procedure could not be adopted for the social system, i.e., relegating the non-logical element to the residues, assuming these as data of fact and then studying the logical actions which originate from these residues. Such an approach would indeed give us a science similar to pure, or even applied, economics. But unfortunately the similarity breaks down over the question of correspondence with reality. The hypothesis that individuals, in order to satisfy their tastes, perform economic actions which may, on the whole, be considered as logical, is not too far removed from reality. The inferences drawn from such an hypothesis as this give to the phenomenon a general form which diverges from reality only to a small and not very considerable extent, except in a few cases, the most important of which concerns savings. On the other hand, there is a wide divergence from reality in the hypothesis that individuals draw logical inferences from residues and act according to these inferences. In this kind of behaviour individuals use derivations more often than strictly logical reasonings. Therefore, to try to base predictions about men's behaviour on their reasoning would be to depart from reality altogether. Residues are not only the origins of actions—like tastes—but they also operate on the whole course of the actions emanating from the origin: a fact made clear to us by the substitution of derivations for logical reasonings. Hence a science based on the hypothesis that logical inferences are drawn from certain given residues would produce a general form of the phenomenon which would have little or no correspondence with reality. It would entail an intellectual system roughly akin to non-euclidian geometry or to the geometry of four-dimensional space. If we want to remain within the bounds of reality, we must seek to discover from experience, not only certain fundamental residues, but also the various modes in which they operate to determine the behaviour of human beings.

(2080) ... Individual human beings constitute the molecules of the social system, containing within themselves certain sentiments manifested by residues. For the sake of brevity, we indicate these sentiments simply by the term 'residues'. We can say that within individual people are mixtures of groups of residues which are analogous to the amalgams of chemical compounds found in nature; the groups of residues themselves are analogous to chemical compounds. As we have already seen from our study of the characteristics of these amalgams and groups, while some appear to be well nigh independent, others are dependent in that the increase of one is offset by the diminution of the other, and *vice versa*. ... These amalgams and groups, whether independent or dependent, are now to be considered among the elements of the social equilibrium.

(2081) Residues are manifested by derivations, which are a reflection of the forces operating on the social molecules. ...

(iii) Composition of social forces*

(2087) So far we have considered separate groups of residues. We must now see how they operate when considered together. . . . (2088) . . . We cannot—as is usually done—assess separately the effects of each group of residues or of the variation in the intensity of each group. If there is a variation in the intensity of one group of residues, then, for the equilibrium to be maintained, variations have generally to ensue in other groups. . . . We shall employ the term 'first type of interdependence' for the direct dependence between different groups of residues, and the term 'second type of interdependence' for the indirect dependence deriving from the requirement that the equilibrium be maintained, or from similar requirements. . . .

(2089) . . . For example, the proclivity of the Romans to formalism in practical life served to produce, maintain and amplify formalism in religion, law and politics, and *vice versa*. This is an interdependence of the first type. But we find an interdependence of the second type in the fact that it was due to a political formalism which avoided the perils of anarchy that the Roman inclination to independence was able to survive for so long. This factor effectively operated right up to the end of the Republic. Then, with the weakening of the proclivity to political formalism (mainly because the Romans had become diluted with people of other nations), the inclination to independence also diminished and Rome had to accept imperial despotism as the lesser evil. If there had not been a weakening of this factor, Roman society would have collapsed, either through internal upheavals or through foreign conquest, as was the case with Poland and for the same reasons. There is here no direct interdependence between the residues of Class II (inclination to political formalism) and the residues of Class V (inclination to independence), which would be an interdependence of the first type. There is, however, an indirect interdependence arising from the fact that, for the Roman community at that time and in those circumstances, there would have been no equilibrium had the inclination to independence (residues of personal integrity) remained constant while the index of political formalism (residues of aggregate-persistence) diminished. This represents an interdependence of the second type. . . .

2. PROPERTIES OF THE SOCIAL SYSTEM

(2105) A system of material atoms and molecules has certain thermal, electrical and other properties; similarly a system composed of social molecules also has certain properties which demand attention. One of these has throughout history been intuitively grasped, albeit in a crude way: the property which, with scant precision, has been called 'utility', 'prosperity', and such like. . . .

(i) Maximum of utility FOR *a community in sociology†*

(2131) . . . Every individual, in as much as he acts logically, endeavours to obtain a maximum of individual utility. . . . If we assume the removal of

---

* Chapter XII, §§2087–9. † Chapter XII, §§2131, 2133, 2134, 2136, 2137.

some of the limitations imposed by public authority without others being put in their place, then an infinite number of positions of equilibrium with the requirements of individual maxima of utility becomes possible. Public authority intervenes to impose some and exclude others. Let us suppose it operates logically and with the sole aim of achieving a certain utility (of course, such is very rarely the case, but this need not preoccupy us since we are not dealing with a real, concrete case, but rather with a theoretical, hypothetical one). If such be its aim, the public authority must necessarily compare—by what criteria we need not here enquire—the various utilities. When, for example, it imprisons a thief it compares the pain it is inflicting on the thief with the utility his imprisonment has for honest men. In a rough and ready way it estimates that the common utility outweighs the private pain—otherwise it would let the thief go free. For brevity's sake we have here compared only two utilities, but of course the public authority— as well as it can, and admittedly this often means pretty badly—takes into comparison all the utilities it is aware of. In substance, it accomplishes by rule of thumb what pure economics accomplishes by exact method, and makes he erogeneous quantities homogeneous through the medium of certain coeff.cients. . . .

(2133) In pure economics, a community cannot be considered as a person, whereas in sociology it can be considered, if not as a person, then at least as a unit. There is no such thing as the ophelimity of a community, but a community utility can, roughly, be assumed. Therefore, while in pure economics there is no danger of confusing the maximum utility *for* a community with the maximum utility *of* a community, it is quite otherwise in sociology where we have to be very wary of confusing the maximum utility *for* with the maximum utility *of* a community, as both utilities are present in it.*

(2134) We can take as an example the question of the increase of population. If the utility *of* a community is mainly thought of in terms of military and political power, it will be advisable to push up its population to a very high level, in fact to the extreme limit beyond which the nation would become impoverished and the race decline. But if we are concerned with the maximum utility *for* a community, we shall fix a much lower limit. It would then be our task to find out in what proportions the various social classes benefit from an increase in military and political power, and in what different proportions they pay for it by their own sacrifices. When the workers say they will not have children, arguing that their children serve only to increase the power and profits of the governing classes, their reasoning entails a problem of maximum utility *for* the community. It matters little what derivations they may employ—derivations, as it might be, of the religion of socialism or of pacifism. It is what underlies their thinking which matters. In rebutting this, the governing classes frequently merge a problem of maximum utility *of* with maximum utility *for* the community. They also endeavour to bring the problem back to the search for a maximum individual utility, and try to make the subject classes believe that there is an indirect utility which, when the account is properly reckoned up,

---

* Cf. *Cours*, p. 103 above.

transmutes the sacrifice demanded of them into a benefit. The governing classes can indeed succeed in achieving this aim, but not always. There are many cases in which, even when the indirect utility is very liberally estimated, the final sum shows, not an advantage, but a sacrifice for the subject classes. In reality, it is only through the influence of non-logical factors that men will allow themselves to neglect the maximum individual utility and hold by the maximum utility *of* the community—or rather simply *of* the governing class. The latter has very often intuitively grasped this.

(2136) There is a theory—we will not examine here to what extent it is in agreement with the facts—according to which slavery was a necessary condition for social progress because, it is argued, it enabled a certain number of men to live in leisure and thereby to take up intellectual pursuits. If this point is accepted, then those who wish to solve a problem of the maximum utility *of* the species and are concerned solely with the utility of the species, will opine that slavery has been 'useful'. Those who wish to solve a problem of the same sort, but consider solely the utility of the men reduced to slavery, will opine that slavery has been harmful, disregarding for the moment certain indirect effects of it. One cannot determine who is right and who is wrong, because, in default here of a criterion on which to base the comparison between the two opinions, 'right' and 'wrong' have no meaning.

(2137) From this we must conclude, not indeed that it is impossible to solve problems which involve at one and the same time various heterogeneous utilities, but rather that, in order to discuss them, some hypothesis or other has to be assumed which can make them comparable. . . .

(ii) *Residues and derivations in relation to utility**

(2140) We have been considering in abstract certain things which may affect the social equilibrium. We shall now specifically consider residues and derivations. . . . (2141) As a preparation for our enquiry, let us for a moment leave aside actual human society and assume that we have two extreme types of abstract societies: 1. A society in which sentiments exclusively are operative, without reasonings of any kind. Animal societies would appear to approach this type closely. 2. A society in which logico-experimental reasoning exclusively is operative. . . .

(2142) In the case of type 1, the form of the society is determined if the sentiments are given together with the external circumstances in which the society exists; or if only the circumstances are given and the sentiments are considered as being determined by the circumstances. . . .

(2143) In the case of type 2, the environment in no way determines the form of society; it is necessary to go further and indicate the nature of the end for which logico-experimental reasoning is to be the means. A society determined exclusively by 'reason' does not and cannot exist (*pace* the humanitarians and positivists), not because the 'prejudices' of men prevent them from following the 'dictates of reason', but because the data are lacking for the problem which it is desired to solve by logico-experimental

---

* Chapter XII, §§2140–3, 2145, 2146.

reasoning. Here we are once again struck by the vagueness of the concept of utility, as we were when earlier we tried to define utility. The concepts which different individuals have about their own good and the good of others are essentially heterogeneous, and there is no way of reducing them to unity.

(2145) Social reformers in the main are not aware of the fact—or at any rate they ignore it—that individuals have different opinions in regard to utility. This is because they derive the data they need from their own sentiments. Social reformers believe they are solving an objective problem: what is the *best* form for a society? But in fact they are dealing with solutions to a subjective problem: what form of society is best fitted to my sentiments? It goes without saying that the reformer is confident that his sentiments must be shared by all honest men, and that his sentiments are not only excellent in themselves but are also highly beneficial to society. Unfortunately such a belief, however confident, cannot alter reality.

(2146) Human society lies between the two types noted above. As well as by environment, its form is determined by sentiments, by interests, by logico-experimental reasonings which serve to satisfy sentiments and interests, and by subordinate derivations which express and sometimes strengthen sentiments and interests, and are in certain cases effective as methods of propaganda. Logico-experimental reasonings have value and importance when the end is assumed and when appropriate means are sought for to achieve this end. Hence we find them employed with great success in the arts and crafts, in agriculture, industry and commerce. Thus it has been possible to create, not only many technical sciences, but also a general science of interests—economics—which presumes that such reasonings are exclusively employed in certain branches of human activity. They are also of great value in warfare and have given rise to such sciences as strategy. They could possibly be highly relevant to the science of government, but—either because the objective is not determined, or, if known, it is considered undesirable to reveal it—they have so far been employed in this field more as an art by particular rulers than as elements in the creation of an abstract science. For these and other reasons, logico-experimental reasonings have in general played little part in the ordering of society. Scientific theories are still lacking in this field; in all that concerns it men are moved much more by sentiments than by reasoning. Some of them know how to profit from this circumstance to satisfy their own interests; as opportunity occurs, and according to the requirements of this or that situation, they employ reasonings which are empirical and to some extent logico-experimental.

(iii) Use of force*

(2170) Societies of all and every kind subsist in virtue of the fact that the sentiments corresponding to the residues of sociality (Class IV) are lively and strong in most of their members. But in human societies there are also individuals in whom at least some of these sentiments are weak or have

---

* Chapter XII, §§2170, 2171, 2178–81.

even disappeared. This produces two notable and apparently contrary effects: the first threatens the dissolution of the society concerned; the second promotes its progress in civilisation. Substantially, there is always movement, but the movement can be in several directions.

(2171) Clearly, if the need for uniformity were so powerfully operative in each individual as to prevent the detachment of even one man from the uniformities subsisting in his society, then there would be in this society no internal causes tending to dissolution. But equally, it would have no causes tending to change, whether in the direction of an increase or of a decrease in the utility of individuals or of the society. Conversely, if the need for uniformity were absent, society would not continue in being and each individual would 'walk by himself' after the fashion of lions and tigers, birds of prey and other animals. Societies which continue in being and change are therefore in a state intermediate between these two extremes.

(2178) In considering the governing class, there are five main categories of facts to be noted. 1. A small group of citizens, if prepared to use violence, can impose its will on governing circles which are unwilling to meet violence with equal violence. If humanitarian sentiments are mainly at the root of the governing authorities' abstention from force, the violent minority easily achieves success. But if the authorities refrain from using force because they think it wiser to employ other means, the effect is often as follows: 2. To prevent or resist violence, the governing class may use guile, cunning, fraud and corruption—in short, government passes from the lions to the foxes. The governing class bows before the threat of violence, but only appears to give way, endeavouring to manoeuvre round the obstacle it cannot openly surmount. In the long term, this way of dealing with the problem exerts a dominant influence on the selection of the governing class: the foxes alone are called to serve in its ranks, the lions are rejected. In such circumstances those best equipped for government are those who are most adept in the art of undermining opponents by bribery and corruption and of regaining by fraud and deception what appeared to have been conceded under the threat of force. Individuals whose impulse is to resist and are incapable of giving way as time and occasion require are of small value to a governing class, and they can maintain their membership of it only if they make up for this prime defect by outstanding qualities in other respects. 3. Thus the residues of the instinct of combinations (Class I) increase in the ruling class while the residues of aggregate-persistence (Class II) decrease, since the Class I residues foster precisely the skills and the flair for expedients which are necessary for devising ingenious ploys as substitutes for open resistance, while the Class II residues inculcate open resistance—a strong sentiment of aggregate-persistence militates against flexibility. 4. The policies of the governing class are not planned very far forward in time. The predominant influence of instincts of combination and the weakening of sentiments of aggregate-persistence have the effect of making the governing class more satisfied with the present and less inclined to take thought for the future. The individual comes markedly to prevail over the family, the community, the nation. Material interests and the interests of the present or the very near future come to prevail over the ideal interests of the community and nation and over the interests of the distant future. The enjoyment of the present is pursued without much preoccupation about the future. 5. Some of these phenomena are observable also in international relations. Wars become essentially economic. A policy is attempted of avoiding war with strong nations and of engaging in armed conflict only with the weak. A country often unwittingly pushes itself into war by nurturing economic conflicts which are expected never to go so far as armed conflict. War then comes to be imposed on it by peoples who have not developed so far as it has in the evolution which brings about the predominance of the residues of Class I.

(2179) In considering the subject class, the following relations are to be noted, which correspond in part to the foregoing: 1. In cases where there is within the subject class a certain number of individuals who are prepared to use force and have leaders capable of organising them, it often happens that the governing class is dispossessed and its place taken by another class. ... The maximum instability is that of a humanitarian aristocracy which is closed or virtually exclusive. 2. Conversely, it is much more difficult to seize power from a governing class which shrewdly knows how to employ cunning, fraud and corruption. Its overthrow becomes very difficult indeed if it succeeds in assimilating to itself most of the individuals in the subject class who are adept in the same skills and who therefore are potential leaders of those in the subject class who are disposed to use violence. A subject class which is thus bereft of leadership almost always remains impotent. 3. ... But since the governing class is composed of a smaller number of individuals, it changes considerably in character by the adding to it or withdrawing from it of relatively small numbers of individuals; on the other hand, such cross-movements of identical numbers produce only slight effects in the enormously greater total of the subject class. Such changes still leave in the subject class many individuals endowed with combination-instincts which they apply, not to politics or to activities associated with politics, but to arts and crafts independent of politics. This circumstance gives stability to a society because its governing class need only open its ranks to admit a limited number of 'new men' in order effectively to deprive the subject class of leaders. Nevertheless, in the long run the difference of temperament between the rulers and the ruled becomes more marked. In the former the combination-instincts tend to predominate more and more, while in the subject class the instincts of aggregate-persistence prevail. When the difference becomes sufficiently great, revolutions ensue. 4. These revolutions frequently put power into the hands of a new governing class whose instincts of aggregate-persistence are intensified and which therefore engrafts ideal designs to be pursued in the future on to its intentions of present enjoyment of power. To a certain extent scepticism yields place to faith. 5. These considerations must be applied in some measure to international relations. ... The potency of an ideal as a guiding force to victory is observable as much in international as in internal conflicts. Those who lose the habit of using force, who become accustomed to assessing a course of action solely in commercial terms of profitability, are easily induced to buy peace. It may well be that such an approach, in itself, has much to recommend it, for a war very likely would prove more expensive than the purchasing price of peace. But experience shows that in the long term such a policy, when account is taken of the other things which it inevitably entails, ruins the nation practising it. We should note that it is very rare for this phenomenon of the intensification of combination-instincts to become prevalent in the whole population of a society. Usually it is to be found only in the upper strata of society; it exists scarcely or not at all in the lower and larger strata. Hence, when war breaks out, one stands amazed at the energy shown by the masses; knowledge of the upper classes alone would never have led one to expect this. Sometimes, as was the case with Carthage, this popular energy may not suffice to save the nation if the classes in control have been incompetent in preparing and conducting war against an enemy country whose governing class has made better provision for war and has a more competent military leadership. At other times, as the French revolutionary wars show, popular energy may be such as to save the nation in the case where, albeit its leaders have made poor preparations for war, the enemy's ruling class proves to be even more incompetent in military affairs. . . . Or, as happened in Germany after Jena, popular energy may permeate the superior classes and stimulate them to action, the effectiveness of which derives from the combination of able leadership with vitality of faith.

(2180) Such, in outline, are the principal phenomena, but very many secondary phenomena are associated with them. For example, we should specially note the fact that, if the governing class is incompetent, unwilling or unable to use force to suppress transgressions against the uniformities in private life, the vacuum created by its inaction is filled by anarchic action on the part of the subject class. The evidence of history clearly shows that the private vendetta waxes or wanes in ratio to the public authority's failure or success in replacing it as a means of suppressing crime. It has been seen to re-emerge in the form of lynch-law in America and even in Europe. Moreover, it is noticeable that, where the influence of public authority is weak, little states are formed within the state itself. . . . In international relations, beneath all the surface tinsel of humanitarian and ethical declamation, what prevails is force alone. The Chinese considered themselves to be greatly the superiors of the Japanese in civilisation—and perhaps they were. But they were lacking in the military capacity and vigour which the Japanese had in abundance, thanks to the survival in their society of elements of feudal 'barbarism'. And so we see the poor Chinese attacked by hordes of Europeans whose conduct in China forcibly recalls, as Georges Sorel has well said, the exploits of the Spanish conquistadores in America. . . . On the other hand, we find the Japanese treated with the highest respect by everybody ever since they worsted the Russians in battle. . . . A few centuries ago, the subtle diplomatic skill of the christian lords of Constantinople could not save them from ruin under the onslaught of Turkish fanaticism and power. And in 1913, in the very same place, the conquerors of 1453, diminished both in fanaticism and power and in their turn relying with vain hope on the arts of diplomacy, were utterly vanquished by the power of their former subjects. Politicians who imagine they can make unarmed law a substitute for armed force delude themselves most grievously. . . . The constitution of Sulla collapsed because the armed force which could have ensured respect for it was not maintained. The constitution of Augustus endured because his successors had the power of the legions to support them. Thiers believed that his government should be sustained by the rule of law rather than by armed force; his laws were scattered like leaves in the wind before the hurricane of democratic plutocracy. . . :

(2181) As a general rule all such facts appear in the guise of derivations. On the one hand we have theories which condemn the use of violence by the subordinate classes in all cases whatsoever; and on the other hand, we have theories which censure its exercise by the public authority.

3. CYCLES OF INTERDEPENDENCE

(i) *Principle of 'interaction'**

(2205) We now turn to consider the question of interdependence among the categories. For brevity's sake, we will indicate alphabetically the following elements: (a) residues; (b) interests;† (c) derivations; (d) social heterogeneity and circulation. . . .

(2206) We can therefore say that: 1. (a) acts on (b), (c) and (d); 2. (b) acts on (a), (c) and (d); 3. (c) acts on (a), (b) and (d); 4. (d) acts on (a), (b) and (c). . . . *Interaction 1*‡ produces a very substantial part of the social phenomena. This perhaps was perceived, albeit remotely and imperfectly, by those thinkers who considered ethics to be the foundation of society. It also accounts for such particles of reality as can be found in metaphysical theories which subordinate facts to 'concepts', since 'concepts' reflect, though misshapenly, sentiments and their corresponding residues. Moreover it is *Interaction 1* which also assures the historical continuity of human societies since the category (a) varies only slightly and slowly in time. . . . *Interaction 2* also provides a considerable part of the social phenomena, and it likewise fosters social continuity, varying but little and slowly in time. The importance of *Interaction 2* was perceived by the advocates of 'historical materialism', who fell however into the error of substituting the part for the whole and neglecting the other interactions. *Interaction 3* is the least important of the four. It is their failure to realise this which renders erroneous, inconclusive and inane the lucubrations of humanitarians, 'intellectuals' and worshippers of the goddess Reason. But since it figures more prominently in literature than the other interactions, a greater importance is commonly given it than it merits in reality. *Interaction 4* is of no small importance. Its significance was in some measure appreciated by Plato and Aristotle, not to mention other ancient writers. In our day the work of

---

* Chapter XII, §§2205–7.

† Pareto defines interests as 'means to some personal end' [*T.* §1138] and as desires 'prompted by instinct and reason to acquire possession of material goods which are useful, or simply pleasurable, for the purposes of living, and also to seek considerations and honours' [§2009]. For interests as an agency of government, see below p. 267 [§2250].

‡ Pareto uses 'combinazione' here. It is translated as 'interaction' to avoid confusion with residue combination.

Lapouge, Hamon and others—although to some degree erroneous and inadequate—has had the great merit of giving due emphasis to this very important interaction. It is their disregard of it which radically vitiates the so-called 'democratic' theories.

(2207) It must be borne in mind that action and reaction follow one another indefinitely, as in a circle; the process, starting with *Interaction 1*, moves on to *Interaction 4*, and goes back again from *4* to *1*. In *Interaction 1*, the element (a) was acting on (d); in *Interaction 4*, the element (d) is acting on (a); then one goes back again to *Interaction 1*, so that (a) is once more acting on (d), and so on. Hence, a variation in (a), in virtue of *Interaction 1*, produces variations in the other elements (b), (c) and (d). Simply to make the matter clearer, we will use the term *immediate effects* to indicate these variations of (a), (b), (c) and (d) which arise in virtue of *Interaction 1*. But in virtue of other interactions, variations in (b), (c) and (d) also produce variations in (a). Because of the circular movement already referred to, this variation has repercussions on *Interaction 1* and gives rise to new variations in (a), (b), (c) and (d). As before, simply to clarify matters, we will indicate these variations by the term *mediate effects*. Sometimes it is necessary to consider two or more interactions simultaneously. . . . The state of concrete equilibrium in a given society is a product of all these effects, actions and reactions. In this it differs from a state of theoretical equilibrium obtained by considering one or more of the elements (a), (b), (c) and (d) instead of all of them.

(ii) Military and industrial cycles*

(2223) . . . The protection of the military classes which occurs when individuals acquire wealth, distinction and power mainly through war, has an influence . . . on social heterogeneity . . . in that it tends to increase Class II residues in the governing class. . . . It intensifies circulation and gives people with bellicose instincts the opportunity to rise from the lower strata to the governing class. Where this is the case, the effects on residues are marked—within the limits, we must add, imposed by their relative stability. War tends to increase the intensity of Class II residues. As usual, its effects on derivations are considerable, although less than is the case with economic protectionism, since war has little or no need of theories; to see this clearly in an extreme form one has only to compare Sparta and Athens. For this reason also derivations exert little influence on social heterogeneity, although their influence on residues is somewhat greater. Finally, in particular regard to *Interaction 4*, we find that protection of war interests gives an incentive to military pursuits in a country; this constitutes . . . a *mediate* effect.

(2224) From this situation also arise forces which tend to produce a movement running counter to that of the cycle we are considering. . . . While on one hand frequent warfare raises individuals of bellicose instincts into the governing class, on the other hand it destroys them. All in all, these two contrary movements—according to the case—may make a

---

* Chapter XII, §§2223-7.

governing class richer or poorer in bellicose elements, and consequently there will be an increase or a diminution in the strength of certain residues. Modern warfare demands not only men but also enormous outlays of money, and this is only possible by intensive economic production. Hence, if wars increase the bellicose element in the governing class, the preparations necessary for modern warfare have the effect of reducing it by bringing industrial and commercial elements into prominence in the governing class. This second effect is at present preponderant in France, England and Italy. It is much less marked in Germany.*

(2225) In considering the circumstances which make possible the cycles in question, we should note that, while the 'war cycle' depends on the existence of rich countries which can be exploited by conquest, the 'industrial cycle' benefits from the existence—though this is not an indispensable condition—of peoples economically less developed who are exploitable by industrial production. And here we should note something which has hitherto escaped due attention: industrialism requires for its growth a large class of savers, yet its general tendency is to undermine the savings instinct and to induce people to spend all they earn. . . . Generally speaking, and this is valid for all periods, the movement of the war cycle has within itself greater contradictions than are contained within the industrial cycle. In fact, the industrial cycle is self-sufficient up to a point: it produces the wealth it consumes. When prosperity begins to increase in the poorer nations who are being exploited, their consumption-potential also increases and in consequence the richer industrial nations make even greater profits. The situation becomes adverse for the latter only if, later on, the poorer nations succeed in approaching to parity with them. We know that residues change very slowly and so, in regard to savings, there is an appreciable delay in the effects of the industrial cycle on the sentiments which foster the habit of saving. For a long time savings may continue to increase, thus reducing the risk of a drying up of those reserves of exploitable wealth which are indispensable to the continuation of industrialism. On the other hand, in order to profit by the arts of war a nation needs to be able to exercise these arts on nations of considerable wealth. If such nations disappear from the scene, the nation which lives mainly by and for war wastes away. . . .

(2226) The prosperity of Carthage and Venice was based in part on the exploitation of economically backward peoples, and this to some extent is the case with the industrial and commercial nations of our own day. . . . The prosperity of Carthage was shattered by the military power of Rome; the Turkish conquests grievously damaged the prosperity of Venice. The prosperity of modern industrial nations does not appear to be threatened by dangers of this sort—at least not for the present. In general, where there is a collision between a country which is moving through one of the two cycles—war or industrialism—and another which is moving through the other cycle, the question of who vanquishes and who succumbs will probably be determined by the stage they have each reached in their respective evolutions. Modern countries which are far advanced in industrial develop-

---

* I.e., *c.* 1912.

ment conquer, subjugate or destroy barbarous or semi-barbarous countries which are not yet far advanced in the war cycle. On the other hand, the countries with the highest economic development in the Mediterranean basin were conquered by Rome, then at the height of its military development; and in its turn the Roman Empire succumbed to the barbarians. Between the cyclical stages reached by the various civilised countries in modern times there are only very small differences, and the effects of disparities of evolution—though important—are not decisive.

(2227) Among the effects ensuing from changes in the proportions of Class I and Class II residues in the governing class, we should give particular attention to those which undermine this class's resistance to the subject class: To gain a first general notion of these very important phenomena, we may say that, very roughly, the relationship between rulers and ruled is somewhat akin to that between two nations. A predominance of interests which are mainly industrial and commercial makes the governing class richer in individuals who are cunning, shrewd and well-endowed with instincts of combination, and poorer in individuals of bold, resolute character and well-endowed with instincts of aggregate-persistence. This may also come about for other reasons; taking them into general consideration with *Interaction 4*, we might well opine that, if the exercise of government consisted solely of astuteness, cunning and artful devices, then the power of the group in which Class I residues greatly predominated would be very long enduring, and would come to an end only if that group destroyed itself through senile degeneration of the breed. But force also is essential to the exercise of government. As within the governing class there develops a gradual intensification of Class I residues and a corresponding weakening of Class II residues, so those who govern become less and less adept in the use of force. This produces an unstable equilibrium and revolutions ensue, like that of protestantism against the governing class of the Renascence and of the French people against its rulers in 1789. Such revolutions succeed for reasons similar to those through which a rude and uncultivated Rome was able to conquer a civilised and cultivated Greece. ... The populace, in whom Class II residues predominate, carry them upwards into the governing class either by infiltration (circulation of the elites) or in sudden bursts through revolutions.

(iii) *Speculators and rentiers**

(2230) ... We have earlier referred to social classification in terms of aristocracies. There is more to be said about the matter than this. ... Among other considerations there is one of extreme importance. (2231) People have confused, and the confusion continues, in the single term 'capitalists' two different categories: (a) property-owners and owners of savings; and (b) entrepreneurs. This greatly militates against a proper understanding of the economic phenomenon, and even more the social phenomenon. In reality, these two categories of 'capitalists' often have different interests; sometimes indeed their interests are opposed and create an even greater conflict than those dividing 'capitalists' and 'proletarians'.

---

* Chapter XII, §§2230–6.

(2232) The conflict is as marked socially as economically. The entrepreneurial class embraces individuals in whom combination-instincts—indispensable for success in commerce and industry—are well developed, whereas among the class of people who are simply savers individuals in whom residues of aggregate-persistence predominate are strongly represented. As a general rule, therefore, entrepreneurs are adventuresome and always on the look-out for novelty as much in the social as in the economic domain; they are prone to accept change, indeed they hope to profit from it. Mere owners of savings, however, are often quiet, timorous people, like rabbits ever ready to take alarm; they hope little and fear much from change for bitter experience has taught them that it is they who will have to pay for it. . . .

(2233) . . . To make a more general classification . . . let us put in one category, which we will call *s*, those individuals whose income is essentially variable and dependent on their resourcefulness in finding new opportunities for gain. Taking a general view and disregarding exceptions, this category will contain the entrepreneurs. . . . With them will be, to some extent at least, shareholders in industrial and commercial firms—but not bondholders, who more properly belong with the following category. The *s* category will also include owners of property in towns and country districts where there is vigorous speculation in real estate and land values, together with stock-exchange speculators and bankers who deal in public and commercial loans. To their number can be added all those who depend on them: the lawyers, technical advisers, politicians, office-staff and workers who benefit from such operations. In short, category *s* embraces all those who directly or indirectly depend on speculation and in various ways increase their income by ingeniously taking advantage of circumstances.

(2234) In the second category, which we will call *R*, we will group people with fixed or virtually fixed incomes which consequently depend very little on the imaginative use of ingenious combinations. It will include, roughly speaking, simple owners of savings who deposit them in savings-banks or invest them in annuities; people living mainly on the income from government bonds or other fixed-interest securities; owners of property in areas where there is no speculation; and finally the farmers, workers and clerical personnel depending on such people and deriving no sort of advantage from the operations of speculators. In short, category *R* embraces all those who depend neither directly nor indirectly on speculation and whose incomes in the main are fixed or are at least only slightly variable.

(2235) Simply for the sake of convenience we will use the term 'speculators'* for people in the *s* category and the term 'rentiers' for those

---

* Cf. §2254: '. . . When we speak of "speculators", we are not to think of them as characters in a melodrama—conspiratorial figures devising sinister deep-laid schemes for the mastery and governance of the world. This is a fairy-tale picture and quite unreal. "Speculators" are simply people who have a fixed concern for their own affairs. Possessing Class I residues in large measure, they put them to work to make money. They follow the line of least resistance—just as, in fact, everybody else does. . . .'

in the *R* category. . . . Class I residues predominate among the speculators, Class II residues among the rentiers. . . . The two groups fulfil functions of differing utility in society. The speculator category is primarily responsible for changes and progress in economic and social affairs. The rentiers, on the other hand, are a powerful element making for stability, and in many cases they safeguard society against the risky ventures of the speculator class. A society in which the rentiers almost exclusively predominate remains immobile and so to speak petrified. A society in which the speculators predominate lacks stability and is in a state of uneasy equilibrium which can be destroyed by a trifling accident from outside or within. The *R* types must not be assumed to be 'conservatives' and the *s* 'progressives'. . . . There are evolutions, innovations and revolutions which the rentiers will support . . . particularly movements tending to restore to the governing class certain residues of aggregate-persistence which had been eliminated by the speculators. A revolution may be made against the speculators—for instance, of the kind which founded the Roman Empire and, to some extent, the protestant Reformation. Due precisely to the fact that residues of aggregate-persistence predominate among them, the rentiers may be blinded by the sentiments associated with these residues to the point of acting against their own interests, allowing themselves to be easily gulled by those who make appeal to their sentiments. And thus it is that time and time again they have been the architects of their own ruin. . . . Similarly the *R* and the *s* categories must not be confused with groupings based on economic occupation. . . . There may be an overlapping but not a full coincidence. . . . An individual of the speculator type founds an industry as a result of fortunate speculations; when it produces, or seems to produce, handsome returns, he may turn it into a limited company, retire from business and pass over into the rentier category. . . .

(2236) The different proportions in which speculators and rentiers are combined amid the governing class correspond to different types of civilisation; these proportions are among the chief characteristics which have to be considered in social heterogeneity. . . .*

4. THE SYSTEM OF GOVERNMENT

(i) *Political forms*†

(2237) Among the various complex phenomena observable in a society, the regime or system of government is of very great importance, for it is intimately associated with the character of the governing class, and both of them are in a relationship of interdependence with other social phenomena.

(2239) Those for whom the form of government is of highest importance are much exercised by the question: 'What is the best form of governmental system?' But this question has little or no meaning unless the

---

* For further discussion of speculators and rentiers, see below p. 277.
† Chapter XII, §§2237, 2239, 2240.

particular society is indicated to which the system is to be applied, and unless the term 'best' is explained for it refers in a very indefinite way to the various individual and social utilities.* Although now and then this has sometimes been discerned intuitively, consideration of forms of governmental system has begotten endless numbers of derivations which ultimately appear as various myths. Both myths and derivations are worth nothing at all from the logico-experimental viewpoint, but both of them (or rather the sentiments they manifest) may have effects of great significance in motivating human behaviour. It is certain that the sentiments manifested by belief in such political forms as monarchy, republic, oligarchy and democracy have played, and continue to play, no small part in social phenomena—this they have in common with the sentiments manifested by other religions. 'Divine right', be it of prince, aristocracy, people, proletariat, majority or any other imaginable divine right, has not the least experimental validity. We must accordingly consider these forms of divine right only extrinsically, as facts, as manifestations of sentiments which, like other characteristics in the human beings composing a given society, operate to determine that society's ethos and form. In observing that such 'rights' have no experimental basis whatever, we are not in any way imputing invalidity to any social utility which may be attributed to any one of them. Certainly, if the observation were a derivation, then such an imputation would stick since in such reasonings it is generally assumed automatically that 'what is not rational is harmful'. But the question of utility is not affected one way or the other when the proposition is strictly logico-experimental since it makes no such assumption. The study of political forms properly belongs to *special* sociology. Here we are concerned with forms only for the purpose of ascertaining the substance underlying derivations and of studying the relationships between the various types of governing-class composition and other social phenomena.

(2240) As in other matters of this kind, we immediately come up against the stumbling-block of terminology. This is to be expected since the objective investigations we are making require an objective terminology, whereas the subjective discussions customary in these matters are served well enough by a subjective terminology drawn from everyday language. For example, everyone recognises that at the present time 'democracy' is tending to become the political system of all civilised peoples. But what is the precise meaning of this term 'democracy'? It is even more vague than that vaguest of terms, 'religion'. We must therefore set it aside and turn to study the facts it covers.

(ii) *Agencies of government*†

(2244) We will not linger over the fiction of 'popular representation'—fine words butter no parsnips. Let us rather see what is the substance beneath the various forms of power in the governing class. Discounting exceptions,

---

* For further discussion of the impossibility of fixing optima, see *Trasformazione*, pp. 300–1 below.

† Chapter XII, §§2244, 2246, 2249–52.

which are few and of short duration, there is everywhere a governing class, not large in membership, which maintains itself in power partly by force and partly by consent of the governed, who are very numerous. Between one governing class and another the difference lies mainly, in regard to substance, in the ratio of force to consent, and, in regard to form, in the ways by which force is used and consent procured.

(2246) . . . Dominant peoples sometimes endeavour to assimilate their subject peoples. Success in achieving this assimilation is certainly the best way of ensuring their power. But often they fail because they seek to change residues violently instead of making use of existing residues. Rome brought the policy of assimilation to a fine art and was thereby able to extend and maintain its power over peoples in Latium, Italy and the Mediterranean basin.

(2249) Utilising the existing sentiments in a society is in itself neither useful nor harmful to society. The utility and the harm depend on the outcome. If this benefits society there is utility; if it is detrimental there is harm. Nor can it be said, when the governing class pursues an end which is to its own advantage and without concern whether this be advantageous for the subject class, that this necessarily is detrimental to the subject class. There are very many cases in which the governing class exclusively pursues its own best interests and yet in so doing also promotes the best interests of the subject class. In short, utilising the existing residues of a society is only a means, and its value is determined by the value of its outcome.

(2250) Interests should be included with residues as agencies of government. Sometimes it is interests alone which are able to modify residues. Even so, although interests on their own, unalloyed with sentiments, can well be a powerful agency affecting individuals in whom residues of the instinct of combinations (Class I) predominate—therein affecting many members of the governing class—we must take note that, on the other hand, interests on their own and unconnected with sentiments have very little effect on people in whom residues of aggregate-persistence predominate, which is to say the greater part of the subject class. Speaking generally and very roughly, it can be said that the governing class has a better view of its own interests because it wears thinner veils of sentiment, while the subject class has a less clear view of its interests because it is more heavily shrouded in veils of sentiment. As a result the governing class is able to gull the subject class into serving the interests of the governing class. Such interests are not necessarily opposed to those of the subject class; often the two sets of interests coincide to a degree which makes the deception advantageous to the subject class.

(2251) Throughout history consent and force appear as agencies of government. . . . (2252) In the same way that derivations are much more variable than the residues they manifest, so do the forms in which force and consent appear vary much more than the sentiments and interests originating them; the differences in the proportions of force and consent largely arise from differences in the proportions of sentiments and interests. . . . Both derivations and forms of government . . . have much less influence on the social equilibrium than the sentiments and interests sustaining them. . . .

(iii) The governing class: character and methods*

(2253) Everywhere there exists a governing class, even in a despotism, but the forms in which it appears vary. In absolute governments there is only one figure on the stage: the sovereign. In so-called democratic governments it is parliament. But all the time behind the scenes are people who have very important functions in the practical work of government. Certainly from time to time these have to bow the head to the caprices of ignorant and overbearing sovereigns or parliaments; but soon enough they return to their tenacious, patient, unwavering work, the effects of which are of much greater significance. We find in the Roman *Digesta* admirable constitutions bearing the names of quite deplorable emperors, just as in our own day tolerably good legal codes emanate from parliaments which, heaven knows, are stupid enough. In both cases the reason is the same: the sovereign gives a free hand to his legal advisers, in some cases being quite unaware of what he is being made to do. This is even more so the case with parliaments, which are apt to be even less discerning in these matters than some kings and potentates. Even less percipient is His Majesty Demos, and at times this has made it possible to achieve, against the current of his prejudices, improvements in social conditions, not to speak of timely measures for national defence. The worthy Demos thinks he is following his own wishes, whereas in fact he is following the behests of his rulers. But this very often serves only the interests of his rulers for these, from the days of Aristophanes down to our own, have practised on a large scale the art of pulling the wool over the eyes of Demos. Like men of the same kidney at the end of the Roman Republic, our own plutocrats are absorbed in making money, either for themselves or to sate the greed of their partisans and accomplices. They give little or no thought to anything else. Among the various derivations they deploy to show the nation that their being in power is of benefit to it, there is the assertion that the people are better equipped to make decisions on general questions than on special questions. In fact, the exact reverse is the case. One only has to talk a little with uneducated people to discover that they can understand special questions, which are usually concrete, much better than general questions, which are usually abstract. But abstract questions have this merit for those in power: whatever the views of the public about them, political leaders will indubitably be able to make what they like of them. For example, the people elect members of parliament whose policy is to abolish interest on capital and 'surplus value' in industry and to check the 'greed' of the speculators. These are general questions. The elected representatives, directly or indirectly, make enormous increases in the public debt, and therefore in the interest paid to capital; they maintain and indeed increase the 'surplus value' enjoyed by manufacturers, many of whom grow rich on demagogy, and make over the government of the state to speculators. Some of the most prominent of these become diplomatists—like Volpi who concluded the Peace of Lausanne—or ministers—like Caillaux and Lloyd George.

(2254) The governing class is not homogeneous; it has within itself a

---

* Chapter XII, §§2253, 2254, 2257, 2259, 2260, 2267.

governing authority—a more exclusive class or a leader or a power-group—which exercises control in effect and practice. Sometimes the fact is obvious, as with the Ephors at Sparta, the Council of Ten at Venice, the favourite ministers of an absolute sovereign, or the political 'bosses' in parliament. At other times the centre of control is to some extent under cover, as with the 'caucus' in England, the party conventions in the United States, the wire-pulling financiers in France and Italy, and so on. The inclination to personify abstractions or even simply to give them an objective reality leads many people to think of the ruling class as a person, or at least as a concrete unit, and to suppose that it has a single will, implementing preconceived plans by logical procedures. Many anti-semites think in this way of the Jews; likewise many socialists of the bourgeoisie—though others, approaching nearer to reality, see the bourgeoisie as a system for whose operations the individual bourgeois, to some extent, is not directly responsible. The governing class, like other groups in society, performs logical and non-logical actions. The main factor in the matter is really the system in which they subsist, not the conscious will of individuals, who may indeed in many cases be carried along by the system to positions they would never have arrived at by deliberate choice. . . .

(2257) To maintain its power, the governing class makes use of individuals from the subject class. These fall into two different categories which correspond to the two principal agencies for retaining power. In the first category, force is the instrument; it embraces soldiers, police and the *bravi*—the hired cut-throats of former centuries. In the second, the instrument is artifice; from the days of the Roman *clientela* to the henchmen of modern politicians, individuals in this category exhibit similar characteristics. These two categories are always present in public life, but not in the same actual proportions and even less in the same visible proportions. Rome under the praetorians marks one extreme: here the main *de facto* instrument is armed force. The United States exemplifies the other extreme: here political cliques are the main actual, and to a somewhat lesser extent also the apparent, instruments. These cliques work in various ways. The principal way is the least obvious: the government 'looks after' the interests of the speculators, often without having any explicit understanding with them. A protectionist government, for example, wins the confidence and support of the manufacturers it protects without necessarily making an explicit agreement with all of them, although it may come to a direct understanding with leading individual manufacturers. . . . There are other more obvious ways, less important from the social viewpoint but which are held to be of great importance from the ethical viewpoint—for example, the bribing of voters, elected representatives, government officials and ministers, journalists and similar people. This is the modern version of the bribery, under absolute governments, of courtiers, male and female favourites, government officials, generals and so on—nor has this older form of corruption entirely disappeared. . . .

(2259) There seems to be a very close correlation between 'democratic' evolution and increasing use of that method of governing which resorts to artifice and clique-politics as opposed to the method which has recourse to force. This opposition between the two agencies is observable in the history of the late Republican period in Rome; force finally emerged the victor in the shape of the Empire. It is even more evident at the present time. The political system of many 'democratic' countries could very well be defined as mainly an economic feudalism in which the skilful deployment of political cliques constitutes the main instrument of government. In this it differs from the military feudalism of the medieval period, the main instrument of which was force based on vassalage. A political system in which the 'people' expresses its 'will' (supposing it to have one, which is arguable) without cliques, intrigues, lobbies and factions, exists only as a pious wish of theorists. It is not observable in reality in the past or the present, either in the West or anywhere else.

(2260) These phenomena have attracted wide attention, but usually have been described as deviations or 'degenerations' of democracy. But when or where we are to find the perfect, or at least tolerably healthy, state of affairs from which these unpleasant things are a degeneration, this no-one has ever been able to say. All one can say is that when democracy was a political movement in opposition, it had fewer of the blemishes it now exhibits; but this is a characteristic common to almost all opposition parties, for these lack not so much the will as the opportunity for malpractice.

(2267) If we consider all these facts objectively, freeing our thinking as far as possible from the influence of sectarian passions and from the prejudices of country, party, perfectionist and idealist passions and the like, we see that in reality—whatever the form of political system—the men who govern have, as a rule, a definite tendency to use their power to keep control of affairs and to abuse it in order to obtain personal advantages and gains, which sometimes they do not distinguish from party advantages and gains, and almost always identify with national advantages and gains. It follows that: 1. From this point of view, the various forms of political system do not differ markedly from one another. The differences existing between them lie not in the form but in the substance; that is to say, in the sentiments of the people. The more—or less—honest the general population of a country, the more—or less—honest its government. 2. The uses and abuses of power will be the more considerable the greater the intervention of government in private affairs. As exploitable material increases, so do potential gains. . . . 3. The governing class sets itself to appropriate other people's goods and property not only for its own use but also to share its booty with individuals and groups in the subject class who defend it and support its power—as the client supports his patron—whether by force or guile. 4. Usually neither patrons nor clients are fully aware that their conduct transgresses the moral norms prevailing in their society, and even when they are so aware they readily find excuses either by arguing that, when all is said and done, other people would do just the same, or else by recourse to the convenient pretext that the end justifies the means—and for them there can be no more excellent end than maintaining themselves in power. 5. The government machine consumes in all sorts of ways a quantity of wealth which correlates not only with the total amount of wealth represented by the private interests which are subject to government intervention, but also with the relative proportions of Class I and Class II residues among the governors and the governed.

(iv) *Elements in the governing class**

(2268) . . . We can divide these elements into two broad categories. Type A comprises the individuals who aim resolutely at ideal ends, adopting and strictly following certain rules of conduct. Type B comprises those whose aim is to promote the well being of themselves and their dependants or henchmen. This general category is divisible into two subtypes. We will indicate as B-*a* those who are content with the enjoyment of power and honours, leaving the material benefits to their associates; and as B-*b* those who seek material benefits—generally money—both for themselves and for their adherents. People who favour a particular party call the A types in it 'honest men' and set them up for admiration. Opponents of that party term them fanatics and sectarians and hold them in odium. The men of the B-*a* sort are generally regarded as 'honest' by those well disposed to the party, and are viewed with indifference, in regard to honesty, by its opponents. When the existence of men of the B-*b* sort is discovered, every-one calls them 'dishonest', but the friends of the party try to cover up their existence, and to achieve this they are quite capable of saying that black is white. The B-*a* are usually much more costly to a country than the B-*b* because their veneer of honesty makes possible all sorts of manoeuvres directed towards transferring other people's property into the hands of their political cliques. Moreover, the B-*a* umbrella also covers a fair number of people who, while taking nothing for themselves, go to great lengths to enrich their families. The relative proportions of these two main categories A and B depend to a great extent on the relative proportions of Class I and Class II residues. Among the A, Class II residues greatly predominate and so, according to one's point of view, the A may be called 'honest' or 'fanatic and sectarian'. Class I residues prevail among the Bs; hence these are better fitted to rule. When the B attain power they find the A a heavy drag on their party, though they serve to give the party a tinge of respect-ability. But this purpose is better fulfilled by the B-*a*; these are a rather rare commodity and much sought after by parties. The relative proportions of Class I and Class II residues among the party's voters, active supporters and those of its members not in government correspond, without being identical, to the relative proportions of these residues in the group which actually governs—the party's general staff. Only a party abundant in Class II residues can elect many individuals of the A category; but it also elects, without realising it, some men of the B category because these, being astute and circumspect and masters of the art of combinations, can easily pull wool over the eyes of ingenuous voters in whom Class II residues predomin-ate.

In our western political systems, parties are divisible into two broad classes: 1. parties which alternate with one another in government; 2. intransigent, uncompromising parties which do not get into government. It therefore follows that in parties which alternate in power there will be a minimum of the A and a maximum of the B; in intransigent parties the relative proportions will be reversed. Another way of stating the same thing

---

* Chapter XII, §2268.

would be to say that the parties which do not get into government are often more honest, but also more fanatical and sectarian, than parties which do exercise power. Hence the French aphorism: 'The Republic was a fine thing under the Empire.' . . . In the parties which get into power, there is a first 'weeding out' at the hustings. With few exceptions, a man cannot become a member of parliament unless he pays for the honour and unless he is prepared to dole out—and even more freely to promise—favours from the government. Very few of the A ever get beyond this hurdle. Yet candidates who are rich enough to buy parliamentary seats, regarding them as luxuries, come very near to being A for, strange as it may first appear, they are next to the A the most honest of politicians. In our day their numbers are growing smaller due to the enormous increase in the cost of buying votes. Those who meet the cost themselves aim at recouping the outlay by making money out of their political position, while those who will not or cannot find the money themselves get the administration to foot the bill in the form of various kinds of concessions and favours. The competitition is tremendous and only those exceptionally well equipped with combination-instincts can come out on top.

A second and more thorough test is the choice of ministers. Parliamentary candidates have to make promises to the electorate; ministerial candidates have to make promises to members of parliament and must be able to satisfy them that they and their political supporters will be well looked after. Ingenuous people are greatly mistaken in thinking that, to cope with these matters, it is enough for a man to be a knave. In fact, exceptional talents are required: shrewd intelligence and a marked aptitude for combinations of all kinds. Ministers do not have at their disposal great treasure chests which they can dip into at any time to scatter largesse among their adherents. They have to survey the world of business and industry with a shrewd eye to devise subtle combinations of economic favouritism, adroit ways of being agreeable to banks and business corporations, of promoting monopolies, of manipulating the incidence of taxation, and so forth. They have to know the ins and outs of bringing influence to bear on the law courts and of awarding titles and honours and such things to the benefit of those on whom they depend for continuation in power. And all along the A men in other parties must somehow be prevented from joining together. Those in a party who have a firm faith which is opposed to the firm faith of these A will not accomplish much in this direction. But if one has no faith or convictions whatever, with practically no residues save those of Class I (combinations), then it will not be too difficult to influence the A, or indeed profit from their very convictions to bring them over to one's own side, or at least to weaken the strength of their opposition. It is certain therefore that in the parties which alternate in governing a country, Class I residues greatly preponderate. It is for this reason that our political system is tending to become more and more a demagogic plutocracy. The various parties continually accuse one another of dishonesty. . . . Since almost all parties contain B-*b* types in them, considering that element exclusively would justify an accusation of dishonesty against almost every party. Parties also have their B-*a*, so that if one considers these exclusively, one may or may not accuse a party of dishonesty, depending on how one defines the term 'dishonesty'. Moreover, there are very few parties which do not have some A types; if one considers *them* exclusively, one may well say that a given party is honest. If instead we consider the relative proportions of A and B types in a party, we shall certainly find some parties in which the A predominate and which therefore may be called 'honest'. But in very many other cases it is not possible to determine whether there is any significant difference in the proportion of the A to the B. All one can say is that in the various parties which clash in the struggle for power, the A are remarkable for their rarity.

At the same time, since the lower classes are still rich in Class II residues, it behoves administrations which in reality are motivated solely by material interests at least to pretend that they are inspired by ideals. Politicians have to swaddle themselves in veils—often pretty diaphanous—of honesty. When one of them is trapped with his finger in the till, the opposition raises a great clamour of indignation—which does not prevent it from doing all it can to turn the scandal to its own advantage. If the alleged culprit's party fails in its efforts to exculpate him, it will cast him off as a ship in a storm throws out ballast. The public watches the affair develop with the fascinated interest of an audience at the theatre, and it becomes high drama free of charge if by any chance there is in the affair an element of sex or human interest. Trivial minor issues push the main issues aside, and the real issue—the social and political system which begets such scandals—is entirely disregarded. . . . Moralists assume that it is the fortuitous rise to power and influence of a 'dishonest' man which has provoked the scandal, arguing as if it were equivalent to a cashier's embezzling his firm. But there is no parallel between the two cases. It is not by fortuitous circumstance that such a man is raised to a position of power; it is by selection at the dictates of the very nature of the system. For the comparison with the dishonest cashier to have point, we would have to assume that the cashier was not appointed in the normal way but that his employer deliberately recruited him from among potential till-pilferers with outstanding gifts for fraud and peculation.

(v) Typology of government*

(2274) . . . We must note that very often the governing class, aiming at certain ends, indirectly produces other results, some of which it neither foresaw nor desired. For example, governments which impose protective tariffs in order to favour the interests of their clique may unintentionally promote thereby the circulation of elites. From the ethical viewpoint, a measure may be judged independently of all other social phenomena, but from the viewpoint of social utility one cannot so judge matters; one has to consider how this measure affects the social equilibrium as a whole. . . . To gain a general notion of this aspect, let us consider certain types of government as revealed by history.

Type I. *Governments which rely mainly on physical force and on*

---

* Chapter XII, §§2274–8.

religious or other similar sentiments. These include, for example, the governments of the Greek cities in the era of the 'tyrants', of Sparta, of Rome under Augustus and Tiberius, of the Venetian Republic in the last centuries of its existence, and of many European countries in the eighteenth century. In all there is a governing class in which Class II residues predominate over Class I residues. Elite-circulation generally speaking is slow. They are not expensive governments, but on the other hand they provide no stimulus to economic production, either because they have an innate repugnance for new things or because they set little value, in terms of elite-circulation, on individuals with a marked propensity for economic combinations. If, however, such a propensity exists in the population as a whole, society may enjoy a fair degree of economic prosperity (as was the case with Rome under the High Empire) provided government sets no obstacles in the way. But often in the long run there proves to be a substantial obstacle arising from the fact that the ideal of governments of this type is a nation petrified in its institutions (Sparta, Rome during the Low Empire, Venice during its decadence). They may grow wealthy by conquests, but this wealth is necessarily precarious since conquest produces no new riches (Sparta, Rome). Moreover, such regimes have in the past often degenerated into rule by armed bands (praetorians, janissaries) which are fit only to squander wealth.

Type II. *Governments which rely mainly on intelligence and cunning.* (2275) Here we can distinguish two subtypes. II-*a*: If intelligence and cunning are mainly used to influence sentiments, the outcome is some kind of theocratic government. This type has disappeared in modern Europe and we need not linger over it. . . . II-*b*: If intelligence and cunning are mainly used to operate on interests (which is not to say that they neglect sentiments), the outcome is governments like Athenian demagogy, the Roman aristocracy at various periods during the Republic, many of the medieval republics, and finally—a very important variety—the 'speculator' governments of our own day. (2276) In all governments of Type II, even those which play on sentiments, the governing class has a predominance of Class I over Class II residues. . . . The circulation of elites is normally slow in subtype II-*a* but rapid, sometimes very rapid, in subtype II-*b*, attaining its maximum rapidity under our 'speculator' governments. Regimes of the II-*a* subtype are usually not expensive, but neither are they productive. They lull their people into lassitude and stifle all stimulus to economic production. Not using force to any significant extent, they are unable to compensate for this lack of productivity by wealth gained through conquest. Indeed they become easy prey to neighbours who are adept in the use of force, and hence they disappear either by conquest or internal decadence. Regimes of the II-*b* subtype are expensive, sometimes very expensive indeed, but they are also productive of wealth, outstandingly so in some cases. There may therefore be such an excess of production of wealth over costs as to ensure great prosperity for the country. But it cannot by any means be assumed that, with increasing expenditure, the surplus will not become smaller, disappear and perhaps even turn into a deficit. . . . Such regimes may degenerate into rule by astute but irresolute people who are easily overthrown by violence from within or without. Such was the fate of many democratic governments in Greek cities, and this factor played an appreciable part in the fall of the republics of Rome and Venice.

(2277) In actual experience one finds mixtures of these various types; sometimes one type predominates, sometimes another. Governments mainly of Type I mixed with an element of subtype II-*b* may endure for a long time, based on force and without reduction in economic prosperity. Rome under the High Empire provides an example. Such governments run the risk of the degeneration to which Type I is prone and of a serious reduction in the proportions of the II-*b* element in them. Governments which are mainly of subtype II-*b* mixed with an element of Type I also may endure for a long time because they combine sufficient strength to defend themselves with the ability to achieve considerable economic prosperity. They run the risk of the degeneration to which the II-*b* subtype is prone and of a serious reduction in the proportions of the Type I element in them, and this almost invariably entails the danger of foreign invasion. This factor can be seen contributing to the destruction of Carthage and the Roman conquest of Greece. (2278) There may be a mixture of I and II-*b* in governments which rely mainly on force in international relations and on intelligence in internal affairs. The government of the aristocracy at the zenith of the Roman Republic was in many respects such a mixture.

(vi) Economic periodicity and government*

(2299) Confining ourselves to the economic and social state of western peoples from the beginning of the nineteenth century to the present day, we find that the most important interactions [see p. 260 above] are 2 (interests on residues, etc.) and 4 (social heterogeneity and circulation on residues, etc.). Concentrating on the most important element of the phenomenon, we may in fact consider, in a first approximation, a restricted cycle in which interests (b) act upon elite-circulation (d) and then in turn elite-circulation acts upon interests. It would be difficult, indeed probably impossible, to separate the two elements in the cycle, so it is better to consider the latter as a whole.

(2301) Although at the present day the circulation of elites . . . raises to the governing class many people who destroy wealth, it brings to the fore an even greater number of producers of wealth. The fact that the economic prosperity of civilised countries has increased enormously in recent times proves beyond doubt that the activity of the producers of wealth outstrips the activity of the destroyers. . . . (2302) In periods of rapid economic growth . . . governing is a much easier task than when the economy stagnates. . . . For example, the successes of the Second Empire coincided with the period of economic prosperity which began in 1854. Later on difficulties arose, and it is possible that, even without the war of 1870, the Empire would have faced very serious dangers in the period 1873–96. . . . Almost everywhere in Europe this was the heroic age of socialism and anarchism. Even so powerful a ruler as Bismarck had to have recourse to exceptional laws dealing with the socialists in order to be able to govern at

---

* Chapter XII, §§2299, 2301, 2302, 2304–7, 2309–14; Chapter XIII, §2565.

all. . . . And then, from 1898 to the present day,* there is again a period of easy—or at least not too difficult—government. In Italy this culminates in 1912 in the discomfiture of the opposition parties and Giolitti's easy dictatorship; while in Germany the socialists in the Reichstag—how times change!—approve new and enormous estimates for armaments; and in England the non-violent successors of the Fenians of 1873–98 easily obtain Home Rule for Ireland. . . .

(2304) . . . Famines used to provoke peoples to revolt as hunger drives the wolf out of the forest, but the relation between economic conditions and the temper of the people is far more complicated in economically highly developed societies like those of today. (2305) In their case we need mainly to consider, as was said at §2299, the restricted cycle in which (b)— interests—act upon (d)—social circulation—and *vice versa*. . . . Since modern governments are kept in power less and less by resort to force and more and more by an expensive art of government, they have a very urgent need of economic prosperity in order to carry on their activities, and they are also much more sensitive to variations in prosperity. . . . (2306) In deploying the combinations indispensable to their rule, modern governments are driven to spend over a given period more than their revenues would justify. They meet the difference by contracting new debts, avowed or disguised, which enable them to cover their immediate expenses and leave the burden to be shouldered by the future. This future becomes increasingly remote the more rapid the growth of economic prosperity, for the revenue from existing taxation increases with the rise in prosperity and so obviates the need for heavier taxation. It is held that future government surpluses will, in part at least, cover past deficits. Modern governments have gradually grown accustomed to this state of affairs—so convenient and agreeable for them—and they now regularly budget for present expenditure by taking into account future increases of revenue. . . . (2307) In periods of rapid economic growth this method encounters no serious difficulties. . . . But serious difficulties arise in periods of economic depression, and they would be far worse if such a depression were to prove protracted. The social order at the present time is such that probably no government could remain unaffected during such a period, and tremendous catastrophes could well occur more intense and extensive than any yet known to history.

(2309) In a situation where both economic circulation and elite-circulation stagnate, the individuals who are highly skilled in those economico-political combinations on which modern governments rely go unrewarded. . . . The government is hard put to it to cajole its adversaries out of sharp hostility because of the difficulty in finding the wherewithal to sweeten them. And even if something can be scraped from the barrel for the leaders, their henchmen—whose hunger must needs go unsatisfied— refuse to follow them. . . . So opposition to the government and to those of its leading opponents who have in various ways taken its shilling grows more widespread and intense.

---

* I.e., the eve of the first world war.

(2310) We are now in a position to take a stage further our discussion of the differences between 'rentiers' and 'speculators' [see above p. 263]. Periods of rapid growth in economic prosperity are favourable to speculators, who grow rich and enter the governing class if they are not already part of it. But such periods are unfavourable to 'rentiers' living to all intents and purposes on fixed incomes. Their position deteriorates either because of the natural rise in prices or because of their inability to compete with the speculators in gaining favour with politicians and the general public. The situation is reversed, generally speaking, during periods of economic stagnation. (2311) It follows from this that, when the prevailing trend is for periods of rapid economic growth to outnumber periods of depression, the governing class takes in an increasing recruitment from the speculator group which strengthens the representation of Class I residues in it. . . . Correspondingly it experiences a reduction in the numbers of the rentier group belonging to it in which Class II residues generally preponderate. This change in the composition of the governing class has the effect of further stimulating people to engage in economic enterprise. The economic prosperity it promotes goes on increasing until new forces come into operation which neutralise the movement. . . . The situation is reversed when the prevailing trend is towards periods of economic stagnation, the reversal being sharper if an actual economic decline sets in. Modern civilised societies provide examples of the first situation; examples of the second can be found in Mediterranean societies from the decline of the Roman Empire through the period of the barbarian invasions and into the Middle Ages. . . .

(2312) In civilised societies the producers of savings fulfil a highly important function—akin to that of the honey-bee; and one can indeed attach to them the tag, *Sic vos non vobis mellificatis, apes*! It is not stretching the truth to say that the level of civilisation in a society is in direct ratio to the quantity of savings it possesses or deploys. If economic prosperity increases, there is an increase also in the quantity of savings invested in production; if economic prosperity stagnates, there is a corresponding decrease in the productive use of savings. (2313) . . . As we have noted earlier, people in the R group are very different in character from those belonging to the s group [see above p. 265]. . . . They are easily handled and indeed despoiled by those who can make opportune use of the sentiments corresponding to residues of aggregate-persistence (Class II) which are strongly represented in R types. Speculators on the other hand . . . although seeming to be always submissive to the strong, work underground and know how to grasp the substance of power, leaving the outward forms to others. . . . Their opinions are always the opinions most useful to them at the moment; yesterday conservatives, today they are liberals, and tomorrow they will be anarchists if anarchism seems likely to gain power. But they know enough to avoid giving the impression that they are all of one colour, and they understand the value of friendly relations with all parties of any importance. The political scene may present speculators in battle with one another in the struggles of catholics with pro-semites, monarchists with republicans, free traders with socialists. But behind the scenes they are hand-in-glove and push forward together in any venture which offers the chance of making money. When one of their group falls, his opposing fellow-speculators deal mercifully with him in the expectation of receiving similar gentle treatment should they in turn take a tumble. Neither r nor s types are very good at using force and both categories are fearful of it. Those who wield force make up a third category; these find it easy to despoil the rentiers but somewhat more difficult to despoil the speculators since the s, defeated today, return to power the day after.

(2314) Clear evidence of the paucity of courage among rentiers is revealed in the faint-hearted and stupid resignation with which they accept conversions and fundings of the public debts. At one time it could perhaps have been not unreasonable to think that there might be some advantage, along with the disadvantages, in accepting such conversions. But today, with so many examples of bonds falling below par after conversion, one would have to be perversely dense to entertain the hope that a new conversion could have any different result. . . . It would require agreement among only a small number of bondholders to scotch any sort of debt-conversion by the public authorities; yet in truth it would be easier to get a flock of sheep to attack a lion than arouse such people to make the least gesture of energetic action. They bow the head and let their throats be cut. . . .

(2565) . . . The weak feature of 'speculator governments' is lack of courage among the speculators and their meagre aptitude for the use of force. Such governments therefore are usually destroyed by people—be they internal or external adversaries—who do know how to use force. Speculator governments succumb through civil or foreign wars. In the case of internal revolutions, the final catastrophe is often preceded by attempts at revolt which are repressed and defeated.

5. OSCILLATIONS AMONG DERIVATIONS AND THEIR CORRELATION WITH OSCILLATIONS IN SOCIETY*

(2329) This phenomenon is of great importance. As a manifestation of ideas and doctrines, it appears in conflicts between the various sentimental, theological and metaphysical derivations, and between these and the rational processes of the logico-experimental sciences. To write their history would be to write the history of human thought. As a manifestation of the forces at work in society, the phenomenon appears in the conflict between the sentiments corresponding to various residues, and chiefly between the sentiments corresponding to Class I and Class II residues respectively. Hence it appears also in conflicts between actions of logical and non-logical behaviour. It is therefore a very general phenomenon and one which, under different forms, dominates the whole history of human societies. . . . In considering doctrines which transcend experience we came up against the question: how is it that experience works so differently in sentimental, theological, metaphysical derivations and in scientific reasonings? . . . Further on, in considering derivations, we were brought to

---

* Chapter XII, §§2329–38, 2386–93.

enquire how and why certain derivations, palpably false, fatuous and absurd from the experimental point of view, nevertheless persist and recur generation after generation? . . . We could then neither ignore nor yet satisfactorily answer these questions. . . . As we pursued our investigation we found that the scope of the problem grew wider. It now confronts us in the form of a mutual correlation between an undulatory movement in residues and an undulatory movement in derivations, and between both these movements and other social phenomena, especially economic phenomena. Over a long period of time there may be very marked variations in the relative proportions of Class I and Class II residues, particularly among the intellectual classes in a society. In such cases there are very significant developments in regard to derivations.

(2330) The problem is therefore very wide-ranging, yet it is itself only a particular aspect of an even more general problem: the problem of undulations in the various elements which constitute social phenomena, and of the reciprocal relationship between these elements and their undulations. At all times people seem to have had some notion of a rhythmical, periodic, oscillatory, undulatory movement in natural phenomena, including social phenomena. The notion . . . probably derives from observation of the periodic alternation of night and day and of the seasons . . . from the movements of the celestial bodies . . . from the alternation of good and bad harvests . . . and from the succession of human generations—childhood, manhood and old age. The idea of such a succession comes to be applied to families, cities, nations and to humanity as a whole as tradition or history reaches over a certain extent of time and as the curiosity of the intelligent is stimulated. Moreover, the influence of persisting abstractions (residues Class II-d) draws from the phenomenon of natural cataclysm inferences which lead to a more or less deliberate application of the principle of rhythmic movement to the universe as a whole. In all these different cases, the need felt for logical explanations (Class I-e) and the residues of persisting uniformity (Class II-e) lead to the devising of doctrines which flourish vigorously with metaphysical and pseudo-experimental attachments. It would seem very probable that those who reason *a priori* or dogmatically, along with the great majority of metaphysicists, instinctively apply to the whole universe the impressions derived from particular groups of facts; hence their assertion that everything is subject to rhythmical movement. Some writers, however, come to the same conclusion by rash and premature generalisations far outstripping the facts, which they not infrequently distort. . . .

(2331) Small oscillations do not usually appear in correlation. They are transient manifestations in which it is very difficult, indeed impossible, to descry uniformities. In large oscillations it is easy to perceive correlations; they are manifestations of long duration in which we are at times able to detect a law or a uniformity either in connection with some given phenomenon considered separately from others, or in connection with phenomena in correlation with others. . . . Various errors are usually committed in the study of these uniformities. They are of two kinds. A: errors arising from not taking due account of the undulatory form of the phenomenon. B: errors in interpreting this undulatory form.

(2332) A-1. The wave lines disclose what we may call periods of rise and fall in the phenomenon. If these periods are at all prolonged, those who live during them get the idea that the movement must proceed indefinitely in the direction apparent in their own day, or that at least it will eventuate in a stationary situation without subsequent contrary movements. (2333) A-2. The foregoing error is lessened when it is assumed that there is a mean line around which the movement oscillates, but the error still remains because it is held that this mean line coincides with the line of one of the ascending periods of the phenomenon. It is never, or hardly ever, made to coincide with the line of a descending period.

(2334) B-1. It is realised that in the past the phenomenon appears in the form of oscillations, but it is implicitly assumed that the normal movement is a movement favourable to society and tending towards an ever-increasing good, or at the very least that it is constant and does not decline. The case of a continuously unfavourable movement is usually excluded from consideration. Oscillations which are indisputable are regarded as abnormal, secondary, accidental: each has a 'cause' which *could be* and *should be* dealt with; this done, the oscillation would disappear. Derivations in this general form are not common; they are, however, widespread in the following form, B-2. The reason for this, it is plain, derives simply from man's inclination to seek his advantage and evade anything detrimental to him. (2335) B-2. It is supposed that oscillations can be separated and that, by removing the 'cause', favourable oscillations can be maintained and unfavourable ones eliminated. Almost all historians accept this theorem, at least implicitly, and go to great lengths in declaring what various nations should have done to continue for ever in favourable periods without ever sinking into unfavourable periods. Even a good many economists know and benignly instruct us how we might avoid 'crises', employing this term exclusively to indicate the descending period in an oscillation. All these derivations are as a rule brought into play whenever social prosperity is under discussion. They are dear to very many writers who ingenuously imagine they are carrying out a scientific work when they are in fact engaged in moral, humanitarian or patriotic sermonising. (2336) B-3. Simply as a reminder—for all too often we have had to mention it in this enquiry—let us note the error of transforming relationships of interdependence into relationships of cause and effect. In the present context, the assumption is that the oscillations in a particular phenomenon have causes of their own which are independent of oscillations in other phenomena. (2337) B-4. Wholly disregarding the factor of interdependence yet intent on finding some 'cause' or other for the oscillations in a particular phenomenon, some thinkers seek this cause in theology, metaphysics or stray occurrences which are experimental only in appearance. The Hebrew prophets attributed the cause of the descending periods in Israel's prosperity to the wrath of God. The Romans were persuaded that every evil suffered by their city was the outcome of some breach or omission in divine ritual. Very many historians, even modern ones, look for and find similar causes in the 'corruption of manners', in the *auri sacra fames*, in transgressions against the rules of morality, law or humanitarianism, in the sins of an oppressive oligarchy, in excessive inequalities of wealth, in capitalism, and so on and so forth. There are sufficient derivations of this sort to satisfy all tastes.

(2338) In reality oscillations in the various elements composing a social phenomenon are interdependent, like the elements themselves, and are simply manifestations of changes in these elements. If one is determined to use the deceptive term 'cause', one could say that the descending period is the 'cause' of the ascending period which follows it, and *vice versa*. But it must be understood that this is so only in the sense that the ascending period is indissolubly linked with the preceding descending period, and *vice versa*; and therefore, in general, the various periods are only manifestations of a single state of affairs, and observation shows them as succeeding one another—a process of succession which constitutes an experimental uniformity. These oscillations are of various kinds according to the time they take in their fulfilment. It may be very brief, brief, long or very long. As we have already noted, very brief oscillations are usually accidental in the sense that they are manifestations of ephemeral forces. Those which take a fairly long period for their fulfilment are usually manifestations of enduring forces. Due to our lack of knowledge about very remote times and our inability to predict the future, very long oscillations may not appear as oscillations at all but rather as manifestations of a continuous unwavering movement in a given direction.

(2386) Towards the end of the eighteenth century there was a period of economic prosperity which saw the first dawn of modern transformations in agriculture, commerce and industry. This circumstance promoted, as is usual, the predominance of Class I residues and was itself favoured by that predominance. The tide of economic prosperity first rose in England, and hence it is in this country that there is first registered a fall in the curve of Class II residues in ratio to residues of Class I. This is also why England—because of the undulatory movement characteristic of this curve even when economic conditions remain well nigh constant—is the first country to experience the reaction precipitating a rise in the curve of Class II residues. The movements of action and reaction in England accordingly anticipate the corresponding movements in France. In both countries the action carried similar 'philosophic' trappings; in both, the reaction was substantially the same but it took different forms, being in the main christian in England and democratic in France. The French Revolution was a religious reaction, analogous—in a different form—to the religious reaction in contemporary England and to the earlier religious reaction of the Reformation. But it soon changed its livery; democratic and humanitarian at the start of the Revolution, it became patriotic and militarist under Napoleon, and eventually catholic under Lewis XVIII. In Europe as a whole, the residues of Class II reach the zenith of their curve in ratio to Class I residues shortly after 1815, and almost everywhere the outward form is christian.

(2387) But since such movements are essentially undulatory, there occurred a further fall in the curve. The fall was rapid because it corresponded to a new rapid and powerful wave of economic prosperity. Economic production was being transformed; large-scale industry and commerce and international finance were emerging and prospering. Class I residues slowly regained supremacy. The 'positivists', 'free-thinkers' and 'intellectuals' of the nineteenth century revert to the customary task of their species: eroding the bastions of prejudice. In this they prove themselves heirs of the eighteenth-century *philosophes*. They campaign, not in the name of paganism (like the humanists) or of 'common sense' (like the *philosophes*), but under the holy banner of science. The movement they represent reaches its maximum intensity between 1860 and 1870; thereafter it begins to weaken, and by the first decade of the twentieth century a reaction begins in favour of residues of aggregate-persistence (Class II).

(2388) As is usual, particular eddies occur on the surface of the general tide of movement. We must guard against confusing the eddies with the tide. This mistake is made all too easily because the eddy or short wave immediately under our gaze acquires through proximity to us a much greater importance than it merits when the general movement over a long period of time is taken into consideration. (2389) Notable among short wave-movements of this kind is the undulation which ensued after the Franco-Prussian war of 1870 and which, although largely determined by the situation then prevailing in European societies, was yet due in some small measure to the personal initiative of Prince von Bismarck. Through his *Kulturkampf* he contributed, albeit involuntarily, to the pressures on Class II residues, and hence prolonged the predominance of Class I residues. To achieve momentary ends, he protected the Old Catholics against Rome without realising that this was detrimental to his imperial policy. Later on he perceived his blunder and set himself to make peace with the Roman Curia. In these matters Emperor William II proved to be more discerning than the Iron Chancellor, for he saw clearly that conflicts which had the effect of weakening aggregate-persistence factors could in no way advantage the German Empire. Furthermore, Bismarck—again impelled by the momentary exigencies of policy—protected the anti-clerical republic in France, and this also had the effect of prolonging the predominance of Class I residues. On the other hand, his aversion from bourgeois liberalism, against which he had grievances, led him to establish universal suffrage in the German Empire, thereby favouring the socialist party and reinforcing certain residues of Class II. Other residues of this class were intensified by the creation of the catholic 'centre party' and by the spread of anti-semitism.

(2390) At the present time the prosperity of Class II residues seems mainly to be committed to the growing vigour of patriotism in various forms, like nationalism and imperialism. Socialism is also envigorating other residues of Class II which conflict with patriotism. But at the moment of writing [1912] socialism is in process of declining into political combinations and is being subjected to the influence of Class I residues, with the result that it is not making a very effective resistance to nationalism and imperialism. Indeed we find that many socialists are changing the form of their faith and are associating themselves under various pretexts with nationalists and imperialists. On a lower level revivals are now occurring in various religions, ranging from christian denominations down to the sex and teetotal religions. At the same time metaphysics is enjoying a renascence and high-sounding twaddle which seemed to have been utterly discredited fifty years ago is now becoming respectable again. It is not given us to foresee what will befall this oscillation which we can now observe in its early stages—how long it will last, how far it will go. But the evidence of the past permits us to affirm that this trend will eventually give rise to a new oscillation in a contrary direction.

(2391) If one takes a rather detached view of all these phenomena so regularly occurring and recurring in history from the remotest past down to the present day, one cannot but conclude that these oscillations are the rule and that they are not likely to cease very soon. What will befall in the far distant future we cannot say, but it is highly probable that a course of events which has already lasted for so long is not going to be changed in the near future.

(2392) . . . Taking account of modern life as a whole, we may safely conclude that Class I residues and the findings of logico-experimental science have widened the field of their sway. To this fact, indeed, is largely due the great diversity of characteristics in contemporary societies as compared with the societies of ancient Greece and Rome. (2393) We would not be mistaken, therefore, in ascribing to 'reason' an increasingly important role in human activity; indeed, such a view is wholly in accord with the facts. Even so, we must take note that this proposition, like all the formulations which literature substitutes for the theorems of science, is imprecise and conducive to errors. . . .

Part Three

The Application

I

Fatti e Teorie

(1920)

PREDOMINANT DERIVATIONS AT THE TIME OF THE FIRST
WORLD WAR AND IN THE IMMEDIATE POST-WAR PERIOD*

(IX) The defeat of the Central Powers is a phenomenon of great significance. In the first phase of the war, Germany's armies were successful; its
military capacity contrasted sharply with the inadequate military preparations of the Entente plutocracies and Italy's utter unreadiness for war.
But this phase was followed by another which eventually terminated in the
total victory of Germany's enemies. There are many reasons for this outcome, and clearly one of them lies in the enormous disproportion of manpower and financial resources between the two sides—a factor of over-
riding importance given the new character of modern warfare. Another
factor in Germany's defeat is the mastery at sea of England and later of the
United States. But we must go further than this and investigate how this
distribution of forces came about. The first phase is easily explained: it is
the natural consequence of the particular character of demagogic plutocracies. But how do we explain the second phase?
    A comparison of events leading up to Germany's campaigns against
Austria in 1866 and against France in 1870–1 with the events leading up to
the war of 1914–18 will help us to find an answer to that question. If we
study the preparations made for these wars, we shall see that, although in
all three cases Germany's internal provisions were similar, its external
provision for the third war was markedly different from that made for the
other two. On the political chessboard of 1865, the positions occupied by
Prussia, Austria and France were very similar to the positions of Germany,

    * *Fatti e Teorie*, Epilogue, pp. 335–46, 366–8, 378–9. The roman numerals
in curved brackets relate to the sections of the original.

France and England in 1913. But the movements of the pieces were entirely different. In 1865 the diplomatic moves on the board were arranged with farsighted care by an expert and outstandingly shrewd player. No move was made without the full weighing up of its consequences beforehand. In contrast to this, on the eve of the first world war Germany was diplomatically unprepared and wholly entrusted to the military forces of a player who was obsessed by form, not substance, a player who had for every problem only one simple solution: the terror he assumed he must arouse, and who moved his pieces heedlessly without giving the least thought to the indirect or eventual consequences of his moves.

Ollivier says very truly, when writing of the meeting at Biarritz between Bismarck and Napoleon III, that the former 'sought only for the certainty of our neutrality so as to be free at the decisive moment to disable the Rhineland provinces and bring all his power to bear on Bohemia. However great was the confidence of the king and Moltke in their splendid army, they were not so presumptuous as to think it capable of holding its own at one and the same time against the three armies of Austria, the German Confederation and France. If Napoleon III were to march on the Rhine while the German forces were advancing on Bohemia, they would be forced to halt and retire . . . and lose the opportunity of threatening Vienna.' (*L'Empire Libérale*, Vol. VII, pp. 477–8.) Paraphrasing Ollivier word by word, we can say of the directors of German policy before 1914 that they did *not* endeavour to secure the neutrality of England which would, at the decisive moment, have freed them from the threat by sea and have enabled them to concentrate their forces on the enemy frontier. Because they had so much confidence in their splendid army, they *did* have the presumption to suppose it strong enough to engage simultaneously the French and the Russian armies, disregarding the Belgian army, ignoring Italy's and reckoning England's to be innocuous. If, while German troops were invading France, England were to close the sea-routes and send an army to the continent, they would be compelled to stop short and then retire, and so lose the opportunity of marching on Paris.

Bismarck went to Biarritz; Bethmann-Hollweg neither went himself to London nor sent a special mission. He seemed to be unaware of the existence of Italy. These omissions cannot be attributed to ignorance of England's power or of the possible consequences of Italian intervention. Indeed, not to make a long story of it, it is enough to record, in regard to England, Bethmann-Hollweg's stupefied anguish when the British ambassador gave him notice that the invasion of Belgium constituted a *casus belli*. Some indication of Italy's place in official German thinking is given by Marshall Konrad von Hoetzendorf in an interview published in *Correspondenz Bureau*, July 16, 1919: 'The intervention of Italy was the cause of the disaster. Had this not occurred, the Central Powers would certainly have won the war. All along we were hoping that Italy would remain faithful to the Triple Alliance.'

But really, prudence and wisdom are hard to seek in a policy which did nothing to ensure this desired fidelity of Italy to the Triple Alliance. And what conclusion does von Hoetzendorf draw from all this? Does he subscribe to the prudent view that it was necessary to come to terms with Italy and that, to win the high prize of victory, some rather considerable sacrifices had to be made? Not at all. His rash and ill-considered conclusion is that it was necessary first of all to make war on Italy. He says: 'It was impossible to have freedom of action against Serbia without first subduing Italy. To this end it had been proposed that there should be a campaign against Italy in 1906, and after.this, in 1908 and 1913, a war with Serbia.' The worthy marshal fashions the future to his own liking. It never crosses his mind that these wars, so nonchalantly projected by him, were capable of having repercussions throughout Europe.

It might be argued, though with some difficulty, that consequences of this kind are simply the outcome of mistakes from which even the most cautious and astute governments are not exempt. But such an explanation falls to the ground when we consider that this sort of thing occurs again and again—which all goes to show that these things do not come about by fortuitous chance but have a constant uniform cause.

(X) Nor has the result of the war succeeded in opening the eyes of the majority of Germany's statesmen. Take Gottlieb von Jagow, for example. This former foreign minister exhibits an utter lack of understanding of the consequences of facts which are yet apparent to him. He gives an excellent analysis of the sentiments motivating Germany's future adversaries.* Speaking of Russia, he says: 'Alexander III directly favoured panslavist tendencies. The alliance with France was concluded in the autumn of 1893. Friction grew sharper with the Danube monarchy in the Balkans and with us in Turkey in consequence of our *Bagdadpolitik*. There is a well-known Russian saying: "The road to Constantinople passes through Berlin." The Straits Question was quite vital for Russia; the Russian people have always kept alive the dream of being masters of Byzantium, and this has always had power to inspire them to struggle and make sacrifices' (pp. 15–16).

Later on, as if he had forgotten what he has said here, he comes out with the following statement: 'As has been said, our efforts were in the direction of avoiding a European conflagration and of limiting the affair to an Austro-Serbian conflict in which other powers ought not to become involved' (p. 115). But however could he hope to succeed in this, aware as he is of the circumstances he had earlier described? What sort of foresight is this which permits a statesman to go blindly forward without taking due care whether the venture to which he is committing himself is possible or not? 'But Serbian interests in the eyes of M. Sazonoff ... were in this matter identical with "Russian interests".' (This is hardly surprising in view of what von Jagow has said on page 16!) 'A communiqué from Petersburg on July 24 announced that Russia could not remain indifferent in the Austro-Serbian conflict' (pp. 115–16). But according to von Jagow, Russia *ought* to have remained indifferent; the 'ought' is decreed by the author's religion of patriotism. 'Russia's bristling, curt attitude appeared all the more strange in view of the fact that Count Berchtold had already declared to the Russian chargé d'affairs in Vienna ... that if it should turn out that Austria were compelled to take up the struggle with Serbia, it would only be as a means of self-preservation, but Austria was not aiming

---

* *Ursachen und Ausbruch des Weltkrieges*, 1919.

at conquest and did not contemplate impairing Serbia's sovereignty' (p. 117). But what is so 'strange' about Russia's attitude? It was on the contrary the natural consequence of all that von Jagow had noted on pages 15 and 16. Whether genuine or feigned, his position is a trifle too naïve, for his knowledge of history cannot be so lamentably feeble for him to be unaware that the subservience of a state can be achieved by other means than direct conquest. And if he really thinks that Russia, after abandoning Serbia in a life-and-death struggle with Austria, could have maintained its authority in the Balkans, then it is high time he gave up writing about politics and turned his pen to composing tales for the nursery.

But von Jagow's way of thinking is much more reasonable if it is seen as the product of his religious-patriotic sentiments, according to which everything which directly or indirectly damages Germany's interests is unjustifiable and illegitimate. A good deal of his book is taken up with ethico-metaphysical disquisitions, as learned as they are useless, about the violation of Belgian neutrality. We have served up to us the familiar argument that 'necessity knows no law': an argument which, according to Alphons Rivier, enjoys the support of international law or the law of nations. Rivier writes*: 'When a conflict arises between a State's right of self-preservation and its obligation to respect the rights of another State, the right of self-preservation takes precedence over the obligation. *Primum vivere*. An individual man is free to sacrifice himself, but it is never legitimate for a Government to sacrifice the State whose destiny has been entrusted to it. . . . There is a distinction between the honour of a private person, which may in certain circumstances be sacrificed, and the honour of a Government which must not sacrifice the State.'

The reader will have little difficulty in recognising in these remarks that derivation which asserts that the end justifies the means. A ready tool for all forms of fanaticism, this derivation has been employed time and again in politics. A classic example is the invoking of it to justify Nelson's treacherous violation of Danish neutrality. But, of course, it goes without saying that these high-flying notions have no validity unless those subscribing to them are victorious or powerful!

Von Jagow describes French sentiments and attitudes with the same perception he shows in his account of the Russian state of mind. 'France, Russia's ally since 1893, had remained irreconcilable ever since the war of 1870. French *amour-propre*, the national pride of a highly bellicose people which had given fresh proofs of its traditional valour in this war, could not adjust itself to the idea of defeat and of the dimming of France's ancient glory. Hatred of the victorious enemy and the thirst for vengeance were crystallised in grief over the "stolen provinces". The French made no allowance for the fact that these were German imperial territories in former times [*What an argument to advance! Playing politics with history like this is too childish for words—excusable only by fanaticism and quite extraneous to factual reality*] and that they are still German-speaking to a very considerable extent. [*German in language, yes—but not in sentiment.*] All the efforts made to come to an understanding with France were in vain' (p. 22).

---

* Probably *Lehrbuch des Volkerrechts*, 1899.

This was surely to be foreseen from what the writer himself has already said, since Germany was unwilling to make the sacrifices necessary for an accommodation with France. The same holds true in regard to an understanding with England. Von Jagow desired this but was not prepared to pay the price. It was crystal clear that such an understanding could not fail to be highly precarious so long as Germany continued to evince the intention of competing with England for supremacy at sea.

It would seem that he was not unaware of the circumstances which were modifying Italy's alliance with Germany. 'Italy's rancour over Tunis had died down. [*Bismarck had fed the flames of Italy's resentment against France; his successors had allowed it to 'die down'.*] Friction with France was progressively diminishing and relations between the two countries were becoming smoother. Italians began to speak readily of their "Latin sister" and to stress that Italy had a "friend" in France as well as in the Triple Alliance. . . . Moreover, there still survived, especially in northern Italy, the old hatred of Austria, and points of friction with the Danube monarchy were being sharpened by Italian aspirations in the Balkans' (p. 40). And not by Austrian aspirations in the Balkans? Only eyes blinded by dogmatic obsession could fail to perceive what was so obvious.

(XI) If all this and much more beside were known in Germany, how is it that the ruling circles in Germany acted as if entirely uninformed in these matters? How is it that certain questions went unasked? Why were certain problems not posed, as for example: Given such and such pieces disposed thus and thus on the chess-board, what kind of game must we play? What sentiments and interests must we make use of? How best can we implement the policy of *divide et impera*? Which are the enemies whom, according to Machiavelli's precept, we should conciliate if we cannot crush them? What sacrifices must we make to achieve victory? Should we give up the distant and uncertain prospect of maritime supremacy in order to ingratiate ourselves with England? Would it be to Austria's advantage to make the cession of Trentino and Trieste to Italy the purchase price of a free hand to extend the Dual Monarchy's influence in the Balkans and the Near East? These and other questions were highly relevant to any examination of the existing state of affairs and of the possibilities it held for furthering the interests of the Central Powers.

When war broke out with Russia and France, and with England very soon joining in, Germany's rulers at last began to realise the importance of a possible intervention by Italy. Had the neglect of such an important factor as Italian intervention been due to simple error, then they surely ought to have taken urgent steps to correct the mistake, employing all appropriate means. Now, though it is true they did seek to amend their blunder, they did so in a woefully makeshift fashion, quite unequal to the seriousness of the situation. Von Bülow was sent to Rome, but there he performed like the heavy father in a melodrama. He returned to Germany empty-handed. His government could not be bothered with such trivialities as are implicit in the old maxim: those who will an end must also will the means.

Nor is this all. It eventually became apparent that the United States of America was contemplating intervention in Europe. American imperialism came into prominence in Theodore Roosevelt's presidency. A little later, under Woodrow Wilson, it began to envisage more ambitious ventures. Wilson had first cast his eye over Mexico, but his gaze shifted to another direction when bigger and better prizes loomed up on the other side of the Atlantic. American intentions being apparent, it was quite inexcusable for Germany's rulers to ignore the heavy weight the United States could bring to bear with all its vast resources in wealth and manpower. It is conceivable that they could have turned this intervention to their own advantage. Political common sense demanded that they should at least attempt this. The war might very well have ended differently if, when Wilson asked the belligerents to define their war aims, Germany's rulers had proposed that the matter be settled by the arbitration of the United States. But pride, arrogance and overweening presumption militated against this. Pride and arrogance forbad sacrificing a part to save the whole; overweening presumption rendered them incapable of a correct appraisal of Germany's strength and that of its enemies.

Thus was determined the intervention of the United States on the side of the Entente and the consequent ruin of Germany. The latter's total defeat might possibly still have been avoided if some opportunity or other had been seized to make peace. Certainly this would have entailed heavy sacrifices, but nowhere near so heavy as those which the Central Empires had to suffer in the end. We can put this forward only as a conjecture since the evidence for it is not so obvious as in the other cases cited.

(XII) In the way Germany's rulers acted before and after the declaration of war, are there not clear indications of the same kind of sentiments as are exhibited by religious believers? Faith in 'Germany's destiny', in its military strength and in the power of its 'organisation', the dogma of 'vital interests'—all this clouded the vision of its rulers. To employ the terminology used in the *Treatise*, we can say that in Germany's rulers Class II residues (persistence of aggregates) were potent, while among the rulers of the Entente nations, with the exception of Russia, Class I residues (instinct of combination) predominated. Russia's rulers, with their dreams of the illimitable power of Holy Russia and with their emperor under the sway of Rasputin, were heavily endowed, like Germany's, with Class II residues. And as in Germany, so in Russia it was this which dragged the nation and its rulers to ruin: a fate they could have easily avoided if only Russia had maintained its former alliance with Germany.

Bismarck was able to achieve great things when working in concert with William I, for in Bismarck, who governed, there was a prevalence of Class I residues, while in William I, who executed, Class II residues predominated. In contrast, the mystical William II, dominated by Class II residues, had no countervailing influence in government. He would not tolerate chancellors who used their heads as instruments for intelligent calculation. He got rid of Bismarck, stupidly presuming that he could do better, and would accept no one who might have been able to take Bismarck's place.

(XXIX) To gain a clear grasp of the phenomenon under consideration, we should note the presence within the Entente of two divergent sections of opinion. One section wished to persevere with a policy of diplomatic finesse and was opposed to war. The other favoured resort to force, seeing in war opportunities for splendid gains and advantages. The first section was, more or less covertly, pacifist; the second cloaked its cupidity in democratic and humanitarian derivations to which they strove to add juridical derivations by passing off their policy as a 'defence of right and justice'. They sought to destroy the first section; this intention was manifested in many ways, especially in certain political trials. Notable examples of these were the Caillaux affair in France and the Cavallini trial in Italy. This latter dragged on for several years; in the end the court ruled that there was no case to answer. The whole business was a shameless insult to every principle of law, and was initiated solely to quell the political opponents of the government of the day.

In support of the first section's viewpoint, it can be argued that it is always dangerous to set the masses of the people in motion. Once started, there is no knowing where things will end. It is better to rest content with the little one has, which is at least certain, than to let oneself be won over by blind cupidity and set off in the uncertain pursuit of more. The outcome of Germany's unrestrained greed is eloquent testimony to the wisdom of this view.

Demagogic plutocracies risk two dangers in waging war. 1. If the military forces engaged are relatively small in number, the war may throw up a victorious general capable, without much difficulty, of gaining the absolute loyalty of a small army and so be in a position to drive out the plutocrats. Caesar and very many other successful military leaders did precisely this. It does not require a very long purse to satisfy the demands of a small body of henchmen. 2. If, as is the case today, war is carried on by an army recruited from the majority of men in the country capable of bearing arms then, although the first danger is avoided, it remains to be seen how, after victory, pledges can be kept and satisfaction given to the very great numbers involved. Multitudes of hangers-on inevitably prove very expensive. Since all past experience went to show that it was by the 'arts of the fox' that demagogic plutocracy had grown in power, why then —the anti-war party could argue—abandon these well-tried, known, safe and easy methods for the 'arts of the lion' and their novel, unknown, perilous and arduous methods?

But this argument ran up against the fact that in certain countries internal developments appeared more and more every day to be leading to the abyss of revolution. Somehow then the possibility of revolution had to be forestalled. To this end governments at all times have had recourse to international wars, calculating that thereby civil conflict could be avoided. Such a consideration was not absent from the thoughts of the Russian bureaucracy when it decided to go to war; and it may well have played a part, albeit a small part, in the corresponding decision of Germany and Austria, the latter in particular being fearful of the rebellion of its oppressed nationalities.

In the case of the second section of opinion in the plutocracies—the 'war party'—the terms of the case made out for the first section have to be inverted, its weak points being strong points for the interventionists and *vice versa*. It is truly amazing to see what subtle refinements of skill these sections have employed in making use of the interests and sentiments subsisting in the various nations concerned. We shall be able to tell which of them is making better provision for its own interests when we know whether the plutocracies, aided and abetted by the rhetoric of the intellectuals, are going to find the mass of the people in these nations as effectively gullible in the future as they have been in the past. . . .

The world war let loose a swarm of derivations of all kinds and flavoured to suit all tastes. Some of them are puerile, like the theme of the 'scrap of paper' which is harped on in and out of reason by countless numbers of people. Derivations *habent sua fata*. Alexander I's remark, 'treaties are made to be broken', did not acquire anything like the same notoriety as the very similar remark of the German chancellor. Those who speak of his curt dismissal of the treaty guaranteeing Belgian neutrality as if it were something new, unheard of and typical of German 'barbarity', must have forgotten their history; the evidence of history shows that treaties are much more honoured in the breach than in the observance. Germany's violation of Belgian neutrality is not, after all, very much removed from the English violation of Danish neutrality at the hand of the great Nelson.

Similarly, the cruelty and havoc wreaked on Belgium and northern France by the invading German troops are not by any means examples of a peculiarly German 'barbarity'. Such things are of very common occurrence whenever human animals take turns in tearing each other to pieces. At all times and among all peoples this has been so. Everywhere and everlastingly human beings brutally ill-treat, slaughter and destroy their kind. When they cannot behave thus to men of their own race, they mete out this treatment to men of what they call 'inferior' races. When they cannot vent their ferocity in foreign wars, they commit ghastly cruelties in civil wars. One notes with a certain wry amusement that it was General Sherman, a fellow countryman, no less, of Woodrow Wilson's, who recommended that the civilian populations of enemy countries should be treated with extreme brutality.

Many writers, Herbert Spencer among them, hold up to derision those who, in such matters, see the mote in their neighbour's eye but do not perceive the beam in their own. But it is useless to press this point home because it is a waste of breath to use logico-experimental arguments with people who are swayed by their sentiments. The proofs for this are legion; it is impossible for us to bring forward even a mere fraction of them since to do no more than this would involve us in writing a sizeable part of the history of the human race.

In the unceasing succession of crimes, cruelties, barbarities, massacres and infamies recorded by history, and in which individuals, races and nations in course of time become by turns the tormentors and the victims, people with a theological inclination may see the hand of a god who punishes the individual for his wrongdoing, visits the sins of the fathers upon the children, and makes a whole community responsible for the transgressions of its individual members. This is a derivation 'in accord with supernatural entities', Class IIIf.* Those who are inclined to metaphysics

---

* See classification of derivations, *Treatise*, §1419, pp. 237–8 above.

may speak of the 'inherent justice of things' or of some similar entity. This would be a derivation 'in accord with metaphysical entities', Class IIIe. Those who delight in literary precepts may say with Aeschylus 'it is the law that the murdered victim's blood shed on the earth requires blood in retribution'. This is a derivation 'in accord with juridical entities', Class IIId. And so one could go on. But those who adhere to experience simply see in these things manifestations of human nature. With the passage of time, it is true, human nature tends to become milder, but it does so very slowly and with sudden reversions to primitive ferocity.

In the very copious literature incriminating and vindicating the various belligerents in the world war there are readily apparent many derivations of Class I (assertions of facts, assertions of sentiments, and mixtures of facts and sentiments). Extensive use is made of derivations involving metaphysical entities (Class IIIe). The cause of the Entente and its allies was sustained by Truth, Justice, Law, Humanity, Democracy. On the side of the Central Empires stood Vital Interests, the Great German Fatherland and Organisation, sustained by a theological entity (Class IIIf), the Good Old German God. To a lesser degree juridical entities (Class IIId) also made an appearance. Their classic manifestation is in the arguments advanced for bringing the former emperor of Germany to trial. The campaign to put him in the dock came to nothing when Holland refused to co-operate and thereby rescued the Allies in the nick of time from a very awkward situation. Derivations from authority (Class II) appear in the great quantity of written material in praise of the various powers. They lie at the heart of the *Manifesto of the German Intellectuals* and of the retorts which this provoked. Here we see a clear example of Class IIa derivations, those invoking the authority of one individual or a number of individuals.

To learn whether or not massacres of the civilian population in Belgium did occur, the evidence of eye-witnesses or at least of people who report eye-witness evidence is certainly worth a good deal more than any assertions by all the world's most sublime 'intellects'. What did the ninety-three very learned 'intellectuals' who signed the German Manifesto know about what took place in Belgium? They were not there to see what was happening. A professor of theology may fittingly deal with theological matters; a professor of Scandinavian philology may properly instruct us in Nordic literature; a professor of chemistry can teach us how chemical bodies combine; and so on and so forth. But pray let these very excellent people spare us the time-wasting tedium of testifying to us of matters about which they are totally ignorant or dependent solely on hearsay. It is by sheer divine or metaphysical inspiration that they declare: 'It is not true that our soldiers have raised their hands against the life or property of a single Belgian citizen [*note the certainty of their knowledge: not even one!*]) without having been constrained by the hard necessity of legitimate defence. For, in spite of our warnings, the population has not refrained from treacherously firing on our troops, from mutilating the wounded and butchering doctors in the exercise of their humane profession.'

Derivations such as these, it is evident, can be accepted only on the authority of those who produce them or because they accord with the sentiments of those to whom they are addressed; that is to say, they are chiefly derivations of Class IIa (authority of individuals) and secondarily of Class IIIa (accord with sentiments).

In the reply given by the Allies, June 16, 1919, to the representations of the German government [seeking to modify the Versailles peace terms], there is a veritable firework display of derivations. Germany must be punished because its rulers 'have by all the means in their power conditioned the minds of their people to the doctrine that, in international affairs, Might is Right'. Metaphysical warfare has broken out. There is a doctrine about the relationship of 'force' and 'law' which is orthodox and another doctrine which is heretical and must be put down by the Holy Inquisition into heretical pravity, seconded by the secular arm. Logically, not only Germany but all the writers professing the perverse doctrine should be hunted down and punished, and their works burned by the public executioner.

Every religion has its mysteries. A very significant mystique appears in President Wilson's speech of April 6, 1918*: 'Let everything we say, my fellow countrymen, everything that we henceforth plan and accomplish, ring true to this response till the majesty and might of our concerted power shall fill the thought and utterly defeat the force of those who flout and misprize what we call honor and hold dear. Germany has once more said that force, and force alone, shall decide whether Justice and Peace shall reign in the affairs of men, whether Right as America conceives it or Dominion as she conceives it shall determine the destiny of mankind. There is, therefore, but one response possible from us. Force, Force to the utmost, Force without stint or limit, the righteous and triumphant Force which shall make Right the law of the world, and cast every selfish dominion down in the dust.'

Here we see appear a new entity, Selfishness, which had not hitherto been alluded to. The contradiction between calling perverse the doctrine that force produces right, and praiseworthy the doctrine that force must impose right—this passes unnoticed for the simple reason that, in the logic of sentiment, two contradictory propositions can subsist together. Derivations of accord with sentiments are such that the self-same proposition, if advanced by one's enemies, is reckoned perverse, and if by one's friends, then praiseworthy.

There might perhaps be a way of removing the contradiction by having recourse to a derivation of metaphysical entities (Class IIIe) or of theological entities (Class IIIf). Let us suppose for the sake of argument that there is an absolute entity, or indeed a god, called Right. It is heretical to maintain that this deity is *created by might*, but orthodox to assert that might has been *created by the deity* for whom it is natural to employ it in imposing his doctrine. It would be blasphemous to say that the god of the mussulman was the creation of the might of the Arabs, but pious to say that the Arab god created Arab might and then availed himself of this might to impose his faith. Whosoever believeth this not, let him be put to the sword.

---

* This was Wilson's speech at Baltimore in which he condemned Germany's peace treaties with Russia and Rumania and took up the German challenge of force.

Addressing the workers of the Creusot factor, M. Thomas—then under-secretary of state for Munitions, today head of the International Labour Office at Geneva, and at all times a socialist—said (August 24, 1915): 'We speak of victory because we have gained, in our unremitting effort, the certitude of victory. We had this certitude from the beginning since we are the upholders of Right. But when we see the increase of the material means . . . who then can still doubt it?' It would seem that this worthy personnage, Right, is a *quid simile* of the Zeus of the *Iliad*—only it is not told us if this Right confirms the promise of victory by a nod of the head whereat all Olympus trembles.

There was great play made of derivations to put up a case for that juridical monster, the projected trial of the former emperor of Germany: a trial in which the accuser was to be the judge, conducting the case, passing sentence and, in the absence of any competent law, being guided solely by sentiment. A rich example of such derivations is the assertion that such a trial would have the effect of preventing future wars because those contemplating starting them would be deterred by the threat of being sentenced to death by a similar trial. As if the possibility of a 'war crimes' trial were the only risk to life in warfare, and as if such a risk had ever deterred any prominent man from taking part in wars, rebellions and struggles for power! Only derivations by accord of sentiments can blind people to this. As proof we would have to invoke the testimony of the whole of human history. But really, such derivations cannot be taken seriously. The only appropriate answer to them is a mocking smile.

In the use of derivations, none of the belligerents can claim more credit than the others. We find a Germanophile, Konrad Falke, writing thus in the *Journal de Génève*, June 2/3, 1915: 'When in the opposite camp they speak of brutal "policy of expansion", we on the other hand see in this a cruel necessity [*a*]. Such powerful growth and development [*as Germany's*] needs must lead to a nation's bursting its clothes at the seams [*b*]; society, instead of waxing indignant about it, would do better to accept tranquilly the need for a new tape-measure [*c*]. The present war is perhaps above all else the tragic struggle of a nation which, sword in hand, is constrained [*d*] to prove to the world its right [*e*] to exist.'

The following derivations appear clearly in this passage: (*a*) This is a derivation by verbal proofs, Class IVb (terms designating things and arousing incidental sentiments). The term *necessity* induces the sentiment that the will of the German people has no part in the war. The term *cruel* is a concession to opponents. (*b*) This is a classic example of Class IVd derivations (metaphors, allegories, analogies). It is an exact equivalent of the metaphor of the sun and the moon employed at the time of the investiture contest between the Papacy and the Holy Roman Emperors. . . . Germany's garments have become too small for it; other peoples must provide it with a more ample suit, and therefore permit themselves to be conquered by Germany. It is most unfortunate that the military tailor called in to make this refitting tightened instead of enlarging the German suit. According to its logic, Falke's metaphor has held good! (*c*) This also is a Class IVd derivation. Take away the derivation and there is here the simple concept that other states must submit to what Germany wills.

Derivations are useful for modifying the feelings which would arise from the naked and crude enunciations of this proposition. (*d*) This is a derivation similar to (*a*). By whom or what is Germany *constrained*? Is it some metaphysical or theological entity? And is it not possible that such an entity should *constrain* other nations to resist Germany? It is all verbose metaphysical drivel. (*e*) This is a derivation of Class IIIe (accord with metaphysical entities). This *Heilige Recht* has clearly nothing to do with that *Holy Right* which is the object of President Wilson's devotion. Since the latter got the better of the former, he is comparable with Zeus and Falke's deity with Poseidon. We can, moreover, say that one of these two Rights represents the principle of Good and the other the principle of Evil. So long as we do not specify which is which, we shall please everyone.

Let us note that Mr Falke in no way intends to imply that Might creates Right; in this he concurs with President Wilson. He desires only that might shall impose a right which is pre-existent. I regret there should be this agreement between the friend and the enemy of Germany since, because of this, there is much less reliability in the explanation I had devised for resolving the contradiction between Wilson's statements. And yet, Woodrow Wilson—doctor *honoris causa* of so many European universities, associate of so many eminent academies—cannot for certain be anything other than a scholar of the very first order. There must assuredly be therefore some way of removing this contradiction. But to the uninitiate it remains hidden, like the meaning of Dante's demon chorus in Canto VII of the *Inferno*: 'Papé Satan, papé Satan aleppe.'

II

Trasformazione della Democrazia (1921)

1. CONTINUITY OF SOCIAL MOVEMENTS

*(i) Human society as a perpetual 'becoming'**

The social order is never at perfect rest; it is in a perpetual state of becoming; but the speed of the movement varies. In antiquity the movement is detectable as much at Sparta as at Athens; in our own day it is at work in societies as diverse as China and England. The difference lies in the degree to which the motion is slow, as at Sparta or in China, or rapid, as at Athens or in England. Similar differences exist in a particular country at different times. For example, there has never been any pause in the movement in Italy from the legendary days of Romulus down to the present time, but its intensity is not constant from year to year.

It is easy to understand how a new era is signalled for the devout christian by the advent of Christ, for the mohammedan by the Hegira, for the believer in 'democratic' religions by the French Revolution of 1789, for the faithful adherents of one of the religions of the Third International by the revolution of Lenin, and so on. Nor does logico-experimental science make any contention over this, since there is involved here an argument of faith which wholly transcends the experimental field of enquiry. But those of us who keep within this field, studying events solely as facts and leaving aside the question of faith, very soon come to realise that these eras are new only in form and that essentially they are points corresponding to peaks in the continuous curve of perpetual social development. Arguing retrospectively, there was a christianity before Christ, a mohammedanism before Mohammed, a 'democracy' before the French Revolution, and a bolshevism before the revolution of Lenin.

---

* *Trasformazione*, pp. 11–12.

Looking at events in this way, putting oneself deliberately outside faith is useful and indeed indispensable for experimental science; and yet it can often be very harmful for creative action. Scepticism produces theory, faith stimulates activity, and it is creative action which constitutes practical life. Ideal aims can at one and the same time be absurd and highly useful for society. This point must be emphasised for it is easily ignored. Such a distinction between the utility of experimental science and social utility is fundamental. . . . *

(ii) *The impossibility of defining democracy†*

. . . Democracy is an imprecise term, like many other terms in current usage. Sir Henry Maine thought to avoid the difficulty arising from this by substituting for 'democracy' the term 'popular government', and made this the title of his principal work. But 'popular government' is no more precise as a term than 'democracy'. There is indeed no hope of devising a strict and precise term for something which is inherently indeterminate and transient.

There is in fact no sudden transformation from one set of circumstances to another, but rather a continuous mutation similar to that which time produces in living creatures. It is our purpose to study a stage in this continuous movement in society. Experimentally we have to place it not only in its own context but also in the context of social phenomena as a whole, otherwise we would run the risk of making a subjective evaluation of the sentiments aroused by a close-up view of this latest stage, and our enquiry would lack objectivity.

(iii) *The impossibility of fixing optima‡*

Since every social situation is the product of past situations and the origin of future situations, it follows that anyone wishing to make about it an absolute judgement of 'good' or 'bad' would have to know all future situations to infinity.§ This is not possible and therefore no such judgement can be made. We must abandon the absolute and resort to the contingent in order to define these terms 'good' and 'bad', investigating only the *proximate* effects of the social situation we are studying, and working within the limits indicated by this term *proximate*.

The proscriptions of the Roman triumvirate, the 'reign of terror' of the first French Revolution and of the bolshevists of our own day—are these 'good' or 'bad'? Sentiment and faith and the reasoning which proceeds

---

* Cf. *Systèmes*, p. 128 above; *Manuel*, p. 150 above; and *Treatise*, §§401 and 843–4, pp. 207, 216 above.

† *Trasformazione*, p. 6.   ‡ *Trasformazione*, pp. 14–19.

§ Pareto here refers to *Treatise* §§2238, 2548, B-2. The point in question—his differentiating between the form and the substance of political systems—is discussed at §2239 *et seq.*, p. 265 above. Note: in these extracts from the *Trasformazione*, Pareto's references to sections of the *Treatise* which are included in Part Two of this volume are given in footnotes; his references to sections not included are given in square brackets in the text.

from *a priori* metaphysical concepts and the like can make shift to answer this question: pure logico-experimental science cannot.

There is a faint notion of the interdependence of diverse phenomena in Clemenceau's statement that the French Revolution must be considered as a whole, 'en bloc'; i.e., whoever accepts a part must accept the whole. Now here the difference between derivations and scientific methods of reasoning becomes apparent for, to be logical, Clemenceau would have to extend this principle to include the present Russian Revolution. But instead he dispenses with it without giving any reasons. He does not consider the Russian Revolution 'en bloc'; he condemns it for its *terror*, while refusing to condemn the French Revolution on the same grounds.

This is a particular example of something which is of very general relevance. Little that is truly new can be said of social facts which recur in all periods, since they cannot fail in the end to have made some sort of impression on intelligent observers, and the difference between this impression and a scientific evaluation is simply that of a closer approximation to experimental truth. Thus, an uninformed man's impressions about 'fat' and 'thin', fertile and barren soils will differ from those of a chemist who knows something the other does not know, namely, the constituent elements of the two types of soil called respectively 'fat' and 'thin'. The chemist's use of these terms is to be accepted as exact; the ignorant man's is devoid of precision and hence is to be rejected by all strictly scientific reasoning. It would therefore be a monstrous stupidity to deny the progress made by chemistry or to say that the chemist is plagiarising the ignorant man. But this in fact is the shape and size of the observations of those worthy people who assert that every new theory is to be found in the works of past authors, going so far as to discern the theories of Darwin in the works of Aristotle.

In the context of economics, there is a concept of oscillations in the biblical account of the seven fat and seven lean kine, just as there is in Clément Juglar's work on economic crises. But Juglar and *Genesis* have different approximations to reality. The same observation can be made, in the social context, about the metaphysical theory of Vico, the theory of Ferrari and the modern theory of logico-experimental science.*

Close study of the facts reveals something of high importance, i.e., that 'oscillations of the various elements in social phenomena are interdependent, like the elements themselves, and are simply manifestations of changes in these elements. . . . These oscillations are of various kinds according to the time they take in their fulfilment. It may be very brief, brief, long or very long.'† We shall therefore have to investigate whether the transformation we are witnessing today belongs to the category of brief, incidental oscillations, or whether it indicates a mean movement or a movement of long duration.‡

A further conclusion, justifying the argument we are advancing about optima, is that the search for the 'optimum government' is vain and

---

* Pareto here refers to *Treatise* §2330. See p. 279 above for his discussion of incomplete notions of the oscillatory movements of social phenomena.

† *Treatise*, §2338, p. 281 above.   ‡ *Treatise*, §1718, p. 243 above.

chimerical, not only because of the imprecision of the term 'optimum' [*T.*, §2110], but because in addition it envisages the possibility of something which is quite impossible: the cessation or suspension of movement in that state said to be 'the best'. . . .

If we study the many theories expounded in the last century about parliamentary and constitutional states, we shall be struck by the fact that none of them has any relevance to what is taking place at the present time. They go one way: current events move in quite a different direction. For example, if we read John Stuart Mill's *Representative Government* and *Liberty*—books which at one time enjoyed an enormous reputation—we find ourselves breathing the intellectual atmosphere of a society which has no relation at all with contemporary English society, and which indeed now seems altogether unreal. Who bothers any more about the 'balance of powers' in society, or about the 'just' balance between the 'rights' of the state and the 'rights' of the individual? Is the highly revered *ethical state* still with us? The *hegelian state* is certainly a beautiful vision, kept alive for the use and benefit of poetic and metaphysical sociologists; but the workers prefer the tangible benefits of higher wages, progressive taxation and greater leisure—a preference they exercise while freely entertaining myths of their own: the myth of the holy proletariat, the myth of the inherent evil of the capitalist system [*T.*, §1890], the myth of an ideal government under worker-soldier soviets, and so on.

(iv) *Accord between myths and sentiments**

Myths and prophecies are proliferating anew in our day. Peace and joy are infallibly to be achieved in the world, according to some, by the League of Nations, by the 'triumph of right and justice'—a few would add 'of liberty'. According to others these desirable things will be achieved by bolshevism. A good many people are certainly insincere in professing these beliefs, but very many others are genuinely moved by a living faith in them. However strange it may seem, there are large numbers of people who, even today with the onset of disillusionment, are convinced that the League of Nations is the panacea to cure all the world's ills. There are some—but not many, it must be admitted—who hold faithfully to the Fourteen Points of Woodrow Wilson: that great man who knew so much better than all other thinkers who have ever lived what are the fundamentals on which to base the *respublica optima*. Why should we be surprised at this? After all, there are still people among us who believe in magic—nay, it is rumoured that the Devil is still invoked; and look at the large following which Christian Science is attracting.

. . . When one asks if a measure or policy is 'good, just, fair, moral, religious, patriotic' etc., one is in fact enquiring if it is in accord with the sentiments of a given community at a given time—sentiments which generally lack precision. This sort of enquiry is useful if one wants to know the consensus of opinion in this community, but it is of little or no use if what is wanted is to know whether a particular measure or policy can be

---

* *Trasformazione*, pp. 19–21, 23.

given practical effect and, if so, what its economic and social consequences will be. It is of little use because the very fact of a concept's subsisting for a long time within a society demonstrates that it is compatible with the prevailing circumstances of that society, and hence it is highly probable that a measure or policy which is in accord with this concept will also be in accord with the prevailing social circumstances. [*T.*, §§1778, 2520.] It is wholly useless when the accord between proposal and concept is governed by that element in the concept—often a substantial element—which does not correspond to reality.

For example, it was of great help in predicting the attitude to the Crusades of firm believers in christianity to know if going to the East to free the Holy Sepulchre constituted a religious act; but it was no value at all for understanding the economic, political and social consequences of the Crusades. The baron who went campaigning in the Holy Land may well have been a first-rate christian (often enough he was simply a restless adventurer), but it is quite certain that he was a bad feudal lord since he was digging the grave of his own caste. The bourgeois of our own day who are so keen to wage war may well be first-rate patriots (there are also profiteers among them), but they are, in part, engineering the impending ruin of their class. . . . It may be 'just, laudable, desirable, morally necessary' that the workers should labour only a few hours each day and receive enormous salaries; but this is a problem of a wholly different order from that posed by the questions: is this in reality possible, that is, in terms of real, not merely nominal, wages? And what will be the consequence of this state of affairs?

2. COUNTERVAILING FORCES IN SOCIETY

(i) Residues as a psychological link with the past*

An institution or a social situation observable at a given time may be, but is not necessarily, a direct mutation of some other institution, some other social situation. As a general rule, evolution does not proceed in a straight line,† and the fact that there are certain elements in common between a given institution or situation and a previous institution or situation must not lead us to assume that the one descends directly from the other. In the classifications of birds and mammals, there are analogies between the raptors and the felines, but no one, not even the most extreme darwinian, has ever asserted that the felines descend from the raptors. The trade unions of our day have resemblances with the gilds of the Middle Ages, but any attempt by overenthusiastic devotees of evolutionary theory to argue that this resemblance indicates direct descent of the modern from the medieval institution would be resolutely rejected by those who pay closer attention to the facts of experience. . . .

In every human collectivity, there are two contradictory forces at work: a centripetal force operating in favour of the concentration of power at the centre, and a centrifugal force working towards the dispersal of the central

---

* *Trasformazione*, pp. 25, 31–4, 36.   † *Treatise*, §217, p. 187 above.

power. . . . In essence they are bound up, not only with some subclasses of Class IV residues (those connected with sociality), but also with that subclass of residues (Class II-a) which we have termed 'persistence of relations between a person and other persons and places'.

The following factors influence the relationship of centrifugal and centripetal forces in favour of the former: 1. An increase in the strength of residues (Class II-a) of family relationships and of kindred groups—even when these are independent of the family; 2. An increase in the strength of the residues (Class IV-a) of the need for particularist social groupings, which is often connected with economic conditions; 3. A diminution of the residues (Class IV-b) of the need for uniformity, which is very frequently connected with residues of sentiments termed 'religious'; 4. An overall increase in certain sentiments of hierarchy (Class IV-e) as opposed to others in this class. The effect of such factors is to weaken the centripetal tendency and strengthen the centrifugal.

We know that the movement of residues takes the form of an undulating curve. We can therefore predict that the effects produced by residues— the centrifugal and centripetal forces—will also take this form. The point of equilibrium of these two forces is in perpetual alternation, shifting now to one side, now to the other. This shift in the equilibrium follows no regular, identical pattern but varies from one period to another. Such oscillations are manifested in many and varied phenomena. One such, occurring in the Middle Ages in Europe, has come to be called the feudal period.

In France, this period is, properly speaking, a second and fuller oscillation, being preceded by a first and less extensive oscillation of the same kind. The power of the central authority under the earlier Merovingians had been considerable, but this had disintegrated by the time the Carolingian dynasty emerged. For a time, a strong central power was reconstituted under these monarchs, but under the later sovereigns of this dynasty it once again crumbled away, to be restored after a long passage of time in another form by the kings of France.

A general study of the history of different epochs and different countries reveals periods which have characteristics similar to those of medieval Europe. To these periods, by synecdoche, taking the part for the whole, the term 'feudal' has also been applied. Intelligent men noted that these periods had a rhythm of rise and fall; in other words, that they were dynamic phenomena—more precisely, oscillations. It is this which gives Vico's theory of 'recursals' (*ricorsi*) some consonance with reality. But he errs in giving identical forms to the various oscillations, and in certain particulars he is led into error by conjectures which trespass beyond the bounds of experimental enquiry.

. . . The phenomenon of feudalism in Europe has given rise to innumerable theories. I do not intend—far from it—to relate the history of these theories, not simply for reasons of space but because in any case to do so would be superfluous and of no value to the purpose of this present study. Even so it may be useful to cite examples which show how theories diverse in form have, in substance, something in common.

Montesquieu interprets the phenomenon in terms of that evolution in direct line which we have already referred to. In the peoples of ancient Germany he detects the origin of vassalage which ultimately, by successive transformations, produces the fief and the system of feudal tenure. Theories of this kind have continued to be elaborated up to the present day. They are held in special favour, naturally, by the Germans because people are always inclined to prefer the derivations which are most consonant with their sentiments. For the very same reason, adherents of the theory of direct evolution in France and other Latin countries seek the origin of feudalism, not in Germany, but in Roman society, detecting it—on very precarious evidence—in the *clientela*. What such theories in fact manifest is the need for particular social groups, and changes in the residues of sociality. This is particularly the case with Falch's theory which makes the 'clan' the origin of the feudal society of the eleventh and twelfth centuries.

We find similar theories being employed to explain the phenomenon of the modern trade unions. Some writers go as far back as the craft associations of imperial Rome; others, with rather more discretion, delve no deeper than the gilds or the journeymen's associations of the medieval period. Such theories are rightly refuted by the Webbs in their *History of Trade Unionism*.

(ii) Centripetal and centrifugal forces*

Shifts in the point of equilibrium of centripetal and centrifugal forces have the following characteristics. In periods when the point of equilibrium shifts in the direction of centrifugal force, the central power grows steadily weaker. It matters little whether the central power's form be monarchic, oligarchic, popular or of the masses. What is called its 'sovereignty' tends to become a term devoid of meaning; it disintegrates, littering the country with its ruins. As the central power declines, there is a corresponding growth in the power of certain individuals, certain collective bodies which, though still in theory subordinate to the central power, for all practical purposes achieve independence. As a result, those who do not come under these categories—the weak—find that they are no longer protected by the sovereign power; accordingly they seek elsewhere for protection and justice. They may swear fealty to some powerful man or band together, publicly or secretly, with other weak persons to form a corporate body, a commune, an association for protecting common interests.

Eventually this development turns against itself. As the situation evolves, 'protection' is transformed little by little into 'subjection'; this leads to an increase in the numbers of those hostile to the existing system, and also, if social and especially economic conditions are favourable, to an increase in their strength. On the other hand, there sets in a decline in the strength of the many and various participants in sovereignty: a decline which is attributable to the fact that, as their fear of the central power gradually diminishes, the rivalry amongst them grows greater. Their struggles with one another very easily break out into open conflicts, leading

---

* *Trasformazione*, pp. 41–57.

to anarchy, and these persist even when the central power begins to acquire new vigour.

The need of the weak for protection is constant and universal,* and seeks fulfilment at the hands of whoever possesses power. In a period when centrifugal forces prevail, this protection will be sought for at the hands of certain outstandingly powerful men: the great lords and magnates. When centripetal forces are dominant, the central government will be called on to provide it. Whenever circumstances turn in favour of this second, centripetal phase, a pre-existing central government, or a central authority new both in form and substance, asserts itself sooner or later. Either by sudden violence or by protracted effort it subdues the dominant oligarchy and sets about the task of concentrating all sovereignty in itself.

A remarkable thing about this transformation is that it is often promoted by one of the phenomena termed 'religious'. This can be observed in Europe towards the close of the medieval period; in Russia at the time of Ivan the Terrible; in Japan in the latter part of the nineteenth century; and in many other cases. This must not be regarded as fortuitous coincidence; on the contrary it is the natural consequence of the relationships revealed to us by experience, for the strengthening of religious sentiment is a manifestation of increased activity by the sentiments we have called persistence of aggregates—sentiments which are the cement of all human societies.

International conflicts likewise exert influence in a centripetal or a centrifugal direction. The military defeat of the central power in a society may bring about its fall and thereby promote centrifugal movements. Victory may have the opposite effect, but this is not invariably so. If victory is to a large measure the outcome of the efforts and sacrifices of the masses, the central power may be weakened. There was little likelihood of this happening when wars were waged by professional, limited armies. Alexander's successors were long able to engage in wars among themselves. Similarly, the Roman Empire managed to subsist in an almost continuous state of war, while the great monarchies of Europe for a considerable period could indulge the luxury of incessant wars which bled their peoples white. But it is quite otherwise with modern warfare. The recent world war flung whole peoples into battle and thereby dealt a powerful blow to the central power, as much in the victorious as in the defeated countries.

The world war, moreover, has had no small effect in accelerating an evolution which otherwise, though certain to occur, would have developed much more slowly. As a result of their failure to live in harmony, Russia on the one side, Germany and Austro-Hungary on the other—those 'conservative' empires which, united, would have been invincible—have come crashing to the ground and have been replaced by 'democratic' governments or the like. As a result of the discords provoked by excessive stupidity and of the consequent long drawn-out war, demagogic plutocracy as a political form and the entire bourgeois system are reeling under the impact. The ruling circles in the European bourgeoisie did not simply make use of the religion of imperialism: they abused it. If they had made peace in 1917,

---

* *Treatise*, §2180, p. 259 above.

they would have had good hopes of prolonging their lifespan; but on the one side there was a desire for total victory, and on the other a determination not to confess to being beaten. Thus the bourgeois ruling class will probably prove to have been the author of its own ruin. Its adversaries know well enough what they are about as they watch it struggling in vain to free itself from inextricable difficulties.

There are many examples of similar oscillations in the movement of the point of equilibrium between centripetal and centrigual forces. For example, studying the state of western Europe from 774 to 800, we find at the centre an indisputably preponderant power. Charlemagne imposes his authority not only on his lay subordinates but also on the church. No one in his vast empire dares to set up against him. But subsequently there is a rapid transformation, and when the last Carolingian emperor dies in 899 he leaves western Europe in a state of anarchy. It has taken scarcely a century for the effecting of a significant oscillation in the point of equilibrium between centripetal and centrifugal forces. Some hold that the Norman invasions were the 'cause' of the break-up of the Carolingian empire. But if this were so, how is it that the invasions of the Saracens—even more fearsome enemies—helped to bring about the establishment of that empire? In reality, the effects of external conflicts on an internal situation are conditioned by prevailing internal circumstances. They contribute to the effects of these circumstances but they are not of themselves the initial determining factor.

At the beginning of the nineteenth century, the point of balance in England is poised in the direction of centripetal force. Parliament at this time is truly sovereign. It would have been ludicrous to set up associations like our modern trade unions against its power, just as it would have appeared ridiculous for the power of the glorious Charlemagne to be opposed by the power of petty lords of the manor who were at that time the royal feudatories. More than a century has elapsed since the days of that omnipotent parliament which, as they used to say in England, could do everything except change a man into a woman; today parliament finds its power has been considerably diminished by slow erosion. It has been inherited by the trade unions which treat as equals with parliament and with its executive committee, the government. In a Commons debate on February 10, 1920, Lloyd George said:* 'The difficulties in the way of providing low-cost housing originate in the shortage of workers in the building industry and in the attitude of the trade unions which will not permit the employment of the 350,000 demobilised workers capable of taking on jobs in the building industry.' So these men need to have the permission of the trade unions in order to work. Will parliament protect their right to work? Not at all! Lloyd George goes on to say: 'It is the Labour party's responsibility to consider that the needs of a particular organisation must not be preferred to the needs of the nation.' Yet only a few years earlier he had been saying the opposite, holding that it was the

---

* Pareto's quotation is not a wholly accurate précis (probably based on a newspaper report) of Lloyd George's speech. Cf. Hansard, 5th Series, Vol. 125, Cols. 34–5.

responsibility of parliament, not of private associations, to ensure that private interests should not prevail over the general interest.

This sort of thing leads to very odd consequences. In Italy it is decreed that, in order to prevent exhaustion of the nation's livestock resources, the consumption of meat shall be strictly forbidden on Fridays and Saturdays. Condign punishment awaits any one destroying a beefsteak on these days. But if he happens to be a member of a trade union, he is allowed to destroy the entire animal with impunity. At the very moment when government was decreeing these hypocritical regulations, there was an outbreak of agricultural strikes. Under the benevolent paternal gaze of the public authorities, the strikers prevented the feeding and watering of livestock, going so far as to beat up owners of cattle who tried to give food and water to their animals, and at the same time preventing them from selling the cattle for consumption.

Charlemagne holds his subjects in direct dependence as king of the Franks and as emperor, and it is to him in this capacity that they swear fealty. Reviving and enlarging an earlier institution, he sends his *missi dominici* through the length and breadth of the empire 'to the end that they diligently enquire if any man complain of injustice done to him by others'. He ordains his emissaries to adhere unswervingly to this duty against 'flattery, reward, any ties of kinship whatever, or fear of the strong', In another capitulary we read: 'If perchance any bishop or count should neglect his proper function, he is to be corrected by the admonition of the *missi*; for let all men know that the charge of the *missi* is such that whosoever is unable to obtain justice, by negligence or unconcern or defect of power of the count, he may bring his complaint directly to them and by their help obtain justice; and if any man, induced by necessity, shall have recourse to Us, We may give them mandate to determine the matter.' The *missi dominici* are still in being under Charlemagne's successors, but their power and importance gradually diminish and in the end amount to nothing. Charles the Bald threatens to send forth officials to enforce his prohibition against the building of new castles; but this is an empty threat. More and increasingly stronger castles will go on being built. Petty local sovereignties are rising up out of the ruins of the central sovereignty.

We must be careful to avoid confusing the *de facto* situation with the *ideal* or *legal* situation, to use modern terminology. In France the *de facto* authority of the king disappears with the accession of Hugh Capet; the *ideal* authority continues in being, survives all the storms and buffetings of feudalism, and eventually serves to justify and strengthen the revival of the monarchy's *de facto* authority. According to very many theories, the relationship is the reverse of this; it is argued that it is the *ideal* authority which is the origin or 'cause' of the new *de facto* authority. But such theories are vitiated by the error of seeking *a priori* explanations of facts by ideas. Experience, on the contrary, teaches us that it is much more usual for ideas to be the consequences of facts.

The progress of feudalism is somewhat similar to the progress of trade unionism in our day. . . . In studying what is taking place under our eyes in respect to trade unions, we can gain a better understanding of the more remote and less well documented phenomenon of feudalism. Similarly, such limited information as we have of the older phenomenon has some usefulness in helping us to get a clearer concept of the modern phenomenon.

Subject to the proviso that the substitution of discontinuous for continuous transformation is admissible only for the purpose of making it easier to present the matter clearly, we may accept the divisions which the Webbs have made in the history of trade unionism. These are as follows: 1799 to 1825: the struggle for existence; 1829 to 1842: the revolutionary period; 1843 to 1860: the new spirit and new model of trade unionism; 1860 to 1875: the Junta and its allies; 1875 to 1889: the old and the new unionism; 1892 to 1894: trade unionism 'arrives'. This last period, it should be noted, continues up to the start of the world war. After this war a new period opens up which may be called the era of the triumph of trade unionism. At all events, its progress is definite and considerable and is, moreover, not confined to England but is generally observable in other countries. In respect to the central power, we have reached a point at which a dichotomy is becoming more and more acute between the form and the reality of the prevailing system.

Fustel de Coulanges has confuted the theory which argues that the Articles of Kiersy of 877 should be considered as the starting point of the feudal society. His treatment of the evidence seems valid for the transformation-point of the *ideal* situation, but not for the transformation-point of the *de facto* situation. He himself recognises this when he says:* 'Now that our analysis has given to the Articles of Kiersy their true meaning, it behoves us to see if, as sometimes is the case, they may not have had a larger and more general significance than their author intended to give them. Let us note first the usages and practices contained in them. We shall not speak of Article 1, which indicates the great position which the church has made for itself in the state. This does not, in any case, represent an innovation.' (*What applies here to the church now applies in our day to socialism, especially to 'transformist' socialism.*) 'Nor shall we say anything further about certain articles like 2 and 5 and 18 to 22, in which Charles the Bald, albeit using the language of masterful authority, clearly shows how fearful he is of not being obeyed.' (*Similarly our parliaments and governments issue laws and decrees in the full knowledge that the trade unions will give them little or no obedience. For example, public employees are forbidden to strike, but trade unions pay no attention whatever to this prohibition. . . . Ordinances and laws are made for the protection of private property, and trade unions are then allowed to violate them. Like the man who, when he fell off his horse, exclaimed, 'It was my intention to dismount', governments and parliaments put their heads together to devise a legal or pseudo-legal form for the ensuing usurpation.*) 'We shall not insist on Article 18, in which the king finds it necessary to remind the counts that they are functionaries'—(*This is exactly what our governments say to the railway workers, who pay even less attention to them than the magnates of Charles the Bald did to the admonitions of their monarch*)—'and speaks of their duties as administrators and judges as if they had forgotten these duties. It seems that even the *missi* themselves were neglecting their specific duties.' (*And what then of our*

---

* *Nouvelles recherches sur quelques problèmes d'histoire*, 1891, pp. 473–5.

magistrates?) 'Article 4 and the reply the magnates make to it merit special attention. Here the king and his faithful subjects are seen entering into engagements with one another.' (*This is precisely what is involved nowadays in the treaties of peace between governments and powerful trade unions, like the Miners' Union in England and the railway unions almost everywhere.*)

There is a further analogy with our contemporary situation: 'The king still pronounces the word "obedience", but it is transparent that what is involved here is no longer that general, obligatory obedience, superior to will and inclination, which is owed to the king by the subjects in a monarchical state. Obedience here is simply the obedience a man owes to somebody to whom he has promised it.' . . . 'The fascinating thing here is the simplicity with which these ideas are expressed as generally received, commonplace, natural and incontestable verities.'

Similarly today it seems a natural thing for trade unions to treat with the government as equals—something about which there is no dispute. The railway workers, employed and paid by the state, refuse to carry by rail the state's property: soldiers and policemen. There appears here the concept— if not the fully established fact—of a state of affairs analogous to the medieval system of *immunities*. The railway workers are taking the view, albeit not yet very precisely formulated, that the power of the central government stops short at the frontiers of their own domain: the domain of railway transportation. Ideas of more or less the same sort are making headway in the thinking of other trade unions.

A sure index of the disintegration of the central power is the ability of groups and individuals to remove themselves from the protection of its justice and from the concurrent obligation of submitting to its enforcement of justice. In this respect also the *de facto* situation precedes the *ideal, legal* situation into which it is transformed only gradually. At the present time we are witnessing such a transformation. Trade union *immunity* has not yet attained precisely the same degree of immunity which ecclesiastical and lay bodies obtained under the Carolingians, but it is taking shape little by little. In many cases—the number and importance of which are daily on the increase—the trade unions are challenging the assumption that laws and regulations are to be obeyed; and in this they have the support of a substantial body of public opinion.

If the state were brought to annul such laws and regulations, there would then be scope for a way of dealing with the situation which would, in form at least, have regard for the central power. But if the latter continues on the present course of letting its own decisions go by the board, it can only destroy—in form as well as in substance—the foundations of its sovereignty. The 'solidarity' and 'sympathy' strikes indicate that against the sovereignty of the central power there is arising a league of lesser particular sovereignties which aim at independence.

Any occurrence, often of little or no importance in itself, is capable of providing an opportunity for the resistance and offensive action of trade unions, singly or in alliance with one another. For example, in France—in conformity with a provision in the railway regulations—an employee of the Paris-Lyons-Mediterranean line was, in February 1920, suspended from work for two days because he took time off without permission. This was enough for the railway unions to decide on and put into effect a general strike of railway workers. In such cases an intention to implement laws and regulations is called 'violation of trade union liberties'; it is exactly akin to the violation of a medieval 'immunity'.

There is observable a tendency for trade union privilege not to be limited to conflicts with employers, but for it to be extended to conflicts between trade unionists and other workers who do not belong to a union. These latter are dragged into the privileged jurisdiction of the trade unions; if the central power resists, strike action is threatened and taken. Under the feudal system, the vassal was not entirely outside the king's justice. Certainly, he had to make his way up through the feudal hierarchy, but in the end justice could be had of the king. The immediate lord could not refuse to give justice or to present the vassal to the justice of the superior lord. Perhaps there will one day be a similar provision in the law affecting trade unions; at the present time it does not exist.

The emergence and development of the present anarchic system has a consequence which has so far not received much attention, although there is enough evidence for it. If the movement already begun proceeds further, conflicts between the various trade unions will become more numerous and considerable. There will be a struggle not only between workers' organisations and the rest of the population, but also between the different categories of trade unions. A similar phenomenon occurred in the Middle Ages when conflicts broke out among those who had divided the spoils of the central power. So long as the central power remained a force to be reckoned with, its rivals held together in unity, or at least kept their disunity within bounds, for their common advantage. The predominant concern of the magnates under the Carolingians was to liberate themselves from imperial or regal power; for the trade unions of the present day, the main concern is to prevail over the authority of parliaments and over the interests of the rest of the population. On January 27, 1920, at a meeting of the International Labour Office, M. Jouhaux—retorting to M. Guerin's statement that the competence of parliaments remained intact—said that the international labour organisation was an economic parliament of a superior order, the decisions of which were only to be ratified by the various states.

As the central power gradually weakens, signs of rivalry among its opponents increase. Private wars ensued between the feudatories of the Capetian monarchs; and so will trade unions in the future engage in struggle with one another. Signs of this future development can be seen in the outbursts of physical violence between organised workers and black-legs, between Reds and Yellows, Reds and Whites—I almost wrote Guelphs and Ghibellines. And all these conflicts are taking place under the benign gaze of the central power, just as at one time the private wars of the barons were waged under the eye of the king.

(iii) Reconstruction of the central power and intellectual revaluation*

It is in the interests of the dominant groups and individuals in a society to hide the fact that their privileges weigh heavily on the rest of the population.

---

* *Trasformazione*, pp. 59–61, 67–70.

They have willing adulators who assert that the weight falls only on the 'rich'. But this error is eventually exposed by the facts. In any case, all theories apart, those who have to pay the price for these privileges will incline to rebellion; nor will they give much heed to the honeyed words, the sugary mincing homilies of those greasy characters who, consciously invoking tolstoyan theories, go around exhorting the people not to struggle against 'new times' but to resign themselves to the 'inevitable', to accept the gospel of the 'divine proletariat', of the 'sacrosanct toilers', to 'submit to change in order to avoid being destroyed'—which is as much as to say 'commit suicide to avoid being murdered.' All this may have some influence on a weak-kneed and stupid bourgeoisie, degenerate like all decadent elites, but it will make little headway with the energetic men of the new elite—for example, the adherents of a leader like Lenin.

When inter-union conflicts and struggles between the various sections of society begin to increase in number and intensity, they will have to be resolved if society is not to break up in anarchy. Attempts to tackle this problem have so far availed very little because, as experience shows, it is generally only in practical terms—not in a prevenient theory—that a solution can be found for such problems. The theory of parliamentary government in England did not precede, it followed, practice and was modified gradually as the system was transformed. Similarly it was not abstract and desired theories but practical acts—often unrelated to theory—which transformed parliamentary government of the type established by the Albertine Statute in Piedmont into the present system of government in Italy. There is no reason for believing that, where similar developments are concerned, the future will differ from the past. Moreover, it will not suffice, as some think, to look for a solution to the problems of the present situation regarding trade unions in the replacement of present-day parliaments by assemblies of trade union delegates. This would provide merely the form, not the substance of a solution.

The theory that our parliaments represent the complex of the nation is a pure fiction. In reality they represent only that part of the nation which is dominant over the others, either by the arts of the fox when the prevailing situation accords with the first stage of demagogic plutocracy, or by sheer weight of numbers when the second stage is in full vigour. The old maxim, which lies at the heart of the parliamentary system, that taxes are to be subject to the approval of those who have to pay them, has now given way, implicitly or explicitly, to another maxim: taxes are to be approved and imposed by those who do not pay them. Once upon a time, it was the serfs who were mercilessly oppressed; now it is the well-to-do. In the past, the underdogs of the feudal system had to provide the wherewithal for meeting the costs of the bellicose follies of their masters; today this is the function of the people of independent means. At one time, the emigration of serfs from their native manor was strictly forbidden; in our day there is a similar restriction on the free movement of 'capital'. Within a single generation there have been significant oscillations in this particular segment of the social circle. Before the world war, the Italian government was seriously considering inhibiting the emigration of workers on the grounds that it was proving disadvantageous to the 'capitalists'. Today the object of official concern is to prevent the exportation of 'capital', for this, it is said, is proving harmful to the interests of the workers. Depretis* despatched troops to fire on the crowd to protect landowners in their struggles with agrarian strikers. Today it is to these latter that the protection of our governments is extended, even when the strikers use force to prevent the gathering in of the harvest which they intend to let rot so as to bring pressure to bear on the landowners. Yet from the days of Depretis to our own, theory and legislation have remained unchanged. In the universities they still continue to teach the theory which was being taught in the days of Depretis, and one would search the statute book in vain for a single legislative act sanctioning the changes which have occurred in practice. . . .

Outstanding among the forces working in favour of the central power there are—in practical terms—the interests of the plutocrats, and—in terms of ideas—the religion of the state, with its myths and its theology. This latter is a common feature of two schools of thought, otherwise poles apart: the school of nationalism or imperialism, and the school of marxist or 'classical' socialism which is opposed to 'anarchy', to free competition and to syndicalism. At the present time there is a weakening in the strength of both of these political tendencies. The first is affected by post-war disillusionment. Had the war ended earlier, the nationalists would have emerged from it with a greatly increased influence. But they damaged their cause by prolonging the conflict to the bitter end. As for the strict school of socialism: its adherents have lost ground in the domain of ideas by associating themselves, for an ephemeral political advantage, with the 'democrats', co-operating with them under a variety of patriotic pretexts not only in the conduct of the war but also in the formation of governments. Even so, although at the moment the forces of these two sections are not very effective in promoting the strength of the central power, the day may well come when, with a swing back to centripetalism, these forces—or let us rather say the successors of the present-day nationalists and marxists—will exert a notable and effective influence.

A similar alternation of circumstance is observable in the growth and then the decline of feudalism. For example, marxist idealism's loss of credit at the present time has some analogy with what befell the imperialist doctrine of Charlemagne's *proceres* after the death of the great emperor. Likewise the Third International's supersession of the First and the Second is not without some points of similarity with feudalism's supersession of Carolingian imperialism. But just as imperialism eventually re-emerged in the form of the doctrine of regal authority, so it may well be that classical socialism will come to the fore again—albeit in another shape—when syndicalism or something of the same kind suffers a decline.

The catholic faith endorsed the doctrine of regal authority; the humanitarian faith sustained socialism and will perform the same service for the party into which socialism is eventually transformed. Our judgement of the political activities and influence of the church in the medieval period must not be based on its theology, on the derivations of orthodoxy

---

* The leading figure in 'transformist' governments in Italy between 1876 and his death in 1887.

or heresy, nor yet on the conduct of its prelates. Equally, classical socialism does not stand or fall in virtue of its theories or the inordinate greed of social democracy. Faith is one thing: priests another. In regard to derivations, there is not a great deal of difference between the mystery of the Holy Trinity and Marx's theory of surplus value; between loathing of the Great Enemy of mankind and loathing of capitalism. In regard to substance, medieval theocracy's aim was to get control of the central power, but by no means to destroy it; indeed, albeit without deliberate intention, it promoted the central power. Classical socialism also aims at getting control of the central power, which it intends to use so as to control economic life in its entirety. It is firmly opposed to the 'anarchy of capitalist production', nor does it look with any greater favour on the anarchy of syndicalist production.

If practical implementation could be given to the utterly puerile notion that the manual labourer is the only real factor in production (and to think it could is an absurd hypothesis), the effects would be directly contrary to those desired by the enemies of the intellect and by the worshippers of the Holy Proletariat, for the simple reason that, as they became rarer, so would intellectuals become more highly prized, necessary, indispensable and powerful. This was the main reason for the power of the medieval priesthood. The feudal gentry, worthy precursors of our modern despisers of intellect, prided themselves on not even knowing how to write their own names. The power of the church declined with the increase of educated laymen, especially when lay culture diverged from established theology, the character of which is not so dissimilar from modern proletarian theology. . . .

3. THE PLUTOCRATIC CYCLE

(i) Elements composing demagogic plutocracy*

If we consider the economic and social development which has occurred in our society over the last hundred years, and endeavour to distinguish the mean trend from various disturbing secondary factors, we shall recognise the following characteristics:

1. A very large increase in wealth and savings and in the capital engaged in production.

2. An unequal distribution of this wealth. Some people try to make out that this inequality has increased; others contend that it has diminished. Probably the norm of distribution has remained about the same.

3. The ever-growing importance of two social classes: rich speculators, and those whom we may generally term 'workers'. This period appears notable for the growth and flourishing vigour of 'plutocracy' if particular consideration is given to the first of these two phenomena. If emphasis is placed on the second, then the period can be seen as marking the growth and flourishing of 'democracy'. Of course, we are here using the terms

---

* *Trasformazione*, pp. 73–7.

'plutocracy' and 'democracy' in the rather vague sense they have as employed in everyday speech.

4. A partial alliance between these two elements; this is especially noticeable from the end of the nineteenth century and up to the present day. Although as a general rule speculators and workers do not altogether share common interests, it nevertheless happens that some among both groups find it profitable to travel in the same direction, with the object of getting the upper hand over the state and of exploiting other social classes. At times the plutocrats are able to achieve this kind of alliance by cunningly playing on the sentiments (residues) of the masses, thereby pulling the wool over their eyes. Herein lies the origin of the phenomenon which ordinary people and empirical observers identify by the name of 'demagogic plutocracy'.

5. While the power of the two forementioned classes increases, there is a decline of the power of two others: (a) the rich propertied class, or simply the well-to-do who are not speculators; and (b) the military class. The power of the latter has now indeed been reduced to very small dimensions. Before the 1914–18 war one would have had to make an exception in the case of Germany, for until then the power of the military was still very considerable there. But this is no longer the case. A clear sign of the strength and prevalence of this phenomenon is the ever-increasing extension of the suffrage from the 'haves' to the 'have-nots'. It must be noted that among the 'haves' there are many who are not speculators, while among the 'have-nots' there are some who share common interests with the speculators, and yet others whose sentiments (residues) the speculators can make use of. Hence it is of advantage to the speculators—an advantage which they have frequently seized—to weaken the power of the 'haves' and increase that of the 'have-nots'.

6. Slowly but surely the use of force passes from the upper to the lower classes. This characteristic forms, with the following factor, one of the features of the disintegration of the central power.

7. The modern parliamentary system, to all intents and purposes, is the effective instrument of demagogic plutocracy. Through elections and then through political transactions in parliament, considerable scope is given to the activities of individuals who are well endowed with instincts of combination. Indeed it now seems clear that the modern parliamentary system is to a great extent bound up with the fate of plutocracy—prospering with it, declining with it. Transformations of the parliamentary system —which can also be termed transformations of democracy—closely follow the vicissitudes of plutocracy.

What is now occurring in our society is in no way unique. To understand them correctly, the main features of the present situation need to be placed in their proper historical context. We must resist the tendency to give exaggerated and exclusive importance to what is happening under our eyes, disconnecting it from the evidence of past history. Equally we must avoid the opposite error of purporting to see in the present situation a faithful and exact reduplication of the past. Movements recorded by history which have points of similarity with present developments do not tend uniformly in the same direction; they fluctuate now in one direction, now in another. None the less, we can perceive in them a general trend, a basic line of development discernible amid the various fluctuations. These undulations in the general line of movement result from the very nature of human beings who, where government is concerned, are regulated in the main by two agencies: consent and force.* The social system oscillates between these two poles.

Consent is achieved by means of subsidiary agencies; 'identity of interest' is one such, and another derives from religious sentiments, customs, prejudices and so forth, corresponding to the residues which in the *Treatise* we have termed residues of aggregate-persistence (Class II). Persuasion is often employed in the operation of these agencies; sometimes genuine sound reasoning is used, but much more often sophistries (derivations) are deployed, corresponding to the residues we have classified under the term of instinct of combinations (Class I).

We have to bear in mind the different roles played in matters of government by two major groups of citizens. One group consists of farmers and owners of landed property; the other consists of merchants, industrialists, public works contractors, financial operators, 'speculators' and the like. The tendency of the first category is almost invariably in the direction of reinforcing the persistence of aggregates, while that of the second fosters the instinct of combinations. The prevalence of one or the other gives rise to markedly different types of society. When the first is dominant, its own inherent qualities may serve to maintain it. The predominance of the second category usually produces plutocratic societies and therefore, since plutocracy is deficient in inherent strength, the end-result is almost inevitably demagogic or military plutocracy. . . .

The readiness to use force and the preference for obtaining consent are manifestations not only of distinct but also of conflicting attitudes. Exceptional individuals may possibly possess both attitudes in equal measure, but in the majority of men within the governing class one or the other attitude predominates; and we find that the circulation between the various social classes is very closely linked with the oscillations in the social order.

As is the case with living creatures, every type of society contains within itself the seeds of its florescence and its eventual decay; the major oscillations correspond to these periods of rise and fall in societies. . . . †

---

* *Treatise*, §2251, p. 267 above.

† Pareto refers here to *Treatise* §2541: Many historians of the Roman Republic 'consider it axiomatic that its decline must have had a "cause" and that all that is necessary is to seek for this "cause" in the actions of the men of the period. It is assumed that the "cause" of the decline must be essentially different from the "cause" of the vigour of the Republic, contrary conditions necessarily having contrary causes. They never entertain the idea that successive circumstances, although with opposite characteristics, have a common "cause", an identical origin. If the term "cause" is used in this sense, then one can just as well say that, in respect to the individual, life is the "cause" of death since the latter indisputably follows on the former; and that, in respect to the species, death is the "cause" of life for, so long as the species endures, the death of certain individuals is followed by the life of other individuals. Just as birth can be called the "cause" or common origin both of life and death, so

(ii) The end of the plutocratic cycle*

Modern Italy was established by the bourgeoisie against the indifference and at times the opposition of the agrarian masses. The new regime soon turned into a demagogic plutocracy which reached the height of its power at the time of Depretis and a little after. As might be expected, it is now suffering from the consequences of the war, but it is far from being overcome.

Demagogic plutocracy now seems in general to be wholly triumphant. In England it may well be able to hold its own for a long time to come, thanks to the benefits accruing from the hegemony England has created and to which all other countries, America only excepted, now willy nilly submit. Rome exploited merely the Mediterranean basin: England is exploiting vast areas of the world's surface. It remains to be seen whether effective forces within England will arise against its demagogic plutocracy, or whether military plutocracy in other countries will emerge and challenge England's hegemony. It also remains to be seen what part will be played in the future by those two unknown quantities: Russia and Asia.

Plutocracy is in much greater danger in other European countries; but at all times and in all countries it is rich in expedients for turning to its own advantage circumstances which on the face of it seem to be overwhelmingly unfavourable. To all appearances plutocracy gives way to hostile forces. But it does so with the set purpose of regaining by devious means what it has had to abandon to force, outflanking the obstacle which cannot be overcome by frontal attack—and, in conformity with its general rule, passing on payment of the bill of the conflict to the savers and investors: those meek sheep who lend themselves so readily to fleecing. It has by now devised innumerable expedients: vast public debts which it knows very well cannot in the end be honoured; capital levies; taxes which sap and exhaust the incomes of the ordinary, non-speculating investor; sumptuary laws, proved ineffective time and time again in the past—all these and many other devices of the same sort are employed with the set purpose of gulling the masses.

In Italy, Signor Falcioni's proposed legislation for dealing with the large landed estates and for granting land to the peasants will prove no more harmful to the interests of our plutocrats than were, after a brief period of storm and stress, the agrarian laws of the Gracchi to the interests of the Roman plutocracy. Our plutocrats stand to suffer much more harm from the proposal, if it is implemented, of the 'populists' who are aiming at increasing the numbers of small proprietors, for this group in the agrarian class is the sole adversary plutocracy need fear.

As long as the increment from savings is not too severely curtailed, as

---

certain social facts can be called the "cause" or common origin first of the florescence and then of the decay of a given society, and *vice versa*. This observation should not be taken as valid for all facts and all circumstances, but simply as applicable to some situations. Our only purpose in making it is to emphasise that the answer to the problem must be sought for, not in any axiomatic solution, but solely in experimental investigation.'

* *Trasformazione*, pp. 83–6.

long as food-prices and rents are kept low, and provided there are on tap all the other benefits which the plutocracy can make available to its supporters and dependants, there is nothing in the present state of affairs to prevent the plutocrats from continuing to make fat profits, just as the general prosperity of the Roman plutocracy was in no way jeopardised by the corn doles and the annonary laws introduced under the Republic, maintained and then extended under the Empire. This similarity between the conditions prevailing and the measures taken in ancient Rome and the conditions and measures obtaining in our own society derives from the intrinsic nature of things. As it was and is, so will it continue to be in the future. In the decadence of the Roman plutocracy we discern what could very well be, to some degree at least, the image of the decadence which is threatening our own plutocracy.

It is certain that we have now reached a point where there are close parallels with the situation of the Roman plutocracy towards the end of the Republic. By analogy with cycles observed in other periods and in other countries, it is probable—highly probable—that, being close to the peak, we are close also to the downward slope. Realisation of this does not of itself amount to much and we would not want to know far more about it. Yet something, however small, is better than nothing, and a limited knowledge now does not preclude—on the contrary, it lays the foundation for—a fuller knowledge in the future. The only trustworthy guide we have in attaining this is experimental science.

(iii) Bourgeois sentiments and proletarian sentiments*

We can have no direct knowledge of sentiments; they are to be understood only from their observable manifestations. For the purposes of our enquiry, it is advisable not to linger over the qualitative factor, but direct our attention, as far as possible, to the quantitative factor. For the purposes of logico-experimental science, the opinion of a single individual may be of great importance. But this opinion is worth practically nothing in determining the social equilibrium. In celestial mechanics, the opinion of a Newton is worth more than the opinion of millions of his contemporary fellow-countrymen; but in determining the social and economic condition of England, it is the latter opinion alone which counts for anything.

Even a very superficial glance at present society makes us aware of certain great currents of opinion, revealing sentiments and interests, i.e., the forces which operate on the social equilibrium. They should be studied as such, without lingering over outward appearances or extreme cases in which reason and experience play a small part. In such cases they assume a religious form; in less extreme cases they take on metaphysical or pseudo-experimental forms, for it is all along a common human characteristic to seek to attain the absolute and to evade experimental contingencies.

Those who accept and adopt this way of thinking avoid the difficulties and the discipline of scientific study, and are able to give firm judgements on all social facts, employing particular *a priori* principles, more especially

---

* *Trasformazione*, pp. 89–99, 106–9.

ethical, metaphysical and theological principles. For example, a good deal is said at the present time about 'the defence of law, right and justice'. Certain people enjoy the privilege of sustaining this defence, wherefrom they derive no small advantage, resembling in this the mohammedans, sole guardians of the true faith to whom God, for the propagation of this faith, granted the right of conquering vast territories—which later on they lost. We have the doctrine of the *fatale andare*, the ineluctable advance of democracy, Queen of the World, and its derivative: the dogma of the 'sanctity of the proletariat' which now, in good or bad faith, has so very many believers—devoted adherents who are renewing against the intellect and its works all the anathemas formerly hurled by the early christians against pagan culture and learning. Or again, there is the principle of patriotism which, having set neighbouring cities in arms against each other —Sparta against Athens, Florence against Pisa—is now inciting whole nations to war in an outburst of imperialism. And finally there is all-holy humanitarianism which makes its early appearance, albeit still wearing patriotic garb, in the orations of Isocrates. Later, disencumbering itself, like Beatrice and Dante, from terrestial veils, it shines forth in the numerous, but so far stillborn, projects for universal peace, notable among which is Kant's—that universal peace we are now privileged to contemplate in the formation of the League of Nations.

These opinions and manifestations are here considered by us with detachment; in no sense whatever do we seek to praise or censure them, even less to defend or attack, propagate or combat them. We relate facts; we strive to understand the relationships between facts; and that is all.

In all religions there may be different levels of faith among believers. Faith may be uncomplicated and fervent. While still genuinely held, it may be more of a myth. It may be weakening and affected by scepticism. It may be regarded as only partially true, or kept up as a pretence when wholly abandoned, becoming sheer hypocrisy. For people whose thinking is governed by sentiment, the presence of hypocrites among believers in a given religion is an argument for depreciating its importance and often for condemning it. But for those who reason experimentally, the fact that a religion has hypocritical supporters is an indication of the faith's power, since men feign belief in something only if it is widely accepted by large numbers of their fellow men. From this point of view there is a great deal of truth in that tale of Boccaccio's which tells of the Jew who was converted to the catholic religion because he realised that by so doing he would escape destruction at the hands of malevolent Roman prelates. It is today a sure index of the power of the belief in democracy to see so many people pretending to share the belief, while it is a certain sign of the decline of the belief in aristocracy that among this belief's supporters there remains not one hypocrite. Similarly, it has for long been noticed that heresies appear when a religion is in a flourishing state and disappear when it is declining and moribund.

We must therefore reject that facile censure of religions which fastens on the fact that many people make a living out of them and often get wealth, honours and power from their religious professions. For example, if a vociferous patriotism has worked to the advantage of the plutocrats, if a war has proved to be the foundation of the fortunes of many individuals and created *nouveaux riches*, it should not for all that be concluded that there were not, on the other hand, many people, moved by pure idealism, who made an all-out effort in patriotic activities and war-service, offering their possessions and lives. Nor should we assume that people of this sort are outnumbered by the former sort. In evaluating great currents of opinion, therefore, we must consider as incidental factors the artifices and deceptions which accompany them.

In any given society there are manifestations of conflicts between social classes which point to a general law of rhythm, now quickening in pace, now slackening. In the oscillation occurring at the present time, the following features are prominent.* Among the working class or proletariat there are signs of an intensification of the sentiments of hatred for the 'haves' and for those who are superior in culture or in other respects. Such sentiments attain their most extreme form of expression in bolshevism, but in varying degrees of intensity they are in evidence on a worldwide scale. On the other hand, among the 'haves' and in the upper class as a whole all manifestation of sentiments hostile to the lower class has disappeared, in many cases giving place to fawning flattery of a kind not so very different from that formerly bestowed on absolute sovereigns. On one side the trumpets are sounding and the troops moving to the assault; on the other, heads are bowed in submission; they surrender or—what is thought the better part of wisdom—they go over to the side of the enemy and sell themselves for thirty pieces of silver.

In all this, what relationship do such manifestations have with sentiments? Where the lower classes are concerned, it may be that hatred for the upper class now appears all the greater because of the removal of the restraints which in the past curbed its expression—greater than it would be if its manifestations corresponded exactly to the actual increase in the intensity of the sentiments involved. But even if we make allowance for this factor in the calculation, the sum total outstanding is pretty considerable. This is clearly shown in particular cases. We have only to compare, for example, the attitude of the Tuscan sharecropper to the landowner today and fifty years ago; or the attitude to the state of the lower-grade civil servant of our own day and that of his predecessor, enshrined as a distinct character-type—*l'impiegato regio*—in Piedmontese literature. The celebrated play, *Le Miserie di Monsù Travet*, is now so outdated as almost to be archæological. Similar changes are clearly observable in other sectors of the lower classes. They have been evident for a long time among industrial workers. Some assign the cause of these changes to the transition from small-scale to large-scale industry. But the fact that the situation is very much the same even where such a transition has not yet occurred, clearly makes this only a partial explanation of the phenomenon. Fundamentally,

---

* Pareto notes: 'The conflicts we are studying here involve the residues defined in the *Treatise* as those of Class IV (sociality) and Class V (integrity of the individual and his appurtenances). With the latter are to be identified the sentiments of hate which had such a great influence in the war. . . .'

a general change is taking place among large numbers of the common people who, to use the modern jargon, are more 'aware', more 'developed'.

Very many in the upper class are also more highly 'developed', but in a directly opposite sense to that in which the term is applied to the masses. While these latter have become more staunch and demanding in the defence of their person and interests, the upper classes on the whole have become gutless and demoralised. They patiently endure every insult, threat and oppression; they are only too anxious to avoid irritating their enemies, kissing the hand that strikes them, and seeking to further their interests by relying, not on courage and force, but on underhand tricks. At the end of a strike, they cravenly abandon to the strikers' wrath those workers who refused to strike—the 'blacklegs'—and whose support they had appealed for, making promises only to break them. Even when a strike is beaten, they are too weak-kneed to follow up their victory; instead, to 'conciliate the men', they pay them the wages lost due to strike action. This 'conciliation' to all intents and purposes is an inducement to fresh conflicts since, whatever the outcome of the struggle, the workers stand to lose nothing.

Among the 'haves', the sentiments sustaining firm attitudes about personal and property rights are fast being extinguished. These are being transformed into a nebulous and precarious concept of 'social function'— some call it 'social duty'—which subordinates them to the new 'rights' of labour. In some parts of Italy, for example, agricultural workers are swarming into the fields and insisting, at their own will and pleasure, on doing work which is virtually useless, thus acquiring the 'right' of claiming wages as and when it suits them, for the farmer and landowner have a 'duty' to pay them. This meets with the approval of many in the bourgeoisie.

Discussing the oligarchies of his own day, Aristotle writes: 'Instead of swearing as they do now in some oligarchies, "I will be a foe of the commons and will devise whatsoever ill I may against them", they should take or pretend to take a precisely opposite point of view, emphasising in their oaths the pledge, "I will do the commons no wrong".'* The upper classes have followed this advice throughout the nineteenth century and up to the present day. Many are sincere in their attitude; others, especially the plutocrats, pretend—exactly as Aristotle recommended.

When the French Estates General were summoned in 1614, the Third Estate, although of a lower order, sought to meet together with the clergy and nobility. The latter, indignant at such impudence, obtained audience of the king and Baron Senecey, the nobles' spokesman, uttered these words: 'Sire, it is shameful to me to tell you of the terms by which we are once again insulted. They say that the ecclesiastic order is the eldest son, ours is the second son and they are the younger sons, and that it often happens that families ruined by the older sons are raised up again by the younger. . . . And, not content with calling themselves our brothers, they attribute to themselves the restoration of the State.' Today we can see the workers taking this high tone with the 'capitalists', disdaining to be compared with such folk not only in the realm of the Soviets but also in other countries.

---

* *Politics*, J. E. C. Welldon's translation (1883): Bekker's text, Book VIII, chapter IX; otherwise Book V, chapter IX.

As they are so well known, I will say nothing of the innumerable broils in our medieval republics, where the *popolani* and the nobles were fired with equal boldness and vigour, although even then chicanery and deception were rife. They are one example among very many of oscillations in social phenomena. Treating of the old communes, Muratori writes: 'To regain influence in the government of their city, or to control it entirely, the nobles were perpetually devising plots, sometimes with success, sometimes not. And here a strange thing appears which must not be allowed to pass unmentioned. When the nobles, in their eagerness to obtain public offices and honours, could see no other way of achieving their intentions, not a few of them took to getting their names inscribed in the lists of the merchant and artisan gilds (for, as it happened, this was not forbidden them), and by this means, as gild-members, they became capable of assuming public duties, succeeding through this demonstration of their love and esteem of the commonalty in gaining the mastery over their masters. [*Just like our plutocrats.*] The nobles of our day would perhaps be ashamed to bring themselves so low, but the nobles of the old days were not so squeamish; they sank in order to rise.'* We may now be reverting to what Muratori called 'the old days'. When a new elite eventually comes to power, it is not at all impossible that there will be a return to the attitudes of Muratori's own day.

Of even greater significance is the change in sentiments in regard to taxation. It was once thought 'just' that the incidence of taxation in all, or almost all, cases should bear on the lower classes, leaving the upper classes wholly, or almost wholly, exempt. Nowadays it is the other way about—which all goes to show, we may note in passing, what a very obliging lady is this Justice who never denies her help to the powerful. At one time the term 'free' was used to describe the system in which those who paid taxes had first to approve and grant them. Today it describes the system whereby taxes are imposed by those who are exempt, or well-nigh exempt, from them—which indicates that the term 'free' is as pliable as the term 'just'.

There is marked disparity between sentiments which, albeit expressed in the same terms, are in essence different and opposed. In the past, the mass of the people was opposed, not so much to the principle of paying taxes as to the manner in which the principle was exercised. Today we find that it is the 'haves' who accept the principle of being squeezed, contenting themselves where and when they can with hair-splitting cavillings aimed at avoiding to some degree the full weight of the burden laid on them. Never uniting to throw off the burden, each one of them strives to push it off on to the next man; by such internal discords they make themselves even weaker as a social group. Governments take the line of least resistance—or what seems to be such. In past centuries they fleeced the common people; today they are despoiling the propertied classes.

From what has been said so far, it seems to me one may conclude that, from the point of view of sentiments, the section of society we call the 'masses' is greatly superior to the section we call the 'haves'. Those com-

---

* Muratori, *Dissertazioni sopra le antichità italiane*, 1790, Vol. 3, Part 1, Diss. LII, pp. 43–4.

posing the former section are more firmly united and staunch, with greater reserves of courage and energy, of abnegation in defending their own ideals, and of good sense and perseverance in pushing directly towards their desired goal. It is true that they are inferior in practising the arts of the fox, but in time of upheaval this deficiency is compensated for by force.

It is thus that the better well-being of society has been furthered in the past; it is therefore likely so to be furthered in the future, these character-istics of the masses procuring, despite the damaging effects of upheavals and clashes, long periods of prosperity. Such was the eventual outcome of the internal class-conflict in Greece; such was the outcome of the medieval period after the fall of the Roman Empire; and such indeed could well be the outcome of a new middle age. . . .

We shall realise the extent and strength of sentiments if we study the energy and perseverance with which workers and wage-earners have now achieved the general establishment of the eight-hour day. They set them-selves an attainable aim, and they have unswervingly pursued it in all countries through united and steadfast efforts. They left it to their adver-saries to chatter about 'the patriotic spirit of sacrifice', and asserted quite plainly: 'After the war we intend to be better off than before; you others must put up with this as best you can.' No one in the lower classes is to be found appealing to his fellows to work harder for the benefit of the 'haves', whereas there are certain people in the propertied class who can be found exhorting their peers to give money to the government, thereby enabling the latter to shower benefits on the lower orders and on the plutocracy—this being a natural consequence in a system based on demagogic pluto-cracy. There are blacklegs, of course, within the popular section just as there are among the 'haves'; but whereas by the former they are detested and persecuted, by the latter they are condoned and frequently held in respect.

By simple strength of sentiments, the masses have managed to increase wages. There is not to be found among them a single representative of that type so frequently found in the well-to-do class: the person who makes it his study to devise all possible means of increasing the incidence of taxation on his peers, many of whom have still not realised that, in present circum-stances, what is withheld from the taxman is withheld from the enemy. The masses grasp intuitively that even extremists who want to go to lengths which, for the time being at least, the rest of them do not desire, are very useful as allies. Hence in all countries we find that there is general approval for the bolshevists. The 'haves' cannot find it in themselves to counter this by supporting the opposite extreme; the terror they feel at the mere name of 'militarism' is positively comical. Cicero perfectly represents, in the terms of his own day, the attitude which is prevalent among our well-to-do middle class. He was utterly bemused by the double dilemma posed by the violence of the rabble and the might of the legions. Nobly, but vainly, he hoped for a government of the optimates based on the favour of the people.

Since the force of the masses is now the stronger of the two forces in conflict in our society, the bourgeois state is lurching on its foundations and its power is disintegrating. Under demagogic plutocracy, plutocracy is weakening and democracy growing ever stronger. Oscillations are being set in motion the extent and duration of which it is as yet impossible to predict.

As we have already said many times, we abstain entirely from making judgements about the facts we are expounding, from awarding praise or blame, and from exploring what short-term or long-term utility these facts may have for society. We cite them with the sole purpose of furthering our appreciation of the extent and intensity of the sentiments which are operating in the contending social groups. We began by studying the outward characteristics of the relevant phenomena; we were drawn to make certain conjectures. We then went more deeply into the matter, arriving at the sentiments which underly the phenomena. Thereby we found confirmation of the conjectures we had made, obtaining, with a great degree of probability, a general concept of the transformations which are taking place in our modern societies.

(iv) The new cycle*

... A general trend has made itself apparent over several years and has been intensified by the war. The question therefore arises: Is this trend going to stick at its present point? Or is it going to continue, albeit irregularly and with alternating phases of immobility and regression, but none the less maintaining on the whole an average rate of perceivable progression? If it stays as it is, it will lead to further developments of the cycle which has already revealed itself to a substantial degree in the twentieth century. If the trend moves forward beyond its present point, it will directly confront our society with insuperable obstacles—such as, for example, the combination of a fall in production with a rise in consumption—and it will initiate, with or without catastrophe, a new cycle. To determine this question requires a statistic of sentiments able to evaluate them and comprehend their possibilities of variation. Science is still unable to do this with any real precision. We can therefore only make rough and ready evaluations of events according to their being more or less probable.

To support the view that the present trend will stick at its present point, there is the example of the past: what has occurred before may occur again. But we have to take account of the fact that two conditions which used to exert influence are now of lesser significance.

First: Formerly there were considerable numbers of individuals whose sentiments underwent little substantial change—individuals who could be said to have 'conservative' inclinations. It was to this class of person that governing circles looked in the main for support, and accordingly it was to them that they granted further extensions of the right to vote. Such was the general policy of England's rulers on several occasions; such was the policy followed by Napoleon III in France and Bismarck in Germany, and which was repeated by Italy's governing class. But in the end it proved a broken reed because it did not sufficiently make allowance for the profound changes which the war produced in sentiments and interests. It is legitimate therefore to wonder if similar attempts are not bound to fail in other

---

* *Trasformazione*, pp. 138–41.

countries. Today this large body of conservatively inclined people no longer exists. Of course, there are still many such individuals in our society, but they are nowhere near so numerous as they once were, and hence they do not constitute a force on which any great reliance can be placed.

Secondly: There was formerly a huge amount of savings and wealth which governments were able to make use of, by ever-increasing taxation, in order to meet growing expenditure without causing undue harm to production. But today, due mainly to the war, the burden of taxation has reached a limit beyond which it is scarcely possible to go without considerably reducing production and also, it may well be, the effective yield of taxation. There is an indication of this phenomenon in the fact that, in several countries, the increase in the incidence of taxation goes hand in hand with a depreciation of the currency. The sources are drying up which governments have been accustomed to tap in order to satisfy the desires, needs and cupidity of their supporters, and to make their adversaries more amenable. Henceforward and for the foreseeable future the burden of taxation will be such as to be incapable of increase. The needs of politics are thereby going to predominate over the needs of the economy. This is what happened towards the end of the Roman Empire and was the main cause of its fall. And this is what could happen in our own day.

We have, of course, to take account of the exploitation of vast regions in Africa and Asia. This will very likely prove to be of special benefit to England, the United States and France; but it can be of little or no benefit to Italy which has picked up merely the scraps which these voracious gourmands have let fall from their festive board. Hence it is only these countries which can refashion for modern times the policy, pursued in the later years of the Roman Republic, of conceding everything to demagogy at home in the knowledge that the bill could be footed abroad. But this policy is impossible for other countries, like Italy, for their opportunities of exploiting overseas territories are severely circumscribed.

We are left then with a question to which as yet there is no answer: How will the balance be struck between these two different types of countries—the 'haves' and the 'have nots' of the western world? Will they inevitably come into conflict? This might well be one of the factors producing the sort of catastrophe which could initiate the new cycle.

Bibliography

I. PARETO'S MAJOR WORKS

Principii Fondamentali della Teoria dell' Elasticità. Florence, 1869. Reprinted in Demaria, G. (ed.), *Scritti Teorici*, Milan, 1952.
Introduction à 'Le Capital' de Marx, Paris, n.d. Italian edn., Turin, 1934.
Cours d'Economie Politique, Lausanne, 1896, 1897. Italian edn., Turin, 1942.
La Liberté Economique et les Evènements d'Italie, Lausanne, 1898. Italian edn., Turin, 1951.
Les Systèmes Socialistes, 2 vols., Paris, 1902; 2nd edn., 1926.
Manuale di Economia Politica, Milan, 1906. French edn., revised (*Manuel d'Economie Politique*), Paris, 1909.
Le Mythe Vertuiste et la Littérature Immorale, Paris, 1911. Italian edn., Rome, 1914.
Trattato di Sociologia Generale, 3 vols., Florence, 1916; 2nd edn., 1923. French edn., *Traité de Sociologie Générale*, 2 vols., Paris, 1917. English edn., *The Mind and Society*, trans. A. Livingston and A. Bongiorno, 4 vols., New York and London, 1935; reprinted, 2 vols., 1963.
Fatti e Teorie, Florence, 1920.
Trasformazione della Democrazia, Milan, 1921; reprinted, Modena, 1946.
Mon Journal, Padua, 1958.

II. COMPENDIA AND SELECTIONS FROM PARETO'S WORKS

Farina, G. (ed.), *Compendio di Sociologia Generale*, Florence, 1920.
Bousquet, G. H. (ed.), *Précis de Sociologie d'après V. Pareto*, Paris, 1926.
Arcari, P. M. (ed.), *Pareto*, Florence, 1948.
Vanni, S. F. (ed.), *The Ruling Class in Italy Before 1900*, New York, 1950. (Various articles by Pareto.)
Demaria, G. (ed.), *Scritti Teorici*, Milan, 1952.

III. PARETO'S CORRESPONDENCE (by date of publication)

Antonucci, A. (ed.), *Alcune Lettere di V. Pareto*, Rome, 1938.
Sensini, G. (ed.), *Corrispondenza di Vilfredo Pareto*, Padua, 1948.

Giacalone-Monaco, T. (ed.), *Vilfredo Pareto dal Carteggio con Carlo Placci*, Padua, 1957.

—— *Pareto-Walras, 1891–1901*, Padua, 1960.

De Rosa, G. (ed.), *Lettere a Maffeo Pantaleoni*, 3 vols., Rome, 1960.

—— *Carteggi Paretiani*, Rome, 1962.

IV. SELECT BIBLIOGRAPHY OF CRITICAL COMMENTARY

Arcari, P. M., 'Umanesimo Italiano di V. Pareto', in *Mélanges d'Histoire et de Littérature Offerts à M. Charles Gillard*, Lausanne, 1944.

Aron, R., 'La Signification de l'Oeuvre de Pareto', *Cahiers Vilfredo Pareto*, Geneva, No. 1, 1963.

Ascoli, M., 'Pareto's Sociology', *Social Research*, February 1936.

Bobbio, N., 'Vilfredo Pareto e la Critica delle Ideologie', *Rivista di Filosofia*, Turin, October 1957.

—— 'Vilfredo Pareto's Sociology in his Letters to Maffeo Pantaleoni', *Banca Nazionale di Lavoro, Quarterly Review*, Rome, September 1958.

Bongiorno, M., 'A Study of Pareto's Treatise of General Sociology', *American Journal of Sociology*, November 1930.

Borkenau, F., *Pareto*, New York and London, 1936.

Bousquet, G. H., *Vilfredo Pareto: Sa Vie et Son Oeuvre*, Paris, 1928.

—— *Pareto: Le Savant et l'Homme*, Lausanne, 1960.

—— 'Vilfredo Pareto: Biographical Notes', *Banca Nazionale di Lavoro, Quarterly Review*, Rome, September 1958.

Braga, G., *Forma ed Equilibrio Sociale*, Bologna, 1959. (Introduction, pp. ix–lix.)

Burnham, J., *The Machiavellians*, London, 1943.

Busino, G., 'Materiali per l'Edizione dell' Epistolario', *Cahiers Vilfredo Pareto*, No. 1, Geneva, 1963.

Busino, G. (ed.), 'Etudes offertes en hommage au professeur Georges-H. Bousquet', *Cahiers Vilfredo Pareto*, No. 5, Geneva, 1965. (Essays by several hands on various aspects of Pareto's life and work.)

De Pietri Tonelli, A., 'Pareto e Mosca', *Rivista Internazionale di Scienze Sociali*, Milan, 1935.

—— *Vilfredo Pareto*, Rome, 1935.

Einaudi, L., 'Dove Si Discorre di Pareto, Mosca ed A. de Viti', *Riforma Sociale*, Turin, 1934.

—— 'Pareto as I Knew Him', *Atlantic Monthly*, 1935.

Eisermann, G., *Vilfredo Pareto: System der Allgemeinen Soziologie*, Stuttgart, 1962.

Faris, E., 'An Estimate of Pareto', ch. 15 in *The Nature of Human Nature*, New York, 1937.

Giacalone-Monaco, T., *Pareto e Sorel: Riflessioni*, 2 vols., Padua, 1961.

Ginsberg, M., 'The Sociology of Pareto', ch. 4 in *Reason and Unreason in Society*, London, 1947.

Handman, M. S., 'The Sociological Method of V. Pareto', in Rice, S. A. (ed.), *Methods in Social Science*, Chicago, 1931.

Henderson, L., *Pareto's Sociology: A Physiologist's Interpretation*, Cambridge, Mass., 1935.

Homans, G. C. and Curtis, C. P., *An Introduction to Pareto: His Sociology*, New York, 1934.

Hughes, H. S., *Consciousness and Society*, London, 1959.

La Ferla, G., *Vilfredo Pareto: Filosofo Volteriano*, Florence, 1954.

Madge, C., *Society in the Mind*, London, 1964.

Meisel, J. H., *The Myth of the Ruling Class: Gaetano Mosca and the Elite*, Ann Arbor, 1962

Millikan, M., 'Pareto's Sociology' *Econometrica*, London, 1936.

Parsons, T., 'Pareto's Central Analytical Scheme', *Journal of Social Philosophy*, New York, 1935.

——— *The Structure of Social Action*, 1937; 2nd edn., New York and London, 1961.

Schneider, E., 'Vilfredo Pareto: The Economist in the Light of His Letters to Maffeo Pantaleoni', *Banca Nazionale di Lavoro, Quarterly Review*, Rome, No. 58, 1961.

Tagliavini, V., 'Comments on Millikan's Review of Pareto's Sociology', *Econometrica*, 1957.

Wollheim, R., 'Vilfredo Pareto: A Case in the Political Pathology of Our Age', *Occidente*, Oxford, 1954.

Index of Subjects

Page numbers in bold type relate to references in the Introduction